Mormonism
FOR
DUMMIES®

Mormonism
FOR
DUMMIES®

by Jana Riess, PhD, and
Christopher Kimball Bigelow

WILEY

Wiley Publishing, Inc.

Mormonism For Dummies®

Published by
Wiley Publishing, Inc.
111 River St.
Hoboken, NJ 07030-5774
www.wiley.com

Copyright © 2005 by Wiley Publishing, Inc., Indianapolis, Indiana

Published simultaneously in Canada

For general information on our other products and services, please contact our Customer Care Department within the U.S. at 800-762-2974, outside the U.S. at 317-572-3993, or fax 317-572-4002.

For technical support, please visit www.wiley.com/techsupport.

Wiley also publishes its books in a variety of electronic formats. Some content that appears in print may not be available in electronic books.

Library of Congress Control Number: 2004117769

ISBN: 0-7645-7195-8

Manufactured in the United States of America

10 9 8 7 6 5 4 3 2 1

1B/RR/QS/QV/IN

About the Authors

Jana Riess, PhD, is the Religion Book Review Editor for *Publishers Weekly* magazine and is also the author of *The Spiritual Traveler: Boston and New England* (HiddenSpring) and *What Would Buffy Do?: The Vampire Slayer as Spiritual Guide* (Jossey-Bass). She holds degrees in religion from Wellesley College and Princeton Theological Seminary, and a PhD in American religious history from Columbia University. She is frequently interviewed by the media on trends in religion and publishing. A convert to the LDS Church, Riess has spoken at Brigham Young University Women's Conference and other Mormon gatherings, as well as professional conferences. She lives in Kentucky with her husband and daughter.

Christopher Kimball Bigelow is the great-great-great-grandson of a Mormon apostle who had more than 40 wives. He served an LDS mission in Melbourne, Australia, and worked as an editor at the LDS Church's official *Ensign* magazine. A graduate of Emerson College and Brigham Young University, Bigelow cofounded and edited the Mormon literary magazine *Irreantum* and the satirical Mormon newspaper *The Sugar Beet,* and he's working on a memoir and a novel. A Hodgkin's disease survivor and the oldest of ten siblings, he lives with his wife and four children in Provo, Utah. You can reach him at chrisbigelow@gmail.com.

Dedication

From Jana: To Sister Wibiral and Sister Lundblade, two of the most caring missionaries to have ever served anywhere, with much gratitude.

From Chris: To the memory of my pioneer Mormon ancestors, who made choices and sacrifices that bless me every day of my life.

Authors' Acknowledgments

We want to thank our mutual agent, Linda Roghaar, who introduced us to each other and encouraged us to collaborate on this project. We also want to thank Kathy Cox, our acquisitions editor, and Chrissy Guthrie, our project editor, who have overseen this book from concept to finished product. Historian Jan Shipps served as our technical review editor and provided important expert commentary on every chapter during the revision stage. We also need to thank those friends, family members, and colleagues who graciously and carefully took the time to comment on some or all of this manuscript: David Allred, Paris Anderson, Ann Bigelow, Mitzie Bigelow, Sylvia Cabus, Andrew Hall, Tona Hangen, Grant and Heather Hardy, Heidi and Tyler Jarvis, Sammie Justesen, Ken Kuykendall, Jonathan and Laurel Langford, Tania and John Lyon, Brian Maxwell, Henry and Carol Miles, Benson Parkinson, Robert Slaven, Phyllis Tickle, Darlene Young, and Margaret Young. Although this book isn't authorized or approved by The Church of Jesus Christ of Latter-day Saints, we appreciate the help of the Church's Public Affairs Department in providing up-to-date information and statistics.

Jana thanks her family, especially her husband Phil, for love and unflagging support, and also her friends Ray, Roberta, and Angela Black for enduring friendship and incomparable hospitality.

Chris thanks his wife, Ann, for her feedback and support, as well as many friends and family members who offered encouragement.

Publisher's Acknowledgments

We're proud of this book; please send us your comments through our Dummies online registration form located at www.dummies.com/register/.

Some of the people who helped bring this book to market include the following:

Acquisitions, Editorial, and Media Development

Project Editor: Christina Guthrie

Acquisitions Editor: Kathy Cox

Copy Editor: Kristin DeMint

Editorial Program Assistant: Courtney Allen

Technical Editor: Jan Shipps, PhD

Editorial Manager: Christine Meloy Beck

Media Development Manager: Laura VanWinkle

Editorial Assistants: Hanna Scott, Melissa Bennett, Nadine Bell

Cover Photo: © Corbis/PictureQuest

Cartoons: Rich Tennant, www.the5thwave.com

Composition

Project Coordinator: Emily Wichlinski

Layout and Graphics: Andrea Dahl, Stephanie D. Jumper, Barry Offringa, Jacque Roth,

Proofreaders: Leeann Harney, Jessica Kramer, TECHBOOKS Production Services

Indexer: TECHBOOKS Production Services

Special Help: Carmen Krikorian

Publishing and Editorial for Consumer Dummies

    Diane Graves Steele, Vice President and Publisher, Consumer Dummies

    Joyce Pepple, Acquisitions Director, Consumer Dummies

    Kristin A. Cocks, Product Development Director, Consumer Dummies

    Michael Spring, Vice President and Publisher, Travel

    Brice Gosnell, Associate Publisher, Travel

    Kelly Regan, Editorial Director, Travel

Publishing for Technology Dummies

    Andy Cummings, Vice President and Publisher, Dummies Technology/General User

Composition Services

    Gerry Fahey, Vice President of Production Services

    Debbie Stailey, Director of Composition Services

Contents at a Glance

Table of Contents

Introduction

. . . .

*I*f you're picking up this book, you may already know that Mormonism is one of the world's fastest-growing religions. With more than 5 million members in the United States, The Church of Jesus Christ of Latter-day Saints is the sixth-largest religious body in the nation. It also has nearly 7 million more people on the rolls around the world. Almost all this growth has happened in the last 25 years, making Mormonism a hot topic that many people want to understand better.

In this book, we help you do just that. If you don't know a Mormon from a Moravian, you find the basics here for most everything you need to understand. We don't assume that you have any background. At the same time, even if you are a Mormon, you may find information in this book that helps you understand your religion more thoroughly and with fresh perspective.

About This Book

Don't feel that you have to read this book straight through from cover to cover. Each chapter is a self-contained unit, designed to give you information about that particular topic. Where relevant, we also include cross-references to show you where to find more information. This way, you can find what you want quickly and skip over the stuff that seems less important to you.

One more thing: Although we're both practicing members of The Church of Jesus Christ of Latter-day Saints, the views you find in this book are unofficial and don't necessarily represent the opinions of the Church's leadership. Furthermore, although we tried our best to capture the broadest cross-section possible and to present a range of viewpoints, we certainly can't claim that every Mormon you meet will agree with everything we say. Throughout the book, we refer you to a few other books that the Church *does* produce and sanction, and we also point you to the Church's official Web site, www. lds.org.

Conventions Used in This Book

The Church of Jesus Christ of Latter-day Saints has some style preferences that we adopted for this book. You won't see the term *Mormon Church* here, because *Mormon* is a nickname and the Church would rather have people use its official name. We do use *LDS Church* for short, instead of spelling out the whole name each time. You'll also see the word *Mormon* used as an adjective or a noun to refer to members of the Church.

In addition, you may notice a bit of fuss about the capitalization of *church*. Here's the deal: Whenever we're referring to other denominations or to churches in general, we use little *c*. But when we're talking about the LDS Church as a specific denomination, we use capital *C*.

When it comes to the Bible, we stick with what Mormons love best: the good ol' King James Version (KJV for short). Because the other Mormon scriptures are distinctively Mormon, they only come in one lingo — and it reads very much like the KJV. When we reference a particular verse or range of verses in any of the scriptures, we follow the standard: For example, in the Bible, Matthew 10:1 refers to Matthew as the book, 10 as the chapter number, and 1 as the verse.

To add a little spice, we threw in a few formatting conventions:

✔ Anytime we introduce a new term, we *italicize* it and define it.

✔ Web sites or e-mail addresses appear in `monofont` to help them stand out.

✔ Anytime we suggest typing keywords into an Internet search engine, we put them in **boldface.**

Foolish Assumptions

While writing this book, we assumed that many of our readers aren't going to be Mormons, but some will be. Maybe you fit into one of these groups:

✔ You've got Mormon friends, neighbors, relatives, or co-workers, and you're naturally curious about their faith.

✔ You've heard something or read an article about Mormonism, and it made you wonder what Mormons believe.

✔ You're thinking of joining the LDS Church and want to know more about it.

- You're a new Mormon convert trying to better understand what you've gotten yourself into.

- You're an established Mormon, and you want this book to give to someone else who fits in one of the first four categories. Or maybe you like to read different perspectives on your own faith.

How This Book Is Organized

Even though Mormonism is a relatively young religion, packing more than 180 years of history and belief into one introductory book is still a tough job. Obviously, we've had to omit some things. Our goal here is to give you the down-and-dirty (actually, make that down-and-squeaky-clean) story of the Mormon religion and its people.

To make it easy for you to find exactly what you're looking for, we divided this book into several parts, each covering a broad topic. Each part contains several chapters that relate more specifically to that topic.

Part 1: What the Mormon Faith Is All About

This part deals with the basics: Who are the Mormons, and what do they believe? Here you find the Mormon view on the meaning of life, the nature of God, and what happens to people after they die. You also read about the Mormon concept of priesthood and the idea of a restored church with 12 apostles and a living prophet. We explore why Mormons emphasize family and what it means to believe that families can be together forever.

Part II: Eternal Rituals and Endless Meetings

This part outlines the day-to-day workings of The Church of Jesus Christ of Latter-day Saints, from the activities and organizations of the local congregations to the hierarchy of leaders at Church headquarters in Salt Lake City. We help you understand what to do if you're invited to a Mormon church service, baptism, or funeral. We also take a sneak peek inside the temple, the most sacred place in Mormon life, and explain why temples are so significant for Mormons.

Part III: Holy Books and Sacred History

In this part, we walk you through the four sacred texts that Latter-day Saints regard as scripture (the Bible, Book of Mormon, Doctrine and Covenants, and Pearl of Great Price) and explain what Mormons believe about continuing revelation. We also spend some time with the pioneers, giving you the highlights — and lowlights — of Mormon history from 1820 onward.

Part IV: Mormonism Today

This part explores Mormonism as a worldwide religion, focusing on its rapid international growth and the role of missionary work. Here you get to understand who those clean-shaven, well-dressed Mormon missionaries are and what their lives are like. We also give you Mormon perspectives on some controversial issues, such as racism, polygamy, homosexuality, and women's roles. Then we delve into Mormon spiritual practices, from paying tithing and remaining chaste to praying daily and reading the scriptures. Finally, we help you understand the Mormon emphasis on self-reliance and look at Mormon culture, from the highbrow (the Mormon Tabernacle Choir) to the lowbrow (green Jell-O salad).

Part V: The Part of Tens

Every *For Dummies* book has a part of tens, which is a quick and entertaining way to get the basics. Here, we include answers to ten frequently asked questions about Mormonism, introduce you to ten (well, almost) famous Latter-day Saints, and profile ten places to visit if you're interested in finding out more about Mormon history.

Icons Used in This Book

This book uses the following icons to help you find information you need or to highlight ideas you may find particularly helpful.

This icon points to areas of disagreement, either within the Mormon community or among outsiders who have criticized the Mormon faith.

This icon calls attention to elements of the Mormon past that are still very relevant to Mormon belief and practice today.

You find this icon next to significant information that you'll want to remember.

This icon appears next to most quotes from the Bible, Book of Mormon, Doctrine and Covenants, or Pearl of Great Price.

This icon points to hands-on information to help you make sense of Mormon belief or practice.

Where to Go from Here

Mormonism For Dummies is like a big Sunday buffet at Grandma's house. You can eat as many of the yeast rolls as you want, and you don't have to touch the peas if you don't want to. In other words, in this book we bring a little bit of everything to the table: history, doctrine, fun facts, spiritual disciplines, culture, and scripture. You can go to any section and discover Mormonism, choosing what interests you the most.

If you're coming to this book with a specific question in mind, feel free to look up that topic in the index or table of contents and start with that section. Others may want to start with Chapter 1, which gives an overview of the whole Mormon topic. There's no wrong way to eat this buffet — just enjoy the meal.

Part I

What the Mormon Faith Is All About

The 5th Wave   By Rich Tennant

©RICHTENNANT

"So, our daughter tells us she's dating a Mormon. Julie's father and I understand that Mormons never curse. Tell me Mr. Stuart, how good a Mormon are you?"

In this part . . .

Here you find out the basics about what Mormons believe, including important stuff about God, Jesus Christ, the premortal life, the plan of salvation, and the afterlife. You also discover what happened in the 19th century when Joseph Smith was called as a prophet to restore the church of Jesus Christ and how the Mormon priesthood is organized and used today. Finally, you get to know more about the family: Why is the family such an important concept in Mormonism? Why do Mormons tend to have larger-than-usual families? Why are they so into genealogy?

Chapter 1

A New World Religion

*B*uddhism, Judaism, Islam, Hinduism, traditional branches of Christianity — and Mormonism? If you ask some demographers and sociologists, the idea of Mormonism emerging as the newest major world religion isn't far fetched. In the Christian sector, although Protestantism grew out of Catholicism, Mormonism bills itself as a completely fresh start, with enough distinctive beliefs and practices to back up that claim.

Mormonism isn't the newest kid on the religious block, but its start during the 1820s seems relatively recent — in fact, compared to other world religions, Mormonism is a toddler, still maturing in terms of culture, identity, growth, government, and other aspects. As a blueprint for the rest of the book, this opening chapter gives an overview of what it means to be a Mormon.

Why Know about Mormonism?

If you ask Mormon missionaries why you should find out more about Mormonism, they'll tell you that the LDS Church is the restoration of the Savior's true church, and he wants you to convert. However, we suspect this answer won't satisfy many of our non-Mormon readers, so here are some other reasons:

> ✔ **It's the quintessential U.S. religion.** Increasingly, historians are acknowledging that Mormonism is the most successful, significant homegrown U.S. religion, founded just 54 years after the Declaration of Independence. In many ways, the story of Mormonism mirrors the story of the United

States, and the faith reflects many American ideals and traits. In fact, Mormons believe God inspired the formation of the U.S. partly as a suitable homeland for the gospel's restoration. (For an overview of early Mormon history, see Chapters 4, 11, 12, and 13.)

✔ **It's one of the fastest-growing religions.** Chances are that one or more of your friends, neighbors, or relatives has already joined the LDS Church or soon will. Consider these statistics:

- At the end of 2003, the Church had 5.5 million members in the U.S. and nearly 12 million members worldwide, almost triple its total in 1978. For several decades, the Church has added about 300,000 new converts every year. (For more on missionary work and Church growth around the world, see Chapter 14.)

- The National Council of Churches reported in 2004 that the LDS Church was the fifth-largest U.S. religious body, after the Roman Catholic Church, Southern Baptist Convention, United Methodist Church, and Church of God in Christ. The LDS Church is now larger than any of the mainline Protestant denominations, such as Lutheran, Presbyterian, or Episcopalian, in the U.S.

- The *Yearbook of American and Canadian Churches, 2004* (Abingdon Press) reports that the LDS Church had the highest rate of growth (1.88 percent per year in the United States) among the 15 largest U.S. Churches. The growth rate abroad is even higher.

✔ **It teaches good principles and practices.** Even for those people who don't embrace Mormonism as a religion, the faith yields many useful ideas that you can adapt to fit any worldview. Following are some highlights:

- **Strengthening families:** Mormons are known for their large, tight-knit, superfunctional families. One main reason is that Mormons believe families can be together forever (for more on this idea, see Chapter 5). Also, the LDS Church teaches practical techniques for strengthening families, such as family home evening (for more info, see Chapter 17).

- **Providing for the needy:** Marshalling its organizational might, the LDS Church has created one of the world's most admired systems for helping people provide for their own material needs. Church-owned farms, ranches, canneries, storehouses, and other enterprises provide not only essential goods but also employment. Increasingly, the Church shares its bounty with people outside the faith. (For more on the Church's welfare program and humanitarian efforts, see Chapter 8.)

- **Maintaining health:** When founding prophet Joseph Smith introduced Mormonism's health code, known as the *Word of Wisdom*, little did he know that science would validate many of these teachings more than 100 years later. Likewise, the Mormon law of chastity helps reduce a host of physical, emotional, and spiritual ills. Today, Mormons are known for enjoying some of the most favorable health rates of any demographic group. (For more on these teachings, see Chapter 16.)

The Mormon Worldview

The following equation best sums up how Mormons understand the universe and the purpose of life: As humans are, God used to be; as God is, humans may become.

One main key to getting the gist of Mormonism is the belief that a person's existence doesn't begin with birth on this earth. Rather, Mormons believe that all people lived as spirits before coming here. For Mormons, this belief helps explain a whole lot about the conditions and purposes of this earthly life, which they view as God's test of his children. In addition, Mormons hold some unusual views about the afterlife, particularly regarding what human beings can become. (For a more detailed treatment of these beliefs, see Chapter 2.)

Life before mortal life

If life doesn't start with conception and birth, when does it start? For Mormons, it *never* really started, because each person has an eternal essence that has always existed. However, Mormons believe that God created spiritual bodies to house each person's eternal essence, so he's the spiritual father of humankind. All human spirits were born before the earth was created.

Sitting at the knee of God and his wife, many spirit children expressed a desire to grow up and become like their Heavenly Parents (for more on them, see Chapter 3). So God set up the *plan of salvation,* which involved creating an earth where his children could gain physical bodies and go through a challenging test of faith and obedience. Those who pass the test with flying colors get the chance to eventually start an eternal family like God's.

In *premortality,* as Mormons call this stage, two of the oldest spirit siblings made a big impression. The first spirit, named Jehovah, volunteered to help everyone overcome the sin and death they'd unavoidably encounter during the earthly test, and this brother was eventually born on earth as Jesus Christ (for more about him, see Chapter 3). Mormons believe he's their Savior and strive to be like him. The other spirit, named Lucifer, rebelled against God's plan of salvation, convincing a bunch of siblings to follow him and start a war. God banished Lucifer and his followers to the earth without bodies, and Mormons believe that these spirits are still trying to win humans to their side and thwart God's plan (for more about the devil, see Chapter 2).

Life on earth

Good news: In the Mormon view, everyone who's born on this earth chose to follow God's plan of salvation and come here. Even those who give in to evil during earthly life will still receive an eternal reward for making the correct choice during premortality. Mormons don't believe that humans are born carrying the stain of Adam's original sin, as Catholics and some Protestants do. But they do believe that each individual's circumstances in this life are at least partly influenced by what that person did in premortality.

One of the most difficult aspects of this mortal test is that humans can't remember what happened in premortality, so they must rediscover their divine origins through faith. However, God sent Jesus Christ not only to overcome sin and death but also to establish the gospel, which serves as a road map back to God. Two kinds of messengers help people understand and follow this gospel: prophets and the *Holy Ghost,* a spiritual being who speaks directly to the human spirit (for more on him, see Chapter 3). By listening to these guides, people can figure out the puzzle of life. Unfortunately, the devil strives to fill the world with distractions and counterfeits.

Another hard aspect of the earthly test is that God generally won't interfere with people's freedom to act, even when they do terrible things to each other or fail miserably. In addition, God allows accidents, natural disasters, illnesses, and other difficulties to challenge his children and prompt them to seek him out. For Mormons, it helps to remember that these temporary trials represent a mere blink of the eye on an eternal scale, and they exercise faith that God will comfort and protect those who ask for his help to endure suffering.

During mortality, Mormons believe that everyone needs to participate in certain rituals in order to live with God in the afterlife and become like him. Someone holding God's priesthood authority, which Mormons believe currently comes only through the LDS Church, must perform these rituals. If a person dies without receiving these ordinances, Mormons perform the rituals in temples on behalf of the deceased person, whose spirit then decides whether or not to accept (for more info, see Chapter 7). These ordinances are

- ✔ Baptism (see Chapter 6)
- ✔ Confirmation, which includes receiving the gift of the Holy Ghost (see Chapter 6)
- ✔ Priesthood ordination (for all worthy males; see Chapter 4)
- ✔ Washing and anointing (see Chapter 7)
- ✔ Endowment (see Chapter 7)
- ✔ Sealing, including celestial marriage for those wedded on earth (see Chapter 7)

Life after mortal life

Mormons believe that when humans die, they slough off their physical bodies and return to the spiritual state. Some go to spirit paradise, and some go to spirit prison. Mormons believe that the spirits in paradise visit the spirits in prison and teach them the gospel, and some choose to accept it and cross over into paradise. Whether they're in paradise or prison, the stopover in the spirit world is only temporary, because God has greater things in store.

Eventually, after God's spirit children have experienced their earthly tests and paid for their sins either by receiving the Savior's Atonement or suffering themselves, he'll resurrect everyone with perfect physical bodies that will last forever. Then he'll sort people into three heavenly kingdoms:

- **Telestial kingdom:** Those who live in sin, die without repenting, and never accept the Savior's Atonement go here, after suffering for their own sins in spirit prison.

- **Terrestrial kingdom:** Those who live good lives but don't embrace the full gospel will inherit this kingdom. Jesus pays for their sins.

  (Both the telestial kingdom and the terrestrial kingdom are glorious paradises, not hell or places of torture. For more on the three tiers of heaven, see Chapter 2.)

- **Celestial kingdom:** This highest kingdom is reserved for those who live the full gospel and receive the proper ordinances. This kingdom is where God lives and where his children can become like him.

Joseph Smith and Mormonism's Beginnings

To Mormons, the term *gospel* means the "good news" that Christ died to save humanity and also refers to a very practical package of tools and instructions that the Savior provides for getting humans back home to God. That package includes doctrines, commandments, ordinances, continually updated revelations, and the priesthood authority to act in God's name (for more on the Mormon priesthood, see Chapter 4). Remember, Mormons believe that the Savior was God's first spirit child way back before the earth was formed, so he's been on deck to reveal his gospel to prophets from Adam onward.

In the Mormon view, the timeline goes like this: First the Savior gave his gospel to Adam, but Adam's descendants eventually lost it through disobedience and corruption. Then the Savior gave it to other prophets, such as Noah and Abraham, but their people gradually lost it, too. Finally, when the Savior was born on the earth to accomplish his mission of overcoming sin and death for all humankind, he reestablished his gospel. However, within a few decades after his resurrection, humans fumbled it away yet again.

During the 1,700-year religious dry spell that Mormons say started after the Savior's New Testament apostles died, he worked behind the scenes and prepared the earth to eventually receive his gospel again. In 1820 he began the process of restoring it for the final time. When a teenager named Joseph Smith knelt in prayer to ask God which church he should join, God the Father and his son Jesus Christ appeared to Joseph and told him that none of the existing churches were true. Within ten years, Joseph Smith launched the Savior's restored gospel in the form of what people now know as the Latter-day Saint religion. (For a more detailed account of Mormonism's founding, see Chapter 4.)

Translating additional scriptures

After Joseph Smith's answer to prayer in 1820, which Mormons refer to as his *First Vision,* an angel began regularly appearing to prepare him for his prophetic calling. Finally, the time arrived for him to perform one of the most important steps in restoring the gospel: bringing forth additional scripture that helped restore correct principles and could serve as a witness and testament of the new faith.

As Mormons understand it, something very special happened in the New World between 600 B.C. and A.D. 400. At the beginning of this 1,000-year time period, God instructed a prophet named Lehi to leave Jerusalem with some other families and move to the Western Hemisphere. Over the centuries, this little tribe grew into to a major civilization that underwent continual cycles of faith and wickedness, prosperity and destruction. In his usual way, the Lord sent prophets to teach these people and call them to repentance.

Soon after the Savior's resurrection, he dropped by to spend a few days with about 2,500 of his followers in the Western Hemisphere, ministering to his "other sheep" (John 10:16). Before the Savior ascended to heaven, he called 12 additional apostles to carry out his work in this part of the world. Under apostolic leadership, the people managed to hold onto the gospel for another 400 years after the Savior's momentous visit. Eventually, however, their lack of faith led to their corruption and extermination, and that was the end of the Book of Mormon civilization.

The New World prophets and apostles kept records on metal plates. A prophet named Mormon made a *For Dummies*–style compilation of the people's spiritual history — well, a shortened version, anyway — and his son Moroni buried it in a hillside. About 1,400 years later, Joseph Smith's family settled near this same hillside in upstate New York. With the help of God, who helpfully provided interpreting devices to go along with the metal plates, Joseph translated and published the ancient record, and today the LDS Church distributes millions of copies each year in over 100 languages. If the proof of Mormonism is in the pudding, then the Book of Mormon *is* the pudding. (For more about the Book of Mormon, see Chapter 9.)

Establishing the Church

While translating the Book of Mormon, Joseph Smith and his helpers came across passages that prompted questions, such as how to properly baptize someone. The questions that Joseph asked Heavenly Father triggered the following key events:

- In 1829, John the Baptist appeared to Joseph and his chief scribe to restore the *Aaronic Priesthood,* the preparatory priesthood authority necessary to perform basic ordinances, including baptism.

- Soon after John the Baptist's visitation, the New Testament apostles Peter, James, and John appeared on earth to give Joseph the *Melchizedek Priesthood,* the full authority to act in God's name within the Church organization. (For more on the two Mormon priesthoods, see Chapter 4.)

- In 1830, Joseph Smith officially organized the Church, which Mormons believe the Savior recognizes as his only "true and living" church.

- Until Joseph's assassination in 1844, he received numerous additional revelations, scriptures, and ordinances that helped fully establish the new religion (for an overview of these additions, see Chapters 10 and 11).

Coming to terms with the M-word

As a prophet who lived somewhere in North or·South America around A.D. 400, Mormon was just one of dozens of important figures in LDS history. Nevertheless, he's the man whose name became the nickname for this whole religious movement. Unfortunately, The Church of Jesus Christ of Latter-day Saints is a tad frustrated with the nickname.

As we say earlier in this section, the prophet Mormon's claim to fame was compiling and abridging the ancient records that became the Book of Mormon, titled that way because of Mormon's central editorial role. After Joseph Smith translated and published the book, it didn't take long for detractors to start calling his followers *Mormonites,* because of their belief in the book. The Mormons got rid of the "ite" part of the nickname, and eventually the term stuck and lost most of its negative connotations.

Still, *Mormon* is just a nickname. What would Mormons rather be called? Although the Church hasn't completely ruled out the terms *Mormon* and *Mormonism* at the cultural level, it asks the media to use the Church's full name on first reference in a story — in other words, The Church of Jesus Christ of Latter-day Saints — and then say "The Church of Jesus Christ" on each subsequent reference. However, that lingo hasn't exactly caught on, even at the daily Salt Lake newspaper owned by the Church.

At Church headquarters, use of the term *Mormon* has been gradually phasing out, with one notable exception: the Mormon Tabernacle Choir. What usually takes the place of *Mormon* is the term *Latter-day Saint,* or *LDS* for short. The Church doesn't exactly love being called the LDS Church, but the leaders like it a heck of a lot better than *Mormon Church,* which they strongly discourage.

Throughout this book, we use the terms *Mormon, LDS,* and *Latter-day Saint* interchangeably to refer to the doctrine, teachings, practices, and members of The Church of Jesus Christ of Latter-day Saints. Some Mormons joke that LDS really stands for "Let's drink Sprite," in reference to many Mormons' decision to keep away from cola (see Chapter 16). Within the Church, some hipsters — yes, Mormon hipsters do exist — have started using the word *Mo* to refer to things Mormon, but we won't go that far.

Day-to-Day Mormon Life

Viewing this mortal life as a time of testing, Mormons see their faith as the textbook for an A+, and they strive to live the religion 24 hours a day, 7 days a week. In fact, one of the primary virtues in Mormonism is obedience to the commandments and counsel of the prophets, as well as to the spiritual promptings of the Holy Ghost. The religion provides standards that Mormons believe will help them become pure and righteous enough to reenter God's presence, with the Savior's crucial help to overcome sin and death.

Following is an overview of what daily life is like for Mormons all over the world. Not everyone lives up to all these standards, of course, but this is pretty much what practicing Mormons believe they ought to be trying to do:

✔ **They follow a disciplined routine.** Each day, most Mormons pray individually, pray as families, and spend time reading the scriptures (for more on these practices, see Chapter 17). They may also devote time on one or more weekdays to fulfilling volunteer Church assignments, such as preparing a Sunday school lesson or helping clean the local meetinghouse (see Chapter 6).

✔ **They embrace a G-rated lifestyle.** To avoid addictions and maintain spiritual purity, Mormons abstain from coffee, tea, tobacco, alcohol, and harmful drugs. In addition, they keep sex strictly within the bonds of heterosexual marriage and shun anything "unholy or impure," including immodest clothes, pornography, profanity, and gambling. Some Mormons even refrain from cola drinks and R-rated movies. (See Chapter 16.)

✔ **They seek a change of pace on Sunday.** On Sundays, Mormons spend the day resting and worshipping with their families, and they attend a three-hour block of classes and meetings at their local meetinghouse, which is open to the public. On the Sabbath, most Mormons avoid work, shopping, sports, and other worldly distractions. (See Chapters 6 and 17.)

✔ **They kiss Monday-night football goodbye.** Mormons devote Monday evenings to spending time and studying the gospel with their families (see Chapters 5 and 17).

✔ **They take part in rituals.** Mormons regularly attend the *temple,* a special building set aside for the faith's most sacred ordinances, such as celestial marriage. Temples aren't open on Sunday or to the public, and most of the ordinances performed there are on behalf of the dead. Mormons who've gone through the temple wear special undergarments each day to remind them of their covenants with God and to provide spiritual protection. (See Chapter 7.)

✔ **They occasionally sacrifice food and money.** Each month, Mormons fast for two meals (about 24 hours) to increase their spirituality, spending that time praying, reading the scriptures, attending church, and otherwise trying to get closer to God. They donate money saved from those meals — and more, if possible — to the Church's fund for helping the needy. In addition, Mormons tithe a full 10 percent of their income to the Church. (See Chapter 16.)

What Makes Mormonism Different?

Although Mormons share a lot in common with other Christian and non-Christian faiths, they hold several uncommon beliefs, especially when compared to Protestant Christianity. Here's a brief overview of some key points where Mormons differ from the norm:

✔ **Premortality:** No other mainstream Christian denomination agrees with Mormons that the essence of each human has always existed and that humans were born spiritually to Heavenly Parents before being born physically on earth. Although people who believe in reincarnation can easily relate with the concept of a life before this life, Mormons believe that everyone gets only one shot at mortality. (See Chapter 2.)

✔ **The Trinity:** Most Christians think of God as a universal spirit that manifests as Father, Son, and Holy Ghost (check out *Christianity For Dummies,* written by Richard Wagner and published by Wiley, for more on that idea). By contrast, Mormons see these deities as three separate, individual beings who are united in purpose. (See Chapter 3.)

✔ **God's nature:** Mormons believe that God the Father underwent a test much like this earthly one, which they argue doesn't deny his eternal nature because *all* individuals have always existed, in one form or another (see "Life before mortal life," earlier in this chapter). Today, God has a glorified body of flesh and bones, and he possesses all possible knowledge and power throughout the universe. (See Chapter 3.)

✔ **The Savior:** Mormons believe that Jesus Christ was God's firstborn spirit child, which means he's the oldest spiritual sibling of all humans. However, Jesus is God's only *earthly* child, which means that he's the only perfect mortal who ever lived. Mormons believe that the name *Jehovah* in the Old Testament refers not to God but to his son, who's taken the lead role in saving humankind since before the earth was formed. (See Chapter 3.)

✔ **The devil and hell:** Mormons believe that God didn't create evil but that each individual being has the ability to choose good or evil. The devil was God's first, most powerful spirit child to choose evil, and he tries to persuade others to do the same, but evil could still exist without him. As far as hell is concerned, Mormons believe that wicked people will suffer consequences for their sins, but only those who personally know God and still rebel against him will go to an eternal hell, which Mormons call *outer darkness.* (See Chapter 2.)

✔ **Adam and Eve:** In the Mormon view, Adam and Eve were heroes who consciously took the steps necessary to begin mortality. Mormons view mortality as an essential test for eternal progression. Without this physical experience in a fallen world, humans can't learn and grow enough to eventually become like God. (See Chapter 2.)

✔ **Grace versus works:** Although many other Christians emphasize salvation solely by God's grace through faith, Mormons believe that people are saved by grace after they've done all they can to obey God and be righteous. Good works alone don't save people, but they do nourish people's faith and make them more open to receiving the grace that saves them. As far as bad works go, all sins require repentance before grace can kick in. (See Chapter 2.)

✔ **The Atonement:** Mormons believe that Jesus Christ paid for humankind's sins not just on the cross but also in the Garden of Gethsemane, where his pain was so great that he sweat blood. Christ pays the price of the sins of anyone who repents and obeys his gospel, but those who refuse will suffer for their sins. Mormons don't use the sign of the cross, as some Christians do, but they believe that Christ broke the bonds of death through his resurrection. (See Chapter 3.)

✔ **Salvation:** In contrast to many Protestant Christians, who believe you're either saved or you're not, Mormons believe all humans will be resurrected and will receive an eternal reward depending on individual worthiness. Although pretty much everyone will receive a measure of salvation in one of three eternal kingdoms, only those who at some point accept the Savior's complete gospel — the same one currently preached and practiced by the Mormons — will receive *full* salvation, which means returning to live with God. In addition, Mormons use the term *exaltation* to refer to humankind's potential to become like God, which happens only for people who reach the highest level of the highest eternal kingdom. (See Chapter 2.)

✔ **Priesthood:** In the Mormon view, the *priesthood* is the authority to act in God's name for the salvation of his children, within the bounds of the LDS Church organization. Instead of ordaining professionals who've completed special training, the Church ordains all worthy and willing Mormon males from age 12 on up, via the laying on of hands by someone already holding the priesthood. Any adult priesthood holder can perform ordinances such as baptism and healing or be called to lead a congregation. In contrast with the traditions of some other churches, Mormon priesthood holders don't get a nickel for their service. (See Chapter 4.)

✔ **Ordinances:** In some Christian denominations, ordinances such as baptism are outward expressions of commitment, not requirements for salvation. Mormons, on the other hand, believe that each individual must receive certain physical ordinances in order to return to God's presence, and authorized priesthood holders must perform them. In addition, Mormons hold the unusual belief that if a person dies without receiving an essential ordinance, a living Mormon can perform it in a temple on the deceased person's behalf, and his or her spirit will decide whether or not to accept it. (See Chapters 6 and 7.)

✔ **Apostles and prophets:** Mormons believe that the Savior issues revelations to whatever prophet is currently leading the LDS Church. These revelations instruct how the leaders should administer the Church under current earthly conditions. In addition, Mormons believe that the Savior calls modern apostles to serve as his special witnesses, similar to the New Testament apostles. (See Chapter 8.)

✔ **Scriptures:** Most Christians believe the Bible is God's only authorized scripture. Although Mormons uphold the Bible and prayerfully study its teachings, they believe it contains some translation errors and omissions. In addition, they believe that other civilizations recorded scriptures equally as valid as the Bible, most notably the New World civilization that gave rise to the Book of Mormon. In fact, they believe that God is still revealing scriptures in this day and age. (See Chapters 9 and 10.)

✔ **God's only true church:** Although most other Christians accept each other's churches as valid in God's sight, Mormons believe their own church is God's only "true and living" church currently on the face of the earth. Mormons respectfully acknowledge that many religions contain elements of God's eternal truths, but they believe that only the LDS Church possesses the full package of God's authorized priesthood, ordinances, and revelations. Mormons see the LDS Church as the complete modern restoration of the same true religion that other groups and civilizations have possessed throughout human history. (See Chapter 4.)

✔ **Family and marriage:** Some people believe that earthly family relationships, including marriage, end at death. Mormons believe that specially ordained temple workers can seal earthly families together for eternity and that couples can keep progressing together to become Heavenly Parents. (See Chapters 2, 5, and 7.)

Chapter 2

The Mormon Plan of Salvation

In This Chapter

▶ Understanding humanity's origins

▶ Fulfilling the purpose of this mortal life

▶ Reaching the intermediate spirit world after death

▶ Going to an eternal heaven — or hell

*W*hen it comes to pondering existence, each human being invariably faces three fundamental questions: Where did I come from? Why am I here? What's on TV tonight? (Er, that last one should've been, Where am I going?)

As a religion, Mormonism prides itself on providing complete, satisfying answers to all three of these eternal questions, answers that together are known as the *plan of salvation.* Mormons are Christians, but their beliefs about humankind's origin, purpose, and destiny differ considerably from those of Catholic or Protestant Christians. In a nutshell, the Mormon plan of salvation takes humans through the following major phases of existence:

✔ **Premortal life:** Before this physical earth was created, the eternal essences of all humans underwent spiritual birth and preparation in God's presence.

✔ **Mortal probation:** Born into a physical body and with their premortal memories veiled, humans face trials and tests. All earth dwellers are at this stage.

✔ **Spirit world:** Depending on their earthly conduct and the desires of their hearts, spirits of the deceased wait in either paradise or prison for resurrection and the final judgment.

✔ **Three degrees of glory:** Except for a few really bad people, each human will spend eternity in one level of a multitiered heaven.

In this chapter, we discuss each of these phases in detail (see Figure 2-1 for a quick graphic summary).

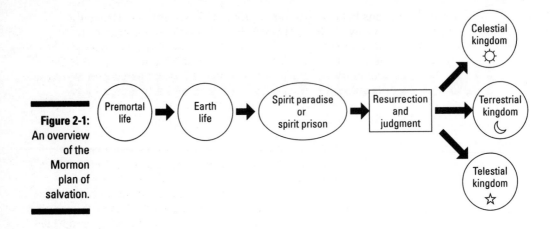

Figure 2-1:
An overview
of the
Mormon
plan of
salvation.

Mormon Karma: The Premortal Life

Every religion makes claims about the afterlife, but one of Mormonism's key concepts is the *before*-life. Mormons aren't the only ones who believe that humans are eternal beings, but Mormons are somewhat unusual — especially among other Christians — for believing that human eternity stretches in *both* directions, before and after mortality.

In Hinduism and Buddhism, a person's actions affect the nature of his or her next life, a process known as *karma*. Mormons don't believe in reincarnation, but they do believe that a person's actions in the premortal life can affect the nature and circumstances of his or her earthly life. It's not uncommon for a Mormon, when faced with some earthly trial, to half-jokingly mutter, "What did I do in the premortal life to deserve this?"

In the Mormon view, each human being arrives on this earth with baggage from the premortal life — and if you're here, it's because you *chose* to come. This section discusses what the concept of premortal life means to Mormons and explains some significant historical premortal events, including the War in Heaven.

From intelligence to spirit

Mormonism's founding prophet, Joseph Smith, taught that the essence of each human being has always existed, as opposed to being created. The Mormon term for an individual human essence is *intelligence,* but exactly what form an intelligence takes is a bit hazy. The important concept to understand, from the Mormon perspective, is that God didn't create our fundamental, individual identities out of nothing.

Instead, Mormons believe that, before this earth was formed, Heavenly Father and Heavenly Mother got together and procreated a spirit body to house each human intelligence. (For more on the infrequently discussed Heavenly Mother, see Chapters 3 and 15.) These spirit bodies resemble God's glorified physical body, but they don't yet have a physical presence. What God does for his spirit children is help them progress into increasingly advanced states of existence, potentially culminating in their becoming an eternal parent like him. After all, they carry his spiritual DNA.

But we're getting ahead of the story. Before the earth's creation, Mormon belief says that billions of spirit children lived in the presence of the Heavenly Parents across eons of premortal time — and, in fact, those spirits who haven't yet been born on the earth are still dwelling in their presence. In this premortal spiritual state, future humans developed their distinctive personalities, attributes, and talents and interacted socially with each other, preparing for the earthly test.

Why do the spirits want to come to earth? Just as an intelligence could progress only so far without a spirit body, a spirit can progress only so far without a physical body. Back before the earth was formed, the spirit children reached a point of maturity where they expressed the desire to gain a perfect, glorified physical body like God's and become like him. Without a physical body, they couldn't do many of the things God could do, including procreate other beings.

Mormons believe that in order to enable his spirit children to become like him, God offered them the plan of salvation, which would allow them to test-drive a physical body on an earth, prove how well they could exercise faith in God and follow his commandments, and strive to eventually return to God's presence. Through a mortal test like the one early Mormon leaders taught that God himself underwent innumerable eons ago, his children could start to learn the godly attributes of disciplining physical appetites, shaping the elements, and loving and serving their offspring.

In addition, they could gain godly wisdom by encountering the opposing forces of good and evil, pain and pleasure, sickness and health, age and youth, sin and virtue, time and eternity, and death and immortality. If they learned these lessons well enough, the potential payoff could be huge: Eventually they could become an eternal parent like God, perfect in love, justice, and mercy. Of course, they would still eternally respect and honor God as their father, even when having spirit children and creating planets of their own.

Relax, you've already passed the first test

Congratulations! As someone who lives here on earth, you've already passed the first test of choosing to follow God's plan of salvation. Due to what Mormons call the War in Heaven, it wasn't an easy choice to make. Allow us to explain.

As his spirit children considered the plan of salvation, God didn't hide the fact that the path would be fraught with danger, difficulty, and sacrifice. To facilitate effective testing conditions, he would place a veil over each spirit's memories of the premortal life. Each person would start over again as a baby and then age and die. God would allow evil to tempt people and chance to affect them for both good and bad. He would continue to absolutely respect human free will (Mormons call it *agency* or *free agency*), even when people chose to do terrible things to each other. In a kind of spiritual survival of the fittest — a process God would oversee with love and concern — only those who made enough progress in learning and obeying God's will would eventually be resurrected as heavenly parents; the rest would be resurrected to lesser degrees of glory, according to their efforts, desires, and faith.

Because all earthly mortals would sin and become unworthy to reenter God's presence, a sinless redeemer would be necessary to pay the price of sin so that those who repented could become clean again. In addition, beings with mortal flesh would need a way to overcome their physical death. Mormons believe that during a great council in heaven before the earth was formed, two of God's spirit children volunteered to serve as redeemer of humankind:

- ✔ A high-ranking, widely influential spirit named Lucifer proposed to save everybody by forcing their obedience, and he would receive all the glory for himself. However, this plan didn't meet God's approval, because true progress is impossible without *agency* and *accountability* — in other words, the freedom to choose and the obligation to face the consequences.

- ✔ The firstborn of all the spirits, named Jehovah, offered to pay the price for everybody's sins, lead those who were willing to follow him back to God, and overcome death through resurrection. In addition, Jehovah promised to obey God's will and give all the glory to God. God chose him as the redeemer, and he was later born on earth as Jesus Christ.

Unfortunately, Lucifer was a sore loser. Declaring war on God and Jehovah, he persuaded a third of the spirit children to take his side. Perhaps these followers of Lucifer feared they'd fail if left to make their own choices on earth, and they wanted someone to guarantee success. Eventually, God cast Lucifer and his followers out of heaven, denying them the opportunity to ever receive a physical body. Lucifer became the devil (also known as Satan) and his followers became demons, and the spiritual war that started in premortality continues here on earth. Lucifer hasn't admitted defeat, and he still lusts for power and tries to thwart God's purposes by destroying human freedom through whatever means possible. (See this chapter's later section "Satan: A necessary evil" for more on Satan's role in Mormon theology.)

If you're holding this book, Mormons believe that you took Jehovah's side in the War in Heaven and thus qualified yourself to be born onto this earth. So, kudos all around.

Premortality in the here and now

Premortality plays a central role in the Mormon religious imagination. However, the subject is also a troublesome area. Because the LDS scriptures don't give many specifics about premortality, much of the Mormon outlook results from semiformal or even folk teachings. Perhaps more than any other Mormon belief, the idea of premortality has been shaped by sentimentalized pop culture, especially the influential Mormon musical *Saturday's Warrior,* performed live for hundreds of thousands during the 1970s and still widely viewed on video. Even worse, Mormon folk beliefs related to premortality have contributed to some harmful attitudes, particularly concerning racial matters.

By the way, although Mormons are unique among Christians for believing in premortality, they've spotted many glimpses of the concept in both the Old and New Testaments of the Bible, especially the following passages: Job 38:4–7, Proverbs 8:22–31, Jeremiah 1:5, John 9:1–3, Acts 17:28, Ephesians 1:4–5, 2 Timothy 1:9, Titus 1:1–2, Hebrews 12:9, Jude 1:6, and Revelation 12:7–9.

The following sections show premortality's effects, both positive and negative, in the here and now.

Effect on earthly circumstances

Mormons tend to wonder and speculate about how premortality affects conditions in mortality. You can imagine the questions. Was someone born into a prosperous Mormon household because he or she fought valiantly on Jehovah's side, or was it because this person was a spiritual weakling who needed a head start on earth? Was a person born into the slums of Calcutta because he or she only barely supported Jehovah, or was it because he or she was a particularly gifted spirit who needed an extrachallenging test? Although only God knows the reasons behind any particular individual's earthly situation, Mormons trust that premortality provides a comforting and reasonable explanation for the great variety of earthly circumstances, instead of attributing them to randomness.

Although Mormons don't believe in predestination, they do believe in *foreordination,* which means that God chose spirits with certain skills and capacities to fulfill special purposes during mortality, such as becoming a prophet. However, being given a particular foreordination doesn't mean the person will necessarily succeed in fulfilling it. In the Mormon view, someone who did well in premortality can screw up on earth, and someone who lagged behind in premortality can catch up here.

On the other hand, Mormons commonly believe that some spirits were so valiant in the premortal life that they simply needed to receive a physical body without being morally tested, which helps account for childhood deaths and people born with mental limitations that make them unaccountable for their actions.

Effect on earthly attitudes

Following are some specific ways in which the Mormon belief in premortality affects earthly attitudes, for better or worse. Although widely prevalent, most of these beliefs aren't official Church doctrine.

- **Dreams and déjà vu:** Although humans have no conscious memories of premortality, some Mormons believe that the subconscious retains ideas, plans, goals, instructions, warnings, and other impressions and impulses from the premortal days. For some, this belief helps explain some dreams, sensations of déjà vu, and perhaps even premonitions that seem to hold spiritual meaning or significance.

- **Friendships and missionary work:** When a Mormon forms an unusually close bond with somebody and gets the feeling they've known each other forever, the Mormon will sometimes assume that the friendship began in the premortal life. Some Mormons believe they promised certain individuals that they'd find them on earth and convert them to Mormonism — in fact, many Mormon missionaries keep such a possibility in mind while knocking on endless doors. As missionaries contact people and try to teach them the gospel, they hope that spiritually sensitive people will recognize the plan of salvation from premortality.

- **The latter days:** As the Church's name indicates, Mormons believe that the period of earthly mortality is approaching its conclusion (for more on the return of Christ, see Chapter 3). Because this modern time is both the most advanced and most challenging era in the earth's history, with more temptations than ever before, Mormons believe that Heavenly Father reserved many of his brightest, strongest spirit children to be born in these latter days. Church leaders frequently repeat this message to the Church's teenage youth, which not only helps build spiritual egos but also gives Mormons a high standard to live up to — and yes, it can also increase guilt about shortcomings.

- **Marriage and family:** Some Mormons believe that during premortality, they formed spiritual bonds with their future earthly spouses, parents, and children. It's not unusual to find a Mormon couple who believes they're meant to be together because of promises made during premortality. Likewise, some Mormon parents conceive another child because they feel a spirit is missing from their family.

- **Race:** In an attempt to explain why some people were born into supposedly inferior races, a few early Church leaders claimed that these people somehow performed inadequately during premortality. Although the LDS Church no longer teaches these politically incorrect ideas, it hasn't publicly withdrawn or apologized for those individuals' earlier racist teachings, and some Church members may continue to hold these beliefs. Other members, however, including some high-ranking leaders, suspect that many individuals of oppressed races may have been *more* valiant in the premortal life than their Caucasian counterparts, and thus are faced with a greater challenge here on earth. (For more on the racial controversies in Mormon theology, see Chapter 15.)

Acing the Test of Mortality

With the successful completion of Phase One — premortality — all those spirits who chose to side with Jehovah in the War in Heaven proceed to Phase Two, which is mortal life, sometimes called "the second estate." In Mormonism, everyone on earth is here because they chose to be, not by accident. That idea may give a spot of comfort when mortal life isn't a bed of roses.

Mormons regard mortality as a test. It offers the chance to come to know the Savior, Jesus Christ, and follow his teachings. Life's trials and triumphs can prepare humans to successfully return to their Heavenly Parents (see the section "The Afterlife: Eternal Progression," later in this chapter), provided they find and keep the faith and live worthily. If people want to be exalted through eternity, they have to go through this mortal life. There's no shortcut.

The basic principle of mortality is *agency,* or free will, and to understand that concept in Mormonism, you have to go way back. Back to a man, a woman, and a garden.

Adam and Eve: Heroes of humanity

In Catholic and Protestant Christianity, Adam and Eve sort of get a bad rap. If they hadn't eaten the fruit and screwed up everything for everyone else, the thinking goes, everyone would be happily cavorting in Eden. But Mormons don't see it that way at all.

In the Mormon view, without Adam and Eve's heroic choice, no one but them would be on earth in the first place. Their decision to eat the forbidden fruit gave everyone the opportunity to experience a mortal life and have a crack at the celestial kingdom (see "Reaching the three degrees of glory . . . or outer darkness," later in this chapter). The Book of Mormon and the Pearl of Great Price (see Chapters 9 and 10 for an explanation of these LDS scriptures) both agree that Adam and Eve's choice wasn't a mistake or some great cosmic tragedy, but a necessary decision. As the Book of Mormon puts it, "Adam fell that men might be; and men are, that they might have joy" (2 Nephi 2:25). In other words, their decision brought the world potential joy as well as pain — both essential parts of being human. God wouldn't create a fallen world or force his children to inhabit one, but he would let them choose for themselves whether to usher in mortal conditions and undergo such a test, and Adam and Eve paved the way.

In the garden, God gave Adam and Eve two seemingly contradictory commandments:

✔ Be fruitful and multiply, replenishing the earth — in other words, have kids.

✔ Don't eat from the tree of the knowledge of good and evil — in other words, don't usher in the mortal conditions necessary to have kids.

No, God didn't make a mistake or succumb to a divine version of Alzheimer's by giving these apparently opposite pieces of instruction. It was a test of Adam and Eve's strength and determination. The decision to usher in mortality was so fraught with significance, difficulty, and danger that God had to make it crystal clear that they chose it for themselves and he didn't impose it upon them — in fact, he sternly warned them against it. Luckily, Adam and Eve passed this test with flying colors, due in no small part to Eve's particular understanding and vision. In so doing, they resolved two major problems for the human race:

✔ One problem was that Adam and Eve had to eat the fruit before they could be fruitful, so to speak. The Book of Mormon explains that they couldn't have any "seed" (translation: kids) in their state of innocence. So they needed to eat the fruit of mortality — the fruit from the tree of the knowledge of good and evil — in order to become parents, and thus become more like God. If the earth's first people hadn't been able to start procreating, that would've been bad news for all the billions of spirits stuck in the waiting room of premortality, chomping at the bit for their shot at the mortal test.

✔ A second problem with their situation in Eden was that Adam and Eve couldn't spiritually progress in their state of innocence. They were stuck, Peter Pan–like, in permanent immortality, which gave them nothing to lose or gain. In order to get the benefit of God's great plan of salvation, they had to prove themselves in mortality and die in order to return to God in heaven.

According to Mormons, Eve was the first to understand that she would have to disobey one commandment in order to obey the other. They consider her a heroine for making a difficult but correct moral choice, disobeying a lesser law and sacrificing her own peace and life of ease in the garden, where no one could age or die, in order to serve a higher law, enabling countless others to enter mortality and fulfill their earthly missions. By choosing death for herself, she gave the gift of life to all people, thus earning the name Eve, which means life, and the title "mother of all living." Mormons believe that God chose her for this mission in her premortal life and that she was one of the noble and great spirits mentioned in the Pearl of Great Price. In fact, modern LDS leaders have taught that Eve's premortal spirit even participated in the creation of the world.

Although Mormons refer to this event as *the Fall,* they don't regard it as a failure, like some other denominations do. Catholics and some Protestants, for example, view the Fall as the moment that sin entered the world, and they believe that *original sin* — sin that is genetically passed from generation to generation at conception — is the direct result of the sin of Adam and Eve.

Mormons completely reject the idea of original sin; as the second Article of Faith states, Mormons believe that people "will be punished for their own sins, and not for Adam's transgression." Note the use of the word *transgression:* Adam and Eve *transgressed* because their actions literally went beyond a boundary that God had set for them. But Mormons believe their actions weren't *sinful,* because their choice paved the way for the plan of salvation.

Satan: A necessary evil

The Bible says that Eve made her choice in the garden following a proposal from a being who was, as Gollum in *The Lord of the Rings* might say, "very tricksy." Satan, disguised (perhaps figuratively) as a serpent, tried to trick Eve by telling her that the fruit would open her eyes and make her and Adam "as gods," knowing good from evil — all true, according to Mormons. But one of Satan's techniques is to mix the truth with lies so that people become confused. He also told Eve (in the Bible, Genesis 3:5) that she wouldn't die if she ate the fruit, which was a lie. She knew he was wrong but chose to partake anyway and embrace mortality.

So who is this guy? Satan, known in the premortal life as Lucifer, and his demonic followers hold an interesting place in Mormon theology. They make life on earth quite a bit harder. Motivated by selfishness and hate, they declared war on God and everything God represents, and yet God allows them to play an important role in the plan of salvation. Mormons believe these beings entice humans with evil, making mortality a tough road, so people must consciously choose good in order to grow and progress.

In the Mormon view, demons can do only what God permits them to do, even though they think they're rebelling against him. God allows them spiritual access to tempt humans, because temptation puts pressure on humans to choose either good or evil, which is a main purpose of this earthly test. He allows these angels of evil to wreak havoc because that gives people a pressing need to seek out God. Eventually, Mormons believe, when the demons' usefulness in the plan of salvation has ended, God will permanently banish them to outer darkness, which we discuss at the end of this chapter.

Because each being is free to choose right or wrong, evil would exist without Satan, but he certainly fans the flames. He and his followers are miserable on account of their own choices and want everyone else to make the same mistakes, too. Mormons believe that one of the key ways demons work is by counterfeiting love, religion, happiness, family, spirituality, and many other facets of life. For example, human beings are wired to crave spiritual experiences, so demons try to counterfeit spiritual-seeming sensations through drugs and other means. Satan can guess at most people's weaknesses, but God won't let him tempt people beyond what they can bear, if they exercise sufficient resistance and faith (see 1 Corinthians 10:13).

It ain't over till it's over: Enduring to the end

Adam and Eve's choice in the garden was risky but absolutely necessary. It was the first earthly instance of human beings exercising their agency, or the freedom to make a choice between good and evil. As in the garden story, sometimes morally correct choices aren't always easy to discern; decisions don't come ready-made with a Hallmark ending. Of course, humans are going to make mistakes, but Christ's Atonement paved the way for everyone to receive forgiveness for all their sins if they truly repent. For more on the Atonement of Christ, stay tuned for Chapter 3.

Mormons have a phrase for their stay-the-course philosophy: *enduring to the end.* This phrase is actually one of the main principles of the gospel: After faith, repentance, baptism, and receiving the Holy Ghost, all an individual must do to gain full salvation — in other words, return to live with God — is endure to the end in righteousness. These goals are easier said than done, however, because the journey is 24/7. Here are the basic expectations that Mormons consider to be part of hanging tough till the end:

- Exercise faith in the Savior, Jesus Christ.

- Repent and be baptized and confirmed.

- Do good works.

- Strive to keep the commandments and continually repent.

To bump salvation up a notch and achieve *exaltation,* which means becoming an eternal parent like God, enduring to the end includes making and keeping temple covenants, as discussed in Chapter 7.

What's interesting about this enduring cycle is how it feeds upon itself: Doing good works, obeying the commandments, and studying the scriptures spring from faith and simultaneously make people more open to deepening that faith. To Mormons, faith in Christ *is* what saves, but faith isn't a one-time event that you can check off a list. Rather, faith is an ongoing journey that takes people through this life and the next. Faith is always growing, and obeying commandments and doing good deeds play an important part in nurturing and expanding faith. This whole process is what it means to endure to the end.

Sometimes it seems that mortal life is impossibly hard, and the paths people take are strewn with obstacles and suffering. Mormons take comfort from a revelation given to Joseph Smith when he was in jail, where the Lord told him that all the rotten things that had happened in his life — which up to that point included being tarred and feathered, falsely imprisoned, and driven from his home — would give him experience and would be for his gain (Doctrine and Covenants 122:7; for more on the D&C, see Chapter 10). Mormons believe that all life's ordeals and sufferings have the potential to bring people closer to God.

Why do bad things happen to good people?

Every religion must answer the age-old question of why bad things happen in the world. Mormonism is different from traditional Christianity in its basic answer to that question. Traditional Christianity assumes that God is both entirely loving and entirely powerful, so it's very much an unresolved question why he doesn't intervene to save his children from things like famine, heartache, and untimely death. Mormonism also assumes that God is entirely loving but teaches that God limits his own power in order to grant human beings their agency and let them encounter hard realities that will help them grow in godly understanding.

Because free agency is such an important part of his plan of salvation, God won't typically intervene when people do bad things to each other, though Mormons believe he grieves deeply when his children hurt one another or themselves. In addition, God allows chance accidents and mishaps to occur. Mormons exercise faith that God will protect them and help

orchestrate their lives, but even faithful people can't always be sure whether God will intervene to limit, prevent, or reverse something bad. However, God *always* supports and comforts his children in their sufferings, when they turn to him and ask for his loving care. Of course, those who do harmful things to each other will eventually face the consequences.

To Mormons, it's a great comfort to know that God doesn't purposely smite them with difficult circumstances. Rather, he generally just allows people and events to take their natural courses in this fallen world, occasionally tweaking things when people exercise enough faith in accordance with his will. It's another great comfort that God gives his children the spiritual tools to endure and overcome hardships and traumas. Mormons don't feel they know all the answers about why suffering exists, but they trust in God's goodness and strive to exercise their agency righteously so they don't cause unnecessary suffering to themselves or others.

Mormons also believe that this mortal journey can yield great joy, even though trusting that all life's twists and turns will work together for good isn't always easy. One Book of Mormon prophet, Nephi, told people who had been baptized and were trying to stay on the right path to "press forward with a steadfastness in Christ, having a perfect brightness of hope, and a love of God and of all men" (2 Nephi 31:20). Mormons still cling to that advice more than 2,500 years later.

The Afterlife: Eternal Progression

The Mormon afterlife consists of two main phases. In the first phase, which human beings enter at the time of death, their disembodied spirits await resurrection. In the second phase, resurrected people dwell for eternity in one of several levels of heaven, as determined by the Lord's judgment of their worthiness.

A waiting room for spirits

Mormons aren't unusual for believing that when a human being dies, his or her eternal spirit leaves the body and goes to what Mormons term the *spirit world*. In this holding place, spirits temporarily await their resurrection and the final judgment, which won't occur until after all God's qualified spirit children have had a chance to get a body and experience mortality.

When the physical body dies, a person's spirit retains his or her personality, talents, habits, tastes, knowledge, attitudes, and so on. In the spirit world, people don't have tangible bodies but take a spiritual form that resembles their body in life. All spirits are in adult form, even if they died as mortal children, and the spirit body is perfect, with no defects or injuries. Mormon scriptures and prophets teach that the spirit world is divided into paradise for the righteous and prison for the wicked. In addition, prophets have taught that the spirit world is located right here on earth, but mortal eyes can't see it.

Free parking: Spirit paradise

For those people who repented of their sins and lived righteously during mortality, Mormons believe their spirits go to a place of paradise, where they can rest from worldly pains and problems. As in premortality, these spirits enjoy relationships with each other and create social organizations. They can continue learning and progressing, and they can help further God's purposes, particularly by serving as missionaries to those in spirit prison.

Can these spirits observe mortals and influence us? Some Mormon prophets have taught that they can, although most angelic messengers to earth are former mortal prophets who have been resurrected (and no, they don't have wings). Mormons believe that occult efforts to speak with the dead actually summon demons, who masquerade as dead spirits to confuse mortals. Another interesting question is whether unborn premortal spirits can mingle with deceased postmortal spirits. The concept isn't an official doctrine, but some Mormons believe it happens.

Do not pass go: Spirit prison

Mormons don't believe in the same concept of hell as most other Christians — in fact, Mormons don't even use the term *hell* very often. There are two places that Mormons think of when they imagine hell. We'll get to the second one, *outer darkness,* in just a moment. But first we discuss *spirit prison,* a temporary abode — although temporary may mean centuries or even millennia — where people's spirits go if they behaved wickedly on the earth, either because they didn't know or didn't accept the gospel message of Christ's Atonement. Mormon scriptures say that spirit prison is for all people who "died in their sins" and still need the opportunity to repent of them (D&C 138:32–35).

Although spirit prison isn't staffed by pitchfork-wielding horned demons, the place isn't warm, happy, and relaxing, and the devil can still influence people there. One Book of Mormon passage says there's a lot of "weeping, and wailing, and gnashing of teeth" in spirit prison, probably because people recognize the harmful consequences of their choices on earth. Good news, though: In spirit prison, the possibility of parole *does* exist, and someone's sentence there can be drastically cut short by a genuine change of heart and acceptance of Christ's gospel.

Mormons believe that an impassable gulf used to exist between paradise and prison. Jesus Christ bridged this gulf when his spirit visited the spirits in prison during the time between his death and resurrection (see 1 Peter 3:18–20 and 4:6 in the Bible). Ever since then, spirits from paradise have ministered to those in prison, teaching them the gospel and trying to convince them to accept Christ and repent.

For some spirits in prison, such as those who didn't get a fair chance to hear the gospel on the earth, learning the gospel and repenting may take a short time, and then they can cross over into paradise. Presumably, many people will become more eternally focused when they realize that their spirits have survived beyond death, and they'll accept the gospel and repent. For others, however, such as those who rejected the gospel or were grossly immoral on earth, repentance may be a long and painful process, far more difficult than it would've been during mortality. For the most stubborn spirits who never voluntarily accept the gospel and Christ as their Savior, they'll suffer for their own sins even as Christ already suffered on their behalf. However, even those souls eventually will be resurrected and assigned to the lowest degree of eternal glory; only a tiny percentage of people will spend eternity in *outer darkness* (see the next section).

Meanwhile, mortal Mormons continually perform crucial gospel ordinances, such as baptism, on behalf of dead people. If and when a dead person's spirit accepts the gospel in spirit prison, these ordinances allow him or her to potentially enjoy the gospel's full eternal benefits and, for those who qualify, eventually ascend to the highest tier of the celestial kingdom. Why can't a spirit perform its own ordinances? Because ordinances are physical and require a body. (For more on performing ordinances for the dead, see Chapters 5 and 7.)

Reaching the three degrees of glory . . . or outer darkness

One of the unusual features of LDS theology compared to other Christian denominations is that Mormons don't see heaven as a one-size-fits-all sort of place. Mormons believe that as in life, where some people are more spiritually oriented and Christlike than others, heaven will feature considerable diversity as far as who receives what eternal reward. For those who earn the highest blessings, those blessings carry great responsibilities and expectations.

In fact, for Mormons, the singular term *heaven* is a bit of a misnomer, because the afterlife will feature not one but three distinct *kingdoms,* or heavens. Mormons believe that the biblical apostle Paul was referring to this distinction in 2 Corinthians 12:2, when he spoke of having been taken up into "the third heaven" in a vision. In the Old Testament's original Hebrew, the word for *heaven* is always plural, and the Greek New Testament also often renders the term in plural form. So Mormons believe that the idea of a multitiered heaven is biblically based.

As is typical of the Mormon penchant for organization, each of the three kingdoms may have gradations *within* it. LDS leader James Talmage taught that because "innumerable degrees of merit" exist among all the people in the human race, it follows that God provides them with "an infinity of graded glories" in the afterlife.

Judging each person

After Christ returns and reigns on the earth for 1,000 years and all God's children — except the devil and his demons — have been resurrected, God's people and Satan will have one final battle (skip to Chapter 3 for more on the Second Coming and resurrection). If you're one of those who likes to read the end of a good mystery first, here's a clue: God's people win. Then all people will face Judgment Day and find out where they'll cool their heels for eternity.

Mormons believe that the Savior and his apostles from different time periods will carry out the final judgment. LDS scriptures say that a perfect record of all human deeds and thoughts — frighteningly enough! — has been made in heaven, and that people will get to see that record on Judgment Day. Some imagine themselves viewing their best and worst moments on a giant screen, like in the Al Brooks–Meryl Streep movie *Defending Your Life.* Maybe a sympathetic Jesus Christ will stand with them, holding their hand as they cringe at the moments when they screamed at their children or smile at the times they selflessly helped someone in need. Hopefully, the worst scenes will have wound up on the cutting room floor, forever forgotten because the person repented by asking the Savior's forgiveness and cleaning up his or her act.

Whatever the case, Mormon belief is clear on the idea that actions in this life are terribly important in determining what will happen to people in the life to come. Good deeds don't necessarily guarantee a place in heaven, but they're definitely not irrelevant, either. Mormons rely upon Christ's Atonement for salvation, but good works are an important measure of faithfulness and make people more able to receive God's grace and understand his goodness (for more on the Atonement, see Chapter 3). Mormons believe that when Christ spoke of the kingdom of heaven in the New Testament, he regarded it as hard earned rather than easily understood or achieved. The kingdom of heaven, he said, is like the yeast that makes bread grow, or a pearl of great price that people may search for their entire lives, sacrificing everything in order to attain it (Matthew 13:33, 45–46). In other words, the covenant relationship with God established at baptism requires active human participation.

The challenging news about all this judgment business is that simply professing belief in Christ isn't enough; a person's actions must live up to the standard set by Christ's gospel. On the other hand, the good news is that Mormon theology doesn't send non-Christians to "hell" simply for not believing in Christ. In the Mormon view, the idea of a loving God sending whole cultures and peoples who never had the chance to hear of the Savior to eternal damnation makes no sense. Mormon theology teaches that good people of many different religious traditions will live in paradise forever; they may even dwell in the highest of the three kingdoms, if they accept the gospel in the spirit world and so qualify.

The following sections provide a rundown of the three basic kingdoms of the afterlife. Think of each of these kingdoms as layers of a wedding cake.

The bottom layer: Telestial kingdom

The lowest tier of the three-tiered heavenly wedding cake is the telestial kingdom, which is basically for the following kinds of people who died in their sins:

- Adulterers
- Liars
- Murderers
- Rapists
- Those who "received not the gospel of Christ, neither the testimony of Jesus," not even in the spirit world (D&C 76:82)
- Those who know all Celine Dion's songs by heart

You may think that such obvious violators of God's laws would be consigned to everlasting torment, but the telestial kingdom is actually a lovely paradise. Remember that these people, not having accepted Christ's Atonement, suffer for their own sins while they're in spirit prison, and then Heavenly Father in his mercy allows them to head for the telestial kingdom after the great judgment. (Nice guy, that Heavenly Father.) Also, we should point out that Mormons believe there's no forgiveness in this life for criminal murderers; although liars, adulterers, and other serious sinners can choose to repent, murderers automatically go to the telestial kingdom.

So what's the telestial kingdom like? LDS leaders have taught that even this lowest degree of glory is so marvelous that humans can't possibly understand it. The Holy Ghost will minister to this kingdom's inhabitants, and Satan will have no power to tempt or torment them anymore. However, their eternal progress will be curtailed — and in that sense, the word *damnation* applies to them. In addition, they will live singly forever, with no family ties.

The middle layer: Terrestrial kingdom

This kingdom is even more glorious than the telestial, because terrestrial folks were basically decent and honorable during their time on the earth, although they didn't embrace the fullness of the gospel. The terrestrial kingdom will include the following kinds of souls:

- ✔ **Those who are confused about religion:** When it came to spiritual matters, they were "blinded by the craftiness of men" (D&C 76:75).

- ✔ **Lukewarm Mormons:** They were members of the LDS Church but "not valiant in the testimony of Jesus" (D&C 76:79).

- ✔ **Those who waited too long:** They rejected the gospel during their mortal lives but later received it in the spirit world (D&C 76:73–74). This idea doesn't apply to those who never *got* the chance to accept or reject the gospel during their earthly lives.

At this point, you may be wondering why good people won't automatically inherit the most glorious celestial kingdom. Fundamentally, such is the case because they weren't willing to do everything the gospel requires, including participate in sacred ordinances. As the Mormon prophet Brigham Young put it, if people aren't prepared for the celestial kingdom's eternal requirements, then putting them in that kingdom and making them stay there forever isn't kindness on God's part, because they would be uncomfortable there.

For many people, even members of the Church, understanding the difference between the telestial and terrestrial kingdoms is tough, because both are paradises. Here's one key difference: Although the Holy Ghost will visit folks in the telestial kingdom, people in the terrestrial kingdom will also get to spend some time with Christ, whose Atonement will have paid the price of their sins. Church leaders compare the difference between these degrees of glory to the relative brightness of the stars (telestial) and the moon (terrestrial). However, like the telestial people, those in the terrestrial kingdom are limited in their eternal progression and live singly forever, without family relationships.

The top layer: Celestial kingdom

At the top of the three-tiered metaphorical wedding cake is the celestial kingdom. Imagine this kingdom standing high above the others on little pillars, because the difference between its glory and that of the terrestrial kingdom is like the difference in brightness between the sun and the moon.

Getting in on the ground floor

In the Mormon view, to cross the threshold into the celestial kingdom, where God himself lives, people have to

✔ Repent of their sins and accept Christ's Atonement

✔ Receive the saving ordinances of baptism and confirmation from an authorized priesthood holder

✔ Strive to keep God's commandments

In addition, God has promised that the following two kinds of people will receive celestial glory:

✔ "All who have died without a knowledge of this gospel, who would have received it . . . with all their hearts" (D&C 137:7–8)

✔ "All children who die before they arrive at the years of accountability" (D&C 137:10), which Mormons believe is age 8

Rising to the highest level

An entry-level spot living with God in the celestial kingdom is just the beginning. The celestial kingdom has degrees of glory *within* it, and Mormons strive to reach the pinnacle of celestial glory, where they can become eternal parents like God.

Picture a happy bride and groom on the very top of the wedding cake. This figurine is a good image to help people understand the highest tier of the celestial kingdom, because *it takes two to get there* — which makes sense, if they're going to become eternal parents. In Mormon belief, righteous husbands and wives who are sealed to one another for eternity in a holy temple can remain together forever in the celestial kingdom, and their children are also sealed to them. This pinnacle of success is known by several different names, including *exaltation* and *eternal life*. (For more on temples and celestial marriages, see Chapter 7.)

Does that mean single people can't enter the highest level of the celestial kingdom? Well, although the highest level is reserved for married couples, LDS leaders assure righteous, unmarried Church members that they won't be denied any blessings in the hereafter. Some Mormons believe that these people may have the opportunity to marry in the afterlife.

People in the highest level of the celestial kingdom can potentially get it all, including

✔ Unlimited access to God the Father, Christ the Son, and the Holy Ghost

✔ The joy of being with their families for all eternity

✔ A perfected body capable of producing spirit children

✔ The right to continue in eternal progression, even to the point of divinity, although they'll always honor and respect Heavenly Father as their superior

All dogs go to heaven

Many people believe in heaven for animals or feel sure their pets will be waiting for them when they die. Mormonism may well be the only Western religion that directly addresses the eternal fate of Fido and Fluffy through prophetic revelation. Joseph Smith taught that animals have spirits and that after Judgment Day, they'll receive a resurrected body and enjoy eternal bliss through Christ's Atonement. Like people, they had a premortal spiritual life, and like people, they'll continue to progress in knowledge throughout eternity — good news for those dogs who never quite succeeded in obedience school. According to Mormon teaching, they'll be able to praise God forever in a language that God understands.

The LDS Church has no official doctrine about whether people will be reunited with their pets in heaven, though the concept is a popular folk belief for Mormons, as for many other Christians. After all, who will be happy in the celestial kingdom if Rover isn't there to frolic with all those spirit children on the front lawn?

But where much is given, much is also expected. The upper level of the celestial kingdom won't be an eternal resting place like many Christians imagine heaven. This heaven is Mormon, after all, so there's no rest for the righteous, and there's always work to be done! Ultimately, that work entails the parenting of spirit children, who will then start the whole mortality process themselves in some other yet-to-be-created world. (Presumably, raising kids in the celestial kingdom will be a lot easier and less messy than it is here on earth.)

If you're really, really, really bad: Outer darkness

Although Mormons believe that the vast majority of people will one day find themselves somewhere along the win-place-show spectrum of the three degrees of glory, that belief has one catch: outer darkness, which is one of the two "hells" of Mormon theology. (For more on the other, see the earlier section "Do not pass go: Spirit prison.") Because Mormons believe that even murderers, liars, and adulterers who died in their sins can inherit the telestial glory behind Door #3, it must follow that outer darkness is reserved for people who are worse than murderers. Those people include

- The devil himself.

- The one-third of spirits who chose to follow Satan in the War in Heaven (refer to the section "Relax, you've already passed the first test," earlier in this chapter). These spirits never received human bodies, so no one reading this book falls into this category.

- The *sons of perdition* (and presumably daughters too) who *knowingly* and *willfully* turn against the gospel after fully comprehending and embracing it. This doesn't apply to people who never heard the gospel, or who heard it but didn't believe it was true, or who got baptized but then fell away, or who committed terrible sins. It's only for those who, during their lives, completely understood the gospel's truthfulness and received a spiritual witness from the Holy Ghost, but then deliberately chose to despise God and rebel against him. Mormons believe that when the Bible's New Testament speaks about blaspheming against the Holy Ghost as the "unpardonable sin," it refers to this extreme denial. Being a child of *perdition* — which means "loss" — is a one-way ticket to hell, and this time it's forever.

The best way to describe outer darkness is the complete absence of light and warmth. This place offers no forgiveness, no redemption, and no possibility of parole — in essence, outer darkness means permanent misery and perhaps even eventual dissolution. Thankfully, only a minuscule number of those who made it to mortality will inherit outer darkness, due to their fully realized hatred of God.

Chapter 3

Heavenly Parents, Savior, and Holy Ghost

. . . .

In This Chapter

▶ Understanding God's origin, nature, and goals

▶ Appreciating what the Savior does for humankind

▶ Receiving God's love, guidance, and protection through the Holy Ghost

. . . .

*T*he Mormon God — whom they usually refer to as *Heavenly Father* — is quite different from the God most Christians worship. In fact, Mormons reject the traditional concept of the *Trinity,* the idea that the Father, Son, and Holy Ghost are different forms of one entity whose ethereal substance fills the entire universe. Rather, Mormons believe in a godhead staffed by three individual beings — Mormons call them *personages* — who are one in mind and purpose:

> ✔ In the CEO position is God, a physically resurrected man who's achieved a glorified state of eternal *omnipotence* (meaning, he has all the power you could ever want and infinitely more). He's the literal father of human spirits and ruler of the universe.

> ✔ Second in command is God's son, Jesus Christ. He's a separate man whose spirit and physical body were literally procreated by God.

> ✔ Number three is a being whom Mormons commonly call the *Holy Ghost, Holy Spirit, Spirit of God,* or simply the *Spirit.* As a spiritual personage without a physical body, the Holy Ghost is able to directly communicate God's messages to the human spirit.

In addition, Mormons believe that God has a better half. He's eternally married to a glorified, deified woman who's known as *Heavenly Mother,* with whom he has spirit children. Most Mormons discuss their spiritual mother only rarely and briefly — but they do know that, as the *Encyclopedia of Mormonism* states, Heavenly Mother is like Heavenly Father in glory, perfection, compassion, wisdom, and holiness.

The Head Honcho: God the Father

To Mormons, God is the same species as humans, but he's infinitely more advanced. To make a comparison, if humans are like newly hatched tadpoles, then God has already progressed through the frog stage and become a handsome prince. In the Mormon view, God isn't so much a *creator* as an *organizer* of raw materials. As we discuss in this section, he's got a very specific purpose in mind for going to all this trouble to run the universe.

What if God were one of us?

Mormonism's founding prophet Joseph Smith taught, "If men do not comprehend the character of God, they do not comprehend themselves." More specifically, Joseph taught the following as life's great secret: "God himself was once as we are now, and is an exalted man, and sits enthroned in yonder heavens!" A later Mormon prophet put it this way: "As man now is, God once was: as God now is, man may be." (Don't worry — these 19th-century fellows were talking about women, too.)

To Mormons, these all-important concepts mean that God himself has gone through everything his human children have experienced, are now experiencing, and will yet experience. Nineteenth-century Mormon leaders taught that untold eons ago, God's eternal essence was born as a spirit to Heavenly Parents, just like human spirits would later be born to him. He received a physical, mortal body on an earthlike planet and passed his mortal test — evidently with flying colors. After his mortal body died and was resurrected, he advanced to his current position as supreme ruler of this universe. Of course, all this happened long ago and via a more advanced process than any human can comprehend. Modern-day LDS leaders are more reticent about God's origins than those 19th-century freewheelers, though they continue to emphasize that God has a glorified, resurrected physical body.

At some point after giving birth to their first spirit child (see this chapter's later section, "Second Mate: Christ the Son"), God and his eternal wife had other spirit children as well — billions of them. To enable these children to start the cycle all over again by growing up and becoming like their own Heavenly Parents, God taught them the *plan of salvation,* which we describe in detail in Chapter 2. All humans who pass through this earth are God's spirit children who agreed to undergo the most difficult phase of this plan: demonstrating their faith and obedience away from God's presence and thus determining their eternal status.

In the Mormon view, Heavenly Father is the source of everything good, and his attributes include the following:

✔ **A glorified humanlike body:** When the scriptures say that people are created in God's image, Mormons take that claim literally — God looks like a man, with body, parts, and passions. Of course, he doesn't have any flaws or weaknesses, and he's so glorified that mortals would shrivel up in his presence if he didn't preserve them. Mormon scripture reveals that he dwells near the universe's greatest star, Kolob, where one day equals 1,000 earth years.

✔ **Omniscience and omnipotence:** God knows everything there is to know and has complete control of this universe, although he limits his own power somewhat by allowing his children freedom to choose their own actions and consequences. He perfectly comprehends, executes, and — Mormons believe — *obeys* all laws of nature and science. He administers the universe through an all-pervasive power called the *priesthood,* which he shares with his worthy children, as we explain in Chapter 4.

✔ **Perfect love for all his children:** God is the ideal parent. Even when individuals don't comprehend or cooperate with his plan of salvation, God still loves them. Although people who are currently suffering — or watching others suffer — may not believe it, God is infinitely kind and compassionate and wants to help anyone who sincerely seeks him out. (For Mormon ways of connecting with God, see Chapter 17.) However, God practices tough love when it comes to upholding the terms of the plan of salvation, to which everyone agreed before being born on this earth. (To refresh your memory about these terms that Mormons claim you accepted, see Chapter 2.)

With Franklin Planner in hand: God the organizer

As we said earlier in this chapter, Mormons see God as an organizer *of existing elements.* They don't believe he created anything out of nothing. However, even though they believe that all matter is eternal and can't be created out of nothing, they do still sometimes use the term *create* to describe what God does: He can manipulate existing matter any way he wants, whether he's forming comets or beetles. And he lets his children learn how to manipulate it, too.

Mormons recognize two basic kinds of matter: spiritual and physical. Yes, spirit is considered matter, too, but this substance is more delicate and refined than physical matter and is kept veiled from the human eye. God first creates everything from raw spiritual material before he creates it physically, including animals, plants, and even planets themselves. In the case of humans, he procreates their spirits from a mysterious raw material called *intelligence,* about which little is known beyond the belief that this material contains each individual's core identity, which is eternal.

Although God generally reserves initial spiritual creation for himself, he lets his children help in subsequent physical creation. Mormons believe that many of God's brightest spirit children, including Adam and Eve, fulfilled assignments to help form this physical earth under the direction of the Savior. (Kudos to whoever did the fjords in Norway and other cool spots.) Closer to home, God's children help create each other's physical bodies by conceiving and giving birth to babies, and God inspires mortals to make scientific discoveries about manipulating the elements. All this creation is practice for potentially becoming more like God himself.

Why does God go to all this trouble?

The earth isn't merely God's hobby or a windup creation from which he walked away. One of the most quoted scriptures in Mormonism reveals God's basic motivation for everything he does: "Behold, this is my work and my glory — to bring to pass the immortality and eternal life of man" (Moses 1:39; for more about this and other Pearl of Great Price scriptures, see Chapter 10). In other words, what gives God joy and satisfaction is helping his children become like himself. Whenever one of his children succeeds, God succeeds; human progress adds to God's eternal glory. In fact, Mormons believe that God has formed — and is still forming — numberless planets like this one, populated by broods of spirit children who are progressing through the plan of salvation.

Differences in beliefs about God the Father

Mormons differ from "traditional" Christians (such as Protestants and Catholics) in some fundamental ways. To help you understand, we've created Table 3-1 to highlight some of the most important differences in beliefs about God the Father. Even if you don't have time to read the whole chapter, you should be able to master the basic bones of contention from this table and Table 3-2 (later in this chapter), which outlines differences in beliefs about Jesus Christ.

Table 3-1	Mormon View of God versus Other Christian Views	
Qualities of God	*Mormon Christianity*	*Protestant and Catholic Christianity*
God the Creator	God organized all matter but didn't will it into being; matter has always existed.	God created everything out of nothing.
God's substance	Heavenly Father is a being of glorified flesh and bone, like his son, Jesus Christ.	God is spirit and doesn't have a physical body.

Qualities of God	Mormon Christianity	Protestant and Catholic Christianity
God the Father	Human beings are God's pro-created children by nature, born with divine potential.	Human beings are created in God's spiritual image, but they become his spiritual children through adoption by God's grace, not by their nature.
God's peers	Heavenly Father, Jesus Christ, and the Holy Ghost are three separate beings who work together as one.	Heavenly Father, Jesus Christ, and the Holy Ghost are members of the *Trinity*, meaning they're one in substance as well as purpose.
God's family	God is eternally married to Heavenly Mother, and together they've populated the world with their children (us).	God isn't married, and his only son is the Savior, Jesus Christ.
God's limitations	God is subject to certain laws of the universe, which are eternal. God respects human *agency*, or freedom, and won't typically interfere with the natural consequences of human actions.	God has no known limitations.
God's goal for humanity	God wants people to return to him and become like him in glory and love.	God wants people to return to him and praise him eternally.

Second Mate: Christ the Son

Mormons view the New Testament as a mostly accurate account of Jesus's earthly ministry (for more on Mormon views regarding the Bible, see Chapter 9). However, additional revelations to Mormon prophets have clarified aspects of what Jesus did before, during, and after his short mortal life, as well as what he's expected to do in the future.

First and best

In Mormon theology, the being who would become known as Jesus Christ was born first among all God's billions of spirit children, and he was by far the brightest, strongest, and most advanced of all God's children. In the premortal world, where human spirits dwelt with the Heavenly Parents and prepared for earthly birth, this eldest son took a primary leadership role and was known as *Jehovah*. Many people believe the names *Jehovah* and *the Lord* in the Old Testament refer to God the Father, but Mormons believe these names refer to the personage who would later be born as Jesus Christ.

As we mention earlier in the chapter, God instituted the plan of salvation so that his spirit children can progress to become like him. In order for this plan to work, a savior was required to help everybody recover from the sin and death they'd encounter as part of the earthly test. Guess who volunteered?

Among God's oldest spirit children was another gifted and talented son, named Lucifer. As we discuss in more detail in Chapter 2, Lucifer developed the worst-ever case of sibling rivalry and rebelled against God and Jehovah/Jesus Christ, which got him and his followers kicked out of heaven. In the Mormon view, Jesus, the devil, and all humans everywhere are spiritual siblings.

Well before coming to earth to perform his saving mission, the Savior began serving as God's second in command. While God created the earth spiritually, the Savior took primary responsibility for the earth's physical creation. After mortals started wandering the planet with no memory of their premortal life, the Savior communicated with them through prophets and the Holy Ghost. On the rare occasion when God himself directly speaks or appears to a human, it's generally to introduce his Son.

Both mortal and divine

In the Mormon view, God fathered everybody's spirit, but the Savior's *physical* body was the only one literally procreated by God, in partnership with the mortal Mary. (We could discuss what some early Mormons believed about the logistics of that situation, but we won't go there.) Possessing both eternal and mortal DNA, Jesus was able to die and then be resurrected in glorified immortality, thus opening the way for everyone to eventually be resurrected.

Equally as importantly, Jesus paid the price for all the sins of humanity. In the Mormon view, whenever a moral law is broken, justice must be satisfied, and the Savior accomplished that for humankind on a spiritual, eternal level. Having paid this bill that mortals couldn't pay for themselves, he forgives the debt for all people who sincerely repent of their sins and strive to live his gospel. Although many Christians believe that Jesus extends his grace to anyone who simply asks, Mormon Christians believe the Savior picks up the slack as a person makes his or her best effort to be good.

An oft-quoted Book of Mormon scripture states, "It is by grace that we are saved, after all we can do" (2 Nephi 25:23). In contrast, the Bible states, "For by grace are ye saved through faith; and that not of yourselves: it is the gift of God" (Ephesians 2:8), which Mormons see as a true but incomplete assertion. For more on how faith and works go together in the Mormon mind, see Chapter 2; for more on Mormon feelings regarding the Bible, see Chapter 10.

Was Jesus married?

Mormons view marriage as an eternal covenant that all men and women must make in order to be *exalted,* or become like God (for more on Mormon marriage, see Chapter 7). In addition, Mormons believe that Jesus Christ set a perfect example in all things. According to this logic, the Savior must've gotten married at some point.

Some early Mormon leaders speculated that the marriage at Cana, where Jesus turned water into wine, was actually his own wedding, which would help explain why he was trying to be a good host. Additionally, some Mormons believe that Jesus married Mary Magdalene and had children, and they reject the notion that Magdalene was a reformed whore. However, modern Church leaders pretty much publicly avoid this subject altogether.

Together, the Savior's overcoming of death and sin is known as his *Atonement.* Mormons believe that the hardest, most significant phase of the Atonement occurred in the Garden of Gethsemane, during that long night when Jesus literally sweat drops of blood (as described in the Bible, Luke 22:44). Although crucifixion was a horrible way to die, numerous others died that same way. Consequently, Mormons don't place heavy religious significance on the sign of the cross. To Mormons, the most important aspects of the story are that Christ's sacrifice atoned for people's sins and that he lives today.

The Savior's post-crucifixion checklist

After his mortal body died on the cross, the Savior immediately got busy with the following tasks:

- **During the three days between Christ's death and resurrection, Mormons believe his spirit visited the realm of the dead.** Wanting to extend his atonement to every human who ever lived, he organized the righteous spirits to start preaching the gospel to those who died without hearing or accepting it. Until then, an impassable gulf had lain between the righteous and the wicked in the spirit world.

- **Jesus transformed his physical body into a perfect, glorified, immortal vessel for his eternal spirit.** At the time of his resurrection, all the righteous people who'd died before him got resurrected too, all the way back to Adam. Most of the righteous who died after him will wait until his Second Coming to be resurrected. Mormons view the Savior's resurrection as the single most significant and miraculous event in human history.

- **As recorded in the New Testament, the resurrected Savior spent time teaching his apostles.** In addition, Mormons believe he visited the people living in the Western Hemisphere, part of the "other sheep" that the Bible's John 10:16 says he mentioned. Lasting several days, this visit is recounted as the centerpiece of the Book of Mormon, Joseph Smith's translation of the sacred account left behind by these people. (For more on the Book of Mormon, see Chapter 9.) He may have visited additional peoples around the world, who presumably have their own scriptures and sacred records about those encounters.

✔ **After the resurrected Savior ascended to heaven, he kept working behind the scenes among humans.** Mormons believe that, within a few decades after Christ left the earth, persecution and corruption ruined his church, as we discuss in Chapter 4. For about 1,700 years, the Savior didn't reestablish an official church or prophet on the earth, although he continued blessing and inspiring worthy, faithful individuals, especially those who sought religious freedoms.

✔ **Finally, when conditions were right for the restoration of the true religion, God and Jesus appeared to Joseph Smith in 1820.** During the subsequent 24 years, Jesus restored his church, his gospel, and God's priesthood through the Prophet Joseph. Since then, Mormons believe the Savior has been actively leading the Church through whatever man is serving as the current prophet. One of the LDS Church's main purposes is to prepare people for Christ's eventual Second Coming.

As Mormons strive to develop a personal relationship with Heavenly Father, they recognize that Jesus Christ is the middleman, the broker, and the gate-keeper — in theological terms, the mediator — between God and humanity. The only way back to God is through him. Mormons feel deep gratitude and love for the Savior and pledge total allegiance to him. When they pray to the Father or do anything else of a religious nature, they do it in Christ's name (for more on Mormon prayer, see Chapter 17). The Church is Christ's, the gospel is Christ's, and Christ administers God's priesthood among humans.

Although everything centers on Christ, Mormons view him as a means to an end, not an end in himself. Mormons are sometimes accused of blasphemy for believing that humans can become like God. However, from a Mormon perspective, the idea that the Savior accomplished his Atonement just so people can strum harps and sing praises for eternity seems almost blasphemous.

When he comes again

As the bumper sticker says, "Jesus is coming — everyone look busy." No one but God knows exactly when Jesus will return in glory to rule the earth for 1,000 years, but Mormons believe the time is fast approaching and people should prepare.

Signs of the times

Although the Church's restoration is one of the key signs that the Second Coming is near, Mormons believe they must still preach the gospel to all nations before Christ will return. Mormon missionaries have entered most countries, but places like Saudi Arabia and China still aren't open for evangelizing. Some Mormons semiseriously debate whether electronically transmitted missionary work suffices, or if missionaries must personally visit each nation. In addition, Mormons expect to build the New Jerusalem in the state of Missouri before the Savior returns, to serve as his headquarters. (Why Missouri? See Chapter 11.)

Unfortunately, many of the signs preceding the Second Coming don't sound like too much fun. Aware that time is running out, the devil is pulling out all the stops. The last century's wars and social ills — and those of the present day — are mere warm-ups for how much worse things will get. The earth will go haywire with natural calamities, including earthquakes, disease, storms, and famine, and the wicked will run rampant. According to Mormon scripture, "All things shall be in commotion; and . . . fear shall come upon all people" (Doctrine and Covenants 88:91). Of course, the Lord has promised to comfort the righteous during these times of crisis, and many of them will survive to welcome him back.

It's a bird! It's a plane!

At a crucial point during Armageddon, the world's final catastrophic war, Mormons believe the Savior will descend out of the sky to assume control of the earth and accomplish the following tasks:

- ✔ **Levitate the good people:** As the Savior comes down from the heavens, he'll resurrect the righteous dead, who'll be airlifted up to meet him, along with those righteous people who are still living. Together with those who were already resurrected at the time of Jesus's own resurrection, these people will eventually inherit the *celestial kingdom,* where they'll live with God and potentially become like him. (For more on Mormonism's three degrees of heavenly glory, see Chapter 2.)

- ✔ **Say goodbye to bad guys:** With the good people safe, he'll destroy the wicked mortals who are still living, imprison Satan, cleanse the earth with fire, and restore the earth to its Garden of Eden status, with no weeds or carnivores. All the wicked spirits from throughout history will stay in timeout in spirit prison.

- ✔ **Start his own show:** He'll establish a perfectly fair, just, and peaceful worldwide government — run by both Church members and nonmembers — and launch the 1,000-year period of earthly paradise known as the *Millennium.* After the Millennium begins, he'll resurrect the medium-good people from throughout history, those who lived decent lives but didn't fully embrace the gospel. These people will eventually inherit the *terrestrial kingdom.*

Peace on earth, good will toward men: The Millennium

During the Millennium, mortals will still dwell on the earth, having children and living out their lives. However, only people of celestial or terrestrial caliber will experience mortality during the Millennium, and Satan won't be able to tempt or confuse anybody. Even better, no one will have to deal with HMOs, because no one will get sick. Instead of experiencing death and burial, people will turn immortal in the twinkling of an eye.

Not everyone living on the earth during the Millennium will be a member of the Savior's true church. People will still be free to believe and worship as they please, and some will hold onto mistaken beliefs and follow false religions — at least, until missionaries can persuade them otherwise.

Two major religious efforts will continue through Christ's Millennium:

- **Performing ordinances on behalf of the dead:** As discussed in Chapter 7, no one can be saved without receiving certain earthly physical ordinances, such as baptism. Mormons are currently trying to perform these ordinances on behalf of all dead people, who can then decide whether to accept or reject them. However, Mormons have so much work to do that they'll continue in the Millennium.

- **Preaching and teaching:** Missionaries will preach the Savior's true gospel to all people, and eventually everyone will acknowledge Christ as their Savior.

During the Millennium, Jesus and other resurrected beings will visit the earth as needed to oversee the government and help Church members carry out the ordinance work for the dead. At the conclusion of the Millennium, the spirits of the wicked from throughout history will finally finish their 1,000-year timeout and be resurrected, eventually to inherit the *telestial kingdom*.

As great as the Millennium sounds, it has a catch at the end. Satan will be unleashed for one last time, and he'll succeed in turning away more people from God. The armies of the righteous will defeat the armies of evil for the final time, and God will forever cast out Satan and his followers into outer darkness. Then will come the final judgment, when all people receive their eternal reward in one of the three kingdoms of heaven.

Differences in beliefs about Jesus Christ

Table 3-2 illustrates how Mormons view Christ, as opposed to other Christians.

Table 3-2   Mormon View of Christ versus Other Christian Views

Qualities of Christ	Mormon Christianity	Protestant and Catholic Christianity
Nature of Christ	Christ is the Messiah and the literal Son of God. He'll return someday and usher in 1,000 years of peace and glory on earth.	Christ is the Messiah, the Son of God, and also God the Father made flesh. He'll return someday, either just before or just after 1,000 years of peace and glory on earth.
Creation of Christ	Christ is the firstborn of Heavenly Father and the oldest brother of all human beings, spiritually speaking. He's the only one of Heavenly Father's children to be conceived in mortality by a human and God.	Christ is the only-begotten Son of God and is of one substance with the Father. He was "begotten," but not made or created.
Christ in the Godhead	Christ is a separate physical being from God the Father and the Holy Ghost. The three beings are united in purpose and love but not in substance. Christ is subordinate to the Father and does his will (John 14:28).	Christ is part of the Trinity, along with God the Father and the Holy Ghost, who all function as one being. God the Father was physically *incarnated,* or made flesh, in the person of Jesus of Nazareth. Christ is eternally coequal with God the Father.
Christ's activity on earth	Christ taught, healed, and performed miracles before his crucifixion. In the three days between his crucifixion and resurrection, he went to spirit paradise (see Chapter 2) to teach righteous spirits how to help those in spirit prison. After his resurrection, he taught his disciples in Jerusalem and the Nephites in the Western Hemisphere, and he may have taught "lost sheep" scattered in other places. After his ministry among the Nephites, he ascended into heaven.	Christ taught, healed, and performed miracles before his crucifixion and resurrection. After his resurrection, he spent 40 days teaching his disciples before ascending into heaven.

(continued)

Table 3-2 *(continued)*

Qualities of Christ	Mormon Christianity	Protestant and Catholic Christianity
Christ's premortal résumé	Christ implemented the plan of salvation during the council in heaven (see Chapter 2), headed up the earth's creation, and functioned as Jehovah in the Bible's Old Testament.	Christ was spiritually present at creation, but his precise role is unknown.
Christ's Atonement	In the Garden of Gethsemane and on the cross, Christ paid the price for our sins and offered himself as a sacrifice for all people.	On the cross, Christ paid the price for our sins and offered himself as a sacrifice for all people.

God's Whisperer: The Holy Ghost

Mormons are unusual in their belief that God the Father has a physical body, like his Son Jesus Christ. The Holy Ghost, in contrast, is a spiritual being. In fact, Mormons often say *Holy Spirit* rather than *Holy Ghost,* using the two terms interchangeably. (*Ghost* was a term used in the 17th-century King James Version of the Bible to signify "spirit," and the name stuck.)

Mormons believe the Holy Ghost is a witness to truth, a comforter, and a sanctifier. The more pure and obedient that people are, the better they're able to feel the Holy Ghost's spiritual influence. Mormons strive to follow God's commandments so they can retain the companionship of the Holy Ghost as much as possible, and they draw upon his guidance when discerning right from wrong, evaluating spiritual teachings, and pressing on toward perfection. As the Spirit carries out the will of the Father, his influence can be felt everywhere in the world at the same time — in fact, Church leaders compare the Holy Ghost to the sun, which warms the entire earth and sheds light everywhere.

The Spirit who never got a body

The Holy Ghost is unique among the three personages in the Godhead because this member is the only one without a physical body. Church leaders have taught that the Holy Ghost has a *spiritual* body, which is presumably a more advanced, deified version of the spirit body that Mormons believe everyone had in the premortal life.

Mormon theology hasn't offered a definitive statement about the origins and identity of the Holy Ghost, focusing instead on this spirit personage's role in the Godhead and in people's lives. Some Mormons believe the Holy Ghost is one of God's spirit children who was called for this particular mission and will be the last spirit to be blessed with a physical body. Even more controversially, some Mormons would like to think the Holy Ghost is female, perhaps even Heavenly Mother herself. However, this is far from orthodox belief. As one Mormon apostle explained, God hasn't yet given revelation on the Spirit's origin or destiny, and debating it is "speculative and fruitless." In deference to current LDS Church usage, in this book we refer to the Holy Ghost with male pronouns.

Mormons believe that as a spirit, the Holy Ghost can communicate intimately with every person's spirit, though the person needs to strive to live righteously so as not to repel the Holy Spirit. No unclean thing can sustain the presence of God, and the Holy Ghost literally imparts God's presence to humans in a tangible way. With this idea in mind, Mormons who've been baptized and have received the gift of the Holy Ghost (see the next section) are careful to remain worthy of that gift.

Although no one knows everything about the Holy Ghost, the key thing to remember is that he quietly works wonders in the lives of believers. He may *seem* like a silent partner, but the Holy Ghost is actually a key mover and shaker in God's business on earth.

The gift of the Holy Ghost

From time to time and under special circumstances, such as while being taught by the missionaries, Mormons believe anyone can feel the Spirit's influence and his confirmation of the truth of certain teachings. In addition, Mormon leaders have taught that great scientific discoveries and uplifting works of art result from the Holy Ghost's inspiration, whether or not their creators were members of the LDS Church. (Latter-day Saints also believe that every person, Mormon or not, can have constant guidance from something called the *light of Christ*. This light comes from Christ's spirit and provides all accountable people with a basic knowledge of right and wrong.)

Having the Spirit all the time

Mormons believe that LDS Church members can receive the *constant* gift of the Holy Ghost. After people are baptized — see Chapter 6 for more on baptism and its meaning for Mormons — the next ordinance they receive is confirmation, which includes the bestowal of the gift of the Holy Ghost. This happens through the laying on of hands by someone with the proper authority, meaning a Melchizedek Priesthood holder (see Chapter 4). After this ordinance, members can potentially experience the Spirit's influence ever after, not just on an occasional basis.

During the confirmation ordinance, the priesthood holder simply blesses the individual to receive the Holy Ghost. Some Mormons believe that when this blessing takes place, it actually verifies the Holy Ghost's entry into that person's life and heart and imparts the Spirit's influence. Others feel that the ordinance establishes the Mormon's *receptivity* and *willingness* to receive the Holy Ghost, but doesn't dictate where the Spirit goes and what he does. (As the Bible says in John 3:8, the Spirit's influence bloweth where it listeth, meaning it goes wherever the heck it wants to.) Whatever the case, receiving the gift of the Holy Ghost is essential to receiving full salvation.

Confirmation of membership and bestowal of the gift of the Holy Ghost can happen any time after baptism. In some cases, this ordinance is performed immediately following baptism, after the new member has changed into dry clothes and freshened up while those in attendance sing hymns or listen to a talk. In other cases, particularly with adult converts, many wards hold the confirmation ordinance during sacrament meeting the Sunday after the baptism so the whole congregation can witness and welcome the new convert.

One thing you rarely see during these ordinances is something that's more common in Pentecostal services, where the person who's received the Holy Ghost dances, claps, whoops for joy, or falls down in the Spirit. Although Mormons in the 1830s engaged in all manner of ecstatic behaviors during worship, Mormons today are pretty sedate by contrast. The individual who's just received the gift may experience a warm and steady feeling of light or may shed tears of joy. Others report feeling nothing unusual at that time but then have deep spiritual experiences afterward. Mormons believe that receiving the gift of the Holy Ghost isn't a one-time affair but a lifelong experience that can grow in depth, frequency, and intensity.

Receiving specialized gifts of the Spirit

Mormons rejoice to know that scripture promises some beautiful spiritual gifts that go along with receiving the Holy Ghost. Obviously, not all Church members possess every gift that Paul outlines in the New Testament or Joseph Smith and other prophets mention in modern revelations. As Paul put it, "There are diversities of gifts, but the same Spirit"; one person may be a healer and another an interpreter. Early Mormons wore their spiritual gifts on their sleeves a lot more than Latter-day Saints do today, but the fact is that Mormons still believe in miracles and seek them regularly. Some of the more common manifestations of spiritual gifts include the following:

✔ **The gift of healing:** Today, many Mormon men who hold the Melchizedek Priesthood carry a small key chain vial containing consecrated oil. At any time, in any kind of emergency, they're prepared to perform an anointing and blessing to heal someone. Although all priesthood holders possess the authority to administer to the sick, Church leaders teach that some have this gift to a greater degree than others. In addition, Mormon history is rife with stories of women and others who didn't hold the priesthood but who could heal through prayer and the gift of the Spirit.

- ✔ **The gift of tongues:** Hearing spiritual gibberish in a Mormon chapel — other than a particularly long-winded talk in sacrament meeting — or seeing someone else rise up to interpret what's been said is unlikely nowadays. However, such *speaking in tongues* was common among Mormon men and women in the 19th century. Mormons believe that today's most common manifestation of this gift is missionaries quickly and thoroughly learning foreign languages.

- ✔ **The gift of faith:** Mormons believe the Spirit witnesses about the truth of spiritual wisdom and increases faith. Again, some people seem to have the gift of faith more than others, while some have the gift of riding another person's coattails of strong, abiding faith.

- ✔ **The gift of prophecy:** Although the president of the Church is the only person who receives revelations from God that are binding for the entire Church, individual Mormon men and women are entitled to revelations about their own lives, families, and Church callings.

- ✔ **The gift of casting out demons:** As with speaking in tongues, this spiritual gift was more visible in the 19th century than it is today, but Mormons still call upon the Holy Ghost to help them withstand temptation and repel Satan's influence. Such episodes may never be as dramatic as a full-twisting *Exorcist* head spin, but this gift is nevertheless effective. If a Mormon senses the presence of a demon, he or she can verbally cast it out in the name of Jesus Christ.

The most important thing to remember about these gifts is that they usually exist for the spiritual growth of the Church, not just the individual. Miracles should increase the faith and well-being of those who witness them; teaching should enlighten all who hear it. Doctrine and Covenants (D&C) 46 states several times in various ways that the gifts of the Spirit exist "that all might be benefited," so Church members are counseled to seek them for the right reasons, not for selfish ones.

Keeping the Spirit

The Holy Ghost is God's primary way of leading people to Christ, confirming spiritual truth, and helping them endure to the end in righteousness. When people have the Holy Ghost in their lives, they feel more connected to Heavenly Father through prayer and are more able to recognize the needs of people around them.

Mormons believe, however, that the trick is to keep the Spirit at all times. As people study the scriptures, pray regularly, and serve others, they can feel the influence of the Holy Ghost most clearly. But the Spirit won't stick around where he's not wanted. If people don't at least try to keep God's commandments, the Spirit will flee. Yet, he'll return after a person repents and tries again to live righteously.

Sometimes, even people who strive to obey God's commandments and do the right thing experience dry spells when the Spirit feels far away. Most Mormons can point to times in their lives when they felt very close to the Spirit and other times when they felt alone. Perhaps God uses these times to strengthen and test people — difficult times help us grow, and in the Mormon view, spiritual growth is the whole reason we're here on earth. Even Christ, who was sinless and perfect, experienced loneliness when he felt that God had abandoned him (for more on that, check out Mark 15:34 in the Bible).

The Holy Ghost's many roles

So what does the Holy Ghost *do,* exactly? While the Father organizes and sustains all things and the Son redeems mortality, the Holy Ghost kind of keeps the home fires burning. In fact, fire is one symbol of the Holy Ghost that frequently appears in scripture (see, for example, the apostles' experience with "tongues of fire" when they were baptized in the Spirit in the New Testament, recounted in Acts 2). The Holy Ghost performs several vital functions in the Godhead and in bringing people to Christ.

The witness of Christ

Have you ever noticed that in scripture, the Holy Spirit seems to show up just when Christ makes an appearance? When Jesus is baptized in the Bible's New Testament, for example, the Spirit descends — perhaps figuratively — in the form of a dove just as Heavenly Father announces the coming of Christ: "This is my beloved Son" (Matthew 3:16–17). In John 15:26, Jesus promises that the Holy Ghost will *testify* of him. In other words, the Holy Ghost is a witness of Christ, pointing people to Christ's glory and truth.

In Mormonism, the *law of witnesses* dictates that more than one righteous person will confirm a true spiritual principle. This idea seems to be true of the Godhead as well: The Spirit is an additional witness of Christ. In the Savior's baptismal story, for example, God announces Christ's identity while the Spirit rests on Jesus. The other members of the Godhead testify to Christ's divine nature.

The comforter

Shortly before Christ was crucified, he promised his disciples that he wouldn't leave them comfortless but would send a comforter to help them in their path (John 16). This promised helper was the Holy Ghost.

The Holy Ghost exists as a comforter for each person and also as an enabler of sorts: Mormons believe one of the primary ways God answers prayers is through other people, and the Spirit is the still, small voice of God that keeps members in tune with the needs of others. Sometimes Mormons feel a little tug to pray for someone or do something to help someone they know. This urge may be as simple as a phone call to a particular friend, only to find out the friend had a rotten day and needed a boost at just that moment.

Sometimes, the Holy Ghost communicates comfort to an individual by showering that person with what the Bible calls the "peace that passeth all understanding" (Philippians 4:7). After prayer, a Latter-day Saint may feel an unexpected sense of calm about a difficult issue or problem and a knowledge of what to do. In addition, the Holy Ghost can provide the blessed assurance that a person's sins are truly forgiven.

The revealer of truth

In John 16, Jesus says that he has many other things to teach his disciples, but they aren't ready for those additional truths. Jesus assures them the Holy Ghost will be their new teacher after his departure, guiding them into all truth as directed by the Father. Mormons believe that human beings learn spiritual truths "precept upon precept, line upon line" — in other words, slowly but surely (Isaiah 28:10 in the Bible's Old Testament and 2 Nephi 28:30 in the Book of Mormon). People don't learn truth in a vacuum, because the Spirit is with them every step of the way, teaching them and helping them discern truth from error.

Mormons are a prayerful people, and they often bring things to God in prayer that other folks may consider trivial (for more on Mormon prayer, see Chapter 17). They follow James 1:5, which says that if they lack wisdom, they should ask God, who gives to everyone liberally. With this idea in mind, Mormons pray for the answers to tough questions and for guidance in making all kinds of decisions, both major and minor. They believe the Holy Ghost often confirms the truth of something they've prayed about. Sometimes, they receive a tingling or warm sensation running through their bodies, or simply a peaceful sense of calm about a particular course of action. On the other hand, they believe they'll receive a "stupor of thought" if something isn't right.

The end of the Book of Mormon contains an oft-quoted passage about praying to know the truth and receiving spiritual confirmation. Widely shared by Mormon missionaries, the passage is called *Moroni's Promise,* because the Book of Mormon prophet Moroni pledged that people who ask God sincerely in the name of Jesus Christ can receive confirmation of the truth by the power of the Holy Ghost (Moroni 10:3–5). The scripture further guarantees that by the power of the Holy Ghost, people can know the truth of all things.

The sanctifier

The Holy Ghost plays an important role in helping members stay on the straight and narrow path. He *sanctifies,* or helps them become more holy. As we explain earlier in this section, the Holy Ghost is sometimes associated with fire, and fire is the ultimate refiner's tool. The Spirit's goal is to purify an individual.

As we discuss in Chapter 2, one of the most important principles of Mormon life is what they call *enduring to the end.* Having faith in Christ, repenting, and being baptized are all wonderful, but those actions don't help people much in the long run if they backslide or fall away from the faith. Enter the Holy Ghost — the Spirit helps members stay in tune with the will of Heavenly Father and his Son, Jesus Christ. He keeps members honest — who can say the Holy Ghost isn't responsible for those occasional prickings of conscience that help keep them on the right path? The Holy Ghost grants people beautiful spiritual experiences, moments of great joy, and answers to prayer to help them stay on the journey and grow in grace.

The unforgivable sin

Before you finish this chapter thinking everything about the Holy Ghost is warm and fuzzy, you should know one more thing: The Bible says that blaspheming the Holy Ghost is the one unpardonable sin (Matthew 12:31–32). As we discuss in Chapter 2, this kind of blasphemy is one of the few things that absolutely guarantee someone a room reservation in Hotel Outer Darkness.

Just what exactly does it mean to *blaspheme* the Holy Ghost? Well, Church leaders teach that you need to have experienced the full influence of the Spirit and then denied it by willfully, consciously turning away from God. Joseph Smith said that when a person knows all about the plan of salvation, receives a spiritual witness of its truth, and *then* denies Christ, he or she sins against the Holy Ghost. This idea makes sense because, as we explain earlier in this section, one of the Holy Ghost's primary functions is to testify of Christ. When we reject Christ's message, having previously embraced it, we also shoot the messenger, the Holy Ghost.

Chapter 4

Restoring the Priesthood and the Church

*M*ormons respect people's right to worship as they please, and they acknowledge that many religions contain elements of truth. But members of The Church of Jesus Christ of Latter-day Saints believe their church is the only complete, "true and living" church that the Savior recognizes as his own. Other churches, in the Mormon view, can be excellent organizations, but they're human, not godly, institutions whose teachings reflect mostly human philosophies. Their scriptural interpretations and — according to the Mormons — especially their priesthood authority come from human sources, not from God himself.

Looking back on human history, Mormons believe that, from time to time, different societies have received the Savior's true religion but then lost it due to the people's lack of righteousness. When the time and conditions are right, the Savior reinstitutes the true religion by calling a new prophet to restore the gospel principles and ordinances to a different group or generation of people. As we discuss in this chapter, Mormons claim that, most recently, the Savior restored his church and God's true priesthood through Joseph Smith, Mormonism's founding prophet.

In addition, we discuss the basic organization and purposes of the Mormon priesthood, which is the authority to act in God's name and can be held by any worthy Mormon male. To help explain the priesthood to their sons, some fathers even compare it to the Force from *Star Wars*.

Gospel Comings and Goings

Like some other folks, Mormons speak of gospel *dispensations* throughout history, or times when the true religion, including God's authentic priesthood authority, exists somewhere on the earth. Each dispensation is usually tied to one special prophet, who receives revelations from God and leads the people back to him. For example, Adam, Noah, and Moses all led major gospel dispensations. However, those dispensations eventually fizzled out.

Why do gospel dispensations end? Often they end because the people are unwilling to follow the prophet and live the gospel. When the people start getting too rebellious, God lets his true religion pass away from the earth, usually because the last righteous leader dies without transmitting the *priesthood keys* (a term Mormons use for priesthood authority) to a successor. In time, God calls a new prophet to restore the gospel, and the cycle continues.

Before a young prophet named Joseph Smith performed the biggest, grandest gospel restoration of all in the early 1800s, roughly 1,700 years passed without an authorized prophet in the Old World, perhaps the longest stretch in history. Mormons believe that within a few decades after Christ set up his New Testament church, all the apostles died without successors, due mainly to persecution. Some fragments of Christianity survived and evolved over the centuries. However, unauthorized men changed the doctrines and ordinances to suit their own purposes and interpretations. (Over in the New World, the last prophet didn't die until about A.D. 400, as recounted in the Book of Mormon — but that still leaves a span of roughly 1,400 years until Joseph Smith.)

Mormons sometimes refer to this huge gospel gap as the *Great Apostasy,* the major falling away predicted by several biblical prophets (see Amos 8:11–12, Matthew 24:9–12, John 16:1–3, 2 Thessalonians 2:3–4, and 2 Peter 2:1). However, although the Savior didn't authorize any priesthood representatives during this long period of time, he did inspire certain people to help prepare the world for the eventual return of the fullness of his gospel. Mormons believe that movements ranging from the Renaissance to Protestantism and the establishment of religious freedom in the United States all opened the way for one key event: the Savior's final restoration of his gospel through Joseph Smith.

Beginning the Restoration

It's hard to imagine that many Americans have been as hated and beloved as Joseph Smith, the founder of Mormonism (see Figure 4-1 for a portrait). To Mormons, he was a prophet of God, chosen to restore the priesthood and the New Testament church, suffering persecution for his faith and dying a martyr's death. To some outsiders, he was a fraud who falsely claimed to have revelations and instituted the practice of polygamy not to obey the commands of God but to satisfy his own carnal lusts.

Figure 4-1:
Mormon-
ism's
founding
prophet,
Joseph
Smith.

Courtesy of Community of Christ Archives, Independence, Missouri

The debate about Joseph Smith continues today as fervently as it did when he was still alive. In this section, we take a quick look at the man and his controversial spiritual claims and let you decide for yourself.

Joseph Smith's early years

Joseph Smith was born on December 23, 1805, in the small New England village of Sharon, Vermont. His story is pretty similar to that of many families in the early republic: His parents were hardworking farm folk who never seemed to catch a break, moving seven times in 14 years to find better land and more economic opportunities. With a large family to support — the Smiths would eventually have 11 children, though only 9 survived to adulthood — getting ahead was a constant struggle.

Religiously, the Smiths were good Christian people who knew the Bible well but weren't typically involved in any one particular church. Their lack of involvement was partly a result of moving around so much, but it also stemmed from their confusion about the many different religious sects of the day. The early 19th century was a time of great religious revival in northeastern states such as New York, where the Smiths moved when young Joseph was 10 years old.

True grit

Joseph's mother recorded in her memoir that he was a quiet child who was interested in spirituality from an early age. He seems to have been made of tough stuff; when he was about 7 years old, for example, he contracted typhoid fever and endured a horrible secondary infection that lodged itself in the bone marrow of his leg.

Mormon children today are regaled with the story of how Joseph bravely faced the surgeon's knife when the infection was being chipped out of his bone. Parents and teachers trot out the story to demonstrate more than just bravery: Little Joseph famously refused alcohol to help deaden the pain, making him a poster child for the later Mormon attitude toward teetotalism. (For the skinny on why Mormons don't drink, see Chapter 16.)

After about six years of pulling together, with the entire family doing odd jobs, the Smiths were able to afford a farm on the outskirts of Palmyra, New York. There, in 1816, they settled into the backbreaking work of clearing the land and harvesting crops until 1825, when a run of bad luck — including falling grain prices and the death of Joseph's beloved adult brother Alvin — forced them to sell the farm and live there as tenants. This change was a hard blow to Joseph's parents, who were then in their 50s.

To make ends meet, the Smith boys and their father hired themselves out for odd jobs in addition to working the land upon which they lived. They worked at haying, harvesting, clearing trees, digging wells — and searching for treasure. The Church has carefully downplayed this last point in its official history, but the fact is certainly true that, like many other Americans of this period, Joseph Smith was involved in treasure seeking. Anti-Mormons are quick to emphasize this activity because they believe it casts doubt on Smith's later discovery of the ultimate treasure: golden plates that, when translated, became the Book of Mormon. (For more on the Book of Mormon, see Chapter 9.) In their minds, Smith's claim to have "discovered" the Book of Mormon through angelic intervention loses credibility if he already had a history of digging for buried treasure. Latter-day Saints argue that the fact that Smith was occasionally drafted into treasure digging is hardly a stain on his name.

Kneeling in the Sacred Grove

During the same period that the Smiths were experiencing such economic unrest, young Joseph was encountering serious religious turmoil. In the early 1820s, a series of religious revivals in upstate New York caused the teenage Joseph to feel some confusion about which church to join. Methodist, Presbyterian, and Baptist ministers were all vying for the souls of the locals. All these preachers seemed to speak some truth, and Joseph had trouble distinguishing which was right.

SCRIPTURE

What happened next has become the stuff of Mormon canon. Although historians sometimes argue about how old Joseph was when he decided to ask God which church to join, the official LDS position is that he did so in the spring of 1820, when he was just 14. Around that time, he was wondering about spiritual questions when he happened upon James 1:5 in the Bible's New Testament: "If any of you lack wisdom, let him ask of God, that giveth to all men liberally, and upbraideth not; and it shall be given him." Joseph took from this that instead of just fretting about the problem and making his own decision, he should ask God for wisdom about choosing a religion.

Joseph couldn't find any privacy in his family's crowded cottage, so he headed off for the woods to pray in solitude. He knelt in a nearby clearing — which Mormons now refer to as the *Sacred Grove* — and prayed to the Lord for guidance as to which denomination was right. He'd hardly finished talking when he felt some astonishing power seize him, making him feel as if his tongue had been bound, and he was surrounded by utter darkness. "It seemed to me for a time as if I were doomed to sudden destruction," he wrote later.

Mormons believe that Public Enemy Number One — Satan — caused the darkness because he could see that something major was about to go down for the spiritual welfare of humankind and wanted to scare off Joseph before it could continue. Joseph felt himself sinking into despair but called upon God to deliver him out of the enemy's power. It was then that he saw a pillar of light appear directly above his head, shining even brighter than the sun. The light gradually descended, driving out all darkness from the grove.

After he adjusted to this shock, Joseph saw that the light was actually coming from two beings, Heavenly Father and Jesus Christ. (Talk about a dramatic answer to prayer.) One pointed to the other and said, "This is My Beloved Son. Hear Him!"

Now that he had their attention, Joseph asked the question that was in his heart: Which church should he join? Surprisingly, Heavenly Father and Jesus Christ told him to join none of them, because they were all corrupt. Considering how important the First Vision later became in the Mormon story, the fact that this is all Mormons know of the conversation is kind of surprising. Joseph said that Heavenly Father spoke of "many other things," but he either couldn't or was forbidden to write about them.

After the vision

When he came to, Joseph was lying on his back in the clearing, feeling spent and exhausted. He walked home and, in what may have been the understatement of the century, told his anxious mother he'd learned for himself that he wasn't supposed to join any of the existing churches.

Joseph, presumably quite flabbergasted by the unexpected divine visitation, seems to have kept pretty quiet about it. Opponents of Mormonism trumpet this fact as evidence that it never happened. If someone experienced a miraculous and highly personal visit from Heavenly Father and Jesus Christ, wouldn't he or she shout it from the rooftops? Mormons counter that Joseph *did* try to tell someone about it: He confided in a local Methodist preacher a few days later but was disappointed by the minister's contempt. Given that God's revelation to Joseph almost entirely concerned the corruptness of existing churches and ministers, the fact that the minister loathed what Joseph had to say isn't too surprising. After a few more such encounters, Joseph learned to keep his mouth shut about his unusual experience, for the time being.

Joseph Smith's experience in the Sacred Grove is canonized in the Mormon imagination as the "First Vision." One account of the vision appears as part of his personal history in the LDS scripture known as the Pearl of Great Price (which we discuss in Chapter 10). Joseph Smith's three earlier versions of the same story — in which he recorded himself as being older when he had the vision and in which some details are slightly different — also circulate in the LDS Church, but Mormons don't regard them as scripture.

According to the accepted official version, several more years elapsed before Joseph received another heavenly visitor. For more on the Angel Moroni and the coming forth of the Book of Mormon, see Chapter 9.

Bringing Back the Church Step by Step

From the time of Joseph Smith's First Vision, about a decade passed before he officially organized the LDS Church in 1830. Until he was martyred in 1844, 14 years later, he continued restoring gospel principles, translating ancient scriptures, and receiving new revelations. In this section, we provide a chronological overview of the major steps in the latter-day restoration of the Church and show how the modern Church relates back to earlier versions.

A parade of heavenly messengers

In order for Joseph to restore the Church, he had to receive the necessary priesthood keys from the men who'd last held them on the earth. Because those men were all long since dead, they returned to the earth as resurrected beings to make some special deliveries to Joseph and his associates.

> ✔ Joseph Smith and his Book of Mormon translation scribe, Oliver Cowdery, said that the resurrected John the Baptist appeared to them in 1829 to restore the Aaronic Priesthood. (We explain this preparatory priesthood in more detail in the section "For boys: The Aaronic Priesthood.") They

said that John laid his hands on their heads to grant them this priesthood as they stood on the banks of Pennsylvania's Susquehanna River. He then instructed them to baptize each other in the river.

✔ At some unspecified time after that, Joseph and Oliver said that the New Testament apostles Peter, James, and John appeared as resurrected beings to bestow the Melchizedek Priesthood on them. (For more about this priesthood, see the later section "For men: The Melchizedek Priesthood.") This event was a prerequisite to organizing and leading the Savior's authorized church, including performing ordinances and receiving revelations. Mormons believe that Peter served as prophet and president of the New Testament church after Jesus's resurrection, with James and John as his counselors.

✔ On April 6, 1830, Joseph Smith convened a small meeting in a log farmhouse in upstate New York to officially organize the Church with six founding members. About two weeks prior to this, he'd published the first edition of the all-important Book of Mormon, his translation of ancient Western Hemisphere writings about Christ. Hot off the press, this book of scripture became the fledgling religion's calling card to the world. (For more on the Book of Mormon, see Chapter 9.)

✔ Over the next several years, other resurrected prophets — including Moses, Elias, and Elijah — gave Joseph additional priesthood keys, such as the power to seal families for eternity and perform gospel ordinances on behalf of the dead. In addition, Joseph continued to expand and refine the Church's organizational structure, which Church leaders occasionally still tweak today. (For info on the Church's general worldwide leadership, see Chapter 8. For info on local leadership, see Chapter 6.)

Continuing the gospel tradition

Mormons believe that the New Testament church was called the *Church of Christ;* today's restored church is called *The Church of Jesus Christ of Latter-day Saints.* To modern Mormons, the word *saint* simply means a person who strives to become like Christ. The early members of the LDS Church knew that early Christians were called *saints,* so they took that name. The "latter-day" part of the Church's name signifies members' belief that they're living near the End Times.

According to the Mormons, the ancient and modern churches share the same priesthood authority, ordinances, and basic organization. Then and now, the Church is the kingdom of God on earth, and its main purpose is to enable all people, living and dead, to make eternal covenants with God by receiving ordinances, obeying commandments, and following Christ. When people hold up their end of the covenants they make at baptism (see Chapter 6) and in the Mormon temple (see Chapter 7), God provides blessings in return, the greatest of which is *exaltation,* or becoming an eternal parent like God.

What's in a name?

The Church of Jesus Christ of Latter-day Saints hasn't always gone by that name. In the 1830s, Joseph Smith tried out two other names before finally settling on the one that exists today (which was spelled a little differently during his lifetime, with no hyphen).

In April 1830, when the Church was first organized, it was called the Church of Christ. However, that name was already taken by a group led by Alexander Campbell, which similarly claimed it was the restored New Testament church, so the Mormons needed to find some way to distinguish themselves in the public mind. In April 1834, Smith declared that the official name was the "Church of Latter Day Saints." In 1838, Smith put "Jesus Christ" into the name, making it the "Church of Jesus Christ of Latter Day Saints."

Interestingly, some members today argue that the LDS Church is the true church of Jesus Christ because it bears his name. Opponents of Mormonism find this argument simplistic and point out that by this logic, the same organization was *not* the true church for those few years in the 1830s when "Jesus Christ" wasn't part of the official name. They make a darned good point: A mere name does not a restored church make.

Today, the Church asks people to use its full name on first reference and the generic-sounding "Church of Jesus Christ" on subsequent references. However, most people inside and outside the Church continue to use the nicknames "LDS Church," which the Church tolerates, and "Mormon Church," which Church authorities actively discourage. (For more on where the nickname *Mormon* comes from, see Chapter 1.)

In addition, Mormons believe that this new church launched by Joseph Smith includes, as predicted in the Bible, the "restitution of all things, which God hath spoken by the mouth of all his holy prophets since the world began" (Acts 3:21) — including, perhaps most challengingly, Old Testament polygamy. The gospel will never again disappear from the earth, in the Mormon view — in fact, another of the Church's main purposes is to prepare people to eventually welcome back the resurrected Christ, who will reign over the earth for 1,000 years before the final judgment (for more on these beliefs, see Chapter 3).

Understanding the Priesthood

In the Mormon view, the *priesthood* is nothing less than God's power and authority. He can use the priesthood to create worlds, to keep the universe running smoothly, and to perform other godly tasks. In order to give his children — who someday will become godlike — an opportunity to learn the ropes of the family business, God grants priesthood power and authority to all worthy male members of Christ's church. This way, they can help carry out God's purposes on the earth and perform ordinances that hold eternal weight. Of course, a mortal's priesthood power compared to God's is like a candle compared to the sun, but the type of power is basically the same, and it can keep increasing eternally. (For comments on women and the priesthood, see the section, "What about women and the priesthood?")

The Mormon priesthood is divided into two levels. The Aaronic Priesthood, also known as the preparatory priesthood, helps Mormon teens get ready to become Jedi — er, to receive the higher Melchizedek Priesthood, which all worthy adult males can hold. (Don't worry; later in this section we explain where that *M* name comes from and how to pronounce it.)

In Mormonism, the word *priesthood* usually refers to God's power and authority that he delegates to men, but sometimes people use the term to indicate male Mormons in general, as in "The priesthood will be responsible for setting up chairs before the meeting" — which sometimes feels like it's one of the chief priesthood duties, in addition to shoveling snow and helping families move.

For boys: The Aaronic Priesthood

Named after Moses' brother Aaron, the Aaronic Priesthood mainly performs the Church's outward ordinances of repentance, such as baptizing people and administering the sacramental bread and water to congregations. In biblical times, adult descendants of Aaron administered this priesthood. In the modern Church, all worthy teenage boys do.

This section outlines the three ranks of the Aaronic Priesthood, through which Mormon boys advance every two years. Each time a boy advances, he can continue performing the duties of the lower ranks. Before advancing in the priesthood, a boy discusses his worthiness in a private interview with his local congregational leader, who also holds an Aaronic Priesthood office, as we explain.

By the way, when an adult male joins the Church, he's initially ordained to the Aaronic Priesthood, but he usually takes only a few months — rather than six years — to advance to the higher priesthood.

Step 1: Deacon

Turning 12 is a major milestone for a Mormon boy. He leaves the *Primary,* the Church's organization for children, and joins the *Young Men,* the program for boys ages 12 through 17. Even more significantly, if Church leaders deem him worthy, they make him part of the Aaronic Priesthood, starting with the office of deacon.

The main duty of a deacon is to pass the sacramental bread and water to the congregation during *sacrament meeting,* Mormonism's main weekly congregational worship service (for more on sacrament meeting, see Chapter 6). In addition, deacons serve as messengers for priesthood leaders, help take care of the meetinghouse, and in heavily Mormon areas may go house to house collecting *fast offerings* from members. (Once a month, Mormons skip two meals and donate what they would've spent on the food — plus more, if they're able — to the poor and needy. For more on Mormon fasting, see Chapter 16.)

Step 2: Teacher

At age 14, a Mormon boy can become a teacher in the Aaronic Priesthood. A teacher's main job is filling the sacramental trays with bread and water and setting them out to be blessed and passed. In addition, teachers can accompany adult priesthood holders on *home teaching* visits, which is the only teaching they typically do. (In Mormonism, the men visit each household in the congregation once a month — ideally — to see how the members are doing and to deliver a short gospel message. For more on home teaching, see Chapter 17.)

Step 3: Priest

At age 16, LDS boys can become priests. The main job of Mormon priests is to bless the sacramental bread and water, saying the prayer exactly right or repeating it until they do. (Don't worry; they can use a cheat sheet.) In addition, priests can perform baptisms (see Chapter 6), ordain other males to Aaronic Priesthood offices, and conduct meetings when an adult priesthood holder is absent.

The bishop

Okay, this section is a little confusing, so bear with us. The leader of a full-sized Mormon congregation, or *ward,* is called the bishop (his counterpart in a smaller congregation, or *branch,* is called a branch president). Why do we list that role here, under the Aaronic Priesthood? Because, technically, the office of bishop is part of the Aaronic Priesthood. The bishop directly oversees the boys who hold the Aaronic Priesthood, and he uses that priesthood to perform some of his duties, such as handling finances and helping the poor.

However, the bishop of a ward is also a high priest in the Melchizedek Priesthood (see the next section), which gives him authority to act as CEO of the ward and conduct its spiritual affairs. In addition to overseeing the efforts of all the volunteers who typically staff a ward (see Chapter 6), the bishop spends a lot of time interviewing individual members for a variety of reasons, such as issuing temple recommends (see Chapter 7). Bishops act as judges in God's earthly kingdom, and Mormons believe they can receive revelation about how to run the ward, including discerning what individuals are really feeling.

Melchize-who?

Originally, the full name of the Melchizedek Priesthood was the "Holy Priesthood, after the Order of the Son of God." However, to avoid repeating the Lord's title too often, the LDS Church renamed the higher priesthood after Melchizedek, a high priest who lived in Old Testament times. The name is a combination of two Hebrew words meaning "king" and "righteous"; the Roman Catholic Church also has a Melchizedek Priesthood order.

The key to pronouncing *Melchizedek* is to treat the "ch" as a "k" sound. Other than that, the pronunciation is pretty much phonetic: Mel-*kih*-zeh-dek.

For men: The Melchizedek Priesthood

Given to all worthy adult Mormon males, the Melchizedek Priesthood provides men with the power and authority to lead the Church and preside over their own families, including receiving revelations directly from God to help them carry out those stewardships. From the prophet (see Figure 4-2) on down, all men hold the same priesthood, but they have different offices and callings within that priesthood; the prophet is the only single man who can exercise or delegate all the keys of authority. Mormons believe God recognizes the actions of priesthood holders only when they're in complete harmony with the chain of command, so a priesthood holder can't go off and start his own church. (However, plenty of people have launched offshoots of Mormonism, all of which the LDS Church regards as illegitimate.)

Figure 4-2: As of 2004, Gordon B. Hinckley was the current prophet and president of the LDS Church.

Photo by Al Hartmann/The Salt Lake Tribune

Elders

During their 20s and 30s, nearly all Mormon men hold the Melchizedek Priesthood office of elder. This rank allows them to teach and administer in the Church, bestow the gift of the Holy Ghost, do missionary work, attend the temple, and perform a variety of blessings and other ordinances. Elders preside over meetings when no high priest is available.

High Priests

In order to hold a high-ranking leadership position, such as bishop or *stake president* (leader of a grouping of wards), a man is first ordained a high priest. A younger man can become a high priest if God has called him to a senior leadership position, but most high priests are middle-aged or retired. When a man approaches his 40s or 50s, he may become a high priest even if he's not called to a senior leadership position, probably just so he can stay with his peer group.

Patriarchs

Usually retirement-aged priesthood holders, patriarchs are fairly rare in the LDS Church, with many *stakes* (groups of wards) having only one. Typically during the teen years, a Mormon goes to a patriarch to receive a *patriarchal blessing.* This blessing tells the receiver which tribe of Israel he or she belongs to and includes personal advice and revelations that Mormons consider important enough to transcribe and keep handy for lifelong reference. Adult converts to the Church can receive a patriarchal blessing, too. (For more on patriarchal blessings, see Chapter 5.)

Seventies and Apostles

The relatively few men who hold either of the two Melchizedek Priesthood offices of *seventy* and *apostle* typically serve the Church full time, and together they're also known as *General Authorities.* Usually based at Church headquarters in Salt Lake City, Utah, they're assigned to oversee Church functions and departments and to rotate among positions governing the Church in large areas of the world. We discuss the General Authorities in more detail in Chapter 8.

Performing priesthood ordinances

Holders of the Melchizedek Priesthood bring the Savior into people's lives by performing ordinances. Many of these ordinances include *blessings,* which are freestyle words of counsel and promise, as inspired by the Holy Ghost in accordance with God's will. For most of these ordinances, the recipient typically sits down in a chair, and the priesthood holder stands behind the chair and places his hands on the person's head, acting as proxy for the Lord himself. If additional priesthood holders participate, they too place their hands on the recipient's head. Some men like to dress up in Sunday clothes before administering an ordinance, and some like to say a personal prayer first to get themselves spiritually in tune.

Many priesthood ordinances, such as healing the sick or injured and giving blessings of comfort, can be performed at will by any worthy priesthood holder. Others, such as baptism, confirmation, and priesthood ordinations, must be authorized by local priesthood leaders. Following are the main ordinances that holders of the Melchizedek Priesthood perform:

✔ **Blessings of comfort:** Any Church member can ask a priesthood holder for a blessing of comfort in times of difficulty or decision making. Usually the person asks a family member or local leader who's familiar with his or her situation. The priesthood holder simply lays his hands on the person's head, starts the blessing, and offers whatever words he feels inspired to say.

✔ **Confirmation and bestowing the gift of the Holy Ghost:** For new members of the Church, this ordinance takes place immediately following baptism. We discuss it in detail in Chapter 6.

✔ **Dedications:** In a manner similar to blessings but without the laying on of hands, priesthood holders can dedicate a building or gravesite as a place of spiritual sanctuary and protection. Upon moving into a new house or apartment, many Mormon priesthood holders dedicate it as a refuge of safety and happiness for their families, and some Mormons even dedicate their businesses to the Lord. The dedication process is quite simple, not much different from a normal prayer. In a more formal manner, senior Church officials dedicate new or remodeled meeting-houses and temples for their specific religious purposes, and they dedicate entire nations for the preaching of the gospel.

✔ **Fathers' and husbands' blessings:** The Church encourages Mormon dads to give regular priesthood blessings to their children, and wives can ask their husbands for blessings. For example, many fathers bless their children at the beginning of a new school year, when they're getting ready to face new challenges and opportunities. In addition, fathers of newborns perform a special blessing ceremony for the infant, which we discuss in Chapter 6.

✔ **Healing the sick or injured:** Two or more priesthood holders usually perform this two-step ordinance, although one can perform both steps if others aren't available. One priesthood holder dribbles a few drops of *consecrated* olive oil (meaning it's been previously blessed for such use) onto the head of the recipient, lays his hands on the person's head, and says a short prayer of anointing. Another priesthood holder "seals" the anointing and offers a blessing of healing, comfort, and counsel. (A priesthood holder can buy pure olive oil at the grocery store and consecrate it, and many Mormon men carry a small key chain vial of this oil at all times.)

Mormons believe that unless a person is appointed by God to die, a healing blessing can save the person's life. Sometimes priesthood holders feel inspired to use extrapowerful wording, such as rebuking an illness or commanding a body to be healed. At the same time, a priesthood holder can't force a healing against God's will. Mormons are encouraged to seek out appropriate medical treatment, as well as priesthood blessings, when they are ill. Coauthor Christopher Bigelow believes he was healed of Hodgkin's disease via a priesthood blessing, although he still underwent subsequent chemotherapy and radiation. Better safe than sorry!

✔ **Priesthood ordinations:** The priesthood is transmitted from person to person by the laying on of hands. Whenever a boy or man advances in the priesthood, another priesthood holder ordains him to the new rank. After stating the details of the ordination, most priesthood holders include a blessing of advice about exercising the priesthood. Some Mormon men carry a wallet-sized card outlining their priesthood *line of authority* — or genealogy — all the way back to Christ. (Yes, a big time gap lies between the apostle Peter and Joseph Smith.)

✔ **Setting people apart:** Whenever a man or woman accepts a calling to perform a job or fulfill a leadership position in the Church, that person is usually set apart for the calling by a priesthood leader. After stating the facts of the calling, most leaders include a blessing of guidance and encouragement about carrying out the calling. For more about volunteer Church callings, see Chapter 6.

What about women and the priesthood?

Mormonism is adamantly, unapologetically patriarchal. Without exception, men preside over the Church and their families, and, ideally, they're the sole breadwinners, freeing women to bear and rear children. However, lots of Mormon women work outside the home, and Church authorities frequently remind Mormon men that they must respect their wives and the women of the Church as equal partners and consult them in making decisions. In the Mormon view, men and women are equally vital, though different, halves of a whole, and neither can achieve *exaltation* — becoming like God — without the other.

One of the most commonly quoted scriptures in Mormonism warns priest-hood holders against misusing the priesthood. If someone tries to dominate his wife or gratify selfish desires through the priesthood, "the heavens with-draw themselves; the Spirit of the Lord is grieved; and when it is withdrawn, Amen to the priesthood or the authority of that man" (from the Doctrine and Covenants 121:37; for more on the D&C, see Chapter 10). In other words, that man's priesthood authority goes kaput unless and until he repents of being too bossy and selfish. Rather, men must use the priesthood "by persuasion, by long-suffering, by gentleness and meekness, and by love unfeigned" (D&C 121:41). In other words, they need to be kind and use the priesthood to serve others.

Certainly, Mormon attitudes and policies regarding the patriarchal priest-hood and gender roles cause some controversy, even within the Church — for more about that topic, see Chapter 15. But many LDS women express grat-itude for having a priesthood holder in the house who can perform ordi-nances, receive revelations for the family unit, and unscrew stuck jar lids.

Chapter 5

Together Forever: The Eternal Importance of Family

*U*pon hearing that Mormons believe families can be together forever, some people think the idea sounds more like hell than heaven, depending on the state of their own family relationships. Nevertheless, Mormons preach that people reach the highest level of heaven as families, not as individuals. Known for marrying younger, divorcing less often, and having more children than today's average couple, devout Mormons who are sealed to one another in the temple believe they can accomplish nothing greater than building a strong, successful family that will continue throughout eternity.

In addition, Mormons think that discovering their ancestors and taking certain steps to eternally bind together their extended families, all the way back to Adam and Eve, is extremely important. Also, Mormons believe that all humans can become part of God's eternal family by entering into covenants and getting adopted into the *house of Israel*, which is what God calls his covenant people.

The Eternal Family Unit

In the Mormon view, all human beings are the spirit children of Heavenly Parents and can grow up to become like them (we discuss this core concept in more detail in Chapter 2). So that humans can learn how to become parents, God commands them to form family units on this earth, which serve as miniature models of God's own eternal family organization. Mormons have faith that, through the gospel, their earthly families can eventually become like God's eternal family.

Why families are so important

Mormons believe that the traditional nuclear family is part of God's plan and must remain the basic unit of society. In addition, they believe that the LDS Church's main role is to help families gain eternal blessings together, through Jesus Christ.

In the Mormon view, all men and women are commanded to "multiply and replenish the earth" — in other words, have children. As we discuss in Chapter 2, God wants all his spirit children to come to this earth, gain a physical body, and go through a test, and this can happen only if people make babies. However, Mormons insist that all children deserve to be born to a married husband and wife. Although the Church expresses compassion for those people who can't find a partner or bear children, it discourages self-imposed celibacy and has zero tolerance for sexual activity outside marriage (for more on Mormon views regarding chastity, see Chapter 16).

As anyone who's seen a Mormon-produced TV public service announcement knows, Mormons are champions of close-knit families. One of the most repeated sayings in Mormonism is "No other success can compensate for failure in the home," which has given pause to many a career-oriented Mormon. In a one-page document titled "The Family: A Proclamation to the World," which many Mormons hand out in their communities and keep framed on their living room walls, the LDS prophet and apostles declare: "We warn that the disintegration of the family will bring upon individuals, communities, and nations the calamities foretold by ancient and modern prophets." This proclamation hasn't yet been canonized in the Doctrine and Covenants (for more on this modern-day scripture, see Chapter 10), but many members expect that will happen eventually.

Because families are so central and important to their faith, Mormons believe the family is one of the devil's main targets. That's why Mormons get so alarmed about divorce, abortion, and gay marriage, which they view as sinful trends that move society away from traditional families. (Some observers find the Church's opposition to gay marriage ironic because its objections resemble those raised about polygamy in the 19th century, when the Church was on the other side of the table.) Even the 1970s women's liberation movement threw some Mormons into a tizzy, because they believe that a woman's main role should be nurturing children in the home.

"Till never do you part": Eternal sealing

Although many successful couples and families instinctively feel they'll always be together, Mormons believe that love isn't enough to preserve relationships past death. Rather, an eternal *sealing* ordinance is necessary to join husbands, wives, and their children together forever.

How and where

Someone holding the proper authority from God has to perform an eternal family sealing, and Mormons believe their specially ordained sealers are the only ones who currently hold that authority. This authority is what Jesus gave to Peter, the senior apostle: "And I will give unto thee the keys of the kingdom of heaven: and whatsoever thou shalt bind on earth shall be bound in heaven: and whatsoever thou shalt loose on earth shall be loosed in heaven" (Matthew 16:19). Mormons believe that this authority was lost from the earth due to corruption and apostasy but was later restored through Mormonism's founding prophet, Joseph Smith (for more details, see Chapter 4).

Eternal sealings occur in a sacred building called a *temple* (we discuss temples in detail in Chapter 7, including an overview of what goes on inside them). After a Mormon couple is sealed, any children they have after that point are automatically sealed to them at birth. If a couple doesn't get sealed until after children are born, those children participate in a temple sealing ordinance with their parents. However, getting sealed doesn't guarantee that every family member will make it to the eternal reunion — the sin in an unrepentant person's life overrides the sealing ordinance for him or her.

To offer the blessings of eternal families to everyone who's ever lived, Mormons are in the process of performing sealings by proxy in the temple for all husbands, wives, and children throughout history, especially their own ancestors. In the afterlife, these people can decide whether or not to accept the sealing — but there's a catch: The sealing is available only as a package deal that includes allegiance to Christ and his gospel. For more on this idea, see this chapter's section on family history work, as well as Chapter 7.

The eternal payoff

For Mormons, eternal marriage offers several benefits:

- Knowing that marriage can last forever adds a deeper dimension to a relationship and gives couples an important goal to work toward together. When a spouse dies, Mormons find it reassuring to look forward to resuming the relationship in the afterlife.

- Parenthood becomes more meaningful when parents focus on the belief that their relationship with their children can be eternal. Motivation increases for parents to teach their children well and build stronger, happier homes.

- Although someone can be *saved* to live with God in the afterlife without being sealed to a spouse, Mormons believe that only those with an eternal marriage partner can be *exalted* to become like God. Mormons don't often mention Heavenly Mother, but they believe God himself is married — which stands to reason if he's going to produce spiritual offspring. (For more on the Heavenly Parents, see Chapters 2 and 3.)

Breadwinning and homemaking

To keep families strong, Mormons uphold traditional gender roles. Ideally, men earn the money so women can stay home with the kids. However, U.S. demographics show that Mormon women work outside the home just as much as non-Mormon women do. LDS Church authorities still preach the ideal, but they allow for the fact that some families require two incomes to make ends meet. However, authorities warn against women working just so the family can enjoy more luxuries.

In Mormonism, men are expected to preside over their homes and families by exercising their priesthood authority in love and righteousness, not bossiness or intimidation (for more on the Mormon priesthood, see Chapter 4). Mormon men are frequently reminded to treat their wives as equals and consult with them in making decisions. Although "househusbands" aren't unheard of in Mormonism, the idea makes most Mormons uncomfortable because the Church teaches men to provide for their families to the best of their ability.

In addition to encouraging traditional gender roles, Mormonism elevates marital romance to near-religious status. Church leaders encourage men and women to continue courting each other throughout their marriage, including spending an evening alone together on a weekly basis, if possible. Mormon spouses recognize the obligation to do their best to help keep their partners happy.

Raising up seed

When it comes to having children and raising them, Mormons go for both quantity and quality.

Populating the earth

Mormons aren't prohibited from using birth control, but they're still known for having large families (see Chapter 16 for more on Mormon views regarding birth control). For example, coauthor Christopher Bigelow is the oldest of ten children, which his parents spaced out every two years. Although Mormon birth rates typically follow the general trend, which means that Mormons in developed nations are having fewer children nowadays, they still have more kids on average than their non-Mormon contemporaries.

Why do Mormons have so many kids? Beyond simply valuing family life and parenthood, several possible reasons exist.

✔ **To make sure they're not leaving anyone out:** As we discuss in Chapter 2, Mormons believe that everybody's spirits lived together and formed relationships before coming to earth. Mormon parents sometimes have more children because they sense that another spirit who belongs in their family is still waiting to be born, although this widespread belief isn't official doctrine.

✔ **To give premortal spirits the opportunity of a lifetime:** Mormons want to give as many people as possible the opportunity to come to earth and be raised in a Mormon home, where they can learn the gospel and receive the necessary ordinances for salvation, such as baptism.

✔ **To extend their boundaries:** Mormons believe they'll progress together through eternity as families, and having lots of children is good preparation for that. In heaven, after an exalted couple — see Chapter 2 for more about exaltation — produces a sufficient number of spirit children, these heavenly parents will eventually organize their own world over which they'll preside, like God the Father presides over this world. This belief has led evangelical Protestants and other Christians who oppose Mormonism to charge that Mormons believe in many gods, but Mormons point out that they never stop honoring and obeying their own Heavenly Father, even after becoming like him. He remains the only God to them throughout eternity.

Rearing children in the way they should go

Mormons view parenting children as perhaps the most critical aspect of this earthly test. According to the LDS document "The Family: A Proclamation to the World," parents are under solemn obligation to "rear their children in love and righteousness, to provide for their physical and spiritual needs, to teach them to love and serve one another, to observe the commandments of God, and to be law-abiding citizens wherever they live." Mormons believe that parents who fail in these duties will be held accountable before God. (For more on the Proclamation, see Chapter 10.)

As a family-centered organization, the LDS Church teaches members several ways to strengthen their families:

✔ **Family home evening:** Mormons reserve Monday evenings to gather as families and study the gospel, discuss plans and problems, and enjoy a fun activity together. This evening is so sacred that all Church buildings are closed, and Mormons consider even telephoning another Mormon family on Monday evening to be bad form. (We discuss family home evening in more detail in Chapter 17.)

✔ **Family prayer:** Every morning and night, the ideal Mormon family kneels in a circle and says a prayer together. Also, Mormon families say a prayer before each meal.

✔ **Family council:** On a regular basis and especially when a family faces a significant decision or challenge, the LDS Church encourages parents to hold a family meeting so each person can express his or her insights and opinions.

✔ **Family scripture study:** The Church urges Mormons to spend time each day reading from the scriptures together, especially the Book of Mormon. Many families do this in the morning, before school. Mormon children *never* doze through it. (Yeah, right.)

✔ **Family work:** Many Mormon families assign chores and organize family projects to help children learn to work and cooperate together. One of the most common projects is a family vegetable garden, and some Mormon families do service projects for widows or other needy people.

✔ **Family recreation:** Mormon families place a high priority on taking time to play games and sports together and go on outings and vacations. In addition, the LDS Church specifically urges fathers to spend time alone with each child. (Presumably, mothers already do.)

✔ **Extended family relations:** Mormons are typically very big on extended family gatherings, reunions, cousin sleepovers, newsletters, and other traditions. In multigenerational Mormon families, the first cousins alone often number in the dozens.

Shaking the Family Tree: Family History Work

Southeast of Salt Lake City, Utah, the white-topped peaks of the Wasatch Mountains seem to beckon with the promise of powdery snow, great skiing, and . . . millions of rolls of microfilm? Yes, you read that right. The LDS Church, long known for its obsession with eternal families, considers genealogy (more commonly called "family history") to be so important that it has buried the world's largest collection of genealogical records 700 feet deep in the cool, solid earth underneath a granite mountain.

The giant doors of the vault are made to withstand a nuclear blast. (Sure, it may seem like overkill, but remember that the site was built in 1960, at the height of the Cold War.) For four decades, this site — off-limits to anyone who's not a Church employee — has been the nerve center of genealogy research. Here, the LDS Church keeps master copies of genealogical microfilms protected at a constant temperature of 60 degrees Fahrenheit, preserved for the ages and ready to be copied for distribution all over the world.

The reason for the fuss

You may be wondering: why all the fuss? To Mormons, keeping family history records isn't just a quaint practice that helps folks remember their great-grandparents. In fact, the LDS Church urges all Mormons to contribute their time, energy, and prayer to the eventual salvation of all people, and doing family history work is part of that. You can thumb back to Chapter 2 for the full scoop on the Mormon plan of salvation, but here's the nutshell version: Every person has the opportunity to be reunited with God in heaven after living faithfully and receiving certain ordinances, including baptism (see Chapters 6 and 7) and a temple endowment (see Chapter 7). This opportunity is available not only to those who've lived since the restoration of the gospel in Joseph Smith's time but also to everyone who's ever existed on earth, from Adam and Eve on down through the entire human race.

Mormons believe that *proxies* (substitutes) can perform the essential ordinances on behalf of people who didn't have the chance in this mortal life to be baptized and attend the temple. In acting as proxies, Latter-day Saints give those spirits the chance to embrace or reject the gospel in its fullness in the spirit world. (For more on the spirit world and the decisions that spirits there can still make, see Chapter 2.)

Family history is the key to making temple ordinances such as eternal family sealing possible for the dead, because family history work provides the names and essential data for people who still need their ordinance work done. Mormons research their genealogy carefully because they want to be with their own families forever. They also want to give other families that same blessing and extend the opportunity for exaltation to anyone who's ever lived. So the Church does family history research in all parts of the world through the *extraction program,* which we explain in the section "Extracting names," later in this chapter.

Some cultures have readily accepted the Mormon practice of proxy baptism, especially parts of Asia, where paying reverence to ancestors is considered a sacred duty. However, others have criticized it, saying that a posthumous baptism or temple ordinance makes a person a Mormon against his or her will. In 1995, Mormon leaders told Church members to refrain from baptizing Holocaust victims, because some Jewish groups felt that baptizing those who were killed due to their affiliation with Judaism was insulting. (Some Mormons apparently didn't get the memo, however: In 2004, the issue hit the headlines again because some individuals persisted in performing these baptisms despite the official Church position.)

Mormons are a bit puzzled by the hullabaloo, because proxy baptism doesn't *make* the baptized person Mormon or force a spirit world conversion — it just provides deceased spirits with the *choice.* As we explain in Chapter 2, *agency* (free will) is one of the most important principles of LDS theology. No ordinance or ritual can take away a person's right to choose his or her own path.

The cloud of this controversy does have a silver lining: Although Jewish advocacy groups have criticized the practice of proxy baptism, they've also praised Mormon genealogists' efforts to use knowledge of Jewish family history in order to regain property lost in the Holocaust.

The details of the work

The LDS Church has two basic ways of gathering family history records: Mormons and other people who are working on their own genealogies submit some of the records, while Church representatives and volunteers get others from public records.

Submitting names

Individuals around the world have submitted many of the family history records that the LDS Church possesses. Some of these people are Mormon, but most are members of other faiths who've graciously agreed to share the information they glean from their research in return for the free use of local LDS family history libraries and access to all the Church's microfilmed records. (The Church doesn't require that individuals who use its libraries share whatever information they find, but doing so is a nice gesture.)

People used to submit names on a longhand *pedigree chart* that traced a family's history and provided information about marriages, children, births, and deaths. (Actually, these charts looked kind of similar to the ones that are still used for purebred dogs.) These pedigree charts could take hours to fill out, and many ran for pages and pages. The last decade has seen the process of submitting names and sharing genealogical information advance at warp speed. Nowadays, people use software to enter and edit information, export and import their family history to Web sites, create charts, and amaze their friends. The new software saves hours of tedium and does everything for you except slice, dice, and make julienne fries. (In fact, some Mormons believe that God inspired the computer's invention mainly to turbocharge family history work.)

Extracting names

Every year, the Church sends teams of researchers to every corner of the earth to extract local history records. The word *extraction* may call to mind a painful root canal in the dentist's chair, but trust us when we say that extracting genealogical records is a lot more pleasant than pulling teeth. From 1985 to 1990, the extraction program generated 13 million names and records, and the work continues to accelerate. The Church's Web site says that its workers are using 242 cameras at any one time to microfilm records in over 40 countries.

LDS Church researchers copy the originals of each record — often in crumbling, dusty books and registers — onto microfilm or into a digital file. The original records typically remain in the local archives, churches, or libraries that own them, and the master microfilm goes into that granite mountain vault we describe at the beginning of this section. Then researchers make daughter copies of the film for distribution to libraries and individuals around the world.

Some of the sources that the Church puts on microfilm include

- **Parish records:** Local parishes of various Christian denominations have kept records for centuries of births, deaths, marriages, and baptisms within their communities. These records are an invaluable source of information for genealogical researchers.

- **Vital records:** Governments keep tabs on individuals, marking not only their births and deaths but also things like income. (Apparently, the idea that nothing is sure except death and taxes is universally true.) Relevant government documents include Social Security indexes, census records, county tax assessments, and the like.

- **Military records:** Many people who research their genealogy want to know whether a particular ancestor served in a war, as well as details like battles, honors, and so on. In addition, because many veterans receive a pension after their discharge, military records may include information about where the individual lived after military service and when he or she died.

- **Immigration records:** These details can be the missing link for researchers who want to know when their immigrant ancestor left County Kerry for Ellis Island. Immigration records sometimes also offer clues about ages, occupations, and possessions brought to the New World. The Church provides a helpful database of most of the 22 million Ellis Island immigrants who came to the United States between 1892 and 1924.

Some communities have expressed gratitude to the LDS Church for its extensive work in genealogical research. In 2004, for example, a tropical cyclone devastated the island of Niue in the South Pacific. In the village of Alofi, 180-mph winds swept away homes, businesses, and all the village's vital records of births, deaths, immigrations, and marriages. However, only the original records were lost, because the LDS Church had already microfilmed all the records a decade before. The Church presented a copy of the microfilms to the local government so that Alofi's people wouldn't lose their knowledge of their ancestors.

How can I get started with family history?

Just 50 years ago, people who were serious about doing genealogical research would take a two-week vacation from work and embark upon the long journey to the Family History Library in Salt Lake City, Utah, the largest genealogical library in the world. They'd pore over books during the library's open hours, tracking their small victories — a great-great-grandmother found, a link to another family discovered — in fat ledger books filled with names and dates.

Well, hooray for technology. No one needs to brave the Wild West to go to Salt Lake City anymore — most people only need to venture as far as their local LDS meetinghouse or even their own desktop computer. All the information contained in the megalibrary in Salt Lake City is available by ordering microfilms at any one of more than 3,700 Mormon family history centers in 88 nations. (There's a small fee for shipping and processing the loaned roll of film.)

Moreover, most of the information is also available on the Web at www.familysearch.org. Here you can plug in what you already know about your ancestors and see what pops up; in many cases, researchers find that other people have already paved the way for them and they can piggyback on research that distant cousins may have done. If you're not so fortunate, think of yourself as a pioneer, blazing a path that others will be glad to follow. The site allows access to the entire catalog of the main Family History Library in Salt Lake City, and you can order microfilms to be viewed at your closest branch library, which is usually located in a room inside the local Mormon meetinghouse or stake center.

Coauthor Jana Riess, who volunteered for several years as a family history consultant in her former congregation, has a word of advice for people who are thinking about starting their family history: Don't wait. She found that most people who used the services of the center were retired; they had the time to spend doing the research, and they also were more aware of their own mortality and the need for keeping records. But many of these people said they would've given anything just to have their mother or grandmother with them for an hour to answer questions about family history. The moral of this story is . . . don't wait until all the previous generations are gone before you begin making a record. Start it now.

God's People: The Family of Israel

The Mormon concept of family begins with the nuclear family — Mom, Dad, and the pitter-patter of (quite a few, ideally) little feet. Beyond that is the extended family — ancestors and descendants who become sealed forever along patriarchal lines through family history and temple work. But hold your horses: The Mormon concept of family has a third level that binds Latter-day Saints together with lots of people who aren't even their blood relatives.

One of the distinguishing factors of Mormonism compared to other forms of Christianity is its emphasis on the role of Israel in God's plan for the world. By *Israel* Mormons don't mean the modern-day nation-state of Israel, but all the many people in the world who are heirs to particular promises God made in the Bible's Old Testament. Mormons believe that anyone can become part of the *house of Israel* — the chosen people of God — whether or not they're genetic descendants of the ancient Israelites. What's more, one of the LDS Articles of Faith states that Mormons believe in the "literal gathering of Israel and in the restoration of the Ten Tribes" — something that isn't a core belief of other Christian denominations.

Why is the house of Israel so important? The story begins with a guy called Abraham.

Abraham and God shake on it

In the Bible's book of Genesis, God made a *covenant,* or two-way agreement, with Abraham. Basically, God told Abraham that if he and his descendants would be God's people, then he would be their God. In return for love, obedience, and faithfulness, God promised Abraham two basic things:

- A bountiful land where he and his descendants could reside
- Descendants without number

For Abraham, an old nomad, both promises were basically laughable. He was rich in everything *but* land and children — and by the time he was 99 years old, neither had materialized. But God made good on his promise with the birth of Isaac, and today Abraham's descendants number as the stars in the sky, as God told him they would.

But according to Mormons, Abraham's descendants aren't just numbered among his literal biological offspring, the Jewish people. In fact, they believe that the *Abrahamic covenant* — God's promises to Abraham — extends to all people who are worthy to be *grafted in* to the house of Israel. (That term is a spiritual one and not something painful, like a skin graft.) So each and every person has the potential to partake of the Abrahamic covenant. How does a person get grafted into the house of Israel? By joining the LDS Church.

The house of Israel in Mormon scriptures

The concept of Israel as a factor in community identification shows up not just in the Bible, but in distinctively Mormon scriptures as well. The plight of Israel's scattering and promised regathering is one of the major themes of the Book of Mormon, in which the term *house of Israel* appears no fewer than 107 times.

In fact, when the Savior appears to the Nephites as recorded in 3 Nephi 10, the very first thing he does is to greet them as "descendants of Jacob . . . who are of the house of Israel." To Mormons, the fact that Christ got right to the point about the Nephites' lineage is significant: The Book of Mormon is about people who were Abraham's descendants. In its opening chapters, the prophet Lehi receives a vision in which he sees the destruction of Jerusalem and the scattering of Israel, so he and his family flee Jerusalem. Six hundred years later, the promised Messiah visits their descendants over in the New World to gather them, as the Savior put it, as a hen gathers her chickens. In other words, the people were restored to their rightful heritage. (For more on themes in the Book of Mormon, see Chapter 9.)

Although the house of Israel is an important theme in the Book of Mormon, even many Mormons misunderstand it. Various outsiders have taught, and some clueless Mormons have mistakenly believed, that the Book of Mormon tells the story of the ten lost tribes who left northern Israel around 721 B.C. In fact, the Book of Mormon doesn't deal with these lost tribes, whose whereabouts and identity are still known only to the Lord. Presumably, scriptures exist somewhere that describe these tribes' history, which may include holy visitations from the Savior or other biblical figures. Mormons expect more of these scriptures to come to light at a future time.

Gathering God's children

The prophets of old and modern-day Mormon prophets have stated that in the latter days just prior to the Savior's Second Coming, the house of Israel will be gathered once again, with the remnant being assembled from among the nations of the earth (Jeremiah 23:3).

What does it mean to be gathered? The LDS Church teaches that Israel's gathering will happen in two stages:

- First, Israel will be *spiritually* gathered into the LDS Church. This stage is already happening as people all over the world embrace the gospel and come to understand themselves as part of God's great work.

- Second will be the *physical* gathering of Israel, which won't be completed until the Savior's Second Coming, although it has already gotten underway in the Middle East. This gathering will involve an actual, bodily migration as the different tribes of Israel move back to biblical and Book of Mormon lands to reclaim their heritage. (Even the ten "lost" tribes, which we mention in the preceding section, will be restored to their lands, as directed by the descendants of Ephraim. For more on Ephraim, skip ahead to the section on patriarchal blessings.)

Becoming adopted into Israel

Presumably, hundreds of millions of people walking the earth today have some genetic link, however faint, to the 12 tribes of ancient Israel. Because bloodlines have been diluted through the centuries and the Jewish Diaspora was so geographically extensive and prolonged, there's no way of telling who has Israelite heritage and who doesn't. However, it doesn't matter, because those who aren't born into the Abrahamic covenant can become adopted into Israel through baptism.

Personal Prophecy: Patriarchal Blessings

Mormons can discover their personal lineage in the house of Israel through an ordinance called a *patriarchal blessing,* which is also an opportunity to receive some personalized prophecy regarding their individual lives. Many Mormons refer to the typed transcript of their patriarchal blessing throughout life, prayerfully consulting it for insights into personal circumstances and future events. Unlike other priesthood blessings in the Church, a patriarchal blessing is a once-in-a-lifetime experience, never to be repeated. What's more, not just any Melchizedek Priesthood holder can offer it. Only a *stake patriarch* who's specifically ordained to that role and gifted with the insights of the Holy Ghost can give this blessing. (For more about priesthood blessings, see Chapter 4. To understand what a *stake* is, flip ahead to Chapter 6.)

Each stake usually has only one patriarch, though very large stakes may have two. Patriarchs have already been ordained as *high priests* (see Chapter 4) and are usually middle-aged or older. Until very recently, the Quorum of the Twelve Apostles in Salt Lake City individually chose and ordained all patriarchs. Now, with so many stakes around the world, the stake president submits a recommendation to the Twelve, who must approve the proposed patriarch before the stake president ordains him.

Discovering personal lineage

One of the most important aspects of every patriarchal blessing is the declaration of a person's lineage in the house of Israel. Drawing upon the inspiration of the Holy Spirit, the patriarch indicates which *tribe* the individual belongs to. Remember that in the book of Genesis, Abraham's grandson Jacob had 12 sons who became the 12 tribes of Israel.

Most, though not all, Latter-day Saints are declared to be of the tribe of Ephraim — an interesting lineage, because in Genesis 48 this tribe receives a special blessing to be great and to be the source of many nations. Having such a noble lineage is a privilege and responsibility, one that Mormons take seriously. Mormons believe that it doesn't matter whether they became part of the tribe by adoption or by blood; the important thing is to participate in the vital work that the tribe of Ephraim must complete to restore the whole people of Israel.

Other aspects of a patriarchal blessing

Mormons rarely show their patriarchal blessing transcripts to people outside their own families. To them, blessings are sacred; in addition, Church leaders don't want people to covet one another's promised gifts, talents, or destinies. For example, if some teens compared their blessings, one young man may feel pangs of jealousy that his best friend's blessing contains specific information about the woman he'll someday marry. Or a young woman may realize that all her buddies' blessings contain promises of missions they'll serve and worry why hers doesn't.

However, Mormons sometimes mention the promises of their patriarchal blessings when they're relevant to a church discussion or in private conversations. In addition to the declaration of lineage discussed in the preceding section, most patriarchal blessings contain some, though by no means all, of the following aspects. These aren't prepared or researched by the stake patriarch beforehand, but come to him through prayer during the blessing, as directed by the Spirit:

✔ **Discussion of the person's premortal existence:** Often, this statement is simple and general, saying that the person fought valiantly in the War in Heaven. (For more on that topic, see Chapter 2.) But some patriarchal blessings are quite specific about what people did and whom they knew before coming to earth.

✔ **A statement about the person's earthly family:** Some patriarchal blessings make general mention about a person's family situation ("You've been raised by loving parents who've taught you gospel principles," and so on). Others are quite particular about unique circumstances in the person's family life or make predictions about the recipient's future spouse or children.

✔ **Reference to individual strengths and weaknesses:** Some blessings are very personal, as the Spirit inspires the patriarch to talk about the individual's personality traits, spiritual assets, and potential flaws.

✔ **Mention of a full-time mission:** Some blessings for young people mention serving a full-time mission for the Church. (To understand what missionary work means to Mormons, see Chapter 14.) For example, in the mid-1980s, one young man's patriarchal blessing said that he would one day serve a mission to Russia. The Cold War still prevailed, and the Soviet Union didn't exactly welcome the evangelistic efforts of Mormon missionaries, so he rightly wondered if the patriarch had gotten soft in the head. However, by the time this fellow was 19, the Church had just opened its first mission in post-Soviet Russia, and he was among the charter group of missionaries sent to preach the gospel there.

✔ **Message from Heavenly Mother:** Heavenly Mother has been known to make an occasional appearance in patriarchal blessings, especially for young women. In these blessings, the message from Heavenly Father is supplemented by words that Heavenly Mother specifically wants the person to hear: that the individual is dearly loved, has a divine nature, and possesses special and unique qualities (which may or may not be spelled out). The recipients, who don't hear much about Heavenly Mother in church, often cherish these words.

✔ **Predictions of events the individual will personally witness:** Some patriarchal blessings make statements about things the person will someday see, whether they be Church growth or signs of the End Times.

✔ **Specific blessings related to career or Church service:** Patriarchal blessings can vary dramatically in this regard. One of us authors (we're not telling who!) was stunned to receive very detailed guidance about education and individual talents through a patriarchal blessing, despite having never met the stake patriarch before the blessing.

✔ **Loving reminders to live worthily:** Most patriarchal blessings contain counsel to follow the promptings of the Holy Ghost and remain worthy to keep his constant companionship (see Chapter 3). Many also urge the individual to be a good influence in the family, at work, and in all circumstances.

✔ **A final promise to be sealed and protected against the Destroyer:** Many patriarchal blessings close with a benediction for protection against Satan.

Understanding a patriarchal blessing

Most Church members are grateful for their patriarchal blessings, which are tailor-made for them and reflect the guidance of the Holy Ghost. However, they're not always easy to understand.

One of the most interesting aspects of a patriarchal blessing is the high emphasis the Church places on its individuality. If a member has questions about the content of a blessing, the patriarch, bishop, and other Church leaders are explicitly told *not* to interpret the blessing for the member. Church members can, through prayer, bring all their questions directly to Heavenly Father.

The LDS Church encourages Mormons to remember that although patriarchal blessings come from the Holy Ghost, they aren't road maps for life or fortunes from a soothsayer. Some of the elements of a patriarchal blessing may not be realized until late in mortal life, or even in the afterlife. (For example, someone who was told that he'd see peace established on the earth may eventually view that transition from the spirit world, not this one.)

Obtaining a patriarchal blessing

To get a patriarchal blessing, you must be a Mormon in good standing and be considered worthy by your bishop. This worthiness interview isn't as set in stone as an interview for a temple recommend (for more on that process, see Chapter 7), but it's important for the bishop to determine whether you're ready. (The LDS Church doesn't set a fixed age for a person to receive a patriarchal blessing, so Mormons who grow up in the Church don't have absolute guidance about when to seek after it, although most do it during their mid-to-late teens.) By interviewing you, your bishop can figure out whether you're spiritually mature and responsible enough, or if you should wait a little longer. If you're a recent convert, he can see whether you're established enough in the gospel to be ready for the blessing. Unlike the temple, which a new convert must wait a full year to enter, there's no preset waiting period for getting a patriarchal blessing after baptism.

If your interview with the bishop goes swimmingly, make an appointment with the patriarch.

Unless you have a family member who's an ordained stake patriarch, you can't cross stake lines to have the patriarch of another stake perform the blessing. Some patriarchs allow you to bring one or two loved ones to hear the blessing — parents, a spouse, or a good friend.

At the appointed time, you all sit down for a few minutes with the patriarch, usually in his home. The blessing recipient is typically a bit nervous at this point, so you can make some small talk, and many patriarchs ask questions that will help them pray about and personalize the blessing. When the time comes for the blessing to begin, the patriarch stands behind you and places his hands on your head. Every blessing is recorded on audio and then transcribed, often by the patriarch's wife or another family member, so don't worry if you don't catch every word. One copy of the transcript is sent to Church headquarters, and another is mailed to you to consult throughout your life. If you lose your copy, you can request another copy from Church headquarters.

As one Church leader taught, a patriarchal blessing is "a paragraph from the book of our possibilities," and it naturally raises questions about who we are and what we may become. As Mormons reflect on its promises and blessings throughout their lives, they grow in understanding and come to more deeply appreciate God's love for them as unique individuals.

Part II

Eternal Rituals and Endless Meetings

The 5th Wave   By Rich Tennant

"I want them to be happy too. I just don't think Mattel makes a Malibu Dream Temple for Ken and Barbie."

In this part . . .

We look at the Church from the bottom up, so to speak. We start with the *ward* (local congregation) and *stake* (regional gathering of wards) and reveal everything that goes on from day to day and week to week. You find out what to expect if someone invites you to attend a Mormon *sacrament meeting* (Sunday service), baptism, or funeral, and you get the scoop on all the different activities and organizations at the ward and stake levels.

Then you take a trip inside a Mormon temple and see why Mormons feel that temples are so important for the spiritual health of the living — and the dead. Finally, you go on a quick tour of Church headquarters in Salt Lake City, meeting the General Authorities and learning about the semiannual televised meeting led by Church leaders and the welfare and Humanitarian Relief programs that help poor people all over the world.

Chapter 6

Welcome to the Meetinghouse!

*W*hen imagining Mormon life, many non-Mormons immediately picture an eye-popping LDS temple, one of the religion's most instantly recognizable symbols. And though these Magic Kingdom look-alike buildings house some of the most sacred rituals of the Mormon faith — see Chapter 7 for the skinny on that — you need to spend some time in the meetinghouse of the local *ward,* or congregation, in order to understand the heart of what it means to be Mormon.

The ward is the second-most-important unit of Mormon life and culture, after the nuclear family. In fact, wards are a lot like a family, with members addressing each other as Brother or Sister, followed by the surname — collectively, the men are called "brethren" and women "sisters." Led by a bishop, a ward usually encompasses all the Latter-day Saints within certain geographic boundaries, even when they don't have much in common beyond their shared faith.

Also in this chapter, we offer a sneak peek into a Mormon sacrament meeting and tell you what to expect if you find yourself a guest at a Mormon Sunday service, baptism, wedding, or funeral. We take a look at the classes and auxiliary organizations that meet on Sundays before or after sacrament meeting and explain the Church's system of volunteer service, which is one of the most distinctive elements of Mormon spiritual life; because Mormons have no paid clergy, Church members all have assignments, or *callings,* to fulfill. Finally, we talk about the *stake* (a grouping of several wards led by a stake president) and what stake conferences and activities entail.

What's a Ward?

In plain English, a *ward* is simply a local Mormon congregation. Wards usually have about 300 to 350 members who meet for a three-hour block of time on Sundays. Often, the first part is *sacrament meeting,* during which everyone gathers in the chapel to partake of the sacramental bread and water and listen to *talks,* or short informal sermons, from other ward members. For adults and teens, this meeting is followed by 40 minutes of Sunday school classes and 50-minute meetings segregated by age and gender, with 10-minute breaks between each meeting; for the children, the Church provides a program called *Primary.* (See Figure 6-1 for a sample schedule). In some wards, this order of meetings is reversed, with sacrament meeting held last.

Figure 6-1: A Sunday schedule for a typical Mormon ward (meeting order may vary).

Men (18+)	Women (18+)	Teenage boys (12-17)		Teenage girls (12-17)		Children (18 mos. to 11 years)
Sacrament Meeting						
Sunday school — Gospel Doctrine, Gospel Principles, or other specified classes		Sunday school — Young men and young women meet together by age				Primary — Sharing time and classes divided by age (including nursery for the littlest ones)
Priesthood	Relief Society	Priesthood		Young Women		
High priests / Elders quorum		Dea-cons (12-13)	Teach-ers (14-15) / Priests (16-17)	Bee-hives (12-13)	Mia Maids (14-15) / Laurels (16-17)	

Unlike most other Christian denominations, The Church of Jesus Christ of Latter-day Saints is a geographically based organization. Ordinarily, the Church doesn't want members to choose the ward in which they want to participate; instead, the Church expects members to become involved with whatever ward encompasses the neighborhood or area where they live. Not only does this ideal avoid the phenomenon of church hopping, but Mormons also believe that part of the genius of the ward concept is that it puts all kinds of people into communion with each other — people who may not otherwise make a connection. Mormons of all races and socioeconomic backgrounds attend church together and feel more blessed because of it.

The geography of a ward can change when the congregation gets too large for every member to have a *calling* (see "Get to work! Every member has a job," later in this chapter) or otherwise becomes unwieldy. When a ward gets too large, the leaders may split it in half or create three wards out of two.

Latter-day Saints are accustomed to the fact that the Church's rapid growth often causes ward boundaries to change, putting members in a new ward with people they don't know very well. That fact is all part of the adventure.

Specialty wards

Most wards are multigenerational and cater to all ages, including children. But the Church designs some wards to meet certain individual needs, including the following:

- **Singles wards:** Yep, this type of ward is the marriage market in its full gospel expression. (If you don't believe us, rent the 2002 screwball comedy *The Singles Ward,* which is a silly but entertaining glimpse of the Mormon dating scene.) Singles wards operate under the premise that young people and college students enjoy one another's company and learn the gospel best when they're serving as moral and spiritual examples for one another. When a member of a singles ward gets married, he or she leaves that ward and becomes a member of the regular ward. Singles wards are most common in university towns and large cities. When a city has an especially large singles population, the singles are sometimes divided into under-30 and over-30 age groups. (Singles don't *have* to attend these wards, by the way — they can just stick with their regular ward.)

- **Language wards:** As we explain in Chapter 14, the LDS Church has been growing at a phenomenal rate and now includes members of many different nationalities and ethnic groups. Sometimes, the Church operates ethnic wards and *branches* (see the following section) in languages other than the one dominant in the nation where they're located. This offering, however, is usually temporary — in the early years, the Church had German and Danish wards in the United States, for example, but discontinued them when members learned English. In the United States today, you can find Spanish, Portuguese, Korean, Vietnamese, and Tongan wards, as well as other languages. Numerous sign-language congregations for the deaf are in operation and, of course, aren't temporary.

Wards in the making: Branches

Wards don't just spring up full-blown in an area shortly after the missionaries first set foot there to convert new members. In the beginning, only a few converts and the missionaries themselves might meet in members' homes or in a rented building. This would-be ward is called a *branch,* and it can consist of as few as two Mormon families if at least one priesthood holder is available to administer the Sunday *sacrament* (communion of bread and water; see the section "What to do when you're in the pew: Sacrament meetings"). The leader of a branch is called a *branch president.*

As branches grow in membership, they gradually add classes and programs until they become a fully functioning ward. When we say *ward* and *bishop* in this book, we generally mean branches and branch presidents, too.

Participating in the Ward

In contrast to the architectural appeal of LDS temples, most LDS meeting-houses appear, um, *functional*. Older wards were a bit fancier and sported different architectural styles, but newer ones are quite bland and usually very much the same architecturally (see Figure 6-2).

Figure 6-2:
An early
Mormon
meeting-
house
(left) and a
contempo-
rary one
(right).

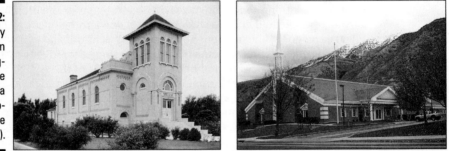

Left-hand photo used by permission, Utah State Historical Society, all rights reserved; right-hand photo courtesy of coauthor Christopher Bigelow.

Some visitors who come to church for the first time wonder aloud at the near-total absence of stained-glass windows, altars, candles, murals, and statues. A few older ward houses sport beautiful murals inside, but for the most part meetinghouse artwork is mass-produced. Various portraits and scenes from the scriptures and LDS Church history often adorn the buildings' halls and classrooms, but never the chapels themselves. Services involve no incense, no priest who changes into different brilliantly colored stoles with the passing of the liturgical seasons, and no objects with cool names like *mitre* and *orb*. You won't see any crucifixes; Mormons prefer to focus on the Savior's resurrection, not his death. Visitors who are used to a more visually stimulating atmosphere — all the "smells and bells," as Catholics may say — are often a little disconcerted at the apparent starkness of Mormon ward buildings and services.

Looks can be deceiving, however, because the life that teems underneath the bland meetinghouse surface is something to behold. Participating in a ward community is a vital and exciting part of being Mormon, plain and simple.

Get to work! Every member has a job

In some other Christian churches, laypersons attend Sunday morning services as spectators of sorts, while professional clergy deliver prepared sermons and teach classes. Churches may have paid staff members who corral the teens, teach the children, counsel members who are grieving, and play the organ. The advantage of such a system is that the sermons are often well conceived and capably delivered, the music holds to the highest standards of excellence, and the congregants receive professional-quality counseling. The disadvantage, from the LDS point of view, is that little may be expected of rank-and-file people, and therefore they don't grow much spiritually.

In Mormonism, only *General Authorities* (such as the prophet, the apostles, and the members of the Seventy; see Chapter 8) and mission presidents (see Chapter 14) receive a living-expense allowance to facilitate their full-time church work. In addition, the Church has a few thousand full-time employees worldwide who work in administrative functions or teach in the Church Educational System (see Chapter 8). Everyone else, including every person you see teaching or leading at the ward level, is a part-time volunteer who has accepted a calling.

Ward members have all kinds of callings: They may teach the *Sunbeams* (3- and 4-year-olds), keep the financial records, administer the sacrament, or plan activities for the youth. Others help people research their genealogy or direct the ward choir. Bishops and other high-level local leaders are also volunteers, often juggling church service with demanding careers and the needs of a large family. (For more on bishop duties, see Chapter 4.) Even the ward upkeep is generally the responsibility of members, who do the everyday cleaning themselves, while professionals attend to the heavy scrubbing.

Ward callings are extended by the bishop or one of his two counselors, who first pray collectively to God for guidance about where to assign various individuals. Some people stay in the same calling for years and years, while others receive temporary assignments (like being the youth summer camp director) or move around every couple of years. In less-populated wards, one person may hold two or more callings at the same time. Mormons can be very busy folks!

The LDS Church encourages members to accept whatever calling their bishop offers them and to regard it as coming directly from the Lord. However, in some circumstances, an individual might refuse a calling because of family issues, personal problems, or severe time constraints. Mormon adults are expected to consult with their spouses (especially if their spouse isn't a member) about a proposed calling from the bishop.

Magnifying your calling

Most Mormons have received a calling for which they felt unprepared, and when they accepted the assignment in faith, they found themselves richly blessed by the experience. In the Church, a popular saying is that the Lord doesn't call people who are already qualified; he qualifies those who are called. In other words, Mormons believe that if they pour themselves into church service, the Lord will help them in their efforts and increase their effectiveness.

Another popular saying is "magnify your calling," whatever it may be. This statement means that if your assignment is to stack chairs after an activity, do it cheerfully and well. If your assignment is to be the stake president, do it cheerfully and well. All such service contributes to God's kingdom and helps the individual become more spiritual and Christ centered.

What to do when you're in the pew: Sacrament meetings

Mormon chapels are always open to visitors on Sundays, and stopping in is a great way to get a glimpse of Mormon life and practice. Here's a quick rundown of what to expect in a Mormon sacrament meeting.

What to wear

Although many churches and denominations have accepted the casual-dress movement, Mormon services are still pretty formal. Men typically wear a suit or jacket and a tie — if you dress like Mormon missionaries, you won't go wrong. In addition, men and boys often wear white shirts, especially if they're participating in rituals like passing the sacrament.

Women generally wear a dress, a suit, or a blouse and skirt; hemlines are conservative and below the knee. A few younger women are starting to wear dressy slacks to church, though such attire is still rarely seen in Utah, which has some of the most conservative dress standards anywhere in the LDS Church.

Where to sit

Seating in Mormon sacrament meetings is on a first-come, first-served basis. Visitors can sit anywhere they want except on the *stand,* an elevated area in front where the pulpit and organ are located. This part of the chapel is reserved for the day's speakers, the choir, and the *bishopric* (the bishop and his two counselors). Also, the front two rows of the chapel on the left or right side are reserved for the young men who pass the sacrament.

What about the kids?

Mormon services differ from those of many other Christian denominations in that children stay with their parents during the entire service. A nursery and classes are available for children during the *other* two hours of the three-hour block, but sacrament meeting is for everyone, from Baby to Grandma and Grandpa. If you have children, bringing quiet games, coloring books, and simple snacks to entertain them during sacrament meeting is perfectly acceptable. Cheerios are a great favorite among the Mormon preschool set (and their parents).

Visitors are sometimes delighted, sometimes dismayed by the din during sacrament meeting in wards with lots of children. Mormons try to be reverent (which in Mormon lingo basically translates to "quiet") during sacrament meeting, but sometimes keeping completely hushed is tough when families are large and the gang's all together. The best advice we can give you is to just bear with the situation, even if a toddler is screaming in the next pew.

Mormons believe that sacrament meeting is for everybody and that the Savior welcomed the littlest ones — tantrums and all. This idea may be confusing to visitors and even to new converts, but it has at least one great advantage: Although adolescents in other denominations sometimes become church dropouts because they aren't accustomed to attending grown-up worship services, Mormon kids get so used to going to sacrament meeting that they tend to remain active through their teenage years.

How the service proceeds

With the exception of the monthly fast and testimony meeting (see the next section), most sacrament meetings follow the same basic order. They're predictable to a fault, which is good news if you're a visitor and don't yet know the score. Many wards provide a bulletin or program that volunteers hand out at the chapel entrance, making it much easier to follow along. Here's the rundown:

- ✔ **Announcements:** The meeting opens with the bishop or one of his counselors making announcements about upcoming activities and meetings in the ward and stake.

- ✔ **Opening hymn:** Hymn singing is important in Mormon services, which feature three or four hymns. The opening hymn is a time to get into the groove of preparing for worship; Mormons use this time to settle their hearts into a more reflective and spiritual mode. Many of the hymns in the LDS hymnbook are recognizable, especially to visitors from a Protestant tradition; others are unique to Mormonism. Unlike most Protestants, however, Mormons usually remain seated while singing hymns. Visitors are always welcome to pick up a hymnbook and join in the singing, although some visitors comment that the slow tempos and serious nature of Mormon hymns are very different from the rollicking hymns of other denominations.

✔ **Opening prayer:** Mormon meetings always begin and end with a prayer. Mormons bow their heads and fold their arms as they remain seated in the pews. One member of the ward, chosen in advance, comes to the front pulpit and offers a short invocation. In English-speaking wards, prayer language is formal, using "thee" and "thou" to address God; other languages may or may not follow similar customs. Every Mormon prayer ends with some variation of the phrase "In the name of Jesus Christ, amen." If you feel comfortable, you're welcome to join the congregation as they respond by saying "Amen" — however, that's the *only* time Mormon congregants say anything out loud. For more on prayer in Mormon life, see Chapter 17.

✔ **Ward business:** At this point, the bishopric member conducting the meeting announces new callings that members have accepted, and the congregation *sustains* them on cue by raising their right hands in support. (Members also have the right to raise their hands in opposition to a calling, but most members go through their entire lives without ever seeing that happen.) Visitors don't vote in these proceedings. If any baby blessings or baptismal confirmations are scheduled to take place on a particular Sunday, they occur at this point in the program (we describe these events later in this chapter).

✔ **The sacrament:** Partaking of the *sacrament* (bread and water that members of the priesthood have blessed) is the main reason everyone gathers. After ward business, the congregation sings a special hymn to remind everyone of Christ's sacrifice and Atonement, which is what they celebrate by taking the sacrament. Then teenage boys who hold the Aaronic Priesthood (see Chapter 4) bless the sacrament and pass it to the congregation (adult men can pass it too, if needed).

According to Mormons, the bread and water don't *become* the body and blood of Christ (a theological concept known as *transubstantiation*), as members of the Catholic faith believe they do. Rather, these elements are symbols that remind Mormons of the Savior's sacrifice and their own willingness to love and serve him. If you listen carefully to the words of the sacrament prayer — which is one of the few prayers in Mormonism that priesthood holders must recite absolutely the same every time — you'll hear the word *remember* a couple of times. Basically, Mormons believe that taking the sacrament of bread and water in a spirit of repentance helps them remember Christ's love, renew their baptismal covenants, and become more worthy of his Atonement.

If you decide to take the sacrament, take a single little piece of bread and put it in your mouth before passing the tray along and then go ahead and chew; Mormons don't wait to partake until the whole congregation is served. When the water is passed, take one of the little cups, chug it down, and drop the empty cup in the tray's waste receptacle before passing the tray to the next person. Mormons give their kids the sacrament, so you may be amused by a toddler grabbing a whole handful of bread or crying "I'm still thirsty" as the tray moves down the row.

Who's allowed to partake of the sacrament?

The $64,000 question visitors always have is whether they should partake of the sacrament when it's passed. In Mormonism, congregants remain seated while teenage boys bring the bread and water to everyone in little trays, so you're expected to pass the tray down your pew whether you take the elements or not.

In the LDS Church, the only people who are forbidden from taking the sacrament are those members or former members who've been disciplined or excommunicated for serious sin. Obviously, if you're a first-time visitor, this doesn't apply to you. At the same time,

partaking of the sacrament isn't a good idea if you know you have major, unresolved sins in your life or you don't believe in God and his Son, Jesus Christ. Otherwise, feel free to partake if you feel prompted by the Spirit to do so — in other words, if you have a good, warm feeling about it.

Mormons believe that they renew their baptismal covenants every time they partake of the sacrament, but those who haven't yet made any LDS baptismal covenants can still grow closer to God and Jesus Christ if they take the sacrament in the proper spirit.

The sacrament is the holiest part of what goes on in a Mormon service; now isn't the best time to take little Timmy to the potty. Latecomers who arrive during the sacrament's passing aren't seated until after it's finished. Mormons try especially hard to keep their children quiet and to preserve a spirit of dignity and reverence during the sacrament. You may see people meditating with their eyes closed or reading their scriptures, trying to turn their minds to the Savior and repent of their sins.

✔ **Talks:** The longest portion of a Mormon sacrament meeting consists of talks given by two to four members of the congregation, ranging anywhere from 2 to 30 minutes long. Laypeople give these short sermons, which are often pretty folksy; doctrine and scripture verses mingle freely with self-help advice, personal experiences, and anecdotes — not all of which may seem relevant to the topic at hand. Occasionally, the last speaker is a representative of the stake high council (see the section "Twice a year: Stake conference," later in this chapter), who addresses a topic assigned by the stake president. (Because these talks are sometimes longish and a bit dull, Mormons often joke that the speaker is a member of the *dry* council.) Before the last speaker, a hymn or special musical number may take place.

✔ **Closing hymn and closing prayer:** The congregation sings a final hymn, and after the closing prayer that follows, the organist or pianist usually plays postlude music as people get up and start chatting and moving to the foyer. This marks the end of the service.

Step up to the mike: Fast and testimony meeting

The first Sunday of each month is usually fast and testimony meeting, which differs from the ordinary pattern in two key ways. First, members come to the meeting having *fasted* (abstained from food and water) for two meals, or about 24 hours. (For more on fasting, see Chapters 16 and 17.) Second, the meeting gives members the opportunity to "bear their testimonies" after the sacrament has been passed. In Mormon tradition, this phrase means that an individual offers a quick personal homily on some gospel truth. Everyone, including the smallest of the small fries, has the opportunity to take a turn at the microphone.

Although the other Sundays of the month feature assigned speakers who come prepared to address the congregation, testimonies are almost never prepared in advance. Members speak when they feel the Spirit move them. Testimonies give members a chance to express gratitude to the Lord for help in difficult times, bear witness of the Savior's love, explain why they believe the gospel, thank family and ward members for their love and support, and talk about struggles they may be facing.

Testimony meeting is fascinating because although a testimony has a certain basic formula ("I know the Church is true," "I know the Book of Mormon is true," and so on), the meeting is one of the most unscripted events in Mormon life. Some meetings are so full of people bursting to share their stories that there's not enough time to accommodate them all. Other meetings suffer awkward pauses between testimonies. Some testimonies are so beautiful and honest that they bring the congregation to tears, but others ramble on, causing people to glance at their watches.

If you're visiting during testimony meeting and find some members' testimonies to be a little loopy, be generous and attribute it to the fact that they're likely fasting and may not be thinking very clearly.

Other special sacrament meetings

Throughout the year, Mormons observe some special sacrament meetings that highlight one of the classes or organizations of the Church. The ward's children usually take one Sunday a year to do a Primary program, during which they present songs they've learned and wow their parents with their scripture memorization and brief prepared talks. In addition, the Young Women, Young Men, Relief Society, and other auxiliaries may receive the spotlight each year during sacrament meeting, as directed by the bishopric (we discuss these groups in the section "Other Sunday meetings," later in this chapter).

At Christmas and Easter, many wards offer lovely programs that feature more music than usual. Don't look for those majestic trumpets that you find in other Christian Easter services, however. The LDS Church handbook stipulates that brass instruments are too loud and prominent for sacrament services. More's the pity. You're not likely to hear anything but piano, organ, and occasionally some classical woodwinds or stringed instruments in LDS meetings. For Mormons, departing from the official hymnbook and playing something by, say, Bach is really swinging out.

Holding ward conference

One weekend a year, each ward typically holds a *conference,* which stake representatives attend. The stake leaders of the Relief Society, Primary, Young Men, and Young Women organizations may meet with ward leaders on Saturday or just before church to assess how they're doing. During ward conference, sacrament meeting sometimes extends longer to allow more leaders a chance to speak, and the usual class schedule may be altered.

Getting dunked

LDS baptisms generally take place in the local meetinghouse — unless someone is already dead, in which case Mormons can perform baptism on that person's behalf in a temple (see Chapter 7). For Mormons, getting baptized — and yes, they do it by full immersion — signifies many important concepts:

- ✔ It marks the beginning of a person's official membership in the Church.

- ✔ It symbolically washes away sins, an effect that a person can renew each week by partaking of the sacrament (see the section "What to do when you're in the pew: Sacrament meetings," earlier in this chapter).

- ✔ It represents a covenant with God to keep his commandments, stand as his witness, and love and serve fellow Church members.

- ✔ It prepares a person to receive the constant companionship of the Holy Ghost (as we discuss in the section "Confirmation: Installing a direct line to God," later in this chapter).

- ✔ It obeys the example that Jesus set in the New Testament.

- ✔ It symbolizes being buried and then resurrected (being lowered into the water and then lifted out).

- ✔ It qualifies a person to receive salvation in the *celestial kingdom,* the highest level of heaven where God himself lives (see Chapter 2).

Preparing for baptism

The earliest someone can receive Mormon baptism is at age 8, which Mormons view as the *age of accountability* — when a person is spiritually mature enough to discern right from wrong. (People with mental disabilities that prevent accountability don't need baptism — they're automatically saved. It's the same for children who die before age 8.) Mormons don't recognize baptisms performed in other religions, so anyone who wants to join the LDS Church must receive Mormon baptism, even if he or she was already baptized in another Christian church. (Why don't Mormons recognize other baptisms? See Chapter 4.) At the same time, some other Christian churches don't recognize Mormon baptism, either.

Following are several ways in which baptismal candidates prepare for baptism. These steps don't necessarily happen in the order that we list them, and they often overlap. In fact, ideally a Latter-day Saint keeps cycling through these steps for the rest of his or her life.

- ✔ **Learn the gospel:** Children raised as Mormons learn the gospel by attending regular Sunday classes and being taught at home. People who've grown up outside the faith take a series of special lessons prior to baptism, usually from the local full-time missionaries. In addition, they study the scriptures and other sources on their own. (For more on missionaries, see Chapter 14.)

- ✔ **Exercise faith:** Preparing for baptism includes developing an abiding faith in Heavenly Father, Jesus Christ, the divine mission of the founding prophet Joseph Smith, and the truthfulness of the Book of Mormon, other scriptures, and the LDS Church itself. Faith begins with the *desire* to believe, and it grows as a person experiences good results from studying, praying, repenting, and living the gospel. (For more on faith, see Chapter 17.)

- ✔ **Repent of sins:** Everyone makes mistakes due to ignorance, weakness, or disobedience. To gain freedom and forgiveness from sins through the Savior, a person feels remorse about his or her sins, asks the Savior's forgiveness in prayer, stops the sinful behavior, confesses and makes restitution to others as necessary, forgives others, and renews his or her commitment to keep the commandments.

- ✔ **Gain a testimony:** Mormons believe that real, lasting conversion comes through a personal experience with the Holy Ghost. As a person puts effort into learning the gospel, exercising faith, and repenting of sins, he or she can pray for confirmation that Mormonism is true. Usually in a private, prayerful moment, God's answer arrives through an unmistakable spiritual impression from the Holy Ghost, often accompanied by warmth, tingles, or other sensations.

- ✔ **Talk with a Church leader:** Before a person receives clearance for baptism, he or she undergoes a private interview with a local priesthood leader to discuss his or her readiness. Even 8-year-old children meet with a leader. The leader asks questions to find out whether the person understands basic gospel principles, has developed sufficient faith, and is committed to living the gospel. Although the leader doesn't typically need to hear a confession of past sins, he makes sure the candidate isn't still committing significant sins, such as having sex outside of marriage. (For an overview of Mormon behavioral standards, see the temple-recommend questions that we summarize in Chapter 7.)

Going through the baptism process

For 8-year-olds reared in the LDS Church, group baptismal services often take place once a month at a larger meetinghouse called a *stake center* (see the section "Participating in the Stake," later in this chapter). For converts, a ward often holds a special individual service. Baptisms can take place any day of the week, and they can occur in any suitable body of water, although meetinghouse fonts are preferred. Here's how the event typically plays out:

✔ Upon arrival at the meetinghouse, the baptismal candidate changes into plain, white clothing in a small dressing room adjacent to the baptismal font. Most congregations keep some baptismal clothes on hand, or the candidate can arrange to borrow some. *Tip:* Women's clothing should be thick enough to avoid the wet T-shirt effect.

✔ Baptismal services generally take place either in the main chapel or in the auxiliary room where the font is actually located. White-clothed and shoeless, the baptismal candidate sits at the front with the baptizer, a priesthood holder who's also dressed in white. The meeting begins and ends with a hymn and prayer, and assigned members give inspirational talks, usually on faith, repentance, baptism, and the gift of the Holy Ghost. At some point, a congregational leader usually offers words of advice and welcome.

✔ When it comes time for the actual baptism, the candidate and baptizer enter the font via steps descending from the dressing room. (In the best-case scenario, the water will be bathtub warm.) If young children are present, they typically cram along the font's front edge for the best view.

✔ After the baptizer gets the candidate situated in the font, he raises his right arm, calls the person by his or her full name, utters a short, scripted baptismal prayer, and then lowers the person back into the water. Two witnesses standing at either side of the font make sure everything goes under — if even a big toe stays out, the baptizer does the ordinance over again. Most baptizers hold the candidate's wrist in such a way that the candidate can reach up and pinch shut his or her nose, and after the immersion, the baptizer pulls the candidate back up into the standing position.

✔ While the Church's newest member changes into regular Sunday-style clothes, the congregation sings hymns or watches a Church video. By the way, bringing along a plastic bag for the wet clothes, in addition to a towel and hair implements, is a good idea.

✔ Confirmation and bestowal of the gift of the Holy Ghost (which we explain in the next section) can happen at the conclusion of the baptismal service or — especially for new adult converts — during sacrament meeting the following Sunday.

Confirmation: Installing a direct line to God

Any human being who's pure and sincere can feel the influence of the Holy Ghost on an extraordinary occasion, such as when praying to know whether a spiritual concept is true. However, Mormons believe that Church members can enjoy the *constant* companionship of the Holy Ghost if they're trying to live worthily. A priesthood holder bestows this gift during an ordinance commonly referred to as *confirmation*. The confirmation ceremony goes something like this:

- ✔ The recently baptized person sits in a chair. The priesthood holder who will act as voice places both hands on the person's head. Other invited priesthood holders can circle around and lay their hands on the new member's head.

- ✔ The priesthood holder calls the person by his or her full name, confirms him or her as a member of the Church, and confers the gift of the Holy Ghost, usually using the phrase "I say unto you, receive the Holy Ghost." These words don't have to be exact, as in the case of the baptismal and sacramental prayers.

- ✔ The priesthood holder blesses the person with some words of encouragement and advice as the Holy Ghost inspires him.

- ✔ Afterward, the person traditionally shakes hands with or hugs everyone in the circle.

Mormons believe that receiving the gift of the Holy Ghost is essential to full salvation, because no one can make it back into God's presence without guidance and purification from the Holy Ghost. However, even with this gift, recognizing the Holy Ghost's promptings still takes effort. To invite his influence, members strive to obey the commandments and keep their thoughts and actions pure. We talk about the Holy Ghost in detail in Chapter 3, but here's an overview of what the Holy Ghost does:

- ✔ Provides spiritual strength and protection

- ✔ Subtly whispers knowledge, peace, and guidance to a person's heart and mind

- ✔ Sanctifies a person's soul in what Mormons refer to as the "baptism of fire"

Baby blessings: Welcoming a new lamb into the flock

A month or two after birth, new Mormon babies receive a blessing in front of the whole congregation during sacrament meeting. These blessings usually occur on Fast Sunday, which is almost always the first Sunday of the month.

- ✔ The father and other invited priesthood holders stand together in a circle, which turns into an oval if too many men are present. (If the baby's father isn't a member or isn't in good standing with the Church, the family can ask another priesthood holder to perform the blessing.)

✔ The father holds the baby securely in both arms, and each man puts his left hand on the shoulder of the man in front of him and his right hand under the baby, helping gently bounce the baby to prevent crying (which doesn't always work). The baby usually wears something white.

✔ With the bishop or a boy holding a microphone near the father's mouth, the father calls on Heavenly Father in prayer, says the baby's full name, and then directly addresses the baby with advice and promises about its future. Typical utterances include telling the baby to always obey its parents and stay close to the Church and promising the baby that he or she will meet the right person to marry at the right time. If the baby's a boy, the blessing almost always includes a mention about serving a full-time mission when he turns 19 (see Chapter 14).

✔ After the blessing, traditionally the father briefly holds up the baby for the congregation to admire. The mother stays seated in the congregation during the blessing, but she often says a few words later in the meeting, during the open-mike testimony-bearing time.

Although Mormons don't believe that a baby blessing is necessary for salvation, it does trigger the official listing of the baby as a *child of record* in the Church, and the parents receive a blessing certificate. Babies aren't yet technically members of the Church because they haven't been baptized, but they're counted in the Church's membership total. In 2003, the Church added 99,457 children of record worldwide.

Funerals: Saying farewell, for now

Usually held in the deceased person's home meetinghouse, Mormon funerals tend to be relatively upbeat, personalized affairs, celebrating the person's progress to the next step as much as mourning his or her departure. As always, the meeting begins and ends with a hymn and prayer, and it mainly consists of family members and friends giving talks and performing musical numbers. The talks tend toward specific personal remembrances of the deceased person, often sprinkled with humorous anecdotes. At least one talk primarily addresses how the Savior's resurrection opens the way for everybody to eventually be resurrected.

Adult Mormons who've been through the temple are buried in their temple clothes (for more on temples, see Chapter 7). After the funeral, a short graveside service usually takes place, during which a priesthood holder dedicates the gravesite as a place of shelter for the remains until the day of resurrection. Back at the meetinghouse, Relief Society sisters (see the next section) typically serve the extended family a luncheon. In Utah and other places, this meal so frequently includes a certain cheesy potato casserole that many Mormons refer to this dish as "funeral potatoes" no matter when it's served.

Mormons in other countries add a gospel spin to their own local customs. By the way, the Church discourages cremation unless the law requires it, as is the case in some countries.

Weddings: For time only

Most Mormon weddings take place inside a temple, not a meetinghouse (see Chapter 7). When solemnized inside a temple, marriage lasts for eternity. When held in a meetinghouse, marriage lasts only until death.

If a couple isn't yet worthy of temple marriage — such as in the case of a shotgun wedding — the bishop can marry them civilly in the meetinghouse, in a ceremony much like that of other faiths. After the couple demonstrates repentance and worthiness for a suitable length of time, they can get eternally sealed together in the temple.

Meetinghouse weddings can occur on other occasions, too. If a woman is married to someone in the temple and becomes a widow, she can remarry "for time only" in a meetinghouse ceremony. (However, a widower can be married in the temple to both his first and second wives, if the second wife wasn't previously sealed to someone — a lingering echo of 19th-century plural marriage.) If a couple doesn't live near a temple, they can wed in a meetinghouse and get sealed later, when they're able to visit a temple. If a couple wants non-Mormon family members to witness the wedding, they can hold it in the meetinghouse and then wait a year to solemnize it in a temple, which only qualified Mormons can enter.

Other Sunday meetings

A good place to see Mormonism's calling system in action is during the other Sunday classes and meetings, which precede or follow sacrament meeting in the three-hour block. For a visitor, the variety of classroom options can be confusing; probably the easiest thing to do is approach someone who looks official, say you're visiting, and wait to be told where to go.

Sunday school and other classes

Adults (ages 18 and above) are divided into two basic tracks for Sunday school, which is usually the middle hour of the three-hour block schedule:

> ✔ *Gospel Doctrine class* is a course of scripture study for established members of the Church. The class is taught on a four-year cycle, with individual years spent on the Old Testament, the New Testament, the Book of Mormon, and the Doctrine and Covenants. This class is intended to supplement the personal scripture study that the Church encourages all members to do daily; for more on this personal study, see Chapter 17.

✔ *Gospel Principles class* is for new converts and investigators (those who are meeting with the missionaries and thinking about joining the Church). You'll probably attend this class if you're visiting for the first time, unless the class isn't currently taught in that ward. The goal of the class is to help new members build their testimonies and understand the core teachings of the LDS Church.

Other special-focus classes (such as a teacher preparation class or a class on conducting genealogical research) may be held during the Sunday school time.

For the men: Priesthood quorums

In the remaining hour of the three-hour block, adult men and women divide into separate meetings. All the men attend priesthood meetings, which are subdivided into two groups. One is the *high priests group,* which includes men who are generally middle aged or retirement aged or who've been called to specific leadership positions. The other group is the *elders quorum,* generally consisting of men in their 20s, 30s, and sometimes older. (For more about priesthood organization and responsibilities, see Chapter 4.)

During this hour, the priesthood enjoys a lesson from the same manual that the women's Relief Society uses. The goal of using the same manual is to encourage husbands and wives to talk about the lesson content at home.

For the women: Relief Society

The Relief Society, founded by the prophet Joseph Smith in 1842, is one of the oldest women's organizations in the world — and with several million members, it's also one of the largest. All adult Mormon women age 18 and over are automatic members of Relief Society, whose motto, "Charity never faileth," reveals one of the organization's main purposes: to provide relief to the poor and needy.

Throughout its history, the Relief Society has founded hospitals, provided many of the resources to begin the Church's welfare program, and assisted untold numbers of needy families. Although the Relief Society no longer builds hospitals, its members devote countless hours to compassionate service on an individual level, which involves fixing meals for families in need, driving sick people to the doctor, and other kindly acts. On Sundays, Relief Society meetings include a lesson taught by one of the sisters. On Fast Sunday, the lesson often ends a little early so the sisters have time to bear their testimonies in the more intimate, all-female setting of Relief Society.

For the teens: Young Men and Young Women

Being a Mormon teen is tough, especially when you live in an area where you may be one of the only LDS students at your high school. Sundays offer a chance for Mormon youths to gather with others who have the same G-rated lifestyles.

Young men and women, ages 12 to 17, meet together in age-sorted classes during Sunday school, and then meet separately in priesthood or Young Women classes to hear gospel lessons. Just as boys advance in the priesthood as they age, becoming first a deacon, and then a teacher, and then a priest (for more about the Young Men priesthood program, see Chapter 4), young women also graduate to higher classes as they age. The names of these stages — we're not making this up — are Beehives (12- and 13-year-olds), Mia Maids (14- and 15-year-olds), and Laurels (16- and 17-year-olds). Those names are all quaint traces of bygone eras of LDS history, and the young women bear them with unusual grace.

The Young Women motto begins with the line, "We stand for truth and righteousness," which reflects the organization's desire to contribute positively to girls' self-images as they in turn contribute to society. Each week, Mormon young women recite that motto and the Young Women values, which are faith, divine nature, individual worth, knowledge, choice and accountability, good works, and integrity. Many of the Sunday lessons for Young Women focus on those seven values.

For the kids: Primary

Kiddies love Primary, the Church's organization for children ages 3 to 11. (In addition, Primary provides a nursery for children from 18 months to 3 years, where they can play with toys, have short lessons, and eat yummy snacks.) During the two-hour Primary time on Sunday, Mormon boys and girls gather with their teachers for sharing time, during which they hear short talks by other kids, learn scripture verses, and sing songs with great enthusiasm. In addition, they break up into smaller classes by age groups. Each month in Primary, children learn certain scriptures and songs, which relate to their annual theme and become part of their annual sacrament meeting presentation. The annual theme is the same for wards around the world.

Senior Primary kids — those who've been baptized and are ages 8 to 11 — enjoy midweek activities outside of Sunday classes. Girls can earn recognition at "Activity Days," not unlike the Cub Scout and Boy Scout awards that boys work toward. Also, Primary children of all ages look forward to special-occasion quarterly activities, which may include gospel-themed events, Halloween parties, service projects, Easter egg hunts, and Christmas with Santa.

Weekday meetings

Mormonism isn't just a Sunday religion, and if you drive by the parking lot of a local meetinghouse you may find it busy every night except Monday, which is *family home evening* (for more on that, see Chapter 17). The other weeknights are fair game for activities, meetings, book clubs, Boy Scouts, sports, holiday parties, wedding receptions, and the like.

Sharing a building

One unusual aspect of Mormonism is that anywhere from two to five congregations may share the same meetinghouse. One ward may hold its Sunday sacrament meeting at 8:30 a.m. and then head off to classes at 9:50, and then another ward will start its sacrament meeting in the same pews that the first ward warmed up for them. These wards also juggle a host of weeknight events, which can be especially tricky at times.

Wards that share a building usually bend over backwards to ensure that the arrangements are fair, and they rotate their meeting times each January to give every ward a turn to enjoy the most favorable Sunday meeting schedule (some members prefer morning, some afternoon). In addition, the wards take turns cleaning the building, shoveling snow, and doing other chores.

Teens meet once a week for Young Men and Young Women activities, and teens and college-aged students may use the meetinghouse for their weekday religious classes called *seminary* and *institute* (for more on those, see Chapter 8). Relief Society women gather monthly for a meeting called "Enrichment." No, this meeting isn't about getting rich, though some lessons do focus on self-reliance and financial responsibility. Enrichment meetings are meant to help sisters learn useful new skills (estate planning, food storage, self-defense, and so on) while sharing fun times, crafts, fellowship, and loads of sugary snacks.

Participating in the Stake

If a ward is the equivalent of a Catholic parish, then a *stake* is like a diocese, a gathering of 5 to 12 adjacent wards that a stake president oversees. The word *stake* comes from the Old Testament prophet Isaiah's prophecies comparing the latter-day Church to a tent held fast by stakes (see Isaiah 33:20 and 54:2).

Each LDS stake usually has about 3,000 members. In heavily Mormon areas such as Utah, this quota is met in a matter of blocks. In other parts of the country and the world, traveling from one end of the stake to another can take several hours — a difficult consideration for unpaid stake leaders who regularly visit all the wards within their jurisdiction.

Unless they have a stake calling, such as stake high councilor or stake Relief Society president, most Mormons don't experience quite the same weekly connection with their stakes as they do with their wards. Their participation usually happens during the semiannual stake conference and in occasional stake activities.

Twice a year: Stake conference

Four Sundays each year, Mormons don't meet with their normal ward. They spend two of those Sundays every April and October watching *General Conference,* a Church-wide meeting that we discuss in Chapter 8. They spend the other two Sundays attending *stake conference,* a twice-yearly meeting that usually takes place at the *stake center,* a largish meetinghouse with overflow space to accommodate the crowds. (In addition, bigger regional meetings are sometimes held every few years, usually in a large, rented auditorium.)

True to the spirit of Mormon pragmatism, stake centers aren't really separate buildings that are used only twice a year; the Church also uses them as a regular meetinghouse for one or more wards. In addition, stake centers usually feature extra office space for stake leaders. Sometimes members refer to a stake center as the "stake house," and uninitiated visitors may feel disappointed not to find steak served there.

Stake conferences usually feature several sessions within the same weekend. At the general two-hour session on Sunday, members of all ages hear from any General Authority who may be visiting, the stake president, and other male and female leaders and members. Members also listen to special music and hear about stake business, including the appointment and release of stake officers. Many stakes hold a Saturday evening session for adults, and special leadership training sessions help members with their callings in ward groups (Primary, Relief Society, Young Men, and Young Women). The sacrament isn't administered during stake conference.

Just a note on one bit of Mormon jargon that may be confusing at stake conference: Each stake president appoints two *counselors* to assist him in his

Changing what's at stake

Stake conferences have changed a great deal since the early days of the Church, when they were quarterly affairs led by a *General Authority* (an official who helps oversee the whole denomination; see Chapters 4 and 8). In 1979, the Church reduced their frequency to twice a year, and in recent years the Church's swift growth has meant that General Authorities can no longer preside directly over each stake conference.

The Church has started using satellite technology to hold multistake conferences, which is possible because each stake center already features a satellite dish to receive transmissions of general Church meetings. The idea is that members in one area can attend the conference at their own stake center and watch a live satellite broadcast that members of other stakes are also viewing at their own stake centers, and these meetings can also include some local speakers and business. This way, General Authorities based in Salt Lake City, Utah, can deliver special messages to stakes without a huge travel burden.

duties, just as each ward bishop appoints two Melchizedek Priesthood holders to be his counselors. Stake presidents also choose 12 *councilors* — pronounced the same, but spelled differently — to serve on the *stake high council.* These 12 men travel to all the wards in the stake and carry out specific assignments in supervising various stake programs.

Finding Grandpa's grandpa: Stake family history centers

Most stake centers in the United States, and many abroad, house a family history center where anybody, Mormon or not, can research his or her genealogy. As we explain in Chapter 5, Mormons are avid researchers into family history, and each stake family history center is a branch library of the largest Family History Library in the world, located in Salt Lake City, Utah. Some ward buildings also house small branch libraries.

Mormons aren't the only ones who use these history centers — in fact, the majority of patrons are *not* LDS. They're often retired (who else has the time to engage in this marvelous but time-consuming hobby?) and are using the free resources to trace their family trees.

You usually don't need an appointment to use a stake family history center, but you should phone ahead to find out when the center is open. They're staffed by volunteers and are often open only during evenings and weekends. If you bring information about your ancestors, a consultant can help you figure out the next step. Some centers offer periodic classes on how to get started in doing family history research.

Stake 'n' shake: Stake activities

The Church encourages members to get together in fun, recreational ways, particularly for the benefit of the teens. Many of these opportunities are organized at the stake level, including sports, cultural arts, and campouts. Often, several stakes join forces for programs and activities, in which case you'll hear the terms *multistake* or *regional.*

Dodging and dunking: Stake sports

In the United States and elsewhere, basketball is so popular among Mormons that nearly every meetinghouse has basketball standards installed in the large, multipurpose room adjacent to the chapel, a gymlike room still known in old-fashioned terms as the *cultural hall.* (In addition, the Church uses this room for overflow seating, dinners and parties, and other activities, and members can arrange to hold wedding receptions there.)

Although stakes organize basketball leagues to provide opportunities for fellowship and exercise, the game is notorious for getting too competitive, with players occasionally losing control of their elbows or their tongues. Many stakes also run softball and volleyball leagues for both men and women.

Hams and cheese: Stake cultural arts

Mormons used to do lots of cultural-type stuff together, such as performing musicals and holding speech contests. One popular event was known as the *road show,* with each ward producing an original short program and performing it for other wards around the stake. Although these kinds of activities still crop up here and there, overall the Church's cultural activities have waned considerably in recent years.

Lately, however, the Church has started renewing its encouragement of stakes to organize cultural activities in the areas of music, dance, drama, speech, and the visual arts. In fact, the Church's Music and Cultural Arts Division accepts submissions of original works from members and selects material to make available to stakes throughout the Church.

For teens and older singles, many stakes hold dances that feature actual worldly pop music, as long as the lyrics aren't blatantly crude. Immodest clothing isn't allowed, and the tongue-in-cheek standard is that couples must dance far enough apart that you can stick a copy of the Book of Mormon between them.

Mosquitoes and no mascara: Stake Young Women camp

Each summer, teenage girls from the entire stake typically get together at an area campsite for a six-day camp experience. They sing songs (both spiritual and silly), cook their own food at least some of the time, enjoy games and activities, and end the week comparing their dozens of mosquito bites. During the week, leaders plan activities that will help young women learn self-reliance and gospel values.

The boys have a weeklong summer camp, too, but it's organized by the local LDS-sponsored Boy Scout troop, not the stake. However, many stakes hold an annual father-and-son overnighter.

Chapter 7

Sacred, Not Secret:
Inside Mormon Temples

. . . .

In This Chapter

▶ Knowing the difference between temples and meetinghouses

▶ Summarizing what goes on inside a temple

▶ Getting ready for temple service

▶ Being initiated into the temple

▶ Becoming a forever family

. . . .

*L*ike Charlie in the movie *Willy Wonka and the Chocolate Factory,* Mormon children grow up wondering just what goes on inside a certain mysterious building. Ideally at least monthly, their parents dress in Sunday best, retrieve small suitcases from the closet, give last-minute instructions to the baby sitter, and disappear into the local temple for several hours. Although Mormon children learn the general purposes of temples, for all they know Oompa Loompas serenade those who go inside. Many non-Mormon observers are equally mystified about what goes on inside temples.

To Mormons, temples symbolize God's entire plan of salvation and provide a safe, private place for performing the faith's most sacred ordinances (for more details about the plan of salvation, see Chapter 2). In this Internet age, the goings-on inside Mormon temples aren't secret to anyone who can use a Web search engine. However, Mormons still revere temple work as too sacred to discuss in detail outside the temple itself. This chapter unfolds the Mormon temple experience in as much detail as practicing Mormons can reasonably discuss without breaking vows of sanctity. As Mormons often say, "It's *sacred,* not *secret.*"

Distinguishing the Temple from the Meetinghouse

Although the LDS Church has built thousands of cookie-cutter meetinghouses globally, so far the Church has erected only about 130 temples worldwide, more than half of them within the past ten years. Many of these temples are magnificent multimillion-dollar whoppers (see Figure 7-1 for an example), but many of the newer temples are much smaller than earlier temples, although still ornate. Meetinghouses sport plain steeples, while temples are topped with a gold-leafed statue of the Angel Moroni, the Book-of-Mormon prophet who buried the golden plates and, as a resurrected angel, led Joseph Smith to them (for more on the Book of Mormon, check out Chapter 9).

Figure 7-1: The Washington, D.C. Temple is one of the LDS Church's largest.

Photo courtesy of Phil Smith

In short, the LDS Church puts more intricate detail and care into these temples than it does into meetinghouses because Mormons consider the temples to be the literal house of the Lord, a place of maximum beauty and reverence where they would feel comfortable hosting the resurrected Savior himself. Mormons use the meetinghouses, on the other hand, for day-to-day worship, instruction, and recreation.

The intricate detail and large size of Mormon temples aren't all that distinguish them from the more common meetinghouses, though. Here are a few of the major differences:

Meetinghouses	*Temples*
Open on the Sabbath (Sunday).	Closed on Sundays.
Visitors are welcome.	Only members who meet certain requirements are allowed to enter, and they must have an entry pass.
Businesslike, no-frills style of worship.	More elaborate rituals; too sacred to discuss in detail outside the temple.
Mormons teach each other gospel lessons, perform simple ordinances, and socialize.	Temple rituals follow scripts, with very little freestyle preaching, praying, or socializing.
Used for both worship and recreation, with casual dress okay on some occasions.	Used strictly for worship, and participants wear white temple clothes. Only whispering is allowed in most areas.
Children of all ages welcome.	Adults only; children allowed entry only in certain extraordinary circumstances.

Temple Ordinances — Why Mormons Go to the Temple

Simply put, temples are where adults — and, to a limited degree, children and teens — perform a variety of eternally vital *ordinances,* or hands-on ceremonies, both for themselves and for people who've died. These ordinances are collectively known as *temple work.*

Understanding the essential ordinances

To appreciate what goes on inside a temple, you first have to familiarize yourself with the basic Mormon ordinances considered necessary for full salvation and exaltation.

In Mormonism, full *salvation* means returning to live with God, and *exaltation* means becoming an eternal parent like God (for more on these concepts, see Chapter 2). In order to gain full salvation, a person needs to be baptized, be confirmed, and receive the gift of the Holy Ghost, which happens during confirmation. In order to qualify for exaltation, a person must receive four additional ordinances: priesthood ordination (if male), washing and anointing, the endowment, and celestial marriage.

Following is a more detailed overview of these six essential ordinances, in the order in which they occur. For living people, the first three ordinances occur in a meetinghouse, and the last three occur in a temple. On behalf of the deceased, Mormons perform all six ordinances inside a temple, which is why we include a summary of all six in this chapter.

- ✔ **Baptism:** Full immersion to wash away sins and commence Church membership (see Chapter 6).

- ✔ **Confirmation:** Laying on of hands to confirm Church membership and bestow the right to spiritual guidance by the Holy Ghost (see Chapters 3 and 6).

- ✔ **Priesthood ordination for all worthy males:** Laying on of hands to confer priesthood power and authority (see Chapter 4).

- ✔ **Washing and anointing:** A temple ordinance to provide spiritual cleansing and empowerment (see the section "Washing and anointing," later in this chapter).

- ✔ **Endowment:** A temple ordinance to teach the plan of salvation (see "Becoming endowed," later in this chapter).

- ✔ **Sealing:** A temple ordinance to bind spouses to each other and children to parents for eternity (flip ahead to "Sealing Families for Eternity," later in this chapter).

Why perform ordinances for the dead?

Before we discuss temple work for the dead, we must clarify one point: Mormons don't dig up decayed corpses and haul them into the temple Igor-style. Rather, genealogical researchers comb through records to extract names and essential data about people who've died all over the world — theoretically, anyone who's ever lived could appear on the list. Mormons who visit the temple perform ordinances as *proxies* (substitutes) on behalf of dead people, whose spirits choose whether or not to accept the ordinances. Why do Mormons do this? Well, allow us to try to explain.

Mormons believe that missionary spirits in the afterlife preach the gospel to all spirits who didn't receive a sufficient opportunity to hear the gospel while alive, thus allowing them to accept the gospel after death. (Head back over to Chapter 2 for more about Mormon beliefs regarding the afterlife.) Mormons feel that during many historical eras, most notably in the Old World during the 1,700 or so years between the New Testament apostles and Joseph Smith, no one held God's true *priesthood authority* (the power to act in God's name; see Chapter 4). In the Mormon view, without the true priesthood the true church doesn't exist, and, as a result, they believe that billions of people died without receiving a fair chance to accept or reject the gospel. Since the time the LDS Church began in 1830, billions more have died before Mormon missionaries could reach them.

LDS theology says that disembodied spirits can't perform the physical ordinances that are essential for full salvation and exaltation. Consequently, earthly beings must do it for them. And because Mormons don't know who will accept the gospel and who will reject it in the afterlife, they aim to perform the necessary gospel ordinances for every person who ever lived so that those spirits potentially may be saved and exalted. After a living person has done temple work for a spirit, that spirit has the option of saying, "Thanks a lot, but no thanks," or of accepting the gospel message. If the spirits accept, they still await the final judgment before receiving their eternal reward (for more details, see Chapter 2).

Beginning in childhood, Mormons are taught about the sacred obligation to perform temple ordinances for the dead, starting with their own ancestors. In fact, the Church teaches that temple work is urgent, because many departed spirits who've already accepted the gospel in the afterlife are anxiously waiting for somebody on earth to complete the ordinances on their behalf. In one commonly told story, a person performing baptisms for the dead reported seeing a queue of patiently waiting spirits. As the workers performed each spirit's baptism by proxy, that spirit disappeared from the line.

Yes, Mormons have undertaken a big job. Completing all the temple ordinances on behalf of one dead person requires several hours of combined labor, and Mormons have already completed the work for well over 100 million deceased people. In order to identify every human being who ever lived, Mormons spend considerable time and money on genealogical research (see Chapter 5 for a more detailed discussion of family history work). Having only just scratched the surface, the Church doesn't expect to complete this project until sometime during the 1,000-year Millennium that they believe will follow the Second Coming of Jesus Christ. (Scratching your noggin? Go to Chapter 3 to find out about the Millennium and the Second Coming.)

By providing the living with the opportunity to serve the dead in this manner, the temple helps draw together the entire family of God. Many have commented on the Christ-like nature of temple service: Just as mortals could never pay for their own sins and must rely on Jesus Christ, spirits can't perform their own ordinances and must rely on the disciples of Jesus Christ. In addition, the repeated visits to the temple help members better understand and remember the ordinances, particularly the lengthy, complex endowment.

A little temple history

Mormons believe that God always commands his people to build temples, from Old Testament times onward. Here's the lowdown on a few temples that are noteworthy because of their influence in the LDS Church:

🖛 The early Mormons built their first temple in Kirtland, Ohio, in 1836. Many spiritual manifestations and heavenly visitations occurred in this temple. Persecution by local settlers led to its abandonment just a few years after its completion, but it still stands today and is owned by the Community of Christ, a denomination started by some Mormons who didn't go west after the murder of the prophet Joseph Smith (for more on the Community of Christ, see Chapter 12).

🖛 The Mormons completed an even grander temple in Nauvoo, Illinois, in 1846. Most of the ordinances and ceremonies that Mormons perform in today's temples originated during this Nauvoo period. Destroyed by arson and tornado soon after local persecution drove the Mormons from Nauvoo, this temple was rebuilt in 2002.

🖛 In Utah, the Mormons completed three temples before finally finishing the flagship Salt Lake Temple in 1893, after 40 years of construction.

🖛 During the first half of the 20th century, temples began to expand outside Utah, first appearing in Hawaii, Arizona, Idaho, and Alberta, Canada.

🖛 The Church built its first temple outside the United States and Canada in Switzerland in 1955. By 1980, it had completed temples in New Zealand, England, Japan, and Brazil.

🖛 More than half of the world's temples have been built since 1995, and temples are now located in about 40 countries. By building a new generation of smaller temples, the Church can locate more temples closer to more people, which is a major development for Mormons living outside Utah.

Becoming Eligible for Temple Ordinances

Entering the temple for your own ordinances requires careful planning and preparation on both the spiritual and practical levels. You have to be 18 or older, and you must have been a baptized Church member for at least a year. In addition, you attend a special temple preparation class, buy or rent some special temple clothes, and allow local Church leaders to evaluate your personal worthiness.

However, before qualifying to perform their own temple ordinances, teenagers and converts who haven't yet reached their one-year baptismal anniversary can get their toes wet — figuratively and literally — by being baptized and receiving the gift of the Holy Ghost on behalf of dead people. Performing these two simple ordinances for the dead in the temple doesn't require as much preparation and provides a good warm-up for the full temple experience.

Getting a temple recommend

The Church is obligated to make sure that only sufficiently pure, worthy individuals (according to the standards set by Mormon prophets) enter the temple. The way the Church safeguards the temple's sanctity is by issuing a special card called a *temple recommend,* which a person must show at the front desk for entry into the temple.

To get a temple recommend for the first time, a member sits down in two private, confidential, one-on-one appointments with local church leaders and candidly answers pointed questions about personal righteousness. Initially, the *bishop* interviews the member, and within a few days the *stake president* interviews the member. (In Mormonism, a *ward,* like a parish, is a single congregation; a *stake* is like a diocese. A bishop oversees a ward, and a stake president oversees several adjacent congregations. See Chapter 6.)

If you're simply performing baptisms for the dead, only your bishop interviews you, and the questions are simpler than those in the bulleted list that follows. In this case, the recommend you receive is called a *limited-use recommend,* because it allows you access only to the temple baptistry area.

A temple-recommend interview usually takes about ten minutes, unless you want to discuss additional matters with the leader. The leader asks whether you obey Church standards in several areas, including the following (not necessarily listed in order of importance):

- ✔ Attendance of Church meetings
- ✔ Abstinence from coffee, tea, alcohol, tobacco, and harmful drugs
- ✔ Avoidance of any form of family-member abuse
- ✔ Avoidance of apostate beliefs and groups
- ✔ Belief in God, Jesus Christ, the Holy Ghost, and other points of Mormon doctrine
- ✔ Chastity outside of marriage and fidelity within marriage
- ✔ For divorced parents, payment of any court-ordered support
- ✔ Honesty
- ✔ Loyalty to general and local church leaders
- ✔ Payment of *tithe* (10 percent of all income)

Mormons renew their temple recommends every two years by going through the same two interviews, which in the case of renewals can be conducted by the bishop and stake president's counselors.

Qualifying for a temple recommend gives members a practical, specific goal for religious discipline. While ever mindful of not being perfect, members take pride in staying current as literal card-carrying Mormons. If any serious sins come to light in a temple-recommend interview, the leader helps the member work out a plan for repentance and may possibly withhold the recommend for a time or initiate disciplinary action, which we discuss in Chapter 16.

Performing baptisms for the dead

Remember, living Mormons don't receive their own baptism, confirmation, and priesthood ordination inside a temple — rather, temple-goers perform these ordinances only for the dead. However, living Mormons do receive their own washing and anointing, endowment, and celestial marriage inside the temple, in addition to performing these ordinances on behalf of the dead. We discuss baptism for the dead here because, like we said earlier, it's a good optional introduction to the temple for teens and new converts before they qualify to receive their own temple ordinances.

In the temple baptistry dressing room, baptismal proxies change into white baptismal clothing that they brought or the temple provided. After they're dressed, proxies gather at the temple baptismal font, which sits atop statues of 12 oxen that represent the 12 tribes of Israel (see Figure 7-2). After saying the brief baptismal prayer, a temple worker fully immerses the proxy on behalf of a dead person, repeating the process for several dead people in rapid succession.

Figure 7-2:
Temple baptismal fonts are patterned after Old Testament fonts.

In addition, baptismal proxies can receive the gift of the Holy Ghost on behalf of deceased people. To complete this ordinance, which is generally known as *confirmation,* priesthood holders (see Chapter 4) lay hands upon the proxy's head, confirm him or her as a member of the Church on behalf of a deceased person, and, most important, bestow the gift of the Holy Ghost.

Regarding baptism for the dead, much has been made of the Apostle Paul's comment in 1 Corinthians 15:29, which is the only biblical mention of the practice: "Else what shall they do which are baptized for the dead, if the dead rise not at all? Why are they then baptized for the dead?" (In other words, why would anyone bother getting baptized for the dead unless our souls continue living after death?) Mormons emphasize this surviving fragment as proof that the practice has ancient validation, while opponents argue that Paul's comment means that he did *not* endorse baptisms for the dead as a Christian practice.

A preparation checklist

When Mormons turn 18 or reach their one-year baptismal anniversary, they can qualify for full temple privileges and receive their own temple ordinances. Most young men "go through the temple," in the common phrasing, a few weeks before leaving on a mission to preach the gospel full time, usually at age 19. Young women don't typically serve missions until they're 21 years old, but they can go through the temple before then if they so desire and qualify. For those who don't serve missions, a common time to go through the temple is prior to getting married in the temple.

The following checklist outlines the tasks that members complete before they arrive at the temple to receive their own ordinances. These items are roughly in chronological order:

- ✔ **Temple preparation class:** Most local congregations provide a temple preparation class for those anticipating going through the temple for their own ordinances. This class typically meets once a week for several weeks.

- ✔ **Temple recommend:** You must have a *temple recommend,* a small card that you show to gain entry into the temple. We discuss the temple recommend in more detail in an earlier section, "Getting a temple recommend."

- ✔ **Temple clothing:** The Church encourages members to purchase their own set of white temple clothing, worn to symbolize purity and equality. However, some larger temples rent out temple clothing for a nominal fee. Temple clothing includes a basic white outfit and some ceremonial accessories.

    • You can purchase the components of the basic outfit at any store, including Church clothing distribution centers — as long as the items meet temple standards. Men wear a long-sleeved white shirt,

Getting a sneak peek during a temple open house

The only time people can enter a temple without a temple recommend is during the open house held upon completion of a temple's construction or remodeling. Before the prophet or an apostle consecrates a temple for sacred use by saying a prayer of dedication, the building is open to the public for a short period of time, usually between a few days and a month. During this time, visitors of all faiths (or no faith) can tour the temple and learn a bit more about the worship services that occur there.

If you want to attend a temple open house, here are some things you should know:

✔ **You generally need a ticket.** The tickets are free, but they can go very quickly — for example, more than 250,000 people toured the rebuilt Nauvoo, Illinois, Temple; and most tickets were claimed several months in advance. If you want to attend an open house, go online to www.lds.org/temples. You can find the open house information under "Events and Notices," and when you click on the name of a

particular temple, you get a listing of the dates and hours that the temple is open for tours. Of course, if you don't have a ticket and there's room for you to join a tour, you're not going to be turned away.

✔ **Dress appropriately.** Visitors typically wear Sunday dress to show respect for the sacred nature of the temple.

✔ **It's movie time.** Before the tour, you usually watch a short film about Latter-day Saint beliefs, and you may walk through an informational exhibit as you wait in line.

✔ **Cover those kickers.** On the tour, you'll probably need to cover your shoes to avoid tracking dirt into the new temple and to show respect. Visitors usually receive little white booties to put over their street shoes as they walk through the temple.

Feel free to ask questions of your tour guide. However, please understand that Latter-day Saints consider the temple ordinances sacred and won't discuss them in much detail.

white tie, white pants, white belt, and white socks and slippers. Women wear a plain white dress, white nylons, and white slippers.

- If you hold a temple recommend, you can purchase the special ceremonial accessories through one of the Church's clothing distribution centers, including via phone or the Internet.

✔ **Temple garment:** As part of the temple ordinances, a Mormon dons a special garment that becomes his or her underwear style for the rest of mortality (and no, we don't mean boxers or briefs — see the section "Receiving the preparatory ordinances," later in this chapter). The first time through the temple, a Mormon brings a pair of new garments to wear home afterward, but doesn't try them on beforehand. Garments are sold only to temple-recommend holders through Church clothing distribution centers, and local leaders can answer any questions about buying and wearing them.

✔ **Special appointment:** Prior to attending the temple for the first time, a member should call the temple to make a special appointment and receive some additional preparatory instructions. (Appointments aren't necessary for subsequent temple visits, except at some small temples with limited hours of operation.) Keep in mind that all temples are closed on Sundays, to encourage Sabbath meetinghouse attendance and home family worship. In addition, temples are closed on Monday evenings for family home evening, which we discuss in Chapter 17.

✔ **Escort:** Oftentimes, Mormons invite some friends and family members to accompany them on their first temple visit, including one individual of the same gender who's officially designated as the escort.

Finally! Receiving Your Own Temple Ordinances

Some Mormons compare receiving the temple ordinances to trying to catch the output of a fire hose in a teacup; you're faced with so much new information that it's hard to absorb much on your first time through. However, Church leaders encourage you to keep returning to perform the same ordinances on behalf of dead people so you can gradually digest the experience.

Receiving the preparatory ordinances

After checking your temple recommend at the front desk, where you leave behind any cameras or recorders, temple workers process your first-timer paperwork and then escort you to the dressing room. To maintain modesty, all patrons are assigned private changing booths.

When an adult receives his or her own temple ordinances, washing and anointing and the endowment take place during the same visit, and sealings often take place on another day. When people perform work for the dead, they can choose whether to do washings and anointings, the endowment, or sealings.

Washing and anointing

The temple ordinance process begins with ceremonial washing and anointing, which takes place in what's called the initiatory area, adjacent to the dressing room. Quite personal yet scrupulously modest, this ceremony involves some dabbing of water and olive oil on the body, accompanied by the pronouncing of blessings of purity, health, and eternal potential.

Donning the temple garment

The washing and anointing process concludes with putting on the white temple undergarment, which then becomes the member's underwear style for life. According to the official Church handbook of instructions, "The

Temple garment wash and wear instructions

One of the temple-recommend questions asks whether members properly wear and care for the garment. The Church gives some instructions and rules regarding garments, encouraging members to seek the guidance of the Holy Spirit in their personal habits and attitudes related to the garment. Following are several expectations for day-to-day life with garments:

✔ Mormons wear both pieces of the garment 24 hours a day, removing them only for such activities as showering, swimming, or sex, and putting them back on again as soon as reasonably possible. Some Latter-day Saints wear them during exercise, and some don't.

✔ Mormons don't wear clothing that reveals any portion of the garment, which rules out tank tops, shorts that rise above the knee, midriff-baring tops, and so on.

✔ Mormons aren't supposed to remove the garment top during yard work, roll up the garment legs to accommodate a favorite pair of shorts, or otherwise "cheat."

✔ Mormons avoid exposing the garment to non-Mormons. For some members, that means changing into regular underwear before visiting the doctor or the gym. Others, however, just try to be discreet.

✔ Mormons launder garments normally with other clothing. Some members try to avoid letting them touch the floor.

✔ Mormons are asked to keep garments in good repair. When a piece wears out, they destroy it before disposal.

garment provides a constant reminder of the covenants made in a temple. When properly worn, it provides protection against temptation and evil. Wearing the garment is also an outward expression of an inward commitment to follow the Savior."

In addition to spiritual protection, many members feel that the garment can provide miraculous physical protection. Hearing stories about someone suffering a catastrophic accident but not sustaining injuries on areas covered by the garment isn't uncommon. For these and other reasons, many members report feeling uneasy while their garments are off. However, plenty of people suffer bodily injury and death while wearing garments, so they don't provide infallible protection.

In earlier times, the garment was a one-piece affair that reached to the ankles and wrists. Today's most-worn garment style comes in two pieces, with the bottom reaching to the knee and the top covering the shoulder and scooping down almost to the bottom of the breastbone. Garments are available in a variety of comfortable, lightweight fabrics, but wearing them still limits one's clothing style choices, especially in hot weather. Often visible through clothing, the distinctive neckline shape is affectionately known as the "celestial smile" and provides a good way to recognize fellow Mormons at first sight.

Becoming endowed

Although most Mormon ordinances are short and simple, the endowment is a megaordinance that takes approximately two hours to complete. And that's relatively short — in the olden days, it took all day.

The first endowment you receive is for yourself. For every endowment you attend after that, a temple worker gives you the name of a deceased person as you leave the dressing room.

Clothed in white, you sit quietly in a chapel until summoned for the next endowment session. Then you walk to a theater-style ordinance room, carrying the packet that holds some clothing accessories you'll don during the session. (In the new generation of smaller temples that don't have room for a chapel, you go straight to the ordinance room.)

In a nutshell, the endowment dramatizes the entire plan of salvation, from the earth's creation to humankind's falling away from God and redemption through the Savior (for more about the plan of salvation, see Chapter 2). After an overview of the creation stages — for long-time temple attendees who are prone to dozing, this can be a tricky stretch — the endowment film portrays the story of Adam and Eve, who represent everyone in the human dilemma. Temple workers stop the film at various points so participants can receive instructions, perform rituals, and make covenants, the details of which they don't discuss outside the temple.

Both symbolically and literally, the temple teaches members how to successfully pass the earthly test and reenter God's presence, where Mormons believe humans can eventually become eternal parents like God. According to the prophet Brigham Young, the gestures and phrases learned during the endowment "are necessary for you, after you have departed this life, to enable you to walk back to the presence of the Father, passing the angels who stand as sentinels."

At the conclusion of the endowment, the projection screen rises, revealing a gauzy white curtain known as the *veil*. After passing through this veil, patrons enter the beautifully furnished *celestial room* — in Mormonism, the word *celestial* refers to the highest degree of heaven, where God the Father resides. This symbolic room provides comfortable chairs and couches for those who want to ponder and pray before returning to the dressing room.

Mormons take their temple covenants extremely seriously. During the endowment, they make several promises, such as to be pure and obedient, follow the Savior's gospel, stay chaste, and serve the cause of righteousness to the best of their ability. In return, they're assured of God's promises regarding their eternal potential.

Another brick in the wall: The Masonry connection

Masonry is an ancient fraternal order that its members believe existed when King Solomon built his temple, as recorded in the Old Testament. Anti-Mormons claim that early Mormons, many of whom were Masons, borrowed elements of the secret Masonic rituals for the Mormon endowment ceremony, including aspects of the temple clothing.

According to the *Encyclopedia of Latter-day Saint History,* "Latter-day Saints, including Joseph Smith, believed that the Masonic ceremony and the temple endowment had a common origin — ancient temple ceremonies — and this accounted for any similarities between the two rituals." Others point out that the meaning and symbolism of the rituals differ vastly, with any similarities largely cosmetic.

Sealing Families for Eternity

In the Mormon faith, the highest earthly ordinance is celestial marriage, also known as eternal marriage, temple marriage, or "getting sealed." This ordinance is necessary for exaltation, or becoming an eternal parent like God. Thanks to the sealing authority restored to Joseph Smith by the resurrected prophet Elijah and handed down since then from Mormon prophet to Mormon prophet, Mormons believe that marriages performed in the temple don't dissolve at death, but last forever.

In addition, Mormons believe that the sealing power eternally binds children to parents, linking each Mormon in a massive eternal family that could conceivably include each person's entire progeny and ancestry, all the way back to Adam and ultimately to God himself. Children who are physically born to a sealed couple are automatically sealed to them, which is known as being "born in the covenant." In all other cases, including adoption, the child is sealed to his or her parents during a special temple ceremony.

From the Mormon viewpoint, the Bible's most significant mention of the sealing power appears in Matthew 16:19, where the Savior says the following to Peter, the senior apostle: "And I will give unto thee the keys of the kingdom of heaven: and whatsoever thou shalt bind on earth shall be bound in heaven: and whatsoever thou shalt loose on earth shall be loosed in heaven." Mormons equate the word *bind* with *seal*. It's possible for sealings to be canceled or revoked — "loosed" — under certain circumstances, which we address in this chapter's later section "When the going gets tough: Sealing complexities."

We don't go into detail in this chapter about all the theological ideas behind eternal families, but you can find a complete discussion on the topic in Chapter 5. Here, we zone in on the ceremony.

Temple sealings for the living

Temple work for the dead includes performing sealings for all husbands, wives, and children who ever lived. In this section, however, we focus on two of Mormonism's most anticipated, celebrated events for the living: temple marriages and the sealing of children to parents.

Before a man and woman can get married in the temple, each must have received all the other essential ordinances. Couples who were married outside the temple can get sealed as early as a year after their civil marriage or a year after their convert baptism into Mormonism, and their children can be sealed to them at that time. Adopted children can be sealed after the adoption is final. In the United States and some other countries, temple sealings are recognized as legal marriages.

Kneeling on opposite sides of a cushiony altar and grasping hands, a couple is sealed together for eternity by one of the church's relatively few priesthood holders who hold the sealing power, given to him by the Church's prophet or an apostle. The brief ceremony is the same whether the couple is getting married for the first time or sealing their previous civil marriage. When children are being sealed, they gather around the altar to participate in a similar ceremony.

Eternal marriages and sealings of children to parents take place in special sealing rooms located near the endowment rooms. Sealings for living people differ from other temple ordinances in several ways:

- ✔ **The family can invite adult guests who hold temple recommends to enter the temple simply to witness the sealing.** These guests don't typically dress in white, but they do remove their shoes in a special waiting area.

- ✔ **Not only can children enter the temple to be sealed to their own parents, but they can also witness the sealing of a sibling.** These are the only occasions on which children under age 12 can enter the temple. Temple workers typically take care of the children in another room until they're needed.

- ✔ **Sealings for the living are generally preceded by a freestyle sermon.** The sealer, who is usually fairly advanced in years, typically offers some practical family advice combined with eternal perspective, oftentimes sprinkled with humor.

Only adults who hold a current temple recommend can attend a temple marriage, which sometimes causes heartache for couples with family members who aren't Mormon. Most temples provide an outer lobby where underage family members and those without a recommend can wait. If a couple decides to get married outside the temple in order to accommodate family pressures, they must wait a full year before getting sealed in the temple.

My Big Fat Mormon Wedding

Whether a couple is getting married for their first time in the temple or eternalizing their previous civil marriage, Mormons celebrate the occasion in the following ways:

✔ The bride can wear a wedding dress in the temple. However, several style limitations and requirements apply, in order to make the dress suitable for the temple. The dress can't be sleeveless or backless, for example.

✔ Right after the ceremony, the couple usually kisses over the altar.

✔ The couple doesn't exchange rings as part of the sealing ceremony. However, they can step away from the altar and informally slip rings onto each other's fingers. Some Mormon couples have a public ring-exchange ceremony later, often as part of the wedding reception.

✔ Most, if not all, sealing rooms are furnished with large mirrors facing each other from opposite walls. At some point, the sealer typically invites the couple to gaze together into these endlessly reflecting mirrors and witness their image perpetuated into infinity.

✔ Afterward, many families gather in the beautiful temple grounds for photos. Some arrange for a professional photographer to meet them there.

✔ If they so desire, families can hold a reception or open house in the local LDS meetinghouse's *cultural hall,* a gymlike room used for sports, parties, and overflow seating.

✔ Mormons follow most other local marriage customs, from bridal showers to honeymoons. Cleaned-up versions of bachelor parties aren't unheard of, either.

If, for some reason, a Mormon couple can't get married in the temple, such as in the case of a shotgun wedding, a Mormon bishop can perform a regular "until death do you part" wedding in an LDS meetinghouse, although this is considered far from ideal, of course. If the couple demonstrates complete worthiness for at least a year, they can get sealed later and have any children sealed to them.

When the going gets tough: Sealing complexities

Eternal sealings can bring up some complex family situations, and sometimes a person must exercise faith that Heavenly Father will eventually work out everything to everyone's satisfaction and fill in any gaps. The bottom line is that Mormonism abhors a sealing vacuum. It's always better for someone to be sealed than not to be sealed, even if the person to whom he or she is sealed doesn't seem ideal in the here and now.

Following are a few tricky situations about which the LDS Church offers some insight:

✔ **Death of a spouse:** The LDS Church stopped practicing earthly polygamy more than 100 years ago, but some hints of heavenly plural marriage remain (for more on 19th-century polygamy, see Chapter 13). If a widower who was sealed to his first wife marries a new wife who isn't already sealed to a husband, the widower can be eternally sealed to both wives. However, a widow who was sealed to her deceased husband generally marries a new earthly husband only for the remainder of mortality. If she has any children with the new husband, the children are automatically sealed by virtue of the original sealing.

✔ **Divorced couple:** If a Mormon couple divorces — which, of course, the Church discourages — their sealing remains intact unless and until the wife finds someone else to be sealed with, at which time she can apply to cancel her sealing with her ex-husband. What's important is that she's not left without a sealing ordinance in place; if she doesn't ever find a new spouse, presumably God will somehow resolve the situation later. On the other hand, the man can receive clearance to be sealed to a new wife even if the sealing is still intact with his ex-wife, another lingering echo of patriarchal plural marriage.

✔ **Divorced parents:** From the standpoint of sons and daughters, what happens if their parents' sealing is canceled? The official Church handbook of instructions simply states, "Children who are born in the covenant or sealed to their parents remain so even if the sealing of the parents is later canceled or revoked." Again, the important principle is that the children don't lose their place in God's eternal family, and Mormons trust that any ambiguities will be resolved in heaven. By the way, if no prior sealings have taken place, a child can be sealed to a legal custodial parent and stepparent as long as the other legal parent gives permission.

✔ **Divorced couple, both passed away:** Interestingly, if a deceased couple was divorced before death and never sealed, their children may arrange for the parents to be sealed by proxy in the temple (see the previous section "Why perform ordinances for the dead?") so that the children can then be sealed to them. According to the Church handbook of instructions, "These sealings often provide the only way for children of such couples to be sealed to parents." Even if the parents don't accept the ordinances in the afterlife, the children still reap the full benefits of being sealed into God's eternal family.

✔ **Parents not Mormon:** Adult converts to Mormonism can perform temple work for their own parents after the parents die, eternalizing their parents' marriage and then getting sealed to their parents. Even if the parents don't accept the ordinances, Mormons believe that the convert will receive the full sealing benefits.

✔ **Spouse who leaves the Church:** If someone gets excommunicated from the Church or officially resigns by requesting removal of his or her name from Church records, that person's sealings are revoked. However, the spouse and children of that person don't lose their sealing blessings if they remain faithful.

✔ **Spouse who doesn't join the Church:** What if two members of another faith (or no faith) get married, and only one of them later converts to Mormonism? Because the non-Mormon spouse won't qualify to be sealed, what happens to the Mormon spouse's eternal prospects? If the quandary is never resolved during the couple's lifetime, the sealing can be performed posthumously in the hopes that the non-Mormon spouse will finally convert in the afterlife. Otherwise, the Mormon spouse simply trusts in Heavenly Father to eventually work things out to everyone's wishes and best advantage.

✔ **Never married:** For those who don't have the opportunity to marry during their earthly lifetime, through no choice or fault of their own, Mormons believe they can still qualify to receive all eternal blessings. Many believe that those who die single and worthy will be provided with an eternal spouse at a future time.

Occasional complexities notwithstanding, sealings imbue earthly family relationships with greater meaning and purpose. When you know you're building something that can last forever, you put more effort into it and value it more. Without a doubt, temples are one of the key ways in which Mormonism strengthens families.

Chapter 8

In and around Church Headquarters

. . . .

In This Chapter

▶ Taking a quick tour of Church headquarters

▶ Understanding the General Authorities and General Conference

▶ Meeting material needs for Mormons and others

▶ Getting an eternally well-rounded education

. . . .

*I*n the heart of Salt Lake City, Utah, the LDS Church makes its headquarters on a sprawling campus of sturdy, staid buildings, many of them made of gray granite. From this headquarters, the prophet (the one man who serves as president and worldwide spiritual leader of the Church), the apostles, and other high-level leaders (collectively known as *General Authorities*), plus several thousand bureaucratic employees, run the affairs of Mormonism worldwide. In addition, some female leaders oversee the Church's programs for women, teenage girls, and children.

Twice a year, during an important worldwide event called *General Conference,* the spotlight focuses on Church headquarters and the General Authorities, with eight hours of general proceedings broadcast around the world via satellite and the Internet. In addition, members can get acquainted with General Authorities when these leaders travel to local areas to speak at large-scale regional gatherings and conduct Church business.

Although many Church headquarters functions are what you'd expect for a multinational religious corporation — finances, membership records, curriculum development, property management, public affairs, and so on — in this chapter, we look more closely at some unique programs administered from Church headquarters: the welfare and humanitarian efforts and the Church Educational System. (How does the Church pay for all this? Mainly through donated tithing funds. For more on that topic, see Chapter 16.)

A Tour of Church Headquarters

Visible from afar, two prominent landmarks show where the Church headquarters is located in downtown Salt Lake City. The 28-story, cream-colored Church Office Building is the city's tallest high-rise, and the gray, six-spire Salt Lake Temple sports a golden statue of the Angel Moroni (see Chapter 9 for an overview of who Moroni is). But an even more important building is the solid, banklike Church Administrative Building at 47 East South Temple Street, where the Church's most important leaders have their offices. Following is a quick overview of what Church headquarters includes, both on the beautifully landscaped downtown campus and at some significant sites elsewhere in the Salt Lake Valley:

- ✔ **Temple Square:** One of the most visited tourist destinations in the western United States, Temple Square is a walled city block dating back to 19th-century pioneer times. Although visitors can view the Salt Lake Temple only from the outside, the other buildings inside Temple Square are open to the public, including

    - Two visitor centers that provide displays and presentations about the Mormon faith

    - The synagogue-looking Assembly Hall, used for various meetings

    - The famous Salt Lake Tabernacle, with its distinctive domed roof and massive pipe organ

- ✔ **Church Office Building plaza:** Filling the block east of Temple Square, this plaza encompasses the following buildings:

    - **Church Administrative Building:** As the home base of the Church's prophet, twelve apostles, Presidency of the Seventy, and other General Authorities, this building isn't open to the public, unless you have an appointment (in which case, you may be trembling in your boots).

    - **Church Office Building:** Visitors can ride an elevator past all the bureaucratic departments to the top floor, which provides a panoramic view of the Salt Lake Valley.

    - **Joseph Smith Memorial Building:** Formerly Salt Lake City's grandest hotel, this elegant building was recently remodeled to house some Church offices, restaurants, tourist attractions, and entertainment facilities. Many Mormons hold wedding luncheons and receptions here.

    - **Lion and Beehive Houses:** Originally built by Brigham Young to house many of his wives and children, these restored homes are now used for historical tours and entertaining. (FYI, the cafeteria-style Lion House Pantry is the premier place to go for Mormon comfort food.)

- **Relief Society Building:** Here, the Church's female executives oversee its worldwide programs for women, young women, and children (for more information on these programs, see Chapter 6).

✔ **Conference Center:** Filling the entire block north of Temple Square, this gigantic auditorium is where General Conference occurs twice a year (see the section "A Two-Day Marathon: General Conference," later in this chapter).

✔ **Family History Library and Museum of Church History and Art:** Sitting adjacent to each other west of Temple Square, the library contains the world's most extensive collection of genealogical records (for more information, see Chapter 5), and the museum features exhibits related to the Mormon experience.

✔ **Other downtown buildings:** All around downtown Salt Lake City, the Church owns numerous office buildings, shopping centers, apartment buildings, and condominiums. Some of the office buildings house for-profit businesses operated by the Church, such as a book publisher and retailer, a newspaper, and TV and radio stations.

✔ **LDS Distribution Center:** Located several miles west of downtown Salt Lake City, this large facility prints and distributes the Church's books, manuals, magazines, and numerous other standard supplies, including over 4.6 million copies of the Book of Mormon annually. Smaller centers distribute the materials around the world, and individuals can buy them at retail-style outlets and online at www.ldscatalog.com.

✔ **Granite Mountain Record Vault:** Bored into solid rock in a canyon above the Salt Lake Valley, this unusual facility is designed to withstand a nuclear blast. Its main purpose is to store master copies of millions of microfilmed genealogical records (see Chapter 5). Because of the records' importance and the need to keep the site at a constant temperature, the vault isn't open to the public.

✔ **Welfare Square:** Located across the freeway west of downtown Salt Lake City, this facility is the central hub for the Church's welfare and humanitarian programs, which we discuss later in this chapter. You can easily spot Welfare Square — just look for its tall, white grain elevator.

Governing the Church: General Authorities

Mormons believe that Jesus Christ directly governs their church, making his will known through revelation to 15 men who together function as the earthly heads of the Church. The most senior apostle — by date of apostleship, not date of birth — is set apart as the prophet and president of the Church, and he selects two other apostles as his counselors to constitute the three-man *First Presidency.* The two counselors work closely with the president, and they're highly visible and respected leaders in the Church.

The remaining 12 leaders constitute the *Quorum of the Twelve Apostles.* Although the president is the only individual who holds all the Church's priesthood *keys* (meaning the authority to perform or delegate priesthood roles and ordinances) and the only one officially known as the prophet, the 15 men are all considered prophets, seers, and revelators who act as "special witnesses of the name of Christ in all the world" (Doctrine and Covenants 107:23; for more on the D&C, see Chapter 10). All 15 of these men generally govern together as an executive board, not taking any significant action without unanimity. Their average age is probably well over 70.

In addition, the Church calls men to serve as *seventies,* a New Testament term referring to the original number of such leaders (see Luke 10). Today's LDS Church has far more than just 70 seventies; organized into several quorums, they function under the apostles and are similar to vice-presidents in a corporation. (In fact, one prominent scholar refers to them as "ecclesiastical middle management.") Many seventies are middle aged rather than retirement aged, and although the president and apostles serve for life, seventies may eventually be given emeritus status or released.

Rounding out the Church's top government is the *Presiding Bishopric* (a bishopric is a three-man supervisory board, consisting of a bishop and two counselors). This bishopric leads the Aaronic Priesthood (described in Chapter 4) and oversees the faith's temporal concerns, such as building meetinghouses and collecting tithes. Together, the president, apostles, seventies, and Presiding Bishopric are known as General Authorities, because they preside over the whole Church. Often referred to informally as *GAs,* they're also known as the *Brethren,* with a capital B.

General Authorities receive no professional training specifically to lead the Church. Before being called as full-time GAs, most of these men establish successful careers in professions such as business, law, education, and medicine, which helps explain why the LDS Church feels so corporate in personality. Undoubtedly, all the General Authorities previously served the Church in many important, demanding volunteer leadership positions, which helped prepare them and bring them to the attention of Church headquarters. As General Authorities, they don't receive salaries, although the Church does provide a modest living allowance.

Following the prophet

Latter-day Saints believe that the man who leads them possesses prophetic powers every bit as real and potent as those of Adam, Noah, Moses, or any other biblical prophet. The prophet's job is to bring people to Christ in

Who's the current prophet?

At this writing, the prophet is 94-year-old Gordon B. Hinckley, who's built numerous temples worldwide, urged members to work harder at retaining new converts and reactivating those who've fallen away, and established a special worldwide fund for helping underprivileged members get better educations.

In addition, President Hinckley is known for cracking up congregations with self-deprecating asides, speaking openly with the national media, and building bridges to those of other faiths. His most-repeated warnings have included staying out of debt, shunning all forms of pornography, treating spouses and children more kindly, and keeping traditional families intact.

The apostle next in line to become Mormon prophet is Thomas S. Monson, who was called to the apostleship while only in his thirties and, at this writing, was serving as President Hinckley's first counselor. He's known for his warm, folksy anecdotes that dramatize how simple, heartfelt acts of service can change lives for the better.

preparation both for the Savior's eventual return to earth (which we discuss in Chapter 3) and for humankind's existence with him in eternity (which we discuss in Chapter 2).

According to Mormons, today's prophet received his prophetic authority through a chain of prophets leading back to founding prophet Joseph Smith, who received it at the hands of resurrected prophets from biblical times. The person chosen to receive this ultimate authority is the apostle with the most seniority in the quorum. The last man that Mormons believe carried the prophetic mantle before Joseph Smith was the New Testament apostle Peter, who led the early Christian church after Christ's resurrection, with James and John as his counselors (for more about Mormon views on priesthood succession, see Chapter 4).

Although Church leaders admit that no one is perfect except the Savior himself, members generally feel tremendous respect and affection for the prophet. Some members believe that Heavenly Father would never allow the prophet to lead the Church astray, so they can pretty much assume that everything the prophet says is the will of God. At the same time, however, they believe that God's will in one era isn't necessarily his will in another, because human conditions and needs change. Therefore, the living prophet's teachings outweigh those of deceased prophets.

What the prophet does

As leader of the Church, the prophet clarifies and interprets the Church's doctrines, policies, and organization; introduces new programs and initiatives; warns members and the world at large about sinful trends; and oversees numerous other aspects of Church administration. Each prophet's

Opinion versus revelation

Undoubtedly, prophets sometimes speak more from their own understanding and opinion than from direct revelation, but most Mormons give the prophet all possible benefit of the doubt and strive to obey his teachings. For example, during a recent sermon, President Hinckley expressed distaste for body piercing beyond one earring in each ear for women. On the spot, some listeners reached up and removed their extra earrings, and the comment triggered similar reactions throughout the Church. Although not on the level of a commandment, this kind of *counsel* — as such prophetic admonitions are commonly called — can fast become a new standard.

Does God himself disapprove of, say, body piercing? If an individual wants personal confirmation that what a prophet says is God's will, Church leaders urge him or her to pray about the matter and receive an answer from the Holy Ghost. Some Mormons feel that simply demonstrating *obedience* to the prophet's counsel is as important as the particulars of the counsel, if not more so. Others emphasize the role of individual agency and personal spiritual confirmation when questions arise. Most Mormons are somewhere in the middle of this spectrum, considering the prophet's counsel together with scripture and personal revelation when making any major decision (or even a relatively minor one, like body piercing).

personality makes a unique impact on the Church as he communicates the ideas and instructions that are most important to Christ's people at any particular time.

As God's spokesman to Church members around the world (and anyone else who will listen), the prophet unifies the whole Church. Often flying in a private jet loaned by a billionaire Mormon industrialist, President Hinckley has made a remarkable number of international visits. By some reports, members have even spotted him simultaneously in places as far apart as Madagascar and Poland (no, not really). During his journeys, the prophet dedicates new temples for sacred use, meets with local officials and dignitaries, speaks to large congregations, and conducts other Church business. When the prophet enters or exits a congregational gathering, everyone typically stands up, and the Latter-day Saints often serenade him with a hymn entitled "We Thank Thee O God for a Prophet."

For the prophet's teachings to become an official commandment, doctrine, or scripture of the Church — something that happens extremely rarely these days — the other 14 top apostolic leaders all need to agree to the elevated status, and the teachings go through an official process, often including presentation to the body of the Church for a sustaining vote during General Conference. (No, the Church isn't a democracy by any stretch of the imagination, but members get the opportunity to demonstrate their acceptance of official actions by raising their right hands when called upon to do so.) The best overview of the Church's *commandments* — as opposed to *counsel* — is the temple-recommend interview, which we explain and summarize in Chapter 7.

Hotline to heaven

How exactly does a modern prophet receive revelation from God? Does the Church Administration Building have a special satellite dish through which God beams down instructions? Um, no. Unlike the early days of Mormonism, there's nothing too dramatic about Mormon revelation anymore. By all appearances, the days when resurrected beings — including the Savior himself — regularly appeared to Mormon leaders are long gone, and today's leaders don't use exotic prophetic devices like Joseph Smith did, devices with names such as *seer stone* and *Urim and Thummim.* (If these kinds of things *are* still happening, leaders don't talk about them. In today's media-saturated culture, you can understand why they wouldn't.)

Judging by what the prophet and other General Authorities say in public, revelation comes to them in much the same way it comes to individuals: through strong, unmistakable impressions inside the mind and heart from God's messenger, the Holy Ghost (for more about the Holy Ghost, see Chapter 3). What's more, revelations seem to come in response to direct, prayerful appeal by leaders on a particular issue; God doesn't just randomly zap the prophet with lightning to make a point. Thus the difference between prophetic and personal revelation is in scope, not method of delivery. Individuals can receive revelation for themselves, their families, and their immediate assignments within the Church, and so can the prophet — but his responsibility includes the *whole* Church, if not the whole world.

Apostles and seventies and bishops — Oh my!

From the First Presidency, the Church hierarchy filters down to the apostles, and then to the Presiding Bishopric and the seventies, and then to the local leaders, whom we discuss in Chapter 6.

Apostles

With 12 apostles, most every member can find at least one or two with whom he or she especially relates — and one or two with whom he or she *doesn't.* Because all 12 apostles give sermons in General Conference every six months and travel widely around the Church, most members get to know their distinctive personalities and gospel outlooks pretty well. Their attributes run the gamut: Some are businesslike, some eloquent, some intellectual, some intensely spiritual, and some folksy.

The First Presidency appoints new apostles to replace those who pass away, presenting their names during General Conference to the whole Church for a sustaining vote, which is always unanimous in the affirmative. (In the days of 1970s women's lib, protesters used to shout out their opposition during General Conference, but that kind of public objection hasn't happened in decades.) Through the laying on of hands by the First Presidency and the other apostles, each new apostle receives the same *priesthood keys* (meaning authority to perform certain duties and ordinances) that the Savior gave to the apostles in the New Testament. These keys include the authority to preach the gospel worldwide and to perform eternal sealing ordinances, such as celestial marriage (for more on sealing ordinances, see Chapter 7).

Under the direction of the First Presidency, each apostle receives assignments to oversee what together amounts to all the administrative departments and geographical areas of the Church. Apostles negotiate with national governments to allow the Church to preach the gospel and establish congregations there. In addition, they supervise the Church's *stakes,* or local groups of 5 to 12 congregations, and direct the work of the seventies.

Seventies

At the beck and call of the apostles, the seventies work to spread the gospel around the world and help manage the Church. Some fulfill assignments at Church headquarters in Salt Lake City, and others move abroad to head up the Church's area offices in foreign lands. (Actually, just recently the Church started a new practice of sending an *apostle* or two at a time to fulfill a long-term assignment in a place that needs special support, such as Chile, the Philippines, and central Europe.)

Seventies are organized into several different quorums, and some receive life-long assignments while others serve for a period of five years. Another layer or two of middle management lies between seventies and local *stake presidents,* who keep an eye on clusters of adjacent congregations, but the Church reorganizes those layers fairly often, so it's hard to keep track of exactly what the org chart looks like.

Presiding Bishopric

The three men in the Presiding Bishopric govern the Church's temporal affairs, or things related more to the physical than the spiritual, such as building meetinghouses. In addition, they preside over the Aaronic Priesthood, also known as the preparatory priesthood (see Chapter 4).

For most members, the term *bishop* brings to mind their local congregational leader, not a member of the Church's Presiding Bishopric. Although nearly all experienced members can name each of the 12 apostles, most probably can't name all three men who serve in the Presiding Bishopric, even though these Brethren usually speak at General Conference, too.

Female auxiliary leaders

Nine women hold leadership positions at Church headquarters under the supervision of the General Authorities. Like the General Authorities, they oversee their areas of assignment on a worldwide scale, speak in General Conference and at other Church-wide or regional meetings, and travel around the world. A presidency of three women — a president and two counselors — leads each of the following three Church auxiliaries:

🗸 **Relief Society:** The Church's worldwide organization for women

🗸 **Young Women:** The program for girls ages 12 to 17

🗸 **Primary:** The program for all children ages 3 to 11

In addition, each auxiliary also has a general board with a flexible number of members. For more information about these auxiliaries, see Chapter 6.

A Two-Day Marathon: General Conference

Twice a year, Mormons get up close and personal with their beloved leaders during General Conference (see Figure 8-1), which occurs on the first weekends of April and October. Rather, most get as up close and personal as their local meetinghouse TV set, because the meetings are broadcast live via satellite to Latter-day Saints all over the world. They're also available over the Internet through live audio and video links. In the past few years, increasing numbers of U.S. Mormons have even been able to watch conference at home in their pajamas, because the BYU-TV channel on the DISH Network carries it. Many Mormons hail the new technology as a latter-day blessing, especially because sitting through eight hours of conference can be a real challenge when children are part of the equation.

Figure 8-1:
A scene from one of the Church's recent General Conference sessions.

Photo by Danny Chan La/The Salt Lake Tribune

Conference is occasionally exciting when Church leaders make key announcements that come as a surprise to members. In 1999, for example, President Hinckley electrified his global audience by announcing the planned reconstruction of the Nauvoo, Illinois, Temple, which had been destroyed soon after the Prophet Joseph Smith's 1844 martyrdom. (For more on the emotional significance of Nauvoo and its temple for Mormons, see Chapter 11.) To outsiders, however, nothing much seems to happen at these meetings. This event isn't like the General Conference of the United Methodist Church, for example, during which delegates vote on controversial issues and their disagreements often make the national news. LDS General Conference is staid by contrast, and leaders don't make key decisions at this time, although they sometimes announce decisions there. General Conference is a time to reaffirm the core teachings of the Church, emphasize the importance of faith and family, and marvel anew at the gospel's reach into many cultures and nations.

General Conference has followed basically the same pattern since the 19th century. On Saturday and Sunday, members participate in two two-hour meetings, during which they hear from the prophet and other leaders and listen to inspirational music from the Mormon Tabernacle Choir and other choirs. A two-hour break between meetings ensures that members have time to eat lunch and rest a bit before continuing. On Saturday evening, the male priesthood holders of the Church participate in an additional two-hour session.

The world's largest religious auditorium

Until the year 2000, Mormons almost always held their General Conferences in the Salt Lake Tabernacle inside Temple Square. Built in the 1860s, the oval Tabernacle has excellent acoustics (an important consideration in the days before microphones) and seating for several thousand people. As the Church grew, however, the Tabernacle proved inadequate for hosting General Conference and other large events, so in the late 1990s the Church built the LDS Conference Center, which is more than 40 times the tabernacle's size. This vast and stately granite building — which some Mormons have affectionately dubbed "the Supernacle" — seats around 21,000 people, more than any other religious auditorium in the world, and covers most of its 10-acre site. Amazingly, the cavernous interior has no visible pillars, so there's no such thing as a bad seat.

One of the most beloved Mormon stories about the new building centers around the pulpit, which was constructed from an old walnut tree that President Hinckley, the LDS prophet at the time of this writing, planted in his backyard in the 1960s. He seemed touched and pleased as he told Church members during General Conference that he was speaking to them from the wood of the same tree his children had played under.

The Conference Center is used for concerts, special events (including President Hinckley's 90th birthday bash in June 2000), and other large meetings and activities. The building also features a state-of-the-art 850-seat theater for plays, shows, and other theatrical events. The entire building is topped by a 4-acre meadow — yes, a meadow — with gardens of wildflowers and native grasses.

Conference talks — Mormons don't call them sermons — are relatively brief but are almost never spontaneous. In this age of simultaneous broadcast in many different languages and cultures, General Authorities submit their talks in advance so they can be translated for the live broadcast. Copies of the talks appear in the May and November issues of the *Ensign,* the official magazine of the LDS Church, and are archived on the Church's Web site at www. lds.org.

For kids, General Conference can be — yes, we're going to say it — a little boring. In fact, an entire cottage industry has arisen to help parents keep children busy during the marathon with games such as "General Conference Bingo" and "Apostle Flashcards." These flashcards may be the *only* flashy aspect of General Conference. However, most adult members find that each conference produces at least one gem of a talk that seems to speak directly to them. "That was just what I needed," one exhausted young mother said after hearing a particularly reassuring conference talk on the eternal value of family relationships. So although this conference is long, Mormons don't see it as an ordeal but as an opportunity for spiritual insight and growth.

The LDS Welfare Program and Humanitarian Relief

Joseph Smith taught that each Christian has a responsibility "to feed the hungry, to clothe the naked, to provide for the widow, to dry up the tear of the orphan, [and] to comfort the afflicted, whether in this church, or in any other, or in no church at all, wherever he finds them." Mormons take this recommendation very seriously. They believe that because they're followers of Jesus Christ, they're supposed to try to be like him, which includes ministering to the poor.

The Church has two basic programs for combating poverty, ignorance, and disease:

- ✔ The *welfare program* helps Church members be self-sufficient and assists them if they're unemployed or facing financial hardship.
- ✔ The *LDS Humanitarian Relief program* sends aid all over the world, primarily to people who aren't members of the Church.

Taking care of their own: The world's largest private welfare program

In 1936, alarmed by the global depression that had left millions in poverty, LDS President Heber J. Grant and his counselors started a coordinated

Church welfare plan that gave food and clothing to Church members who were willing to volunteer their time and work in exchange for the assistance. This plan was far reaching in its intent to help fellow Mormons and get them off "the dole" — government programs that Church leaders believed encouraged a cycle of idleness and poverty. In fact, the LDS welfare program was actually one of the first workfare programs in the United States, because members had to contribute their time and talents if they wanted to receive material help.

The funding for the welfare program comes from Mormons all around the world. Generally on the first Sunday of every month, Mormons everywhere fast for two meals and donate the money they would've spent on their own food to the program — plus more, if possible — in order to share their material blessings with others. (For more on Fast Sunday and other Mormon sacrifices, see Chapter 16.)

As of 2004, the LDS welfare program was the largest private welfare system in the world, with

- 113 *storehouses,* or shops with free groceries for those whom *bishops* (local congregation leaders) clear to shop there.

- 105 *canneries,* where member volunteers process and can fresh food for the welfare program or their own home storage (for more on Mormon teachings regarding food storage and other principles of self-reliance, see Chapter 18).

- 222 employment resource centers, to help members find and train for new jobs.

- 46 Deseret Industries thrift stores scattered throughout the western United States, where people can buy cheap clothing and household items. These stores are similar in function to Goodwill or Salvation Army stores. They're open to anyone — Mormon or not — and you can pick up some great bargains there.

- More than 3,000 volunteer missionaries who serve in the program as language teachers, agricultural specialists, medical doctors and nurses, and employment assistants. Humanitarian missionaries are often older couples and professionals rather than the usual college-aged single men and women. (For more on various kinds of Mormon missionary activities, see Chapter 14.)

Today, the welfare program has three basic goals:

- **To serve the poor and the needy:** Although some Latter-day Saints may imagine that "the poor and needy" are people very different from themselves, the fact is that many members fall on hard times at some point in their lives. A parent may experience a job layoff, or an illness or injury may prevent a family from making ends meet. After the family's resources have been exhausted and the extended family has assisted all they can, the Church steps in to help get a family back on its feet. Most Mormons see government help as a last resort and would rather receive Church assistance than government welfare.

At Welfare Square in Salt Lake City, Church members in financial difficulty can shop in a special grocery store that offers the best food money can't buy — it's fresh, high quality, and free. They can also obtain free clothing, temporary shelter, transportation, and counseling. In other parts of the United States and the world, members in need consult with their bishop and Relief Society president (see Chapter 6), who then determine the best way to get clothes, food, and other items for a needy family.

✔ **To encourage self-reliance and help people learn to help themselves:** The LDS welfare program operates on the principle that people who are trying to help themselves, instead of just receiving handouts from others, will make the most lasting changes in their lives. As the old adage goes, you can catch fish and feed people for a day, or you can teach them how to catch their own fish, thereby feeding them for a lifetime. Many of the people who work at the Church's canneries, thrift stores, farms, and other welfare facilities are the very same people who are getting free food and clothing from the Church. (Others are members of the Church who volunteer their time to help others; see the next bullet.)

Also, the welfare program offers extensive job counseling and employment services, all designed to help people find and keep jobs that suit them. Jobseekers can take computer classes or study a language (in North America, usually English) with a tutor.

✔ **To instill the value of service:** The welfare program not only meets the physical needs of poorer Church members, but it also meets a spiritual need of *all* Church members: to be of service. The Book of Mormon says, "When ye are in the service of your fellow beings ye are only in the service of your God" (Mosiah 2:17). In other words, when Mormons serve other people — whether those people are Mormon or not — they feel blessed because they're also serving God.

The LDS Church owns many welfare farms where Mormons sometimes help out in the fields, harvesting the grains and vegetables that will be canned and used for the welfare program. (Such service is a rite of passage for Mormon teens, who may have to be recruited grudgingly into the task to help them earn a Young Womanhood Recognition Award or Eagle Scout badge.) Even though laboring on the farms is hard work, most Mormons are grateful that they can help out and may wonder as they're husking corn or picking apples just who will be on the receiving end of the harvest.

Relief with a personal touch

One of the most unusual aspects of Mormon humanitarian relief may be termed the "personal touch." Alongside the scratchy, utilitarian wool blankets that keep out the rain and the chill, Mormons also send homemade quilts. At Relief Society events, gatherings, and women's conferences, Mormon hands keep busy tying quilts and making children's blankets.

A 90-year-old woman who's legally blind spends her time sewing children's blankets because she heard that newborns in some nations were being sent home from the hospital wrapped in newspaper or banana leaves. Before she sends them to the Church's humanitarian center to be exported to children all over the world, she hugs each cheery blanket close to her chest and says a prayer for the child who will receive it.

Taking care of others: LDS humanitarian relief

Although the welfare program exists to get rid of want within the Church and to prepare Mormons to be as self-reliant as possible, the Church also runs a marvelous program of sending humanitarian relief all over the world. In addition to giving financial assistance to established relief organizations such as the Red Cross, the LDS Church runs its own extensive international program.

The need for aid might arise in case of

- ✔ **Famine:** In 2003, for example, the Church sent more than 600 tons of *atmit,* a nourishing porridge, to help malnourished and starving people in Ethiopia. In fact, a crisis in Ethiopia is what jumpstarted the LDS Humanitarian Relief Fund in the first place. In 1985, Church members held a special 24-hour fast in addition to their regular monthly fast on Fast Sunday (see Chapter 16 for more on fasting). Church members raised $6 million in one day to aid famine-stricken people in Ethiopia, and the Humanitarian Relief program was born.

- ✔ **Earthquakes and other natural disasters:** In 2001, the Church helped victims of earthquakes in El Salvador and Peru and also sent more than 600,000 pounds of food and supplies to India after it suffered a devastating earthquake in January of that year. When Hurricane Andrew devastated Florida in the 1990s, swarms of Mormon volunteers from several states helped with the relief and cleanup effort.

- ✔ **Displacement:** Although the Church doesn't take sides in wars or political conflicts, it helps political refugees and other victims of conflict. In recent years, sadly, there's been a great need for this assistance, and the Church has helped refugees in Kosovo, Iraq, Liberia, and other parts of Africa.

In the last two decades, the Church has offered an impressive amount of aid internationally. See Table 8-1.

Table 8-1	LDS Humanitarian Assistance, 1985–2003
Number of major disaster relief efforts	155
Nations receiving aid	154
Cash donations	$111.7 million
Food distributed	45,247 tons
Medical equipment distributed	5,943 tons
Clothing distributed	57,227 tons
Educational supplies distributed	5,011 tons
Value of donations and material assistance	$530.9 million

Survival of the Smartest: Mormons and Education

Both secular and religious education are vital to Mormons — in fact, they believe that separating the two is unnatural, and Latter-day Saints avidly pursue all legitimate branches of knowledge. Mormon scripture makes frequent reference to learning and intelligence, and Mormon scripture says, "Whatever principle of intelligence we attain unto in this life, it will rise with us in the resurrection. And if a person gains more knowledge and intelligence in this life through his diligence and obedience than another, he will have so much the advantage in the world to come" (Doctrine and Covenants 130:18–19). In other words, you *can* take it with you, as long as you stow it away inside your brain before you die.

When it comes to education versus religion, Mormons buck the trend. American sociologists say that, in most cases, more education results in less religiosity. However, the more education a Mormon receives, the more devoted his or her religious observance becomes, on average. Perhaps this tendency is because the Church provides so many opportunities for combining secular and spiritual education, reflecting the perspective expressed in a Book of Mormon passage: "To be learned is good if they hearken unto the counsels of God" (2 Nephi 9:29).

The Perpetual Education Fund

Because Mormons value education so much, the Church helps its impoverished members in underprivileged countries pay for college or vocational tuition so they can get better jobs. Funded by donations from Mormons all over the world, this program loans money to LDS students who qualify based on need, and they pay it back after they get jobs, replenishing the fund for future students.

Called the *Perpetual Education Fund,* this program is modeled on the Church's 19th-century emigration program that helped needy pioneers pay for their trip to Utah, back when all Mormons gathered there (see Chapter 12). In 2004, the Church reported that the Perpetual Education Fund had helped more than 10,000 students in 23 countries since its start in 2001, with loan recipients typically tripling or quadrupling their earning potential.

In this section, we look at the Church's ambitious worldwide program for providing every Latter-day Saint high school and college student with religious instruction to complement his or her worldly studies. In addition, we take a gander at Brigham Young University, which in many ways functions as an outgrowth of Church headquarters. Together, these programs and schools fall under the umbrella of the *Church Educational System,* or CES for short. (The Church also runs a business college in Salt Lake City and high schools in several Pacific Islands, but we won't delve into those.)

A daily dose of the gospel

For Mormon students, a spoonful of spirituality helps the secularism go down. Designed to add an eternal Mormon perspective to mainstream education, the religious instruction program for high-school students is called *seminary;* for college students, it's *institute.* Both programs are open to members of other faiths.

Seminary: Instead of sleep

The idea that teenagers love to sleep is a universally acknowledged truth. However, if you were a Mormon high-school student growing up outside the heavily LDS areas of the U.S. Intermountain West, you likely wouldn't get much sleep during the week. Why? Because every school morning, you'd arise at an ungodly hour to attend seminary before school — well, perhaps that would make it a *godly* hour. No, you wouldn't be in special training to become a priest or minister — every Mormon teen is expected to take seminary, which is available in more than 100 countries.

Some would say that the kids living in heavily Mormon areas are spoiled, because the Church builds seminary buildings near most public high schools, and the kids can register to attend seminary like any other class during the day. This idea of mixing church and state has caused some court cases, which succeeded in preventing the awarding of high-school credit for such religious classes.

Each of the four years of seminary (which correspond with U.S. grades 9 through 12) covers one of the main books of Mormon scripture: the Old Testament, the New Testament, the Book of Mormon, and the Doctrine and Covenants, or D&C (for more on Mormon scriptures, see Chapters 9 and 10). In places where not enough Mormons live close enough together to warrant early-morning classes, the Church provides an individual home-study program.

Institute: Giving the gospel the old college try

The full name of the Church's worldwide college-level education program is *institutes of religion,* but most people just call it *institute*. The instructors often hold advanced degrees, and they generally address the subject matter with academic rigor. Most institutes offer a variety of classes covering scriptures, history, and doctrine, as well as topics such as marriage and missionary preparation. All told, the institute program serves Latter-day Saint students attending about 2,000 postsecondary schools around the world.

The Church has constructed institute buildings near many colleges and universities in the United States. In other places, classes are held in regular meetinghouses or rented facilities, often on campus — however, these classes usually happen in the evening, rather than early in the morning. For many Mormon college students, institute becomes not only a place for religious education but also a social and recreational hub. Many members agree that the institute manuals are the best educational books that the Church publishes; these manuals are available at www.ldscatalog.com.

Stone-cold sober: Brigham Young University

When the BYU football team won the national championship in 1984, many people around the country asked, "BY-*who?*" However, BYU's Provo, Utah, campus is the largest privately owned educational institution in the United States, with a bigger enrollment — nearly 30,000 — than many public universities. (The university also has smaller campuses in Idaho and Hawaii.) While BYU football doesn't crack the national top-25 rankings every year, the school does consistently rank atop national college surveys in such categories as "Most Religious" and "Most Stone-Cold Sober."

Not so academically free

BYU's mission is to combine the highest-quality secular teaching with religious education to produce eternally well-rounded graduates. Although most of the secular classes are like those at any other university, occasionally professors bring prayer or spiritual perspective into the classroom. Religion classes are part of the general education requirements for all students, but that stipulation hasn't stopped the school from earning a high academic reputation. In keeping with Mormonism's personality as a corporate-style religion, the university is best known for its business-related programs.

To maintain control over the university, in recent years the Church has increased its oversight of BYU and clamped down on perceived troublemakers. The Church now appoints the university president from among its own General Authorities. LDS professors must hold a current *temple recommend* (explained in Chapter 7), and the handful of non-Mormon faculty must abide by similarly high moral standards. From time to time, BYU declines tenure to faculty members not because of inadequate scholarship but because their expressions aren't in harmony with official Church teachings or standards, particularly in the areas of history, anthropology, and literature. As a result, professional agencies have criticized BYU for its lack of academic freedom.

Cracking the code

BYU's strictly enforced student honor code gives the school a wholesome 1950s aura, compared to most college campuses. Of course, BYU doesn't tolerate premarital sex, smoking, alcohol, coffee, illegal drugs, homosexuality, and pornography. Although you won't get kicked out if you drink a Coke or see an R-rated movie, you can't buy these items on campus — well, unless you count caffeine-free Coke. Dorms have curfews and rules limiting gender interaction, and even if undergraduates live off campus, it must be in BYU-approved housing. Men can't grow beards unless they have a medical waiver (such as for a skin condition), and their hair can't cover their ears or touch their collar. Women can't wear sleeveless or backless clothes or bare their midriffs. For both sexes, shorts must extend to the knees, and extreme or grubby styles aren't allowed.

Non-Mormon students are welcome to attend the university if they abide by the same standards, and a few hundred actually do. One reason is that BYU charges relatively low tuition for its level of quality; although it's a private school, its rates are lower than many public universities. (Non-Mormon students pay half again as much tuition as Mormon students, whose families presumably help support the school by paying tithing, but it's still a great deal by national standards.)

As the Church has grown, getting admitted to BYU's main Provo campus has become tougher because of stiff competition from top Mormon students the world over. However, other options are becoming available for a wholesome Mormon-style college education, and we don't just mean BYU's other campuses. In Buena Vista, Virginia, a group of Mormons has acquired a small college originally founded in the 19th century and renamed it Southern Virginia University. Although this school has no official LDS Church ties, the leaders run it as a sort of "BYU East," with LDS religion classes as part of the core curriculum and a similarly strict honor code. The school is still small, but enrollment is steadily climbing.

Part III
Holy Books and Sacred History

The 5th Wave   By Rich Tennant

THE 4 MAJOR GROUPS MENTIONED IN THE BOOK OF MORMON: THE Nephites, Lamanites, Jaredites, and Mulekites. 4 GROUPS NOT MENTIONED:

The Impolites

Pushed and shoved their way across the New World.

The Parasites

Hitched rides with their in-laws to the New World.

The Appetites

Ran out of food before arriving to the New World.

The Suburbanites

Brought outdoor cooking and lawn games to the New World.

©RICHTENNANT

In this part . . .

We show you a thumbnail sketch of the plot and teachings of the Book of Mormon and give you the rundown on what Mormons believe about the Bible. You also get a taste of the other major books that Mormons regard as scripture: the Doctrine and Covenants and the Pearl of Great Price. Then we go on a whirlwind tour of LDS Church history, from the early days in Ohio, Missouri, and Illinois to the great pioneer trek that led the Mormons to Utah. We also lift the veil on the history of polygamy, which Latter-day Saints no longer practice, and highlight Mormon trends in the 20th century.

Chapter 9

The Bible and the Book of Mormon

· ·

In This Chapter

▶ Knowing what Mormons believe about the Bible

▶ Understanding the Joseph Smith Translation

▶ Getting to know the plot and themes of the Book of Mormon

▶ Bringing forth the Book of Mormon in the 1820s

▶ Seeing how the Book of Mormon impacts life today

· ·

*V*isit any Primary class on Sundays (if you don't know what Primary is, flip back to Chapter 6), and you'll hear song after song about the Bible and the Book of Mormon, including many that teach kids basic values and stories from both books. Mormons believe that both the Bible and the Book of Mormon are the word of God — see the eighth Article of Faith on this book's Cheat Sheet — and that people need to study both books frequently and prayerfully. Mormons also hold up two other books, the Doctrine and Covenants and the Pearl of Great Price, as scripture; we discuss them in the next chapter. Together, these four books of scripture are known as Mormonism's *standard works*.

Like the Bible, the Book of Mormon is a hodgepodge of sacred texts written over the course of many centuries by many different people. Like the Bible, it traces God's dealings with particular groups of people — especially the Nephites — and their trials and triumphs in a promised land. Unlike the Bible, which was translated by hundreds of people (and continues being translated in new versions today), the Book of Mormon had only one modern-day translator, Joseph Smith.

However, when Mormons say *translate* in connection with Joseph Smith, they generally don't mean using human linguistic skills to turn a text originally written in another language into English. Rather, Joseph translated by receiving holy text from God via revelatory devices such as a seer stone or the Urim and Thummim, a prophetic instrument mentioned several times in the Bible. (We discuss this idea more in the section "Seer stones and scribes: Translating the golden plates.")

The Bible: True, with a Few Tweaks

Mormons see their church as the restoration of the religion whose evolution is chronicled in the Old and New Testaments. So, of course the Bible is extremely important to Mormons, and they put a high emphasis on studying it and quoting from it. According to Mormonism's eighth Article of Faith, "We believe the Bible to be the word of God as far as it is translated correctly" (for more on the Articles of Faith, see Chapter 10). However, the ninth Article of Faith states that Mormons believe in continuing revelation — in other words, scripture is open to addition. The other three standard books of scripture work together with the Bible to establish Mormon belief and practice.

Thus saith the King James Version

Mormons recognize the *King James Version* (KJV) as their official Bible. They publish their own edition of the KJV, which stays true to the original text and is also jampacked with LDS-specific supplements and reader aids. For a sampling of Bible teachings that are significant to Mormons, see Table 9-1.

Table 9-1	Significant Bible Teachings for Mormons
Doctrinal Point	*Biblical Support*
Human spirits lived with God before earthly birth (for the modern Mormon outlook on this topic, see Chapter 2).	Job 38:4–7, Proverbs 8:22–31, Jeremiah 1:5, John 9:1–3, Acts 17:28, Ephesians 1:4–5, 2 Timothy 1:9, Titus 1:1–2, Hebrews 12:9, Jude 1:6, and Revelation 12:7–9
God speaks to humans through prophets (see Chapters 4 and 6).	Amos 3:7, Ephesians 2:20, and Ephesians 4:11
God enters into two-way promises with worthy individuals, who are collectively known as his *covenant people* (see Chapters 5 and 7).	Genesis, Exodus, Deuteronomy, and Hebrews (especially 8–10)
God gives his people standards of conduct, including a health code (see Chapter 16).	Leviticus
God leads his chosen people to a Promised Land (see Chapters 11–13).	Exodus
God assigns people to tribes in the house of Israel, either through blood or adoption (see Chapter 5).	Genesis, Matthew 3:9, Luke 3:8, Roman 8:15–17, Galatians 4:5–7, and Ephesians 1:5

Doctrinal Point	Biblical Support
God will prepare the earth for the Savior's Second Coming (see Chapter 3); members must pay a tithe (see Chapter 16); people will seek out their ancestors (see Chapters 5 and 7).	Malachi 3 and 4
The basic principles of Christ's gospel include faith, repentance, baptism, and receiving the gift of the Holy Ghost (see Chapter 6).	Isaiah 1:18, Matthew 3:13–17, John 14:26, Acts 19:1–6, Romans 6:4, 2 Corinthians 7:9–10, and Hebrews 11
Christ's church is organized and administered through certain priesthood offices, such as prophet, apostle, seventy, elder, bishop, and others (see Chapters 4 and 8).	Luke 6:13 and 10:1, Acts 14:23, Ephesians 2:20 and 4:11, and Philippians 1:1
God's priesthood must be transmitted through ordination by one possessing authority from God (see Chapter 4).	Hebrews 5:4 (see also Exodus 28:1 and 40:13–15, Matthew 10, Acts 1:21–26)
God's people should perform ordinances, such as baptism, on behalf of those who died without receiving the ordinances (see Chapter 7).	1 Corinthians 15:29
The Church possesses God's priesthood authority to seal families together for eternity (see Chapters 5 and 7).	Matthew 16:19
After Christ's death, his gospel was absent from the earth for a long time (see Chapter 4).	Amos 8:11–12, Matthew 24:9–12, John 16:1–3, 2 Thessalonians 2:3–4, and 2 Peter 2:1

Why do Mormons stick with the old-fashioned King James Version, even though so many more-accessible Bible versions are available? The main reason is that the KJV is the Bible version that founding prophet Joseph Smith used, as did most people in his time. Many of Joseph's revelations and translations appearing in the other standard works dovetail with KJV passages and style. All the Mormon prophets since Joseph Smith have used the KJV, and apparently no modern versions have impressed Mormon authorities enough to switch.

Not enough by itself

Although Mormons are traditional in sticking with the KJV, they're radical in accepting additional scriptures beyond the Bible. Complaining about this element of Mormonism, many mainstream Christians quote the following passage from Revelation: "For I testify unto every man that heareth the words of the prophecy of this book, If any man shall add unto these things, God shall add unto him the plagues that are written in this book" (22:18). Mormons point out that John was talking only about the *book of Revelation,* not the whole *Bible,* which hadn't yet been compiled. And he was talking about humans adding to God's word, not God revealing new and additional information. Mormons also point out that a similar warning appears in Deuteronomy 4:2, but no one argues that the Bible should stop at that point.

In fact, one of the Book of Mormon's most pointed passages concerns attitudes regarding the Bible. The prophet Nephi predicted that "many of the Gentiles shall say: A Bible! A Bible! We have got a Bible, and there cannot be any more Bible." To which the Lord replies: "Because that ye have a Bible ye need not suppose that it contains all my words; neither need ye suppose that I have not caused more to be written" (2 Nephi 29:3,10) — in other words, the Bible isn't God's final word, and exhibit A is, of course, the Book of Mormon itself.

Joseph Smith's corrections to the Bible

With so many people having translated — by traditional means, not like Joseph Smith — and rewritten the Bible over the centuries, Mormons believe that inaccuracies and omissions have crept into it. Joseph Smith said, "I believe the Bible as it read when it came from the pen of the original writers. Ignorant translators, careless transcribers, or designing and corrupt priests have committed many errors." Even though Joseph didn't possess the original Bible manuscripts, Mormons believe he could identify biblical trouble spots through God's inspiration.

In the Mormon view, many of the Bible's skewed or missing teachings have been amended or restored by other scriptural records, particularly the Book of Mormon. In addition, Joseph Smith received a divine commission to make a "new translation" of the King James Version itself. (Remember, for Mormons the concept of *translation* carries a different meaning when applied to Joseph Smith: He prophetically received text from God, instead of using scholarly skills to rewrite original non-English text into English.)

In carrying out this project, Joseph worked on more than 3,400 individual verses, sometimes tweaking just a few words and other times adding whole new chapters. This translation contains too many significant changes and nuances to summarize in this book, but see Table 9-2 for a few representative tidbits.

Table 9-2	A Sampling of Joseph Smith's Bible Revisions
Original KJV Passage	*Joseph Smith's Revised Passage (Differences Noted in Italics)*
In the time of Noah, "It repented the Lord that he had made man on the earth, and it grieved him at his heart" (Genesis 6:6).	"It repented *Noah, and his heart was pained,* that *the Lord* had made man on the earth."
When 12-year-old Jesus taught in the temple, he was "sitting in the midst of the doctors, both hearing them, and asking them questions" (Luke 2:46).	" . . . *they were* hearing *him,* and asking *him* questions."
"Jesus was led up of the Spirit, into the wilderness, to be tempted of the devil. And when he had fasted forty days and forty nights, he was afterward an hungred" (Matthew 4:1–2).	"Jesus was led up of the Spirit, into the wilderness, to be *with God.* And when he had fasted forty days and forty nights, *and had communed with God,* he was afterwards an hungred, *and was left to be tempted of the devil.*"
Regarding the performance of baptisms, "Jesus himself baptized not, but his disciples" (John 4:2).	"*He* himself baptized not *so many as* his disciples; *for he suffered them for an example, preferring one another.*"
Paul wrote, "It is a shame for women to speak in the church" (1 Corinthians 14:35)	"It is a shame for women to *rule* in the church."

So, where are Joseph's corrections?

After Joseph's 1844 martyrdom, his widow Emma gave his unpublished Bible manuscript to the Reorganized Church of Jesus Christ of Latter Day Saints (RLDS), which split off from the LDS Church and is known today as the Community of Christ (see Chapter 12).

The RLDS Church has published several editions of the Bible that reflect Joseph's translations, but the LDS Church never has. However, the LDS Church has inserted large portions of the *Joseph Smith Translation,* as Mormons call it — or *JST* for short — in various locations inside the LDS scriptures, including footnotes throughout the Old and New Testaments, a 17-page appendix to the Bible, and two books within the Pearl of Great Price (which we discuss in greater detail in Chapter 10).

Confused yet? So are many Mormons, many of whom rarely encounter the JST directly, at least in the somewhat inconvenient Bible footnotes and appendix. One has to ask, "Why doesn't the LDS Church just go ahead and publish an edition of the Bible that fully incorporates Joseph Smith's corrections?" Perhaps one answer lies in the area of missionary work. In sharing the Mormon gospel, missionaries make connections with other Christians through the Bible. If the missionaries used a version of the Bible rewritten by Joseph Smith, mainstream Christians would be quicker to dismiss it.

Although the JST provides many doctrinal insights and clarifications, one of its most valuable roles was immersing Joseph Smith more deeply in the Bible. As he studied and translated it, he asked many questions of God, which led to new revelations, several of which are recorded in the Doctrine and Covenants (see Chapter 10).

Getting Acquainted with the Book of Mormon

The Book of Mormon isn't just a simple batch of sermons or a book of prophetic sayings. The volume is a family saga that stretches over more than 1,000 years of history (roughly 600 B.C. to A.D. 421) and mixes visions, religious symbolism, and prophecies about the Messiah with records of migrations, civil wars, and the difficulties of governing a remote New World society. This book is long — it has about 270,000 words — with a complex, involved story. It features 15 parts generally called *books,* and these parts are divided into chapters and verses, much like the Bible. The parts are in chronological order except for the 14th part, called the Book of Ether, which covers events that happened way *before* the rest of the Book of Mormon.

Hitting the highlights

The Book of Mormon has the feel of a Cecil B. DeMille production from the 1950s, complete with an enormous cast of extras and pumped-up manly men. (Not surprising, considering that Arnold Friberg, one of the chief artists for missionary editions of the Book of Mormon, was also the costume designer and assistant art director for DeMille's movie *The Ten Commandments*.) The bulk of the Book of Mormon takes up the centuries-long civil war between the Nephites and their rebellious cousins, the Lamanites, a war of smoldering hatred that eventually spells doom for the Nephites. One of the key points to remember is that all the good guys die by the end of the book, mostly violently. Table 9-3 highlights a basic timeline of the book's happenings.

Table 9-3	A Beginner's Book of Mormon Timeline	
Approximate Year	*Event*	*Book of Mormon Reference*
600 B.C.	Warned of Jerusalem's impending destruction, the prophet Lehi and his family flee into the wilderness.	1 Nephi 1–7
590 B.C.	Lehi's family builds a ship and sails to the Americas (exact location unknown), where they form a new society.	1 Nephi 18–19
580–150 B.C.	After Lehi's death, his sons split into two factions. The Nephites (descendants of the prophet Nephi) are usually righteous, but their pride occasionally leads them away from God. The Lamanites (descendants of Nephi's rebellious older brothers) are generally barbaric, but some convert to the true religion.	2 Nephi 1–5, books of 2 Nephi, Jacob, Omni, and Mosiah
100 B.C.	Alma the Younger, one of the great prophets of the Book of Mormon, is converted and preaches to the Lamanites for 14 years.	Mosiah 27–28
92 B.C.	The prophet Mosiah translates the records of a separate Israelite civilization that lived earlier in the Western Hemisphere. This relatively short account appears as the Book of Ether, near the end of the Book of Mormon.	Mosiah 21 and 28; Ether
90–1 B.C.	More wars and political treachery, with one of the most inspiring victories won by a Nephite army of 2,000 righteous young men.	Alma 53–62
6 B.C.	Samuel, a righteous Lamanite, prophesies to the Nephites about signs that will attend the coming birth of Christ.	Helaman 13–15
A.D. 1	People in the Americas experience a night with no darkness and see a new star in the sky, as Samuel had predicted, so the Nephites know that Christ has been born.	3 Nephi 1
34	After the Nephite society has almost disintegrated due to wickedness, great calamities visit the earth upon Christ's death and destroy the unrighteous people. Then the resurrected Savior appears and teaches the gospel to about 2,500 survivors.	3 Nephi 8–28

(continued)

Table 9-3 *(continued)*

Approximate Year	Event	Book of Mormon Reference
35–231	All the people live together in righteous harmony and hold property in common.	4 Nephi 1
231–380	War resumes between the Nephites and the Lamanites. As the Nephites drift away from God, the Lamanites gradually get the upper hand.	Mormon 1–5
380–385	The Lamanites launch a devastating attack and wipe out the Nephites, who have become "ripened in iniquity."	Mormon 6
421	Moroni, the lone Nephite survivor, buries the 1,000-year record that he and his father Mormon compiled, abridged, and supplemented with their own writings.	Moroni
1823–1830	Moroni, now a resurrected angel, teaches Joseph Smith about the buried record, which Smith eventually retrieves, translates, and publishes.	Joseph Smith History 1:27–54 (in the Pearl of Great Price)

What a long, strange trip: Lehi's journey to the New World

The Book of Mormon opens with the record of an Israelite man named Lehi who lived around 600 B.C. Lehi had a vision that foretold the destruction of Jerusalem (which actually happened around 587 B.C., when Babylonian invaders destroyed the temple there), so he started urging people to leave the city while they still had time. As you can imagine, most people thought Lehi was a nutcase. They didn't want to follow his counsel and began to threaten his life, so Lehi obeyed a directive from the Lord to gather his family together and escape. The family was fairly wealthy, and several family members were reluctant to leave their comfortable home and social position in Jerusalem. Lehi's oldest sons, Laman and Lemuel, openly rebelled.

The son who obeyed without quibbling was Nephi, a righteous young man who prayed to God for his own confirmation of the spiritual vision his father received. He got that confirmation and more, so he threw himself into his father's work. After several unpleasant years of wandering in the wilderness (probably the Arabian Desert), Nephi and other members of the family constructed a boat to take them to the New World.

The journey by sea was no picnic. Laman and Lemuel resented the fact that Nephi, their younger brother, was their father's favorite and had taken to preaching at them a good deal. They tried to kill him several times, both en route and after arriving in the New World. (We don't know exactly where they lived, though some individual Mormons have identified Central America as a likely place. See Chapter 15 for more on Book of Mormon controversies.) Nephi was brokenhearted about his brothers' treachery, resulting in the "Psalm of Nephi," an achingly honest plea Nephi makes to God in 2 Nephi 4. Although he was sick about it, Nephi knew that he had to separate his followers from his wicked brothers and try to build a just society on his own.

Can't we all just get along? The Nephites and the Lamanites

The majority of the Book of Mormon is taken up with the plots and perils of the *Nephites* (including the descendants of Nephi) and the *Lamanites* (including the descendants of Laman and Lemuel, who became like savages because of their wickedness). The Lamanites outnumber the Nephites throughout the Book of Mormon, causing some scholars to think that they successfully intermarried with natives already in the Americas.

Although good and evil may seem to be cut and dried in the Book of Mormon, with the Nephites always righteous and the Lamanites always sinful, the plot just isn't that simple. At numerous times, they switch roles. Dramatizing one of history's worst cases of *Groundhog Day,* the Book of Mormon tells about the same chain of events happening over and over again to the Nephites throughout the centuries:

- The Nephites love God and take care of their neighbors.
- Because of this righteousness, they prosper.
- They get obsessed with their own wealth, loving money and becoming corrupt and immoral.
- The Lord somehow humbles them, often by allowing the Lamanites to defeat them in battle or bring them into submission via slavery or heavy taxes.
- When the Nephites are humble again and repent of their sins, they resume doing what the Lord wants them to do: worship him and deal justly with one another.
- Sadly, before long, the whole pride-prosperity-greed-war-repentance cycle starts again with a vengeance.

Throughout Nephite history, numerous missionaries risk their lives to preach the gospel to their own people and to the Lamanites, with some success. At one point, the Lamanite king converts, and many of his people follow suit.

Having been saved from their sins, the Lamanite converts decide to bury their swords rather than risk murdering again. In battle, they fall face down before their fellow Lamanites who've come to kill them for adopting the Nephite religion. The result is a horrific massacre, but the sight of so many Lamanites going willingly to the slaughter makes such a deep spiritual impact that some of their countrymen also convert.

Despite occasional alliances or truces between the Nephites and Lamanites, no real or lasting peace exists between them until Christ comes.

The main event: The coming of Christ

The Book of Mormon is a very consciously Christ-centered book, featuring prophets hundreds of years before Jesus's birth who look forward to the event and declare Jesus Christ as the Messiah by name. For example, 600 years before Christ came, Nephi wrote, "And we talk of Christ, we rejoice in Christ, we preach of Christ, we prophesy of Christ, and we write according to our prophecies, that our children may know to what source they may look for a remission of their sins" (2 Nephi 25:26). In other words, Christ is the hero of the Book of Mormon, the one to whom all the people through the ages look for atonement for their sins. (For more on the Mormon concept of atonement, see Chapter 3.)

The Book of Mormon teaches that Christ visited the Nephites after his resurrection and before he ascended into heaven, preaching among them, healing their sick, and calling 12 New World disciples (or apostles). These chapters are the climax of the Book of Mormon and feature some of the most beautiful passages of the text.

Some anti-Mormons claim that the fact that Jesus's teachings in the Book of Mormon are so similar to those in the New Testament proves that Joseph Smith wrote the Book of Mormon himself, copying key passages from the Bible to supplement his own story. Mormons counter that it makes perfect sense that Christ's teachings in Jerusalem would be the same as those in the New World and elsewhere, because the core of the gospel is the same in all times and places. They see the Book of Mormon account as a second witness of these key teachings, fulfilling the Bible's promise that "in the mouth of two or three witnesses every word may be established" (Matthew 18:16).

Among the familiar teachings of Christ in the Book of Mormon, you'll find

- ✔ The Lord's Prayer ("Our Father, who art in heaven . . .")
- ✔ Teachings on faith, repentance, baptism, and the Holy Ghost
- ✔ The Beatitudes ("Blessed are the poor," and so on)
- ✔ Discussion of the last days and the restoration of Israel

Near the end of his visit to the Nephites, Christ promises 9 of his 12 disciples that they'll be with him in his kingdom immediately after they die. He allows the three other disciples, however, to remain on earth as long as they desire, establishing the gospel and helping God's people. As far as Mormons know, they're still ministering on the earth today. These fellows are called the *three Nephites,* and they occupy a delightful place in Mormon folklore. Through the years, Mormons have told stories around the campfire about possible sightings of one or more of the three Nephites, who've reportedly helped Mormons in danger, plowed fields when a person was too sick to do it, and even changed tires on cars when Mormons were headed off on missions of mercy. (We're a little skeptical about this last part, too.)

Biting the dust: The end of the Nephites

After Christ's brief visit to the New World, the people put aside their old divisions, including the terms *Nephite* and *Lamanite.* Now sharing the same religion, they founded a church based on the principles Christ taught them. They shared everything, and no one was rich or poor. They healed the sick and worked mighty miracles. The Book of Mormon reports that during this peaceful time, crime and conflict didn't exist, and the people were united in love.

As in any tragedy worth its salt, the peace, love, and understanding couldn't possibly last. About 200 years after Christ's visit, this utopian society gave in to the same old story: The people prospered and then became full of pride. Class divisions between rich and poor again became a big problem. False religions arose, their leaders persecuted the Church, and the old lines between Nephite and Lamanite were redrawn in the sand. War became inevitable.

As the situation worsened, the Lamanites began to slaughter any Nephite who wouldn't deny Jesus the Christ. Most of the Nephites, in turn, became as wicked as the Lamanites or even more so. Seeing that their end was near, two faithful Nephite prophets named Mormon and his son Moroni set about creating a condensed *Reader's Digest* version of their people's records from Lehi on down, also adding some of their own words of wisdom. In addition, they included a historical summary of an earlier civilization called the *Jaredites,* some Israelites who'd journeyed to the New World hundreds of years before Lehi and his family.

Mormon and Moroni engraved their abridgment onto golden tablets — which Mormons commonly call *plates* — and Moroni buried them in the ground for safekeeping, until that day some 1,400 years later when the time would be right to make them known to the world. Because Mormon did most of the editorial work on the book, it was named the Book of Mormon. Moroni did some of the writing and abridging too, but his reward was to serve as the angel who helped Joseph Smith discover the record.

Abinadi? Rameumptom? A Book of Mormon pronunciation guide

Newcomers to the Book of Mormon often trip and stumble over the funkier names in the book. Heck, even lifers sometimes get tongue-tied at such monikers as Irreantum, Ammonihahite, and our personal favorite, Gidgiddonah. That last one makes us downright giddy.

Here are three basic tips to make your reading a bit less challenging:

✔ If it ends in the letter *i,* you typically pronounce it as a long vowel. Abinadi is pronounced uh-*bin*-uh-dye; Moroni (the angel you see atop most Mormon temples) is pronounced moh-*roh*-nye. (If you say something that sounds like *moron* here, you're on the wrong track.) Nephi, one of the

principal figures in the Book of Mormon, is pronounced *nee*-fye.

✔ The next-to-last syllable is often (but not always) the one that you accent. Limhi is *lim*-hye; Moriantum is mor-ee-*an*-tum. However, in plenty of circumstances this rule isn't true, so your best bet is in the next bullet.

✔ Check out the one-stop-shopping pronunciation guide at the end of the Book of Mormon. However, this guide doesn't appear in some non-English editions, so Spanish-speaking Mormons, for example, pronounce Nephi as *neff*-ee.

How the Book of Mormon Came to Be

When Mormons give their testimonies at fast and testimony meeting on the first Sunday of the month (see Chapter 6), they frequently mention that they know the Book of Mormon is true. What they generally mean by this claim isn't simply that the *teachings* of the book are true, but that it came into being the way Joseph Smith claimed: by a miracle.

In this section, you find out how the Book of Mormon appeared — it didn't exactly fall from the sky, but it was a pretty astonishing event — and what it teaches about sin, repentance, family, and social justice.

An angel in the night

Joseph Smith, as we discuss in Chapter 4, had his first major spiritual experience when he was a young teen. This event, known as the *First Vision* to Mormons, was a direct answer to Joseph's prayer about which church to join. That incident opened the floodgates of Joseph's prophetic calling.

The second major event happened in September 1823, and again it was the direct result of prayer. Seventeen-year-old Joseph was praying for forgiveness of his sins (which apparently included *levity,* or lightheartedness) when a glorious being appeared in his room. The man was dressed in a loose white robe, and his feet didn't touch the floor. His whole body seemed to be luminous, almost glowing white. He called Joseph by name and said that he was named Moroni, sent from God to tell Joseph about the work he was called to do.

As you see in the earlier section "Getting Acquainted with the Book of Mormon," Moroni wasn't just a glow-in-the-dark angelic messenger but a resurrected inhabitant of the Americas who lived and breathed and helped edit the ancient record that became the Book of Mormon. Hovering there in Joseph's bedroom, Moroni discussed the book that he had buried in the ground some 1,400 years earlier and told Joseph how to find it. He also gave Joseph directions for using the *Urim and Thummim,* a biblical device that helped him translate this ancient record. In addition, Moroni instructed Joseph in biblical prophecy.

One of the most unusual features of this story — as if it weren't odd enough! — is that just after Moroni finished his little speech and zoomed back into heaven, leaving Joseph in bed to wonder about it all, the angel reappeared and proceeded to tell Joseph the same information again. And then he came a third time, repeating exactly the same stuff and adding a caution that Satan might try to tempt Joseph to get rich from the Book of Mormon plates, given the poverty of the Smith family. (No, Joseph probably didn't get a very good sleep that night.)

The next day, Joseph found the golden plates buried on the hillside where Moroni had indicated, but the angel wouldn't let him remove them yet. Every September 23 for the next four years, Joseph went to the same spot for instruction. From Joseph's own account, Moroni seems to have been pretty severe with him, repeatedly lecturing him about not losing the plates and not making a profit from them. Finally, in September 1827, Joseph was allowed to take the plates and figure out how to translate them.

Seer stones and scribes: Translating the golden plates

Because word leaked out about the golden plates and many people wanted to see and handle them — something the Lord had forbidden except in special circumstances — Joseph temporarily moved to Pennsylvania with his new wife, Emma. There, with the assistance of several scribes, the translation went forth in earnest during 1829. (See Figure 9-1 for an illustration of what the plates may have looked like.)

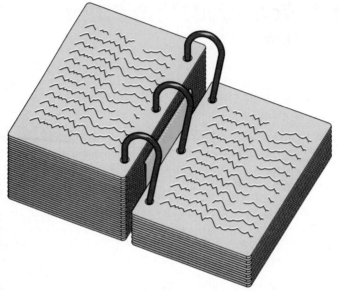

Eyewitnesses to the translation process reported that, aided by a seer stone, Joseph dictated the Book of Mormon aloud while looking into his hat to block the light so he could see each character as it appeared. The plates them- selves weren't even always necessary to the translation, as they were usually still covered by a cloth. Mormons believe that the Lord gave Joseph the translation by revelation, which explains why no one revised or rewrote this complicated narrative.

When Joseph or his scribe needed a break, they resumed work precisely where they left off, because Joseph didn't need to look at the previous dicta- tion to refresh his memory or remind himself where they were. He simply picked up where they stopped before the interruption.

After the long wait to get the plates, the actual translation took only three months. With this 588-page book, Joseph made a remarkable achievement, one that Mormons believe couldn't have happened by natural means. The book displays remarkable self-consistency, especially considering that Joseph wasn't referring back to the English longhand dictation during the process. If the book were of his own creation, Mormons note, he would've had to remember hundreds of character and place names, master a dizzying timeline, be familiar with the history and geography of the ancient Middle East and Nephite lands, and be able to write in many different voices.

"You believe what?!" Reactions to the book

In the spring of 1830, 5,000 copies of the Book of Mormon were printed in Palmyra, New York, and missionaries started selling them to the public. As with many self-published books, however, this one wasn't an overnight sensation. (Joseph and his printer may have the last laugh, though: Today, a first edition of the Book of Mormon in fine condition goes for tens of thousands of dollars.)

As news spread throughout New York State of the "golden Bible" that Joseph Smith had translated, reactions were mixed. Polarized, even. Some professed an immediate recognition that the book was of divine origin. (You can read about Brigham Young's initial reaction in Chapter 12, for example.) Others were horrified that anyone would dare add to the Bible and attempted to discredit both the book and Joseph Smith, the man they presumed had written it. They came up with many different explanations for how the book came into existence: It was the product of Smith's fertile imagination, or Smith plagiarized it from someone else. (For more on some current controversies regarding the Book of Mormon, see Chapter 15.)

What happened to the plates?

According to Joseph Smith, shortly after the translation was finished, he gave the plates back to the angel Moroni. Skeptics see this claim as a convenient excuse for why the LDS Church can't produce the plates or submit them to scientific inquiry. Certainly, the skeptics have a good point. The plates are no longer available, so all we have is Joseph Smith's word on the matter.

Or is it? In the opening pages of every edition of the Book of Mormon, you see the testimony of 11 different witnesses who claimed that they saw the plates and believed Smith had translated them by the gift and power of God. Although several of the key witnesses later left the Church over personal or institutional disagreements, they never denied that Smith translated the Book of Mormon from the plates by divine inspiration.

Interestingly, Joseph translated only a portion of the plates, and not everything he translated got published. He couldn't access the majority of the plates because metal bands kept them locked tight, but Mormons believe that this sealed portion will one day be translated and published, if Moroni would be so kind as to return the plates. In addition, Joseph loaned the first 116 pages of his translation of the manuscript to the Book of Mormon's chief financer, Martin Harris, who lost them. This episode was one of Joseph's most difficult learning experiences as a prophet, and the Lord didn't allow him to retranslate those pages.

The Book of Mormon in Mormon Life

Mormon missionaries today are instantly recognizable by their appearance (see Chapter 14), but also because they offer a unique product: the Book of Mormon. This small navy-blue book with distinctive gold lettering has become a familiar sight around the world: 116 million copies have been printed since Joseph Smith first published it in 1830, and the book is now available in over 100 languages.

Non-Mormons sometimes have a difficult time understanding the tremendous love and respect that Mormons have for this book. To some outsiders, it reads like a string of "and-it-came-to-pass" segments with a few exciting battle scenes thrown in. To Mormons, the book is a guide to life, a story about right-eousness and courage against overwhelming odds. From start to finish, it's a testimony of the Savior, which is why in 1982 the Church began subtitling the Book of Mormon as "Another Testament of Jesus Christ." Like the Bible, the Book of Mormon is a witness of Christ and his Atonement for all people.

Applying what the Book of Mormon teaches

Latter-day Saints look to the Book of Mormon for some distinctly Mormon teachings, such as the spiritual innocence of children, who don't need to be baptized until age 8. However, the bulk of its messages are very similar to those you find in the Old and New Testaments of the Bible, if slightly more detailed. In fact, many people are surprised to discover that some of Mormonism's most distinctive teachings, such as the premortal existence (see Chapter 2), eternal marriage (see Chapter 7), and humanity's potential to become like God (see Chapter 2), don't even really crop up in the Book of Mormon. (In fact, the book specifically condemns polygamy, because God didn't command it for the Book of Mormon peoples like he did for the 19th-century Mormons, as we discuss in Chapter 13.)

Avoiding the sin of pride

As you see in the section "Can't we all just get along? The Nephites and the Lamanites," pride is the source of most of the heartache in the Book of Mormon. (You know the people are in trouble every time the text says they started wearing "costly apparel." It's all downhill from there.) Pride is the most destructive force in Nephite society, a cancer that consumes the culture from the inside. At the end of the book, the prophet Moroni concludes unhap-pily that pride was the root of his people's destruction.

Because Mormons believe that the Book of Mormon was custom edited to suit the needs of 19th-century readers and later, this constant harping on the sin of pride raises an obvious question about the modern era: Will pride be the Mormons' downfall, too? In 1989, LDS prophet Ezra Taft Benson warned of pride being "the great stumbling block of Zion" and chided the Latter-day Saints to become more humble and teachable. This warning is one of the modern Church's most famous talks, and people often quote it in LDS meetings.

Taking care of the poor

Along with pride, one of the other major cautionary tales of the Book of Mormon is the failure of the proud Nephites to care for the poor among them. In the Book of Mormon, the quest for a just society included the goal to have no poor and to share all things, as the people did during the 200-year golden age that followed the Savior's visit.

Repeatedly throughout the Book of Mormon, prophets urge the people to

✔ Feed the hungry

✔ Visit the sick

✔ Clothe the naked

The Book of Mormon prophet Alma, for example, encourages people to "impart their substance" to each other.

Teaching the children

Because the Book of Mormon is at heart a family story, it pays a lot of subtle attention to teaching children right from wrong and showing the essence of true religion. You see numerous examples of righteous parents who raise wayward kids — Lehi worrying over Laman and Lemuel, or Alma coping with his rebellious son Corianton, who gets a stern lecture on sexual immorality. In the Book of Mormon as in Mormon life today, children can exercise their *agency* (free will; see Chapter 2) and choose to reject godly teachings, much to the sorrow of those who try to teach them the correct way. However, you also see cases of children (almost exclusively sons, unfortunately, because the Book of Mormon just doesn't mention a lot of women by name) who follow their parents' righteous examples.

Mosiah 4:14 encourages parents to "teach them to walk in the ways of truth and soberness . . . teach them to love one another, and to serve one another." Mormon parents take such admonitions very seriously. (For more on the importance of the family in Mormonism, see Chapter 5.)

Repenting of sins and receiving forgiveness

Another recurring theme in the Book of Mormon is repentance. In fact, one of the *antichrists* (false teachers) who appears in the book is so dastardly and dangerous precisely because he teaches that repentance is unnecessary. The Book of Mormon makes it clear that repentance is absolutely crucial — the Savior's followers must feel a clear sorrow for sin and develop the desire to never repeat it. (For more on repentance, see the section on baptism in Chapter 6).

Prophets in the Book of Mormon speak often about how, through repentance, all people can receive forgiveness for their sins through Christ's Atonement. "It is expedient that there should be . . . an infinite and eternal sacrifice," Amulek taught in Alma 34. "There can be nothing which is short of an infinite atonement which will suffice for the sins of the world." (For more on the Savior's Atonement, see Chapter 3.)

Finding answers to spiritual questions

Table 9-4 lists some of the spiritual questions for which people can find answers as they read and study the Book of Mormon.

Table 9-4	Spiritual Questions That the Book of Mormon Answers
Question	*Answer*
Do babies need to be baptized?	No. According to Moroni 8:22, little children are "alive in Christ" and don't sin. (Any parent of a strong-willed toddler may disagree, of course.)
What happens to my body after I die?	Good news. At the time of resurrection, all people will be restored to perfection, with bodies and spirits reunited (Alma 40:23).
What's the purpose of my life?	To attain eternal joy, plain and simple (see 2 Nephi 2:25). Also, life is "a probationary state; a time to prepare to meet God; a time to prepare for that endless state . . . after the resurrection of the dead" (Alma 12:24).
How can I be happy?	By obeying God's commandments. "If there be no righteousness, there be no happiness" (2 Nephi 2:13). Even more pointedly, "wickedness never was happiness" (Alma 41:10).
Do I have free will, or is everything predestined?	God gives people free will — generally called *agency* — and permits them to choose and act for themselves (Helaman 14:30–31).
How can my desire to believe be transformed into faith and eventually knowledge?	By experimenting on God's word through putting it into practice and observing its effects on our spiritual feelings (Alma 32).

Increasing emphasis on the Book of Mormon

Although Mormons today carefully read, quote from, and research the Book of Mormon, they haven't always done so. From a historical perspective, the LDS emphasis on reading and studying the Book of Mormon is actually rather new. In the 19th century, Church leaders often trumpeted the fact of the book's existence as a miracle, and members expressed faith that it was indeed an ancient record and the word of God. However, not until late in the 20th century did they begin quoting from it more than occasionally, after LDS Church President Ezra Taft Benson emphasized the book's importance and how God expects members to use it.

Consider the following statistics, compiled by LDS scholar Noel Reynolds:

✔ The earliest LDS publications cite the Bible 19 times for every time they quote the Book of Mormon. In one publication *(Elders' Journal),* biblical references beat the Book of Mormon by 40 to 1.

✔ For most of the 20th century, Book of Mormon citations accounted for just 12 percent of scripture citations in General Conference talks. After President Benson gave his famous speech in 1986 urging Latter-day Saints to read and study the Book of Mormon, such citations spiked to 40 percent before leveling off at about 25 percent, twice the earlier rate.

✔ In the 1980s, the number of books published about the Book of Mormon rose 230 percent.

Using the Book of Mormon in missionary work

The Book of Mormon has become one of the most important vehicles for missionary work in The Church of Jesus Christ of Latter-day Saints. One of the unique aspects of the Book of Mormon is that it is an ancient scripture *intended for our times.* The people who kept the records that became the Book of Mormon saw in visions when it would come forth and what would be most helpful for the people of that future time. They edited their stories accordingly, including only those parts that they thought would be useful for the book's modern readers. In other words, the Book of Mormon was custom made for this modern era, and it addresses many questions that are important now.

Because of this idea, it's not surprising that the book rings true to a whole lot of people. Many people report being unable to put down the book after they start reading it, despite King James-ish language that initially seems outdated and daunting. (It helps if they can make it past the chunk of chapters starting about 70 pages into the book that quote from Isaiah's Old Testament prophecies, which are pretty tough to understand.) The story reels them in, and the book's teachings make them think. Many people feel that the Spirit uses the book to speak directly to them.

When missionaries teach *investigators* (people who are thinking of joining the Church), they encourage them to read the Book of Mormon and pray about it. Many investigators take up the challenge issued by the prophet Moroni in the last chapter of the book: They ask God in the name of Jesus Christ if what they're reading is true. *Moroni's promise,* as Mormons call it, is that anyone who reads and prays with a sincere heart and real intent will receive a confirmation of the Book of Mormon's truthfulness, and thus of the truthfulness of Joseph Smith's prophetic mission and of the LDS Church. Millions of people who've prayed this way testify that they've received the Holy Ghost's confirmation.

Chapter 10

Mormonism's Other Scriptures

. . . .

In This Chapter

▶ Noting key aspects of the Pearl of Great Price

▶ Examining the ins and outs of the Doctrine and Covenants

▶ Making room for modern revelation

. . . .

*I*n addition to the Bible and the Book of Mormon, Mormons recognize two more books of scripture: the *Doctrine and Covenants (D&C)* and *Pearl of Great Price,* which we discuss in this chapter. Together, these four books of scripture are called the *standard works,* and the LDS Church publishes an official edition with all four standard works cross-referenced in one fat volume or two slimmer volumes. Most Mormons bring all four scriptures to church each Sunday, often zippered inside a protective carrier. (For more about why and how Mormons study the scriptures, see Chapter 17.)

If the Bible is the spiritual history of God's people in the Middle East until shortly after the time of Christ, and the Book of Mormon is the spiritual history of God's people living in the Western Hemisphere from about 600 B.C. to A.D. 400, then you can consider the Doctrine and Covenants to be the spiritual history of God's people — er, the Mormons — living in modern times from about 1830 onward, though most of its revelations occurred in America during the earliest days of the Church. And the Pearl of Great Price is a grab bag of scriptural odds and ends, both ancient and modern.

A Scriptural Hodgepodge: The Pearl of Great Price

Although the Pearl of Great Price contains much essential doctrine, it also sometimes seems like the stepchild among Mormon scriptures, for several reasons:

> ✔ At only about 60 pages, this text is considerably shorter than the other three Mormon standard works.

✔ The book is a jumble of several different eras and writing styles.

✔ It creates more than its fair share of ongoing controversy, especially with regard to some of the material's origins.

✔ This scripture is the only one of the four standard works that Church members don't study for a full year in the four-year teaching cycle, which goes through the Old and New Testaments, Book of Mormon, and Doctrine and Covenants. However, teachers touch upon aspects of the Pearl of Great Price in various classes.

✔ Its pages include three funky, Egyptian-looking facsimiles (more on those pictures later in this section).

This book of scripture takes its name from a New Testament passage: "A merchant man, seeking goodly pearls . . . when he had found one pearl of great price, went and sold all that he had, and bought it" (Matthew 13:45–46). The Pearl of Great Price began as a collection of scripture published in England in 1851 by a Mormon apostle, but the Church didn't canonize it as a standard work until 1880. Over the decades, several components have been added or removed, such as in 1979, when Church authorities moved a couple of modern revelations into the Doctrine and Covenants, where all such other revelations were already collected (yes, scriptural change moves at glacial pace).

Revisiting Moses

As we discuss in Chapter 9, Mormonism's founding prophet Joseph Smith received a divine commission to make a new translation of the Bible's King James Version (KJV). Pondering Genesis, which Mormons believe Moses wrote, Joseph wrote an inspired expansion of certain sections, parts of which now appear as "Selections from the Book of Moses" in the Pearl of Great Price.

The eight-chapter book of Moses covers the following territory:

✔ **Details of a vision that Moses experienced but didn't discuss anywhere in his biblical writings:** During this vision, which happened after the burning bush incident but before the parting of the Red Sea episode, Moses is transported to "an exceedingly high mountain," where he meets the premortal Jesus Christ, who was then a spirit personage known as Jehovah, and learns more about the nature of God (for more on the Mormon concept of God, see Chapter 3). In addition, Moses encounters Satan and learns more about the devil's goals, motivations, and methods (for more on the devil, see Chapter 2).

✔ **A recounting of the earth's creation and Adam and Eve's experience, with more particulars than the Genesis account:** For instance, Mormons learn from these chapters that God first created everything spiritually before creating it physically. (When Mormons use the word *create,* they generally mean "form" or "organize," because they believe all spiritual and physical matter is eternal, not created.) In addition, these chapters touch on many aspects of God's plan of salvation and the uniquely positive Mormon outlook regarding the role of Adam and Eve (for more on these topics, see Chapter 2).

✔ **New perspective on Adam's children and descendants:** Although Genesis only briefly mentions the prophet Enoch, the book of Moses provides several pages worth of Enoch's experiences and prophecies, which play an important role in Mormon doctrine, including what will happen in connection with the Savior's Second Coming (for more on that topic, see Chapter 3). According to this section, Enoch led his people in such great righteousness that their entire city was taken up into heaven. This part also includes some additional chilling detail about Adam's bad seed, Cain.

Mummy dearest: Uncovering the writings of Abraham

In 1835, a traveling exhibit of Egyptian mummies and papyri passed through Kirtland, Ohio, where Joseph Smith was then living (see Chapter 11). After the Church purchased the papyri (in a package deal that included the mummies too), Joseph concluded that one papyrus contained writings of the Old Testament prophet Abraham, who lived about 2,000 years before Christ.

In the mid-1960s, a University of Utah professor discovered portions of Joseph Smith's Egyptian papyri in New York City's Metropolitan Museum of Art. Experts dated them as originating between 100 B.C. and A.D. 100, and translators found no resemblance to Joseph Smith's claimed translation. However, defenders point out that the papyri found in the museum may not have included the one containing Abraham's writings. Whatever the case, most Mormons continue exercising faith that divine revelation played a role in Joseph's translation of this document.

The five-chapter Book of Abraham covers the following territory:

✔ **The skinny on Abraham's origins and experiences:** The early chapters go into greater detail, including his ordination to the priesthood and his narrow escape from being sacrificed to pagan gods.

✔ **The Abrahamic covenant:** This covenant includes God's guarantee of a Promised Land, numberless descendants, priesthood authority, and eternal salvation. Mormons believe that anyone can enter into Abraham's covenant by joining the LDS Church, which Mormons view as the modern continuation of the same faith that Abraham practiced. (For more on why God's covenant with Abraham is important to Mormons, see Chapter 5.)

✔ **Details about sacred astronomy, an account of humankind's premortal existence, and a description of the earth's creation:** Abraham taught that the earth was formed from existing materials, not created out of nothing. (This scripture is one of the main reasons why Mormons reject the common Christian notion of creation out of nothing.) In addition, he calls the creative steps *times* rather than *days,* suggesting that the earth's creation took longer than six earthly days.

✔ **Three distinctively Egyptian images:** In 1842, Joseph Smith asked one of his followers to make woodcuts of some drawings from the papyri so he could print these images along with the translation. The pictures depict symbolic figures related to Abraham's experiences and his understanding of astronomy as discussed in the text, and it's not entirely clear to most Mormons why Joseph included these images. Still, during long meetings it's fun to puzzle over these *facsimiles,* as they're called.

Expanding Matthew

During Joseph Smith's prophetic revision — Mormons call it *retranslation* — of the KJV Bible (see Chapter 9), he made a particularly large number of changes to Matthew 24. This revised chapter now appears in the Pearl of Great Price as "Joseph Smith — Matthew." The original KJV chapter contains 1,050 words, but Joseph's version contains about 1,500 words.

In Matthew 24, the Savior gives several prophecies about two future times of trouble and destruction, including what would happen to Jerusalem soon after his death and what would happen before his Second Coming. As the KJV presents them, the chronology of these prophecies is hard to understand. Joseph's translation clarifies Jesus's distinction between the two time periods, which are separated by at least a couple thousand years.

Chronicling Joseph Smith

Although the first two sections in the Pearl of Great Price are from Old Testament times and the third section is from the New Testament era, the fourth section is an autobiographical account of Joseph Smith's early experiences as a prophet, which was first published in 1838. It covers events that occurred during the decade between 1820 and 1830. Titled "Joseph Smith — History," this part relates the following:

✔ **Religious upheaval:** In upstate New York during Joseph's boyhood, many churches were vying for members. Joseph writes that he felt it was vitally important to choose the right one.

✔ **Joseph's First Vision:** A Bible verse informed Joseph how to solve his dilemma: "If any of you lack wisdom, let him ask of God, that giveth to all men liberally, and upbraideth not; and it shall be given him" (James 1:5). In 1820, Joseph found a private grove of trees and knelt down to put

James's promise to the test. Heavenly Father and Jesus Christ appeared to Joseph and told him not to join any of the existing churches. (For more on the First Vision, thumb back to Chapter 4.)

✔ **The visitations of Moroni:** Over the next several years, Joseph was instructed several times by a resurrected being named Moroni, who in A.D. 421 buried the golden plates from which Joseph would translate the Book of Mormon. (See Chapter 9 for more about the coming forth of the Book of Mormon.)

✔ **More angelic visitors:** In 1829, after reading about baptism during the translation of the Book of Mormon, Joseph Smith and his scribe prayed to learn more. In response, the resurrected John the Baptist appeared to them, ordained them to the lower of Mormonism's two priesthoods, and instructed them to baptize each other. Soon after, the resurrected apostles Peter, James, and John ordained them to the higher priesthood. (See Chapter 4 for more about the restoration of the priesthood.)

Here, Joseph's Pearl of Great Price narration ends. Within another year or so, he published the Book of Mormon and formally organized what would subsequently become named The Church of Jesus Christ of Latter-day Saints. Further revelations and events dating from later in Joseph Smith's life are partially chronicled throughout the Doctrine and Covenants, described later in this chapter.

In writing and speaking on different occasions about his early experiences, Joseph apparently made some inconsistent statements about what happened to him and when. Anti-Mormons seize on these inconsistencies as proof that Joseph isn't a true prophet, while Church members attribute any flaws to normal human limitations of memory and communication. After all, the Bible itself contains some inconsistencies among the Gospels and gives conflicting accounts of Paul's vision on the road to Damascus.

Lining up the Articles of Faith

In 1842, two years before his martyrdom, Joseph Smith wrote a letter in response to some questions about Mormonism from a Chicago newspaper editor. Included in this letter were 13 statements of Mormon belief that later became canonized as Mormonism's Articles of Faith. This section occupies only two pages of the Pearl of Great Price, and the individual articles are often the first scriptures that Mormon children memorize.

Although the Articles of Faith touch on several important aspects of Mormonism, they aren't a comprehensive summary of Mormon beliefs. For instance, they don't say anything about humankind's premortal existence, the performance of gospel ordinances for the dead, eternal marriage, or humankind's potential to become like Heavenly Father (for more on these topics, see Chapters 2 and 7). Rather, the Articles of Faith seem to function more as an introductory calling card to the faith, a way of establishing common ground with other Christians while also introducing some unique Mormon beliefs.

The complete text of the Articles of Faith appears on the Cheat Sheet at the beginning of this book. Several of the points aren't that different from what you'll find in any other Christian denomination, but following are highlights of some of the more distinctively Mormon elements:

- ✔ Humans will be punished for their own sins, not for Adam's transgression (for more on this idea, see Chapter 2).

- ✔ Proper priesthood authority and organization are required in God's true church (see Chapter 4).

- ✔ Mormons believe the Bible insofar as it's "translated correctly," meaning that some parts contain errors or omissions, and they believe in additional scriptures (see Chapter 9).

- ✔ Mormons believe that God still reveals his will to humankind through a living prophet (see Chapter 8 and the following section).

- ✔ Mormons believe in the gathering of Israel (see Chapter 5) and that they'll build a New Jerusalem — also known as the City of Zion — in Missouri before the Savior's Second Coming (see Chapters 3 and 11).

So, if the Articles of Faith aren't comprehensive, does a single source exist for an official overview of Mormon beliefs and doctrine? One such aid is the Church-published manual *Gospel Principles,* which is commonly used in Sunday school classes for new converts. In addition, in 2004 the Church released a short, helpful introduction to Mormon belief called *True to the Faith,* which tackles gospel subjects in alphabetical order, from the Aaronic Priesthood to Zion. (These books and other official Church materials are available at www. ldscatalog.com.)

Modern-Day Revelations in the D&C

As the ninth Article of Faith makes clear, Mormons don't see the canon as closed; they believe other scriptures are yet to come. Mormons trust that Heavenly Father is still revealing, and has yet to reveal, many "great and important things pertaining to the kingdom of God."

In this sense Mormonism is a bit of a conundrum. On the one hand, Mormons claim to have fullness of truth, a restored gospel, and a Church organization established by Christ himself. On the other hand, they know that God hasn't yet spoken the last word on every subject, and they remain open to new revelations through the current prophet. At a minimum, Mormons realize that the Church's structure and programs continue to evolve to meet new needs and challenges.

In this section, we look at the Doctrine and Covenants, a canonized book of Mormon scripture that contains modern revelations, mostly from the 19th century.

But wait, there's more: God's revelations to Joseph Smith and others

Every president of the LDS Church is considered a *prophet, seer,* and *revelator,* which basically means that he has the spiritual authority to lead and guide the Church as God directs. Although any members of the Church can receive revelations pertaining to their own families, Church callings, and spiritual lives, Mormons believe that the prophet is the only one who can receive visions and revelations from God for the whole Church. (For more on the role of the LDS prophet, see Chapter 8.) Many of the Church's early revelations — and a handful of more recent prophetic statements — find their home in the Doctrine and Covenants, which Mormons affectionately call "the D&C."

Getting revelations

Almost all the revelations in the D&C came about because a prophet — usually Joseph Smith — had a question and prayed about it. The revelations are God's answers to specific questions, which is why so many of them open with the phrase "thus saith the Lord." For example, D&C 91 begins, "Verily, thus saith the Lord unto you concerning the Apocrypha." (The *Apocrypha* is the collection of ancient books that Catholics have as part of their biblical canon, but Protestants don't.) Joseph Smith was curious about the role of the Apocrypha when he retranslated portions of the Old Testament, so he asked God whether he should translate the Apocrypha, too. (Short answer: Translating it wasn't necessary, but it would be beneficial for study.)

By far, the Mormon leader who received the most revelations is Joseph Smith, the religion's founder. Poor Brigham Young has just one revelation in the entire D&C, and even that was basically how-to advice on organizing the Mormon pioneers for the trek west. (For more on that advice and Young's genius as a manager, see Chapter 12.) The other prophets represented in the D&C include John Taylor, Wilford Woodruff, Joseph F. Smith (a son of Joseph's brother Hyrum), and Spencer W. Kimball. That leaves nine Mormon prophets who haven't added any revelations to the D&C, showing how rarely new scripture surfaces.

Some sections of the D&C deal with issues that are no longer applicable to most Mormons. For instance, D&C 49, which was recorded in 1831, commanded three Mormon men to go and preach the gospel to the Shakers, a celibate religious group that was popular in the 19th century. Because fewer than a dozen Shakers remain in the world today, this revelation doesn't light a fire under many Mormons in the 21st century. However, it does address some timeless spiritual issues as well as concrete historical ones, including the need for missionary work, the importance of marriage, and the Second Coming of Christ, so it remains relevant for Mormons today.

Tracing the evolution of the D&C

The D&C has gone through many different editions since the early 1830s, when the Church first published it under the title *A Book of Commandments.* Through the years, the Church has made changes to the collection's organization, removing some revelations, adding others, and combining others together. The book now contains 138 sections, plus a couple of official declarations (see "Wrapping up: Official declarations," later in this chapter).

The earliest editions contained the *Lectures on Faith,* unsigned discourses on faith that Sidney Rigdon (see Chapter 11) or Joseph Smith may have written. Although Mormons still occasionally quote from these seven lectures, they haven't been part of the D&C since 1921.

How does the Church choose which revelations to include? The First Presidency and Quorum of the Twelve Apostles make this decision, with the consent of Church members who affirm it in General Conference. However, it's unusual nowadays for changes to be made to the D&C, and it hasn't happened in more than 20 years.

If you're new to Mormon culture, you may be surprised to find that Mormons don't use the same chapter and verse system for the D&C that they do for the other standard works. Each revelation is its own *section,* which is then subdivided into verses. So, a Mormon vegetarian might draw on section 89, verse 13 of the D&C to try to persuade a meat-eating Mormon that there's a scriptural precedent for abstaining from meat. Then the meat-eater would quote section 49, verse 19, which seems pretty clear that eating meat is okay.

Key LDS scriptures in the D&C

Here you take a look at some of the most significant revelations of the D&C and find the origins of some of Mormonism's most distinctive teachings.

Understanding the power of the priesthood

In D&C 121, God says that the rights of priesthood (see Chapter 4) are inseparably connected with the powers of heaven. In other words, Mormons believe that all worthy men who hold the Melchizedek Priesthood have the very power of God at their disposal. Think this quality could lead to some serious abuses? Not so fast. The rest of the section details all the many ways a man can lose his heavenly priesthood power: If he's selfish, proud, controlling, ruthlessly ambitious, or unrighteous, the Spirit departs. The scripture says that if a man ever tries to lord his priesthood over someone, he's exercising "unrighteous dominion," and his priesthood goes bye-bye.

Keeping the Mormon version of kosher

In Chapter 16, we take a thorough look at the Word of Wisdom, or the Mormon dietary laws. There, we walk you through what's allowed, what's forbidden, and what falls into a gray area. In the meantime, the basic rules to remember are as follows: no coffee, tea, alcohol, tobacco, or harmful drugs.

The whole idea of the Mormon diet comes from D&C 89, which is commonly called the *Word of Wisdom*. In 1833 Joseph Smith received this revelation when he asked God if the guys were in the clear to use tobacco in their meetings. Joseph's wife, Emma, had already made a stink about it. (She had to clean the floor afterward and didn't appreciate scrubbing up their tobacco-laden spit.) Apparently God agreed with Emma, because the revelation clarifies that tobacco "is not for the body." What's more, it was only one of several items identified as forbidden fruit — showing that you should always be careful what you pray for. This revelation didn't become a full-fledged, rigidly enforced commandment for Mormons until nearly 100 years later.

Marrying for eternity

Several revelations in the D&C speak about marriage, which Mormons believe can be an everlasting covenant. As you discover in Chapters 5 and 7, Mormons don't want to just marry "until death do us part" — well, most Mormons, anyway — but for eternity. D&C 131 and 132 speak of celestial, or eternal, marriage, which is necessary for both men and women if they want to reach the highest level of the celestial kingdom, where they can become eternal parents.

When these revelations were given in the 1840s, Mormon leaders were practicing polygamy, and section 132 explains the theological justification and biblical basis for having multiple wives. This section of the D&C is still printed in its entirety today, indicating that Mormon doctrine still includes plural marriage as an eternal principle, even though Mormons don't practice earthly polygamy anymore. (See Chapters 13 and 15 for more on that topic.)

Distinguishing the three degrees of glory

D&C 88:20–32 offers a pretty comprehensive overview of the Mormon belief regarding a three-tiered heaven, with celestial, terrestrial, and telestial kingdoms. (See Chapter 2 for more on these *three degrees of glory*.) The Lord makes it clear in this revelation that the arrangement is designed so that people will wind up spending eternity in a place that's right for them.

Baptizing new members by immersion

Many of the revelations in the D&C concern Church organization and rituals. Joseph Smith was trying to build a new religious organization without much experience to guide him, so the fact that he often consulted the Lord with rather nit-picky questions about how he should do it isn't surprising. D&C 13 — which is only one verse long — explains that baptism is an ordinance of the Aaronic Priesthood (see Chapter 4) and immersion is the only way to go. In other words, no sprinkling allowed.

Meeting together often

D&C 20 contains important details about such things as how to conduct Church meetings and who's responsible for what in the Church. (Yes, we know it sounds boring, but now you know that Mormons aren't kidding when they say God set up every jot and tittle of the Church's organization.)

Other revelations deal with organizational matters such as General Conference (see Chapter 8) and Church disciplinary actions (see Chapter 16).

Paying an honest tithe

As we discuss in Chapter 16, Mormons are well known for donating ten percent of their income to the Church. In D&C 119, the Lord lays down the law of tithing, which supports the Church's building efforts, missionary work, and other activities.

Understanding humanity's divine nature

Some Mormons cite section 93 as their favorite part of the D&C, because it beautifully sets forth the divine nature of the soul, discusses the relationship between being faithful and receiving wisdom from God, and promises that those who keep the commandments can find "all truth."

Living in the spirit world

The last full section of the D&C is 138, a fairly trippy and fascinating account of visions seen in October 1918 by President Joseph F. Smith, founding prophet Joseph Smith's nephew, who served as prophet from 1901 until his death in November 1918, just six weeks after the visions. He saw that Christ had spent time in spirit paradise in the brief period between his crucifixion and resurrection, preaching liberty to the captive spirits. (For a crash course on the Mormon notion of the afterlife, refer to Chapter 2.)

Although Christ's visit to the spirit world was just a brief weekend stopover with a Saturday-night stay, it was a successful little tour. Christ didn't personally visit the rebellious folks in spirit prison ("unto the wicked he did not go"), but he did organize a missionary force in typical Mormon fashion to carry the gospel there too.

One key element of this revelation is the role of temple work in freeing the spirits of the dead and helping them prepare for their eventual passage to one of the three heavenly kingdoms. In order for them to obtain full celestial glory, Latter-day Saints here on earth must do their temple work for them, and they must accept those ordinances and otherwise qualify. (For more on temples and their meaning to Mormons, see Chapter 7.)

Wrapping up: Official declarations

The closing pages of the Doctrine and Covenants feature two official declarations that represent a different mode of prophetic communication than the preceding 138 sections. Both of these declarations demonstrate that Mormonism is an evolving, dynamic religion in which belief in continuing revelation can cause 180-degree turns in direction, as the Spirit guides.

Making polygamy a no-no

The first of these official declarations is unusual in that it doesn't seem to come directly from the mouth of God. You may even consider it to be more of a press release than a revelation, because it begins with the bureaucratic statement, "Press dispatches having been sent for political purposes." Dated October 6, 1890, and read aloud to the members at General Conference, the statement basically bans the continued practice of plural marriage because of congressional laws forbidding it. (For more about governmental pressure to stop polygamy in the late 19th century, see Chapter 13.)

Now known as the *Woodruff Manifesto* because LDS President Wilford Woodruff wrote it, the document was widely circulated to smooth the Mormons' strained relations with the federal government and pave the way for Utah's statehood, which Congress finally approved in 1896.

Immediately after President Woodruff's declaration, a few members continued quietly entering plural marriage. President Woodruff warned in late 1891 that the Lord had shown him through a vision the trouble the Mormons would face if they didn't abandon polygamy. (An excerpt from this talk is included at the end of the D&C in teeny-tiny type.) In 1904, the Church issued a clearer statement that absolutely prohibited new plural marriages and promised excommunication for anyone who disobeyed. That statement, or *Second Manifesto,* isn't in the D&C, but it's binding on all Latter-day Saints. (For more on why Mormons believe such a flip-flop from go to no on polygamy, for example, is okay, head to "Day-to-day wisdom from the prophet," later in this chapter.)

Extending the priesthood to all races

The other official declaration in the D&C is from June 1978, when the Church extended the priesthood to "all worthy male members" regardless of race. Before that time, the priesthood was denied to any man of African ancestry, a policy that offended many members and nonmembers alike.

In the declaration, President Spencer W. Kimball spoke of the many hours he'd spent in the upper room of the temple, begging the Lord for guidance. He was apparently heartbroken over the idea that the faithful converts from many nations who were joining the Church in ever-increasing numbers couldn't hold the priesthood or enter the temple. Pleading on their behalf, President Kimball received the answer that the time had come to offer those blessings to all, without consideration of race or color. (For more on the controversial history of race in Mormonism, see Chapter 15.)

The Beat Goes On: Recent Revelations Not Found in the D&C

Just because a prophetic teaching isn't contained in the four standard works of Mormonism doesn't mean that it doesn't carry the weight of scripture for most Mormons. In addition to the canonized revelations that appear in the D&C, recent prophets have made other statements that are widely regarded as modern additions to scripture. In fact, any time a prophet speaks in the capacity of his holy office, Mormons consider his words to be scripture.

Picturing the ideal family

In 1995, the *First Presidency* (the prophet and his two counselors) and Quorum of the Twelve Apostles released a statement that has since assumed the status of gospel. Its official name is "The Family: A Proclamation to the World," but most Latter-day Saints just call it the "Proclamation on the Family." We wouldn't be surprised to see it appear in future editions of LDS scriptures some years from now. In the meantime, the statement is springing up in kitschy, mass-market calligraphic editions that some members frame and display.

Basically, the proclamation sets forth the Church's position on gender and family responsibilities more specifically than ever before, putting it all in theological perspective. Although the language is usually gentle, the message is clear: Mormons believe in traditional gender roles and the sacred nature of the nuclear family. The proclamation explains that

- ✔ **Gender is an eternal characteristic that follows a person before, during, and after mortal life.** In other words, our gender here on earth is the gender we've always been in the premortal world and always will be in the hereafter.

- ✔ **Marriage is between a man and a woman.** Not only does this proclamation rule out homosexual marriage, but it also slams the door on marriage between one man and several women, as some 19th-century Mormons practiced.

- ✔ **Children deserve to be raised in a home where parents honor their marriage vows completely.** The proclamation affirms that sex is a gift from God that people should enjoy only within the bonds of heterosexual marriage (for more on Mormon views regarding chastity, see Chapter 16). What's more, the proclamation clarifies that sexual fidelity alone is not enough to guarantee a happy marriage; husbands and wives also need to practice forgiveness, compassion, and mutual respect. This part of the proclamation gently signals the Church's preference that children born to single mothers should generally be placed for adoption by a couple.

✔ **The primary duty of fathers is to preside over their families and provide for their material needs, while the first responsibility of mothers is to nurture their children.** Husband and wife are expected to honor one another as equal partners in the fulfillment of these responsibilities. Although the proclamation doesn't pronounce dire punishments on women who work outside the home and even makes allowances for special circumstances, the general ideal is clear. (For more on the roles of Mormon men and women, see Chapter 5.)

The proclamation closes with specific warnings against domestic abuse, adultery, and other moral failures, saying that people who engage in such behaviors will be held accountable before God. This proclamation is unusual in that it's worded as a warning to the whole world, not just Mormons.

Day-to-day wisdom from the prophet

In addition to the "Proclamation on the Family," any guidance that the General Authorities give during General Conference assumes the status of *de facto* scripture for Mormons. When the prophet speaks, people listen; in one popular LDS hymn, Mormons sing about how thankful they are for a prophet to guide them in these latter days. They *expect* him to give them guidance about spiritual issues, doctrine, family matters, and the like. What's more, they love him for it.

However, any Mormon who reads history knows that what some prophets (and other Church leaders) spoke in the past isn't necessarily Church doctrine today. The primary example of this situation is polygamy, of course; most 19th-century LDS leaders practiced it and preached glowing sermons about it from the pulpit. Obviously, though, Mormons don't feel this way today, and no prophet of the Church has sanctioned polygamy in over a century.

So what happens when the teachings of LDS prophets seem to collide? The basic rule is that according to the doctrine of continuing revelation, the Lord continues to reveal more light and knowledge on various subjects as people are ready for it. In other words, *a living prophet always trumps a dead prophet.* Mormons expect that some Church programs will change as society evolves and the Lord offers new revelations. Sometimes a lower law is replaced by a higher law, such as in the Bible when Jehovah gave the Mosaic Law and later, after he was born to the earth as Jesus Christ, upgraded it with his gospel. But sometimes the reverse happens as well, when people can't live up to the higher law, such as when tithing replaced the law of consecration (see Chapter 16).

Hearing an LDS leader publicly challenge the statements of a dead or past leader is highly unusual, though it has happened — in the late 1970s, for example, one apostle told Church members to forget everything that Brigham Young or any other 19th-century leader ever said about race. (Brigham Young made some racist remarks about blacks being inferior to whites, which is certainly *not* taught by the Church today — see Chapter 15 for more on this issue.) More often, a former doctrine slowly passes out of existence and is quietly dropped from publications because Church leaders no longer teach it.

No one makes a big deal out of this allowance for change except a segment of angry opponents of the Church who think that continuing revelation means that the Mormon God waffles on important truths. They argue that any alterations to past teachings prove that Mormonism is a false religion. Mormons, on the contrary, believe that *of course* a dynamic God who's interested in people in all times and places offers revelations that pertain to their particular circumstances, and he'll fine-tune the counsel somewhat as their circumstances change, just as he did in biblical times. God may be the same yesterday, today, and forever, but the world isn't, and Mormons have to find ways to live in it. That's where the doctrine of continuing revelation becomes a truly beautiful design.

Chapter 11

Searching for a Home

· ·

In This Chapter

▶ Gathering the Mormons in Ohio, Missouri, and Illinois

▶ Building the first temples and performing the first ordinances

▶ Dealing with persecution and Prophet Joseph Smith's murder

▶ Visiting Mormon history sites today

· ·

*T*o understand today's Mormon culture and mindset, you have to understand what happened during the faith's earliest days, especially the period between Joseph Smith's organization of the Church in 1830 and his martyrdom in 1844. The Church devotes considerable instruction time to early Latterday Saint history, and most Mormons are quite familiar with what happened during the 1830s and 1840s. In contrast to some other religious groups today, Mormons often can not only name the Church's earliest converts but also provide details about those early Mormons' lives, sufferings, and contributions. For Mormons, history *is* theology, so they can't take it lightly.

Mormonism has changed a great deal since the early decades. To many, the spiritual fervor and extreme persecutions of early Mormonism seem downright otherworldly compared to today's stable, wealthy, corporate-style Church. At the same time, some argue that the early persecutions continue to motivate Mormons to blend in with mainstream society so that they don't have to endure the same violent fate. In fact, some even say the Latter-day Saints still have a persecution complex.

This chapter traces Joseph Smith's attempts to settle his people in Ohio, Missouri, and Illinois and analyzes what happened when Mormonism collided with the local populations. In addition, we look at the origins of many ins and outs of Mormonism today.

A Significant Pit Stop: Kirtland, Ohio

Just a few months after officially organizing the Church in upper New York (see Chapter 4), Joseph Smith sent missionaries to the far-off Missouri territory to teach the Indians about this restored gospel. In November 1830, led by chief Book of Mormon scribe Oliver Cowdery, the missionaries took a break from their 1,500-mile journey and preached in the area of Kirtland, Ohio, not far from Cleveland. Little did they know their efforts would be so successful that, because of persecution, Joseph Smith would soon move the fledgling Church's headquarters there from New York.

One of the missionaries wanted to reconnect with a Kirtland-area man who he'd studied religion with a few years before discovering Mormonism. The man, a Campbellite minister named Sidney Rigdon, was actively seeking a return to New Testament Christianity — not unlike what the Mormons were trying to do. Sidney allowed the Mormons to preach to his congregation, and, impressed by the Book of Mormon, he converted. Within a month, more than a hundred others were baptized into the Mormon faith.

Soon after his conversion, Sidney visited Joseph Smith in New York, and the Prophet received a revelation to move to the Kirtland area. A powerful speaker, Sidney played a central role in Mormon leadership for more than a decade, until parting ways with the faith after Joseph was murdered in 1844.

Receiving new revelations and doctrines

During Joseph Smith's Ohio residence of nearly seven years (February 1831 to January 1838), a whole lot happened:

✔ **The Church grew like a weed.** With missionaries traveling from the Kirtland hub into Canada and England, as well as throughout the U.S., worldwide Church membership grew from 280 to more than 16,000.

✔ **People packed up and moved in.** Announcing Kirtland as its official gathering place, the Church encouraged converts to move there, which many did despite severe economic hardships.

✔ **The temple went up.** At great cost and sacrifice, the Church built its first temple, which boosted the people's spirituality and helped the Church's progress.

✔ **Joseph put his own revelations in writing.** During this Ohio phase, Joseph Smith received nearly half of the total revelations contained in the Doctrine and Covenants, one of Mormonism's four main books of scripture (for more on the D&C, as it's commonly called, see Chapter 10). These revelations include

• **The Word of Wisdom,** Mormonism's well-known health code warning against addictive, intoxicating substances (see Chapter 16).

• **The three degrees of glory,** Mormonism's three-tiered heaven that symbolizes humankind's potential eternal rewards (see Chapter 2).

• **Plural marriage,** which would remain confidential until years later. Joseph probably entered into his first polygamous marriage in 1835, with a young neighbor (see Chapters 13 and 15).

✔ **Joseph uncovered scriptural pearls.** Several of Joseph's Kirtland-era scriptural translations were later gathered, along with additional material, into the Pearl of Great Price, the smallest and perhaps most unusual collection of Mormon scripture (see Chapter 10). These key Kirtland writings include

- Portions of the Bible's King James Version, which Joseph retranslated to correct errors introduced by earlier translators (see Chapter 9). In particular, Joseph received additional revelations by Moses.

- Revelations of the Old Testament prophet Abraham, which Joseph Smith translated from ancient Egyptian papyri.

✔ **The Mormons adopted a what's-mine-is-yours philosophy.** Joseph Smith introduced concepts that led to the Mormon ideals of caring for the poor, maintaining self-sufficiency, and sharing common resources. Driven by his concern for poor Church members, Smith created a community storehouse that would meet their needs by pooling the extra dough of more fortunate Saints. (Although these attempts at communal living had fizzled out by the end of the 19th century, their legacy lives on in the Church welfare program, which we discuss in Chapter 8.)

✔ **The Church figured out its org chart.** Its main governors include the *First Presidency,* consisting of the prophet and his two counselors; the Quorum of the Twelve Apostles; and other general and local priesthood offices. (For more about the Church's priesthood organization, see Chapters 4, 6, and 8.)

✔ **Education became the new wave.** Joseph Smith, Sidney Rigdon, and others pioneered the Mormon emphasis on education by teaching classes that mingled religious instruction with secular subjects such as literature, history, and philosophy. Today, Brigham Young University and other LDS schools maintain a similar balance, and the Church provides weekday religion classes all over the world to supplement the secular curriculum of Mormons in high school and college. (For more on Mormon education, see Chapter 8.)

Building the Kirtland Temple

When it came time to start putting up the first temple in 1833, Joseph Smith unveiled unique plans for its construction, which he received via revelation from God. This sacred structure featured large meeting rooms on the first and second floors, each with multilevel pulpits at either end for use by priesthood officials. Mormon women donated china and glassware to be ground up for sparkle in the temple's exterior glaze. Because persecution was constant in the early days of Mormonism, people had to guard the temple day and night against vandals, both during construction and afterward. Take a peek at this temple yourself — see Figure 11-1.

Photo courtesy of Phil Smith

Figure 11-1:
The Kirtland
Temple,
dedicated
in 1836,
remains a
popular
tourist
destination.

Joseph Smith didn't reveal most of the key temple ceremonies to Mormons until the later Nauvoo period, so the Kirtland Temple was more of a glorified meetinghouse than a place to perform rituals and ordinances, like today's temples (for more details on Mormon temples, see Chapter 7). However, one ordinance introduced in the Kirtland Temple was the washing and anointing of feet, similar to what Jesus did in the Bible's New Testament. Versions of this practice continue in Mormon temples today for high-ranking Church leaders.

Empty pockets and loaded threats: Good times come to an end

Unfortunately, the temple added to the Church's large debt burden, which in turn led to financial chaos that ultimately helped trigger Joseph Smith's flight from Kirtland. Joseph decided to fix the situation by forming a banklike organization to issue currency notes. However, people cashed in the notes for real coins faster than the organization could handle, and a national banking panic in 1837 sealed the financial doom. People became upset both inside and outside the Church, contributing to increased persecution and hundreds of excommunications, including 4 of Joseph Smith's handpicked 12 apostles.

Clutching pistols and knives, one group of *apostates* (former Mormons who rebelled against the faith) even tried to take over the temple.

In January 1838, fleeing from lawsuits, arrest warrants, and assassination plots, Joseph Smith moved his family to Missouri, effectively ending Kirtland's role as Church headquarters. With mobs ransacking and burning down their homes, hundreds of Mormons followed him.

Kirtland in the here and now

The days in Kirtland remain a controversial period in Mormon history. Some historians argue that Church leaders caused many of their own problems by participating in land speculation and using credit unwisely. Others say Joseph Smith was blameless and did the best he could, considering the new religion's complex challenges and needs. Despite the controversy, one point is true: The Church learned valuable lessons in Kirtland, and the difficulties revealed who was faithful and who wasn't. (Today, however, the LDS Church doesn't go into debt to build temples or carry out its programs.)

Still standing in excellent condition, the Kirtland Temple is now owned by the *Community of Christ,* the modern version of the largest group that splintered from the main Church after Joseph Smith's 1844 martyrdom (see Chapter 12). As a result, the Kirtland Temple isn't used for sacred ordinances as other Mormon temples are, and the building is open for tours. In addition, the LDS Church has rebuilt a nearby village of stores, homes, and other buildings where important events in Mormon history took place.

Seeking Zion in Missouri

Many people think Utah is the promised land for Mormons, but that arid, mountainous state is just a temporary refuge — with *temporary* measured in centuries — until the promised return to Missouri, home of some cherished, significant geographical locations that will be critical to the faith in the future.

The early Mormons sought to establish *Zion* somewhere on earth, a place where they could practice their religion freely and commune with each other. Zion would be the location where the righteous took refuge when the wicked brought chaos into the world, a site identified in the Book of Mormon as the New Jerusalem. In 1831, Joseph Smith received a revelation directing him to travel from Ohio to Missouri, where God would reveal the location for a permanent Latter-day Saint homeland that would last through the Millennium (see Chapter 3 for more on Christ's Second Coming and the Millennium).

Arriving in the rough-hewn frontier outpost of Independence in Jackson County, Joseph Smith declared that the town would become the center place of Zion and the site for the New Jerusalem, and he identified the spot where the Latter-day Saints would build a temple. (In addition, many Mormons believe that Jackson County was the original site of the Garden of Eden.) While Joseph himself didn't move to Missouri for another seven years because God wanted him to finish his work in Ohio, many of his followers immediately started settling there to stake the Church's claim. Unfortunately, their best shot at Zion lasted only two years.

Getting booted out of Zion

For the early Mormons, *Missouri* could well have been spelled *misery*. Although it's the location of Mormonism's most significant sites, Missouri was also where the early Mormons suffered some of their worst persecutions. In the Mormon mind, that equation makes perfect spiritual sense: the greater the potential good, the greater Satan's opposition.

Persecution starts again

With about 1,200 Mormons living in Jackson County by the summer of 1833 (almost a third of the total local population), other settlers began to worry — and not without good reason — that the Mormons would soon overtake them politically, economically, and culturally. Encouraged by local government officials, a large mob formed in July 1833 to force the Mormons out of Jackson County. They destroyed the Mormon printing office, tarred and feathered leaders, and burned down homes and businesses. Even after the Mormons signed an agreement to leave within several months, daily harassment and violence continued. When appeals to the state government didn't do a lick of good, the Missouri Mormons started arming themselves against the mob, and soon the state militia was called out.

In November 1833, after a second attack in which over 200 Mormon cabins were robbed or burned, the Mormons left Jackson County months earlier than originally agreed. Many of them lost everything they owned. Crossing the Missouri River, they found temporary winter shelter among friendlier settlers in Clay County. Church leaders took their complaints and pleas not only to the Missouri governor but also all the way to the U.S. president, Andrew Jackson. However, fearful of open warfare, the government and courts didn't intervene. Thus, the Church lost its all-important Zion homeland — for the time being, anyway.

Trying to stay in Missouri

If the Mormons couldn't live in Zion, at least they could put down temporary roots nearby while they kept petitioning the government to reclaim their rightful Jackson County properties. For over a year, the local settlers across the river in Clay County allowed the Mormons to live peaceably among them. New converts kept arriving, and Mormons started buying up property. Disregarding a prophetic warning from Joseph Smith, individuals openly spoke of taking over the area. By 1836, the locals again began to resent the Mormons.

Clay County locals, however, took a more civilized, diplomatic approach to ridding themselves of the Mormons than did their Jackson County counterparts, refraining from violence and negotiating comparatively reasonable agreements. When Mormon explorers found some sparsely populated land in northern Missouri, Church leaders asked the government to set aside territory for the Mormons to call their own. In December 1836 the state created Caldwell County just for the Mormons.

With a temporary homeland secured, the Mormons started building a new city called Far West and establishing other settlements in the area. Despite the promising new arrangements, however, hostilities started festering again. When some Mormons threatened violence against a handful of internal troublemakers living in Far West, these rebels fled, triggering anti-Mormon feelings in nearby communities. An underground gang known as the *Danites* arose, falsely claiming that Church leaders authorized them to use extreme measures — including robbery and murder — against Mormonism's enemies.

Although the Church didn't sanction the Danites' activities, the words of some Mormon leaders seemed to justify such actions. On Independence Day in 1838, Sidney Rigdon delivered a no-tolerance pledge against any future persecutors. Although the Mormons had repeatedly taken the abuse without fighting back, Rigdon declared that they wouldn't do so anymore. Unfortunately, copies of this speech circulated widely in pamphlet form.

Going to war

Tensions continued to increase between the Mormons and their non-Mormon neighbors. After a brawl broke out when residents of a nearby county tried to stop some Mormons from voting, anti-Mormon agitation swept throughout Missouri. Joseph Smith, who had recently moved to Missouri, submitted to arrest on false charges, but his action didn't diffuse the hostility. Soon both sides began forming militias, capturing prisoners, and robbing each other. Mob militias invaded settlements, destroyed property, and tortured Mormons, many of whom fled to Far West.

Believing exaggerated reports of Mormon "outrages," Missouri governor Lilburn W. Boggs signed an infamous order in October 1838 stating that the Mormons must either be killed or driven entirely from the state, an order that wasn't officially repealed until 1976.

During the Mormon War, most of the Mormon deaths occurred at the small settlement of Haun's Mill. On the afternoon of October 30, 1838, a mob of over 200 men attacked the settlement, shooting at Mormon men, women, and children alike. In a blacksmith shop, a concealed 7-year-old boy watched the invaders kill his father and 10-year-old brother. Later justifying the boy's murder, the triggerman said, "Nits will make lice, and if he had lived he would have become a Mormon."

At least 17 Mormons died in the massacre, with another 13 wounded. Only three Missourians were injured. Joseph Smith lamented that the slain Saints would've been spared if they'd followed his direction and fled earlier to Far West. About 20 years later, a desire to avenge Haun's Mill was one factor that helped motivate some Mormons to commit a much worse massacre; for more on that, see Chapter 13.

At the end of October 1838, approximately 2,000 mob soldiers surrounded the barricaded Far West, outnumbering the Mormon soldiers five to one. Apostle Parley P. Pratt recorded that many in the mob disguised themselves as Indians and were making a racket like "bloodhounds let loose upon their prey." A Mormon military commander made a secret deal to end the standoff, putting Joseph Smith and other Church leaders into the hands of the mob.

Meanwhile, the again-impoverished Latter-day Saints crossed the Mississippi River eastward into Illinois (see Figure 11-2 for a map of their journey). For many, it was their fifth forced exodus in less than a decade. When Missouri officials eventually decided they couldn't convict Joseph on charges of murder and treason, they allowed him to escape in April 1839 and rejoin his exiled people in Illinois. Before long, they built a beautiful city that, by 1846, rivaled Chicago in population.

Figure 11-2:
Map of the Mormon migrations from New York to Ohio, Missouri, and Illinois.

Missouri in the here and now

Mormons still believe that they'll eventually reclaim Jackson County as the center of Zion. In the meantime, they believe that Zion exists in the hearts and minds of the righteous, as well as wherever a stake of the Church exists. (The term *stake* is Mormonism's equivalent of *diocese,* meaning a grouping of local congregations; see Chapter 6.) As odd as it may sound to outsiders, Mormons believe they'll someday build the New Jerusalem at Independence, Missouri, which is now a suburb of Kansas City. This long-prophesied city will serve as Jesus Christ's headquarters during the Millennium, the 1,000-year period of paradise ushered in by his Second Coming (see Chapter 3).

Today, three competing Mormon-related groups own portions of the Independence land where Joseph Smith identified that a temple should be built. A small offshoot known as the Church of Christ (Temple Lot) controls the spot where Joseph actually stood. The Community of Christ, the same denomination that now owns the Kirtland Temple in Ohio, has built two significant structures at the site, a tabernacle and a beautiful temple that is open to the public and bears almost no functional resemblance to the temples of the Utah-based Church. In addition, the LDS Church built a visitors' center at the site.

Nauvoo, Illinois: A Refuge on the Mississippi

After the devastating persecutions of Missouri, the Mormons welcomed the shelter of Illinois, where they were granted their own community on the banks of the Mississippi. The Mormons named it *Nauvoo*, a Hebrew word meaning "beautiful, lovely, or comely." Under the terms of their charter from the state of Illinois, the Mormons received the following:

- ✔ A court system through which they could be tried by judges elected by the Nauvoo residents themselves, with juries composed of Nauvoo residents. This factor was important because it meant that no court could come up with false charges just to persecute — or, more literally, prosecute — the Mormons.

- ✔ A state-authorized militia, the Nauvoo Legion, with as many as 5,000 men. After the Haun's Mill Massacre and the violence in Missouri, the Mormons were glad for a chance to protect themselves if the need arose. (Not surprisingly, it eventually did.)

- ✔ A liberal amount of land and great opportunities for economic prosperity through the profitable Mississippi River trade.

Come on over!

The Nauvoo period marked the first significant migration of Mormon converts from England and continental Europe. In 1840, Brigham Young noted that even if he and other missionaries had tried to prevent the British Latter-day Saints from emigrating, they wouldn't have been able to stop them. Part of the appeal was certainly religious — in Nauvoo they could live among other Latter-day Saints, meet the prophet Joseph Smith, and enjoy the blessings of the temple under construction. But the reasons were economic as well; many of the European converts were poor or working class, and America offered them cheap land and much more opportunity for economic advancement.

Between 1840 and 1846, approximately 4,800 British converts made the voyage, braving the Atlantic Ocean in passenger ships and then taking steamboats up the Mississippi to Nauvoo.

Building a community

When winter turned to spring and the Mormons set about building their new community in earnest, they got some good news: Joseph Smith was freed by his Missouri jailer and permitted to join the Latter-day Saints in Nauvoo. With Smith to lead them, the Mormons were confident that they could make the city flourish.

However, the reality was that they'd settled in a mosquito-infested swamp. Many of the already weakened Saints got malaria, and Joseph and Emma Smith filled every bed in their home with ill Church members, moving their own family to a tent in the yard. Eventually Joseph and other members of his family became ill as well.

Mormons are known as planners (case in point: the Franklin Planner system, which was invented by a Mormon), and the early days of the religion were no exception. Despite the hurried purchase of the land and the onset of disease when the Mormons settled there, the city was carefully planned to the last detail. Because Nauvoo was intended to be as self-sufficient as possible, individual family lots were large: each city block was 4 acres, divided into 1-acre plots. Here, the Mormons could raise livestock and enough crops to sustain themselves. As the city grew, they divided many of those 1-acre lots into quarter-acres to accommodate the newcomers.

Constructing the Nauvoo Temple

In April 1841, the Latter-day Saints laid the cornerstones for what would become the Nauvoo Temple, an enormous limestone structure that housed their most sacred rituals. With almost 50,000 square feet of interior space, it was the largest building the Saints had ever attempted — three times the size of the Kirtland Temple. Construction of the temple was an arduous five-year process, and tragically, the Prophet was killed before he could see its completion.

The temple funding came from the *tithe* of the Latter-day Saints — defined as 10 percent of their "increase," whether in cash, quilts, chickens, jewelry, food, or other items. Many of Nauvoo's men gave a tithe of their time, working every tenth day to build the temple rather than doing their usual jobs. The women of the community sewed shirts for the construction workers, and the Church asked each sister to donate a penny each week — a significant sum for the time — to purchase supplies.

One of the most distinctive features of the Nauvoo Temple was the symbolism of the sun, moon, and stars carved into its limestone exterior. (For an example of a sunstone, see Figure 11-3.) At the base of its 30 stone columns, the temple featured a quarter-moon facing downward, and each capstone bore an image of a rising sun. Also dotting the temple's frieze were stars that extended around the top of the building. This symbolism — sun, moon, and the stars above them — may be a reference to the third chapter of the Book of Abraham, part of the Pearl of Great Price (see Chapter 10). This scripture refers to the sun, moon, and stars and their proximity to God. Another possible explanation is that the symbols represent the three degrees of glory in the afterlife: the stars for the *telestial* kingdom, the moon for the *terrestrial,* and the sun for the *celestial* kingdom, the highest tier of heaven. For more on the three degrees, see Chapter 2.

Figure 11-3:
Nauvoo
Temple
sunstone.

Although the Kirtland Temple served primarily as an assembly hall or chapel and housed many different kinds of functions, the Nauvoo Temple represented a whole new order. Or rather, a whole *old* order, as the Latter-day Saints believed that the rituals Joseph Smith taught them in the 1840s were part of the Lord's restoration of ancient ideas. Although Mormons used the middle floors of the temple for public meetings, they reserved the top and bottom floors for these ordinances, including baptism for the dead, endowment, and celestial marriage. (For more info on these and other temple ordinances, refer to Chapter 7.)

Trouble in Nauvoo

In 1844, anti-Mormon sentiment spilled over once again. Some of the reasons this time were familiar from the Ohio and Missouri days: The Mormons became very powerful, with a population of more than 20,000 people, making Nauvoo the largest town in Illinois at the time. They were prosperous, and people considered their doctrines strange.

But there were other reasons as well, and the Mormons weren't entirely blameless victims of persecution. Many people in Illinois and elsewhere worried that Joseph Smith had accumulated too much power. He was mayor of the city, leader of the Church, and the lieutenant general of Illinois's largest militia force. He also ran for President of the United States in 1844.

After several key Mormons left the Church in 1842 and 1843, they publicized the Prophet's then-secret teaching of plural marriage, which had been the reason for their leaving. They challenged polygamy and claimed it was an insult to Christian morality (to better understand the Mormon rationale, see Chapter 13). In June 1844 the protesters printed a rival newspaper, the *Nauvoo Expositor,* in which they publicly exposed polygamy and claimed that Joseph Smith was a fraud. They demanded the repeal of the Nauvoo Charter, saying that the Mormons had violated its provisions by merging church and state too closely.

Joseph Smith, as mayor of Nauvoo, called his city council together and deliberated with them. In the end, they decided that the press was a public nuisance and that its printers were disturbers of the peace. But instead of closing it down, which would've been legal, Smith instructed the city marshal to "destroy the printing press, scatter the type in the street, and burn all remaining copies of the newspaper and its advertising handbills," as one LDS historian summarized. In doing so the Prophet may have overstepped his legal bounds and verified the charges against him: that he inappropriately meshed religion and government.

Arrest and martyrdom

Joseph Smith's mistake in handling the *Expositor* debacle had fatal consequences. All over the state, anti-Mormon sentiment was stirred into a frenzy, and agitators often urged citizens to take action against the Mormons. Reacting to such attitudes — and undoubtedly remembering the violent persecutions of Missouri — Smith used the Nauvoo Charter and encouraged all Mormon men to prepare to defend Nauvoo if an attack should come. He held a full-regalia militia rally during which he told the men not to initiate an attack but to defend their families if necessary.

The governor of Illinois traveled up to Carthage, the county seat, to hear evidence on both sides of the matter. He ruled that Smith and the city council had violated the protesters' constitutional rights by unlawfully taking and destroying their property and by not heeding the law by allowing a jury trial.

The Prophet fled Nauvoo in an attempt to draw public hostility away from the city and its people. However, after hearing that the governor intended to bring him to trial and had pledged full protection for him, Smith returned to Nauvoo and surrendered. He also laid down the state-owned weapons used by the Nauvoo Legion, hoping along with the governor to avoid an armed conflict.

Accompanied by his brother Hyrum and several other men, Joseph Smith was arrested and put in a small second-floor jail in Carthage. In the early evening of June 27, 1844, a mob of about 200 armed men surrounded the building, their faces painted brown or black. Some rushed into the building and up the stairs, where the Smiths and their companions tried to hold the door and fire their own pistols at the intruders. Joseph's beloved older brother Hyrum was killed instantly in the fray. When members of the mob glimpsed Joseph looking through a second-story window, reportedly lifting his arms in the Masonic signal of distress, they shot him. Smith fell through the window to the ground below, where the mob shot him several more times and then stabbed him with a bayonet.

The Mormons were horrified by the news that Joseph and his brother Hyrum had been killed. Contrary to the expectations of many of their Illinois neighbors, they didn't react violently to the martyrdom. However, their troubles weren't over; within two years, the people of Illinois were again gunning for the Mormons and made it clear that they had to leave the state or face consequences — continued violence, robbery, and maybe even death. The Mormons decided to pack up and head out; see the next chapter for more on their famous trek west to what later became Salt Lake City. They were heartbroken to leave their beautiful city and temple, but they looked forward to a place of refuge in the West.

Although nine men were tried for the murders of Joseph and Hyrum, they were all acquitted. In 2004, the Illinois legislature formally expressed regret for the assassinations and for the later expulsion of Mormons from Nauvoo.

Nauvoo in the here and now

For almost a century after the Mormons abandoned Nauvoo, the area saw little development or progress. The temple was gutted by arson not long after the Mormons left the city, and a tornado finished the destruction in 1850.

Gradually, however, the Mormon presence returned. In the 1930s, the LDS Church regained the land where the Nauvoo Temple stood before its destruction. In the 1950s, Dr. J. LeRoy Kimball — grandfather of coauthor Christopher Kimball Bigelow — acquired and started restoring the still-standing redbrick home of Dr. Kimball's great-grandfather, Heber C. Kimball, who served as a right-hand apostle to both Joseph Smith and Brigham Young (another main man in Mormon history, who we discuss in Chapter 12). Dr. Kimball originally intended the home for private family use, but hundreds of people asked to tour the building. Within a few years, Dr. Kimball was spearheading the restoration of 1840s-era Mormon buildings throughout old Nauvoo, with LDS Church financing and oversight.

Today, Nauvoo is the world's second most visited Mormon location, after Temple Square in Salt Lake City, and has been called the "Williamsburg of the Midwest." Although the town has only about 1,500 permanent residents, it attracts upwards of 350,000 tourists each year, which isn't always a source of joy to all the locals. Recently the LDS Church built a fully functioning replica of the Nauvoo Temple on the original site, prompting reverent celebration throughout the faith. (Check out Chapter 21 for a picture of this temple.)

Chapter 12

Moving on to Utah with Brigham Young

. . . .

In This Chapter

▶ Regrouping after the death of Joseph Smith

▶ Following Brigham Young

▶ Surviving the pioneer trek

▶ Suffering internal divisions

. . . .

The Mormons in Nauvoo, Illinois, were devastated by the assassinations of Joseph Smith and his brother, Hyrum, in the neighboring town of Carthage. But soon enough, they found that they could survive, and even thrive, without their beloved founding prophet. In this chapter, we talk about the critical period after Joseph Smith's death, a time when several competing groups fought for leadership of the Mormon movement and angry Illinois neighbors drove the Latter-day Saints out of Nauvoo.

We also introduce you to Brigham Young, who led the majority of Latter-day Saints west in one of the greatest mass migrations in American history. After their ill-fated stints in Ohio, Missouri, and finally Illinois, this group of Mormons headed for Utah, which was then outside the borders of the United States. They hoped that this time their settlement would be for keeps.

A Crisis of Leadership

In today's Utah-based LDS Church, when a Church president dies, a whole system is in place to make sure that the transition to the next president is smooth and uneventful. The most senior member of the Quorum of the Twelve Apostles almost immediately becomes the next prophet and president. When Joseph Smith was killed in 1844, however, the Church hadn't devised an orderly succession process, and Church members weren't sure at the outset how to fill Joseph's shoes. Several people seemed to have legitimate claims to leadership, including the following:

- ✔ Joseph's young son, Joseph Smith III, who received a blessing in the spring of 1844 from his father, which some Mormons believed indicated that one day he'd become prophet.

- ✔ Sidney Rigdon, Joseph's friend and counselor in the First Presidency.

- ✔ Joseph's older brother Samuel, who was the candidate that the Smith family favored the most, at least until Joseph III could come of age. However, Samuel died in July 1844, only a month after his brothers Joseph and Hyrum.

- ✔ Brigham Young, the president of the Quorum of the Twelve.

- ✔ James J. Strang, a recent convert from Wisconsin, who came to Nauvoo announcing that he received a revelation in which God directed him to lead the Church. Church members cooled their heels and didn't make their decision immediately. Shortly after Joseph was killed, they voted unanimously to keep the whole Quorum of the Twelve as a sort of interim presidency. As the quorum's president, Brigham consolidated some (but by no means all) of the various LDS-affiliated groups and, under pressure from local mobs, planned a mass exodus to the Rocky Mountains.

The Lion of the Lord: Brigham Young

Many Latter-day Saints have called Brigham Young the "lion of the Lord" because of his fierce loyalty to the Mormon cause. He was also a lion in longevity, serving the Church for roughly 30 years — longer than any other LDS president. So who was Brigham Young, and how did he come to lead the Latter-day Saints? In this section, we look at this capable and colorful commander in chief, describing his personal life as well as his ability to lead the Church in turbulent times. For a peek at what he looked like, see Figure 12-1.

Figure 12-1: A portrait of Brigham Young, an effective leader in difficult times.

Image courtesy of Community of Christ Archives, Independence, Missouri

Another unschooled boy from Vermont

As you can see from the following table, Brigham shared some interesting parallels in heritage and upbringing with Joseph Smith, the first prophet and president of the LDS Church.

Joseph Smith	*Brigham Young*
Born in 1805	Born in 1801
From rural Vermont	From rural Vermont
5th of 11 children	9th of 11 children
Poor, hardworking farm family	Poor, hardworking farm family
Very little formal schooling	Only 11 days of formal schooling
Moved to upstate New York as a boy	Moved to upstate New York as a boy

Both boys grew up in large families and faced some difficult times. Sadly, Brigham lost his mother to tuberculosis when he was just 14. He left home a couple of years later to make his way as a carpenter, painter, and glazer. A hard worker, Brigham spent his 20s as a skilled craftsman, constructing houses and making furniture. These practical skills served him well when the time came to plan and build the new settlement of Salt Lake City, Utah (for more on settling in the West, see Chapter 13).

Becoming a leader in the Church

Brigham and his young wife, Miriam, discovered the Book of Mormon in 1830, when they received a copy from a family member. When some missionaries came to talk about the book, Brigham asked them to give Miriam a blessing because she was ill. The missionaries expressed their testimonies, and Brigham said that hearing their words "was like a fire in my bones . . . it was light, intelligence, power, and truth." He and Miriam joined the LDS Church in April 1832, using their own millpond in Mendon, New York, for baptisms. Brigham's father, brother, and sisters were also baptized, and all remained Latter-day Saints for the rest of their lives.

After he lost Miriam to tuberculosis later that year, Brigham threw himself with characteristic determination into the fledgling religious movement. He became a trusted friend of the Prophet Joseph Smith and swiftly rose in the ranks of the organization. Here's a quick rundown:

✔ Brigham gained the Latter-day Saints' confidence when he took charge of their flight from Missouri back across the Mississippi River to Illinois in 1838.

✔ He went on several preaching missions, including one to England from 1840 to 1841.

✔ He was instrumental in organizing the emigration of many British converts to Nauvoo and in establishing the LDS Church in the British Isles.

✔ At the time of Joseph Smith's death in June 1844, Brigham was the president of the Quorum of the Twelve.

Before his martyrdom, Joseph Smith was campaigning to become president of the United States. At the time Brigham heard the sad news about his friend's death, he was in the eastern United States combining preaching and political campaigning to make converts to Mormonism who would vote for the Prophet to head the nation.

With a heavy heart, Brigham returned to Nauvoo, where he found the Church in disarray. He and the other 11 apostles quickly asserted their leadership. In a famous episode in Mormon history, Brigham spoke at an outdoor prayer meeting and seemed, at least to some of his hearers, to supernaturally take on the voice and appearance of the dead Prophet Joseph Smith. One audience member, Benjamin Johnson, said, "As soon as he spoke I jumped upon my feet, for in every possible degree it was Joseph's voice, and his person, in look, attitude, dress, and appearance. . . . I knew in a moment the spirit and mantle of Joseph was upon him." For many Latter-day Saints, this event seemed like a miracle and an answer to prayer: God was making it clear to them that Brigham should be their new boss.

Because of the difficulties of the westward trek, Brigham wasn't officially sustained as president of the Church until December 1847, three and a half years after he spoke in the Nauvoo meeting. But the time in between only further proved his determination in leading the Church through one of its toughest periods.

Famous leader and down-to-earth family man

One thing you can say about Brigham Young is that he lived large, both in his public life and behind the scenes. Although Brigham originally resisted when he learned of the doctrine of *polygamy,* or plural marriage (see Chapter 13), he married again after Miriam's death . . . a couple dozen times (including getting hitched to two daughters of Nahum Bigelow, another of coauthor Christopher Bigelow's great-great-great-grandfathers). Brigham was the father of 56 children by 16 of his wives and was by most accounts a loving and involved parent. His personality was firm and steadfast, yet affectionate. He was a man of deep loyalty and constant practicality. He preached economy, frugality, moral behavior, and hard work.

Brigham's leadership style differed a great deal from the first prophet; Joseph was the dreamer, but Brigham was the builder of the kingdom. American history is full of prophets and charismatic founding religious leaders, but what distinguished Mormonism as a successful religious sect wasn't just the quality of its founder, but the quality of his successor. Most other movements failed because no one who survived the founder was capable of carrying out his or her vision.

Today you'd call Brigham a micromanager, because delegating responsibility doesn't seem to have been his strong suit. Most Mormons feel that this quality was one main reason why they needed his leadership at this point in their history. Without Brigham's intense interest in and keen attention to all the tiny details of building the kingdom, the movement may not have thrived. He was methodical and detail oriented, with apparently inexhaustible energy.

Brigham served as president of the Church and governor of the territory of Utah for many years simultaneously, sitting on the board of trustees of numerous businesses and utility companies all the while. (This apparent mixing of religion, government, and commerce made some people uncomfortable, but Brigham felt that having centralized leadership in Utah was important. Today, the separation between church and state in Utah usually stays clearer.)

A legacy to build on

Brigham Young died in 1877 of a ruptured appendix, having served as president and prophet for nearly 30 years. He's famous for many reasons, from his numerous wives (inquiring minds everywhere debate about how many he actually had, by the way) to his unflagging commitment to Mormon independence. Here are a few of his main accomplishments:

- **He welcomed Latter-day Saints of many different nations to Utah, making Salt Lake City a melting pot of Euro American peoples.** On the other hand, Brigham was primarily responsible for establishing the legacy of 19th-century racism that prohibited anyone of African descent from holding the priesthood until 1978; see Chapter 15 for more about that scar on Mormon history.

- **He furthered Joseph Smith's insistence on Mormon independence, saying that the Latter-day Saints should be self-sufficient in every possible way.** To this day, you can trace back to Brigham's presidency the programs that Mormons use to stay out of debt, store food and supplies for emergencies, and help one another. America's first department store, the *Zion Cooperative Mercantile Institution (ZCMI),* was founded under his direction to help the Latter-day Saints keep their economic dealings under their own control.

- ✔ **Although he was unschooled himself, he believed strongly in the value of education.** He founded three colleges, including the institutions that became Brigham Young University (see Chapter 8) and the University of Utah, which today are archrivals. He also sent many Latter-day Saint men and women to the East Coast in the late 19th century for their educations. Under Brigham's initiative, Mormon women were among the first women in America to become physicians.

- ✔ **He instilled in the Latter-day Saints a respect for hard work.** He reveled in work and expected his fellow Mormons to toe the line too. "I have the grit in me," he once said, "and I will do my duty anyhow."

- ✔ **He has many descendants who are visible participants in Mormon life today.** One such descendant is the NFL's former Most Valuable Player, quarterback Steve Young (football fans, see Chapter 19 for more on him).

Westward Ho! The Pioneer Experience

In the summer of 1997, thousands of Mormons participated in a three-month reenactment of the 1846 to 1847 pioneer trek that Brigham led. Beginning in Nauvoo and ending triumphantly in the Salt Lake Valley, these modern-day pioneers endured mosquito invasions, torrential rain, and bloody foot blisters in their quest to understand their ancestors' sacrifices. Some stayed for the whole three months, while others popped in for just a few days to get a taste of the experience. Some less-hardy folks followed along in air-conditioned RVs.

Why did they undertake this reenactment? For Mormons, the pioneers aren't just long-dead people who baked corn bread, sang hymns all day, and wore ankle-length dresses. Mormons today hold up their example as the ideal for what modern Latter-day Saints should be: patient in suffering and willing to sacrifice almost everything for the Savior and his church. (In fact, Church leaders often trot out the pioneer example to spur on contemporary Mormons to better behavior. For example, in *Primary,* the Sunday School program for LDS children, kids learn a song called "Pioneer Children Were Quick to Obey." Sheesh.)

When Mormons speak of the *pioneer trek,* they're not talking about one journey, but many. From 1846 until the railroad reached Salt Lake City in 1869, an estimated 70,000 Mormons made the journey to Utah on foot or in wagons. About 3,000 of them lost their lives on the way. In this section, you find out about the pioneers and their courage in difficult circumstances.

Packing up and leaving Illinois

Mormons today know a great deal about their ancestors' mass exodus to the Rocky Mountains. Although Brigham Young led the migration, it was actually Joseph Smith's idea; while he was still alive, Joseph proposed sending scouts west to investigate the possibility of a new home for the Latter-day Saints. The plan to go west sped up as a result of the ill feeling in Illinois toward the Mormons, who were ordered out of the state in 1846 (see Chapter 11). Mobs burned the homes of Mormon families and poisoned their wells (including the well of Nahum Bigelow, who later died from internal damage caused by mob poison). With heavy hearts, the Mormons reconciled themselves to the idea that they would have to leave their beautiful city of Nauvoo, selling their possessions for far less than they were worth, sometimes for just a few livestock. Although Mormon families lost out on these trades, the livestock proved to be useful for what was coming next: more than a year of overland travel in dangerous conditions.

Pioneer Day: Break out the corn bread!

A calico-clad woman carries a wriggling toddler in one arm and a cellphone in the other. Brass bands strike up patriotic songs in the town square, while young men compete against each other in a log-splitting contest. A parade marches down the main street, featuring folks dressed in sunbonnets and string ties but riding on flatbed trucks. Is this fiesta a time-travel experiment gone horribly awry?

Not quite; it's a Pioneer Day celebration. On July 24, Mormons everywhere break out the corn bread to commemorate the sacrifices and the courage of the pioneers. In Utah, the day is actually a state holiday. In other parts of the country, Mormons go about their business as usual, but many find ways to mark the day with special events: cookouts, minitreks (to get a taste of the pioneer experience), and concerts. Despite the fact that the original pioneers specifically wanted to get *away* from United States influence, Pioneer Day is now a patriotic holiday for Mormons in America, with U.S. flags flying and more fireworks than the Fourth of July. And of course, they enjoy lots of food, although the green Jell-O salad that

Mormons are famous for isn't a historically accurate representation of what their ancestors actually ate on the trail. The bounty of the modern Mormon table on Pioneer Day, loaded with hot dogs, potato salad, and baked beans, reminds Mormons of the heroic sacrifices of the pioneers, some of whom died of starvation on the trail.

As Mormonism has spread outside the United States and become a world religion, Pioneer Day celebrations have multiplied as well, though nowadays Mormons in other countries are likely to use the time to remember their own nations' Mormon pioneers and early converts. In 1997, the 150th anniversary of the Mormons' arrival in Utah, President Gordon B. Hinckley emphasized the global nature of Pioneer Day when he declared it a day of service for Mormons everywhere. Mormons rolled up their sleeves to give blood, made pioneer-style homemade quilts for the needy, and volunteered their services in soup kitchens all over the world on that day. Most felt it was a perfect tribute to the spirit of the pioneers.

The first company

When the Mormons began fleeing Nauvoo early in 1846, Brigham led a group across the frozen Mississippi River to Iowa to rest and figure out their route for the rest of the way. Although the cold was a real hardship for the shivering Mormons, Brigham believed that the river froze as a result of God's provision, allowing them to flee tough times in Illinois just as the ancient Israelites escaped from Egypt through the miraculous parting of the Red Sea (check out Exodus 14 in the Bible). This move was to be a new exodus, another example of God leading people from oppression to a promised land.

However, just as the Israelites experienced a rough time in the wilderness, the Latter-day Saints' journey was no picnic. They encountered famine and disease and sometimes challenged their leaders, wondering aloud whether God had abandoned them. But they also enjoyed a few miracles along the way. In October 1846, for example, some hungry Mormons on the trek experienced what they called "the miracle of the quail" — the sudden landing of flocks of quail in the Mormon camp. The people scooped up the birds, praising God and likening this unexpected bounty to the time when God provided quail to the Israelites in the wilderness (see Exodus 16). One feature of this first pioneer trek was its strict organization according to the pattern the Israelites followed under Moses' leadership. Brigham divided the company into groups of 10, 50, and 100. The leader of each group of 10 reported to the leader of each group of 50, who in turn reported to the leader of each group of 100. This chain of command helped ensure that everyone was accounted for and that they'd help each other if someone's oxen became sick or a wagon wheel got stuck in the mud. Some of the highlights (and lowlights) of this first group included

- ✔ **Composition of the hymn "Come, Come Ye Saints," by English convert William Clayton:** Mormons still sing this song every Pioneer Day and on almost any occasion when they remember the pioneers. This tune acknowledges the hardships and deaths of loved ones on the trail but affirms a hope in God with the refrain, "All is well, all is well." Because this song is one of the signature numbers of the world-famous Mormon Tabernacle Choir (see Chapter 18), many people outside the faith are familiar with it.

- ✔ **Recruitment of 500 Mormon men to serve as United States soldiers in the Mexican War:** In exchange for federal protection as the Mormons were wintering on Indian land, the government asked — or more like *ordered* — the Mormons to provide 500 military volunteers. Despite the fact that they were defending the same government that allowed its citizens to drive them from their homes, Mormon men dutifully went off to war, marching 2,000 miles to San Diego — one of the longest infantry treks in American history.

- ✔ **Terrible months at Winter Quarters, a temporary settlement on the border between Iowa and Nebraska:** Hundreds died from starvation and exposure during the cruel winter of 1846–1847. In some cases, survivors couldn't even bury the dead because the ground was frozen solid.

- ✔ **Preparation along the way for future groups of pioneers:** Because the first company knew they would be followed by many other groups of Mormons, they planted crops and prepared the land so that later Mormon emigrants would have food to eat during the journey. This set a pattern for the cooperative, organized Mormon approach to trail living: Each group harvested some crops and tried to plant others for the folks still to come.

- ✔ **Triumphant arrival in the Salt Lake Valley on July 24, 1847:** Actually, make that July 23. Although Mormons celebrate Pioneer Day on the 24th, most of the members of the first company arrived the day before. By the time an ill Brigham Young brought up the rear on the 24th, the busy Latter-day Saints had already started planting crops and diverting water to irrigate them. See Figure 12-2 for a map of their entire trek.

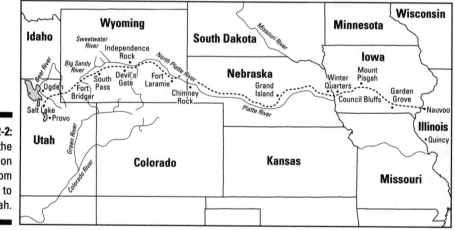

Figure 12-2: Map of the Mormon trek from Illinois to Utah.

The handcart experience

After the initial trek from Illinois, converts to Mormonism in the United States, Canada, and Europe continued to emigrate to join the main body of the Church in Utah. In the 1850s, Brigham and other Church leaders came up with a great idea for helping poorer Latter-day Saints get there. Many converts, especially those from England and Scandinavia, were from the poorest classes of society, and crossing the ocean *and* the plains, when they couldn't afford wagons to carry their belongings, was a huge financial hardship for them.

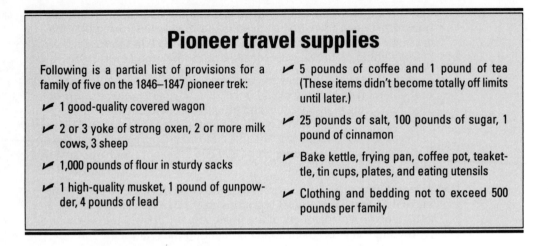

Pioneer travel supplies

Following is a partial list of provisions for a family of five on the 1846–1847 pioneer trek:

✔ 1 good-quality covered wagon

✔ 2 or 3 yoke of strong oxen, 2 or more milk cows, 3 sheep

✔ 1,000 pounds of flour in sturdy sacks

✔ 1 high-quality musket, 1 pound of gunpowder, 4 pounds of lead

✔ 5 pounds of coffee and 1 pound of tea (These items didn't become totally off limits until later.)

✔ 25 pounds of salt, 100 pounds of sugar, 1 pound of cinnamon

✔ Bake kettle, frying pan, coffee pot, teakettle, tin cups, plates, and eating utensils

✔ Clothing and bedding not to exceed 500 pounds per family

The Church's solution was human-powered handcarts, rickshaw-like miniwagons that a strong adult could pull. (To see what a handcart looked like, check out Figure 12-3.) Because the carts were small, each person was limited to 17 pounds of baggage on the journey. Others used the carts to pull small children so they didn't have to walk the 1,200 miles from the usual jumping-off place at the Missouri River to the Salt Lake Valley.

Figure 12-3:
Handcarts are an instantly recognizable symbol of the pioneer experience.

Most *handcart companies* (emigrant trains of several hundred people making their way along the trail) reached their destination without too many mishaps — a broken wheel here, an outbreak of cholera there. But Mormons remember all the handcart companies as tragic because of the unforgettable heartbreak experienced by two of the expeditions, led by James Willie and Edward Martin.

Most companies departed in late spring or early summer at the latest, but the Willie-Martin emigrants suffered numerous delays and didn't get moving until late July 1856. Wondering whether to press on and risk winter weather or wait until the following spring, they voted almost unanimously to continue — a decision they'd come to regret. Winter arrived early and was especially fierce that year, and by October both companies became trapped in Wyoming blizzards. Their provisions gradually gave out, and many died of starvation and exposure.

At the Church's General Conference in October, Brigham told members to go rescue the mired handcart companies. The ever-practical leader enlisted the help of 40 young men and dozens of animals and wagons to leave immediately. Although they were able to save most of the people, casualties were tragically high: 68 of 404 people in the Willie company died, and the death toll in the Martin company was even worse: 145 of 576. Several of the rescuers also lost their lives. (For more about modern-day handcart reenactments at Martin's Cove, Wyoming, see Chapter 21.)

Although pioneers used handcarts for only a few years and only a small fraction of the pioneers used them (about 3,000 of 70,000), this invention has become a recognizable, poignant symbol of the whole pioneer era. When Mormons see a picture of a handcart (and they're hard to miss in Church literature and history books), they think of the pioneers who suffered cruelly yet forged ahead to their promised land.

Keep 'em coming: The Perpetual Emigrating Fund

To help aid European Mormons who converted abroad but wanted to gather with the Latter-day Saints in Utah, the organizationally minded Brigham Young established a revolving fund to meet their needs. The *Perpetual Emigrating Fund (PEF),* which began in 1849, paid expenses for about 50,000 converts as they bought sea passage, crossed the plains, and settled in Utah.

This fund wasn't a free lunch, but it was an interest-free loan. The idea behind the PEF was that emigrants would pay the money back as soon as they became established in their new home, replenishing the fund so other families could borrow for their journeys. (Not everyone was able to pay the loans in full, but that was the original intent.) Brigham encouraged European

Church leaders to choose those families who seemed most committed to the Church and had already proven their faithfulness; that way, the Church wouldn't waste money on people who were just seeking a free trip to America.

By the late 1850s, the PEF was like a well-oiled machine. Emigration became more difficult during the early 1860s because of the U.S. Civil War but picked up again in the 1870s. The LDS Church had to discontinue the program in 1887, when the federal government froze the Church's assets in an attempt to stop polygamy; see Chapter 13 for the story of that trial.

Today, the Church's Perpetual *Education* Fund is modeled on the old emigration program. Through the Education Fund, young Latter-day Saints in designated needy nations can receive loans from the Church to get college or vocational educations in their homelands. Many of the recipients are returned missionaries who've already donated 18 to 24 months of missionary service to the Church. After they finish their education and establish a career, they repay the loan so that other students can receive financial assistance. Since the fund was established in 2001, the Perpetual Education Fund has helped more than 13,000 applicants.

Mormon Groups That Didn't Go West

All this talk of pioneers, trails, and hardships ignores one very important fact: Not all the Latter-day Saints went west with Brother Brigham.

In the crucial period after Joseph Smith's death, when prophetic succession seemed uncertain, the Church split into several groups. Although the largest group by far followed the then-unofficial leadership of Brigham Young and started braving the plains on the way to Utah, several other Mormon-related groups stayed behind, putting down roots in the Midwest.

Sometimes, the differences between the groups were personal, stemming from a dislike of Brigham or other LDS leaders. As Jan Shipps, historian and technical reviewer for this book, makes clear in her work, some Mormons in this period remained within the fold only because of Joseph Smith's charismatic leadership. When he was killed, some of them lost heart.

Most of the time, however, the differences among Joseph's followers were about religious belief and practice. Many who didn't follow Brigham believed that some of the practices that Joseph introduced in the Nauvoo period — including polygamy, the temple endowment, and baptism for the dead — didn't reflect the Lord's original intent for the Church. They wanted to "restore the restoration" — in other words, get the Church back to what they thought it was at its founding in 1830.

Some Utah-based Latter-day Saints (who in the 19th century were sometimes called *Brighamites* because they chose Brigham as their leader) remain pretty ignorant of the beliefs and practices of these other Mormon-related groups. Often, their first real encounter with these groups occurs when they visit Mormon history sites in Kirtland, Ohio; Independence, Missouri; and Nauvoo, Illinois, where other Mormon-related denominations own various buildings that are important in their shared history. (For instance, the Community of Christ owns the Kirtland Temple, as we mention in Chapter 11.) Sometimes, first exposure happens in other contexts — one LDS friend of coauthor Jana Riess attended a wedding in Independence, Missouri, with members of at least five different Mormon-related denominations. The more the merrier, apparently.

This section gives you a glimpse of three different Mormon-heritage churches.

The Community of Christ

The Community of Christ (formerly known as the RLDS Church or Reorganized Church of Jesus Christ of Latter Day Saints) was founded on April 6, 1860 — exactly 30 years after the founding of the original LDS movement — by the Prophet's son Joseph Smith III, who had reached adulthood. Early members included Emma Smith, the Prophet's widow; his mother, Lucy Mack Smith; and his one living brother, William Smith. For well over a century, all the presidents of this institution were direct descendants of the first Mormon prophet. Following is a quick rundown of this church's differences from the LDS Church and its recent history:

- ✔ The reorganized group, often called "Josephites," rejected all the theological innovations of the Nauvoo period, including polygamy and temple rituals. (Members of the RLDS Church taught that Joseph Smith never practiced or taught polygamy. They believed that Brigham Young introduced the practice after Joseph's death. Most historians disagree, however.)

- ✔ Since 1984, the denomination has ordained women to the priesthood, and the highest offices of the organization are available to them. (See Chapters 4, 15, and 20 for the LDS Church stance on this issue.)

- ✔ In 1994, the RLDS Church dedicated a beautiful temple in Independence, Missouri; this building is open to the public and offers communion (the Lord's Supper) for all. In contrast, LDS temples are closed to the public (see Chapter 7), and Mormons administer their sacrament in meetinghouses, which are open to the public.

- ✔ In 1996, the church selected its first president who wasn't a direct descendant of Joseph Smith.

> ✔ Since 2001, this church calls itself "the Community of Christ," the new name reflecting its modern commitment to being an inclusive religious body that works as a witness for world peace. (In addition, some observers feel the name change reflects the church's gradual distancing from its Mormon roots.)
>
> ✔ Today, the church claims to have approximately 250,000 members in more than 50 nations. Other estimates are closer to 200,000 members.

The Strangites

Members of this small group believe that before Joseph Smith died, he appointed a man named James Strang to succeed him. Before the founding of the RLDS Church (see the preceding section), several members of Joseph's family were at least somewhat involved in this group. It had approximately 12,000 members during Strang's lifetime, which was cut short in 1856 when he was assassinated in Michigan.

The group probably only numbers in the hundreds today. Based in the upper Midwest, with branches in Michigan and Wisconsin, the Strangites are sometimes called "Great Lakes Mormons." They believe in a *seventh-day Sabbath* (holding the Sabbath on Saturday, not Sunday), continuing revelation, and animal sacrifice in the manner of the Old Testament.

Church of Christ (Temple Lot)

Like the Community of Christ, the Church of Christ is based in Independence, Missouri, but this denomination is much smaller. The Temple Lot group owns part of the land that Joseph Smith dedicated for a temple in the early 1830s, and they believe that's the spot where Christ's Second Coming will occur.

This group isn't part of the well-known Church of Christ denomination that's widespread in the South and doesn't allow instruments in its worship services. Rather, it's a Mormon-related splinter group that seems to have about 2,000 to 3,000 members, mostly in the general area of Independence. Its 25 Articles of Faith and Practice (similar in some ways to the 13 LDS Articles of Faith that you can find on this book's Cheat Sheet) are posted at www.church ofchrist-tl.org.

Chapter 13

Building the Kingdom in Utah

*W*hen Brigham Young indicated that Salt Lake City was the place for the Latter-day Saints, some of them actually felt a little disappointed — the land seemed so stark and, well, ugly. It wasn't a desert, but it wasn't exactly an oasis, either. Building a prosperous society amidst the mountains took all the Mormons' characteristic commitment to organization and hard work, and they hoped that this time their enemies would leave them alone. However, Mormon conflicts with the outside world actually took a turn for the worse in Utah. What's more, the clash was sometimes their own fault.

Before the Mormons left the Midwest, the practice of polygamy was rumored, but they hid it. After 1852, they practiced it openly in Utah — which didn't go down well with many non-Mormons. In addition, the Mormons made it clear that they had no intention of separating church and state. To make matters worse, the Latter-day Saints stained their own history by instigating one of American history's worst-ever civilian massacres: the Mountain Meadows Massacre of 1857.

In this chapter, we celebrate this period of Mormon history by pointing out the courage of the Mormon pioneers in settling the West and taming the frontier, but we also look at the darker side of the early Utah story. In addition, we explore how the Church made the transition from the 19th to the 20th centuries, from a polygamous fringe movement at odds with the government to a bulwark of traditional values and American patriotism.

Building Zion

When the first company of Mormons arrived in the Salt Lake Valley in July 1847, they took a quick break to thank the Lord for their safe passage and to consecrate the new land to him. Less than two hours after they arrived, they got to work plowing and irrigating that land. Because this place was going to be their new homeland, the Mormons weren't seeking just to survive but to honor God with a flourishing settlement.

The Mormons named their new region *Deseret,* a word from the Book of Mormon that means "honeybee." (Today, you see the symbol of a beehive everywhere in the Mormon world, from the pulpit in the Salt Lake Tabernacle to the logo for the Church's Humanitarian Relief program.) The busy-bee Mormons chose this term because it summed up their labor of building Salt Lake City and sending representatives to establish other Mormon towns throughout the West.

Settling the Salt Lake Valley

The Mormons' first task was to create Salt Lake City, which became the Church headquarters and, after Utah became a U.S. territory in 1850, eventually the region's government headquarters as well.

Laying out the city

Visitors to Salt Lake City today are sometimes surprised by the layout and organization of the downtown area. The place is so clean, so darn *orderly.* Imagine how visitors in the late 19th century felt when they discovered the city's broad streets (wide enough to turn a wagon completely around without backing up the oxen) and temple-in-progress.

Within days of the Mormons' arrival in Salt Lake City, Brigham Young set aside a grade-A spot for building a temple. (Although they got an early start, they didn't exactly rush to get the job done: The Salt Lake Temple took a full 40 years to build, and Brigham didn't live to see the end result.) The temple lot, now called *Temple Square,* was the hub for the entire city.

The Mormons aligned their streets to compass directions and numbered them based on their distance from the temple — and this system still remains in place. For example, if you stand at the corner of 500 South and 200 East, you're five blocks south and two blocks east of the temple. All the city streets radiate from the temple like shuttle probes from a mother ship; getting lost is nearly impossible, though one of the authors of this book has managed it.

Other Mormon settlements used similar patterns and numbering systems. You can often tell exactly where the modern-style suburban development began in Utah communities just by noting where the streets start to get names and run in something other than straight lines.

Taming the frontier

Because Salt Lake City was so far away from suppliers in the East (1,000 miles) and California (700 miles), the Latter-day Saints had to be self-sufficient from the get-go. The land and its accompanying critters didn't make their job easy. That first winter of 1847–48, the Mormons rationed their flour carefully to get them through the cold months, and their sacrifice paid off, because no one died of starvation that first winter. (Compare their situation to the poor Pilgrims, who lost half of the *Mayflower* company in the first year. Ouch.)

But hard times were just ahead. In May 1848, the Mormons suffered a serious setback when a whole mess of crickets (we're talking a plague of Old Testament proportions) destroyed their newly planted crops. The desperate Mormons tried to kill the invaders with brooms and sticks, but to no avail.

What happened next filled the Mormons with faith. Before all the crops were devoured, flocks of seagulls gobbled up the crickets. Some of the crops were saved, and the Mormons didn't starve. Not surprisingly, the seagull is now Utah's state bird, a prominent Mormon bookstore chain has *seagull* in its name, and Temple Square features a lovely monument to the fowl tale. Some cynics point out that seagulls aren't exactly strangers to the Salt Lake area, so their presence in 1848 is no big shocker. (And while we're looking gift gulls in the mouth, can we also ask why the gulls didn't get there earlier and save more crops?) Although Mormons have exaggerated the miraculous aspects of this story over the years, the seagull remains a symbol for Mormons of God's provision in difficult times.

Living alongside Native Americans

The Mormons were the first permanent Euro American settlers in Utah, but they were by no means the only people there. Native American tribes had occupied the region for centuries, and the Mormons who settled in Utah had to learn to negotiate with them.

On the one hand, Mormons treated Native Americans more fairly than other white groups did at the time. They had several reasons for doing so:

- ✔ **Mormon theology said that some Native Americans were descendants of the Lamanites in the Book of Mormon.** In other words, they were considered part of the house of Israel. (For more on the Lamanites in the Book of Mormon, see Chapter 9.)

- ✔ **They faced a common aggressor: the U.S. government.** As the old adage goes, the enemy of one's enemy is one's friend.

- ✔ **Brigham Young, ever the practical leader, thought it was better to feed them than to fight them.** In some cases, Mormon families adopted Native American orphans into their homes to raise and educate.

But Mormons were sometimes guilty of the same racist attitudes toward Native Americans that characterized other white people of the 19th century:

- ✔ **They wanted Native Americans to assimilate.** Although the Mormons sought to improve the lot of Native Americans, they did so with the idea that indigenous people needed to adopt the ways of white settlers in order to become civilized.

- ✔ **They believed that contemporary Native Americans were cursed because of their ancestors' shameful decisions, which accounted for their dark skin.** Earlier editions of the Book of Mormon said that when Native Americans embraced their Hebrew heritage and became righteous, they'd become "a white and a delightsome people." However, that wording has now changed from "white" to "pure." (See Chapter 15 for more on race in Mormon history and belief.)

- ✔ **Mormons were enthusiastic supporters of *manifest destiny,* the belief that whites needed to settle the nation from sea to shining sea.** On a local level, this belief sometimes meant that Mormons were among the first whites to petition the government to open up Indian reservation lands for mining and commercial investment.

Although Mormons had a mixed record in dealing with Native Americans, they were generally peaceable neighbors. Today, many Native Americans are members of The Church of Jesus Christ of Latter-day Saints, and the Church has branches and wards on many reservations throughout the western United States.

Movin' on out: Settling the Jell-O Belt

When pioneers arrived in Utah, most of them thought they could settle down with the other Latter-day Saints and start prospering. But for some, this idea was only a dream. Over the next three decades after the 1847 arrival, President Brigham Young, concerned that the Mormons needed to stake their claim on the surrounding territories so they could have a healthy bit of elbowroom, directed some families to pack their bags yet again.

In all, the Mormons founded nearly 100 communities in their first decade in the West, and more than 500 throughout the 19th century. One of the first and most successful distant communities was St. George, Utah, just north of the modern-day border with Arizona. Attracted to its mild southern climate, Brigham used St. George as a winter home, and many Mormon senior citizens still winter or retire there.

Other Mormon colonies included

- ✔ Cardston, Alberta, Canada, named for the Card family of Mormon settlers
- ✔ Carson City, Nevada

✔ San Bernardino, California

✔ Snowflake, Arizona, founded by Mormon families whose last names, believe it or not, were Snow and Flake

✔ Las Vegas, Nevada

Some Mormons claim that Mormons *founded* Las Vegas, but they're wrong. Someone else discovered the place about ten years before the first Mormons got there. The Mormons were, however, the first European Americans to *settle* in Las Vegas. They did so in the mid-1850s, though they couldn't make a go of it and left after a couple of years. Although the LDS effort was short-lived, the early Mormon presence in Las Vegas is an ironically delightful historical twist, considering that Las Vegas is now known for gambling, drinking, and other decidedly un-Mormon activities. Today, even the Mormon temple in Las Vegas has slot machines in the lobby. (We're just *kidding.*)

Mormon colonization stretched from Utah to all its surrounding territories and was strongest in Nevada, southern Idaho, western Wyoming, eastern Washington, Colorado, and northern Arizona. Today, this core area is called the *Mormon culture region* by demographers and the *Jell-O Belt* by many affectionate Latter-day Saints, because Mormons have a high per-capita consumption rate of that wobbly treat. In Utah, Mormonism is the number-one religion in terms of believers, and in several surrounding states it takes second or third. A smattering of Mormon-heavy communities also shows up in Nevada, California, Washington, New Mexico, and western Canadian provinces such as Alberta, British Columbia, and Saskatchewan.

Conflicts with the Outside World

When the Latter-day Saints arrived in the Salt Lake Valley in 1847, they had reason to hope they'd escaped conflict with the American government forever. At the time, Mexico owned the territory that eventually became known as Utah, and that government was more than willing to leave the Mormons alone. However, only months later, Mexico lost its war with the United States and had to hand over all its lands in the West, including Utah. The Mormons found themselves right back in the thick of controversy.

Today, people often think of Mormons as flag-waving, staunch Republican supporters of the U.S. government. (The extensive presence of Mormons in military leadership, the CIA, and the FBI demonstrates pretty clearly that the U.S. has no lingering concerns about Mormon patriotism.) But in the 19th century, people saw Mormons as fugitives from the long arm of the law. Their stubborn practice of polygamy, as well as their determination to merge church and state in the Rocky Mountains, made the Mormons Public Enemy Number One.

The Utah War and the Mormon Reformation

Utah became a U.S. territory in 1850 with Brigham Young as its governor. Before long, the federal government expressed grave concern about the "Mormon problem." Two basic issues were at stake:

✔ **The Mormons acknowledged in 1852 that they practiced polygamy, or plural marriage.** This topic had long been grist for the rumor mill, but the Latter-day Saints had always publicly denied it. After they let the cat out of the bag, the nation cried foul. The 1856 Republican National Convention denounced polygamy as one of the "twin relics of barbarism" that afflicted the national conscience (the other was slavery). For more on the doctrine of plural marriage and why Mormons practiced it, see the section on polygamy later in this chapter.

✔ **U.S. government officials worried that the Mormons were trying to establish a *theocracy*, or a merging of religion and government.** As a natural outgrowth of its role in promoting and coordinating economic development in Utah, the Church owned prominent businesses and held a stake in many of the industrial enterprises of the region: mines, sugar refineries, textile mills, and the like. It virtually controlled local politics and the judicial bench.

Anticipating war

The tensions between Mormons and the government erupted in 1857–58. When the federal government sent troops to Utah because Brigham Young wouldn't surrender his title as governor to a non-Mormon federal appointee, the so-called Utah War got underway. *War* is actually a bloodier name than the event deserves, because no one was killed — in fact, no one even fired any shots — during the smoldering conflict. But the fact that the government was willing to send the largest peacetime army in the nation's history all the way out to Utah shows how concerned it was about the Mormon question.

To the Mormons, the government's interference appeared to be a rehashing of the same old story that had always ended so badly for the Latter-day Saints in Ohio, Illinois, and Missouri. They saw it as the first strike in renewed persecutions and government attempts to force them to give up their beliefs and way of life.

The lingering image of the Utah War isn't bloodshed but Brigham Young's attempt to prevent it. Rather than risk the lives of any Latter-day Saints when the army arrived, Brigham evacuated 30,000 people from Salt Lake City so that the soldiers arrived to a ghost town. With military combat avoided, the people of Salt Lake returned peacefully to their homes.

Reacting with a reformation

In 1856, when the Mormons realized that the government was sending an army that could destroy them, no one could've predicted the peaceful and uneventful outcome of the controversy. Some Mormons saw the intrusion as a sign of the End Times and believed that they were about to see the obliteration of their beloved Salt Lake City.

With this fear in mind, they entered into a brief period of their history (1856–57) known as the *Mormon Reformation*. To prepare themselves spiritually for the end, they prayed more fervently, met more frequently, and performed round-the-clock ordinances in the Endowment House (the building that substituted for a temple while the temple was under construction). They also made a dizzying number of plural marriages, with some men marrying several women on the same day.

The Mormon Reformation was a time of deep, and even bizarre, fervor in Latter-day Saint history and played an important part in understanding the religion's greatest tragedy: the Mountain Meadows Massacre.

The Mountain Meadows Massacre

Although the 1850s Utah War was bloodless, Mormon history in the 1850s wasn't. The government may not have traded bullets with the Mormons, but many of the Latter-day Saints suspected that civilians in emigrant trains crossing the Utah Territory were in league with the invading army. For this and other complex reasons, a group of Mormons made a large-scale attack on an emigrant train in September 1857. Interestingly enough, the worst of the bloodshed happened on September 11, a day that almost 150 years later similarly became associated with the violence that can stem from religious fanaticism.

The massacre occurred about 200 miles south of Salt Lake City, when a group of men, women, and children passed through southern Utah on their way to settle in California. Some accounts claim that Native Americans initiated the attack and that the Mormons joined in later; others claim that the Mormons planned and executed the whole affair. The latter explanation seems more credible to most historians. At the end of the day, more than 120 men, women, and older children were dead. Young children, the oldest of whom was 6, were left alive, and many were temporarily adopted into the families of local Latter-day Saints before being returned to their homes in Missouri and Arkansas.

Questioning the motive

Why would this group of Mormons, who'd been on the receiving end of violence and persecution themselves, carry out such an unforgivable atrocity? Historians have identified several possible motives for the attack. Some or all of these reasons may help to explain it, though nothing can excuse it. No one will ever know for certain exactly what happened and why, even though a new book on the massacre shows up nearly every year, it seems.

✔ The Mormons, who were expecting an army of 2,500 soldiers to attack them any day, were swept up in a feverish, warlike mentality and believed they stood alone against the world. The emigrant party arrived in Utah at a very bad time.

✔ The emigrant group was from Missouri and northern Arkansas, and historical evidence suggests that they may have taunted the Mormons with boasts of being the wildcats who drove Mormons from Missouri 20 years earlier. The massacre may have been a misguided attempt at Mormon justice for past wrongs, especially the much smaller massacre at Haun's Mill, where some Mormon children died.

✔ One popular history suggests that the Mormons may have committed the massacre because the people of southern Utah were poor and coveted the emigrant party's wealth and livestock. (This theory doesn't satisfactorily explain, though, why the attack happened to this *particular* party at this *particular* time, when other emigrants passed through the region without incident.)

Reacting to the event

We'll probably never know the reason, or reasons, for the attack. The questions remain: How much did Brigham Young know, and when did he know it? Did he order the assault, or did the southern Mormons take matters into their own hands? Apparently, when Brigham found out what the southern settlers planned, he immediately sent a messenger ordering them to allow the emigrants to safely pass through. However, they acted before they received his message.

Unfortunately, the Church — caught up with the impending Utah War and anxious not to give the federal government any reason to attack — chose to cover up the evidence of the massacre for years, blaming local Native Americans even when Mormon involvement was obvious. Gradually, the Church claimed at least some responsibility, but only one man, a local Mormon leader named John D. Lee, was ever tried and executed for the crime.

In 1999, the Mountain Meadows Association, made up of the descendants of the known victims and criminals of the attack, reburied the remains of some of the victims, which were disturbed during construction of a memorial. In his dedicatory remarks, LDS Church President Gordon B. Hinckley promised the descendants that the Church would always treat the two and a half acres as hallowed ground, "a sacred monument to honor all those who fell."

Polygamy: A Divine Principle (But an Outdated Practice)

Today, outsiders sometimes ask Mormons — often in jest, occasionally in concern — whether they practice polygamy. (The Mormon response is usually to roll the eyes and recite for the thousandth time that the Latter-day Saints haven't practiced polygamy for over a century and that anyone who practices it today is excommunicated, yada yada yada.) Although — we'll just say it once more to clear the air — *the Latter-day Saints haven't practiced earthly polygamy for over a century,* Mormonism is forever associated in the public mind with patriarchal polygamy.

In this section, we take a critical look at polygamy, explaining who practiced it and why and exploring the consequences that the Latter-day Saints experienced for doing so.

Who practiced polygamy, and why?

Modern folks aren't the only ones who feel uncomfortable about the idea of polygamy. When Joseph Smith first explained the doctrine of plural marriage to Brigham Young in the early 1840s, Brigham felt repulsed by it. Like Brigham, most of the early Latter-day Saints didn't instantly warm to the idea, but they gradually came to understand it as God's will.

Finding out who was involved

Although in recent years the Church has downplayed the importance of plural marriage to 19th-century Saints in order to keep the current stance clear (today's Church doesn't allow the practice . . . did we mention that?), history shows that polygamy was an extremely important aspect of Mormonism in the 19th century.

Modern LDS apologists have stated that as few as 2 to 4 percent of Latter-day Saints were involved in polygamy in the 19th century, a figure that professional historians know is far too low. Most historians place the figure at anywhere between 20 and 50 percent, depending on the time and place. Rates of polygamous marriages varied at different points throughout the second half of the 19th century in Mormon settlements. The 1850s saw many plural marriages, but the rate seems to have declined afterward due to government persecution and changing social standards. The numbers also varied based on geography; some towns embraced polygamy more than others.

Whatever the statistic, polygamy touched almost all Mormon families, whether they practiced it themselves or not. Almost all their leaders practiced it, and those leaders preached sermons on its importance to rank-and-file Mormons in conference after conference. So despite the understandable de-emphasis on polygamy in official Church publications today, polygamy is a fact of Mormon history, and it deserves to be recognized and understood as a historical and religious phenomenon.

Hearing the defense

Why did the Latter-day Saints practice polygamy, especially when this deviation from what was considered "normal" or moral behavior so angered America's citizens and government? Here are some possible reasons, both theological and social:

- ✔ **God told us to do it. Period.** Most Mormons believe that although they may not understand why, the Lord chose to institute plural marriage for a brief period in the 19th century as the Church was becoming established. The 19th-century Latter-day Saints felt that they were practicing plural marriage in strict obedience to God's will and that the practice was divinely inspired. In fact, Mormonism still acknowledges polygamy as a divine *principle* that may apply in heaven, though it's no longer in *practice* on the earth (see Doctrine and Covenants 132).

- ✔ **It was part of the "restitution of all things."** Mormons saw their practice of polygamy as similar to that of the patriarchs Abraham, Isaac, and Jacob. They believe that their latter-day church includes, as predicted in the Bible, the "restitution of all things, which God hath spoken by the mouth of all his holy prophets since the world began" (Acts 3:21). That includes Old Testament polygamy.

- ✔ **It brought the Latter-day Saints together.** Polygamy made the Mormons more cohesive as a people and gave them a distinct identity. Some plural wives were family members even before marriage (two sisters marrying the same man, for example), and the bonds of marriage expanded family networks. Also, the increased persecution caused by polygamy helped the Mormons bond together even more closely as a people.

- ✔ **It raised up a mighty generation.** Many Mormons believe that one of the reasons the Lord may have sanctioned polygamy for a time was that it allowed the struggling Latter-day Saints to raise up a "righteous seed" of second- and third-generation Mormons to build the kingdom. Because of polygamy, Mormon families in the 19th century were able to obey the Lord's commandment to "be fruitful and multiply," sometimes having two or three times as many children as they may have had with only one child bearer. What's more, polygamy attached women and children to men who had made a strong commitment to the Church, because those men were the most likely to enter into plural marriage.

Women in polygamy

Although some people today imagine the women of 19th-century Utah to be downtrodden slaves, barefoot and perpetually pregnant, the reality is much more complex. Many Mormon women of the period argued that they were far from being oppressed by polygamy — they were actually liberated by it.

✔ Some Mormon women said that because their relations with their "sister-wives" (women also married to their husband) were close, they enjoyed a mutual extended family that gave them emotional as well as practical support. And hey, who can argue with sharing free in-home childcare?

✔ Mormon women, whose polygamous husbands were often away visiting their other families or serving extended unpaid missions, often had to fend for themselves. Some washed laundry, farmed, or took in boarders. Other plural wives were doctors, midwives, shopkeepers, newspaper editors, and teachers. Overall, plural wives were quite independent.

✔ Mormon women had the right to vote 50 years before women were allowed to nationally. Also, they could obtain divorces much more easily, in case polygamy didn't make them happy.

Although some Mormon women felt burdened by polygamy — keeping jealousy at bay and not giving in to resentment was certainly difficult — large numbers of female Latter-day Saints considered living "the principle" to be a privilege. Strong women who believed in the nobility of their cause didn't appreciate being described as oppressed or delusional. According to customs of the time, first wives sometimes initiated the discussions about bringing a new wife into the family and typically had to approve of the new marriage.

Busting a few myths about 19th-century polygamy

Several enduring myths are still bandied about as people try to explain polygamy (or explain it away):

✔ **"Mormons practiced polygamy because women on the frontier far outnumbered men, and plural marriage gave every woman a chance to have a husband."** In actuality, men sometimes outnumbered women, especially in the early years of Mormon settlement. Some towns had three times as many unmarried men as women. In this marriage market of swinging Mormon singles, women had the pick of the litter.

✔ **"Polygamy took care of older women and spinsters so they had a chance to get married."** The truth is that most plural wives were younger than the first wife, so they weren't exactly spinsters rescued by polygamy. This idea was especially true in the 1850s, though as the decades passed, convincing young women to enter into plural marriage got tougher.

✔ **"Polygamous men lived in harems and had about 20 wives each."** Although a few prominent Church leaders like Brigham Young did have wives numbering into the double digits (and coauthor Christopher Kimball Bigelow's great-great-great-grandfather Heber C. Kimball, a right-hand apostle to both Joseph Smith and Brigham Young, married over 40 women), this situation was far from the norm. Most men who entered into polygamy took only one or two additional wives. If the family could afford it, each wife had her own home or apartment.

✔ **"Polygamy was all about sex."** Not really. In fact, some of the plural marriages contracted in Utah were for *eternity only,* meaning that the wife would be on the man's rolls in heaven, but they would have no earthly rolls in the hay. In eternity-only marriages, conjugal relations weren't permitted, and the wife usually supported herself. In marriages for both time and eternity, the couple enjoyed conjugal relations, but the husband was bound to support his wives and any children they had.

✔ **"Only the poorest of the poor practiced polygamy."** Statistics show that most of the men who practiced polygamy in Utah were among the wealthier members of Mormon society. Supporting multiple households required a certain amount of cold, hard cash, so Church leaders were more likely to approve the marriages of men who could support additional wives. (Plural wives, though, often came from economically disadvantaged backgrounds, and plural marriage to a well-established man helped them move up the social ladder.)

Government pressure to end polygamy

After the Mormons' announcement of plural marriage in 1852 kindled the nation's anger, the U.S. government engaged in a vigorous tug of war with the Mormons in Salt Lake City. For nearly 40 years, the government applied as much political and social pressure as possible to get the Mormons to abandon the hated practice. Congress created antipolygamy legislation that gradually tightened the noose around the Church. Here's a thumbnail sketch:

✔ **In 1862, Congress passed the Morrill Antibigamy Act, which made practicing polygamy a felony.** However, this law was full of loopholes (not the least of which was that *bigamy* means only two wives!) and didn't hold any weight in the Mormon-dominated Utah courts.

✔ **In 1874, the government resolved that judicial loophole with the Poland Act.** This law stated that all polygamy cases would be tried in federal courts with federally appointed judges. This way, Mormon judges or juries couldn't just dismiss the cases.

✔ **In 1882, the Edmunds Act made unlawful cohabitation a crime, and anyone who broke the law could be imprisoned for six months.** *Unlawful cohabitation* was a much easier judicial standard to prove than bigamy or polygamy, because prosecutors didn't have to provide evidence of a marriage.

✔ **In 1887, Congress passed the Edmunds-Tucker Act in a final attempt to drive the nail in the coffin of polygamy.** This act accomplished three things:

- It *disfranchised* (took the vote away from) all the women of Utah and polygamous men.

- It froze all the Church's assets in excess of $50,000, basically bankrupting the Church and crippling its missionary efforts.

- It declared all children of plural marriages to be illegitimate in the eyes of the government.

When the Supreme Court declared that this law was constitutional, the Mormons knew that continuing plural marriage could result in the government closing down their temples and threatening the very survival of the Church. Faced with this terrible situation, President Wilford Woodruff issued a document (now known as the *Woodruff Manifesto*) in 1890 ending the practice of plural marriage. Although the manifesto is included in every Mormon's collection of scriptures as part of the Doctrine and Covenants (D&C), they refer to it as an official declaration rather than a revelation, and God isn't mentioned in it at all (see Chapter 10 for more on this document).

The legacy of polygamy

Needless to say, the modern Church has gone to great lengths to distance itself from its polygamous past. For example, in the late 1990s the Church created a stir when it unveiled its new adult curriculum for priesthood and Relief Society. The first manual in the new curriculum was a compilation of the teachings of President Brigham Young, but the book doesn't even mention polygamy, despite the fact that the topic occupied much of Brigham's actual teaching. The Church also omitted the practice from the chronology of his life, which mentions his first two wives — Miriam, who died in 1832, and Mary Ann, whom he married two years later — but none of the others. In other words, the chronology seemed to make Brigham out to be a serial monogamist, not the husband of some two dozen women.

Although Latter-day Saints no longer practice earthly polygamy, Mormon scripture still teaches it as an eternal principle (see D&C 132). A few Mormons believe that the practice will one day be restored again to the earth. Many Mormons assume that the celestial kingdom (see Chapter 2) will include some polygamy, and although Church leaders haven't explicitly mentioned this idea in General Conference or taught it in years, older teaching supports this view.

In fact, the legacy of polygamy is still visible in the way the Church performs eternal sealings of couples. In cases of divorce, for example, a woman has to obtain a cancellation of a previous sealing if she wants to be married again in the temple. A man, however, can apply for clearance to remarry in the temple without canceling the previous sealing. In effect, he can be sealed to two or more women for eternity, while being legally married to only one at a time in this life. Similar conditions apply for widows and widowers who want to remarry. (See Chapter 7 for more details on the complexities of eternal marriage.)

The other major legacy of polygamy is the approximately 30,000 members of fundamentalist Mormon-related groups who still practice it. These folks are the subjects of endless fascination and media attention. The LDS Church doesn't recognize the fundamentalists as legitimate Mormons or Latter-day Saints, but the fundamentalists regard themselves as such because they share much of the same culture, doctrine, and history. In general, fundamentalists feel that President Woodruff led the mainstream Church into *apostasy,* or falling away from God, when he suspended the practice of polygamy in 1890, so they've revived polygamy and other 19th-century Mormon practices. However, the LDS Church promptly excommunicates any participants. Chapter 15 deals with modern-day polygamists in more detail.

Mormonism in Transition

After the Mormons finally cried "uncle" with the 1890 manifesto that ended polygamy, life in Utah started to resemble life elsewhere in the United States. Church leaders emerged from hiding and from prison, and the federal government stopped interfering in Church affairs. Although more than a decade passed before a true nonpolygamous culture emerged, the Church began moving full steam ahead to separate church and state (at least on the surface) and gain statehood for Utah.

Pledging allegiance to the flag

Two events in 1893 seemed to signal that better days lay ahead for the Mormons. At the Chicago World's Fair held that year, the Salt Lake Tabernacle Choir — predecessor of today's world-famous Mormon Tabernacle Choir — won second prize, resulting in positive publicity for the Church. Even more important, the Church finally finished building the Salt Lake Temple, after 40 years of problem-plagued construction. With its thick granite walls and iconic six-spire design, the temple symbolized the faith's determination to stay put in Utah while spreading its influence throughout the world.

With a new constitution banning polygamy and guaranteeing the separation of church and state, Utah finally gained admittance to the union in 1896, after six earlier attempts and almost 50 years after Brigham Young first started campaigning for it. Arid, remote Utah wasn't the Church's first choice for a homeland — to find out what was, see Chapter 11 — but now the Church could operate from a secure, safe base under the protective umbrella of the United States, toward which the Mormons started developing deeper loyalty.

Facing some lingering problems

As things settled down at home, the Church redoubled its worldwide missionary efforts, but with one major change in emphasis: The Church now urged new converts to build up congregations in their home countries rather than gather in Utah. As a result, the flow of converts into Utah became a trickle (good thing, because most of the region's best land was already taken).

Even after gaining statehood, however, the Mormons still faced some challenges. Federal prosecution of polygamy had caused considerable economic trouble for the Church, and it was saddled with debt. By reemphasizing the payment of tithes (see Chapter 16), President Lorenzo Snow put the Church back on sound financial footing. By 1907 the Church had paid all its creditors, never to go into debt again.

In addition, polygamy continued sending out aftershocks. In 1898, when Utah elected a Mormon U.S. Representative who'd married plural wives *before* the manifesto, more than 7 million Americans signed a petition against him, and he was refused his seat. In 1903, when Utah elected a high-ranking Mormon apostle to the U.S. Senate, the Senate commenced an investigation, prompting the Church to issue the *Second Manifesto* to crack down on more than 200 plural marriages that had taken place since 1890, some with the blessing of the First Presidency. The apostle, who was monogamous, managed to keep his Senate seat, but the media muckraked the Mormons well into the 20th century, often with outright fabrications.

Gathering strength for a worldwide boom

Overall, the first half of the 20th century was a time for the Church to lay relatively low, consolidate and refine its methods and messages, and gather strength for the growth boom that began shortly after World War II. (For more details about the modern Church's explosion in membership all over the earth, see Chapter 14.)

As the 20th century progressed, the LDS Church took deliberate steps to overcome its bad public image. Several trends helped the process:

- ✔ **The Church started appealing to tourists, particularly by promoting Temple Square in Salt Lake City.** By 1905, this site was drawing 200,000 annual visitors, and it soon became one of America's most-visited destinations west of the Mississippi. In addition, the Church established visitors' centers at historic Mormon sites around the country, and the Mormon Tabernacle Choir performed for audiences throughout the nation.

- ✔ **The Church reached out to the media.** At first, it focused on rebutting false information and providing accurate portrayals of its controversial history. By the 1920s, Mormonism was getting more-favorable press coverage, with President Heber J. Grant appearing on the cover of *Time* magazine. In time, even Hollywood came around, most notably with the Mormon-friendly movie *Brigham Young,* released in the 1940s.

- ✔ **During the Depression years of the 1930s, the Church gained admiring national attention for its extensive welfare program.** This program helped members survive the dismal economy and allowed many of them to get off the government dole. Mormons became known for taking care of their own. (For more information on the Mormon welfare program, see Chapter 8.)

- ✔ **The Church stepped up its evangelistic efforts by shifting the work from older, married men to younger, single missionaries, including some women.** The missionary force grew from fewer than 900 called annually in 1900 to more than 2,000 by 1940. In addition, the Church made improvements in missionary training and resources. As a result, Church membership mushroomed from about 268,000 in 1900 to almost 1 million by 1945 — but the real exponential growth was yet to come.

- ✔ **Many Latter-day Saints started seeking education and jobs in other parts of the nation, especially California.** This change allowed more Americans to witness firsthand that Mormons weren't weird but could be as conventionally middle class as anyone. As the Church constructed meetinghouses and temples around the nation and started building them overseas, the faith's visibility and respectability increased.

- ✔ **Although the 19th-century Mormons fled the United States because the government failed to protect their rights, 20th-century Mormons became highly patriotic.** Numerous Mormons rose to prominence in American politics, and Mormons did their share — and sometimes more — to support the U.S. in wars and other efforts.

Part IV
Mormonism Today

The 5th Wave   By Rich Tennant

THE MORMON TABERNACLE DOORBELL

In this part . . .

You see a snapshot of Mormon life today, spending a day in the life of a missionary and finding out about the growing pains that naturally go along with the Church's rapid expansion. We also clue you in on some of the hot-button issues in Mormonism, from race and the priesthood to women's roles and Mormon views on homo-sexuality.

Then you look at some daily, weekly, and monthly Mormon disciplines, from the spiritual (prayer, scripture study, fasting, and keeping the Sabbath) to the temporal (food storage, tithing, and emergency preparedness). You discover why Mormons believe that doing these things makes them more devoted followers of Jesus Christ, even if they have to make certain sacrifices. Finally, you dive into Mormon culture, including film, music, and literature.

Chapter 14

Called to Serve: Missionaries and International Growth

*U*pon hearing the word *Mormon,* many people instantly envision two clean-cut young men walking or bicycling through the neighborhood in dark suits, white shirts, ties, and the telltale black missionary badges. These junior gospel executives are the main means by which the LDS Church fulfills its sacred mandate to spread the doctrine of Christ throughout the earth. As we explore in this chapter, full-time missionary service is a huge part of Mormon culture.

Largely because of this dynamic force of about 56,000 — at this writing — gospel representatives, the LDS Church has grown remarkably fast since World War II. In the past 50 years, Mormonism has mushroomed from 1 million members in 1950 to almost 12 million in 2004. Much of this growth has occurred in far-flung places, with more than half the Church's total membership now living outside the United States, in more than 165 nations and territories. As we show you in this chapter, these membership statistics don't tell the whole story of how many members are actually active participants in the LDS Church, but they indicate Mormonism's reach into many nations and cultures.

Missionaries of All Shapes and Sizes

At the age of 3, Mormon boys and girls begin singing a song at church titled, "I Hope They Call Me on a Mission." However, the song is really aimed mostly at the boys, who make up about three-quarters of the total missionary force. Missionary service is practically encoded into the DNA of Mormon-born males, and it's considered a priesthood duty. Young women can serve missions, but Church leaders say they should feel no obligation to do so. On the other hand, Church leaders increasingly encourage retired Mormon couples to serve missions, if they don't have any dependent children and their health and finances allow it, because retirees provide maturity and wisdom that the youngsters can't match.

Citing the rigors and demands of missionary life, the Church has recently raised the bar on qualifications for missionary service, particularly for the boys. Increasingly, leaders are weeding out young people who sow their wild oats and then try to repent or who aren't prepared to succeed on a mission. The Church now expects missionaries to demonstrate real faith and a genuine desire to serve, instead of going to meet social expectations, to try to convert *themselves* to Mormonism, to please girlfriends who will marry only a returned missionary, or to get the new car their parents promised if they serve a mission. Those who are worthy to serve a mission but who suffer from physical or emotional problems often volunteer in local positions rather than in full-time, faraway missions. Not surprisingly, the number of full-time missionaries serving worldwide has dropped by more than 10 percent in recent years, although many people feel that today's missionaries are better qualified and more enthusiastic than ever before.

Boy wonders

For nearly a century, a mission has been Mormonism's rite of passage into adulthood for young men, almost like a two-year tithing on the first 20 years of life. Nearly all begin serving at age 19, after working or attending college for about a year following high school. A male can sign up for a mission as late as his mid-20s — but any later than that and he's expected to stay home and evangelize the single gals until he finds one who's willing to become his wife.

Notwithstanding the Church's raising of the bar, every qualified, able young man is still expected to serve, and the social pressure is enormous. Not going — or going but getting sent home early — can make a young man feel like a second-class Mormon for years afterward. Whether or not a missionary wins many converts, the experience is considered essential preparation for future Church service and leadership.

As the teen years progress, parents and youth advisors help Mormon boys prepare for their missions. This preparation includes both spiritual and practical elements. On the spiritual level, young men are expected to

- Gain an abiding faith in the Savior, Joseph Smith's prophetic mission, and the Church
- Read the entire Book of Mormon, and study the Bible and other Mormon scriptures and manuals
- Develop a personal relationship with Heavenly Father through prayer

✔ Learn to recognize and follow the promptings of the Holy Ghost

✔ Keep themselves morally and ethically pure

✔ Share the gospel with their friends

In addition, the Church encourages teen boys to develop practical skills that will come in handy during their missions, such as how to

✔ Save and budget money

✔ Speak in public and teach individuals of all ages

✔ Work hard and get along with others

✔ Launder, mend, and iron their clothes

✔ Prepare nutritious meals and do basic housework

Girl power

Mormons used to joke that women went on missions only if they couldn't get married. In recent years, however, increasing numbers of young women have chosen to serve missions before getting married. These "sister missionaries" must wait until they're 21 to leave, but they don't have an upper age limit like the men do — even a 50-year-old woman can go on a mission if she's still single.

As far as women waiting longer than men to start serving, perhaps the Church intends this policy to reduce opportunities for same-aged missionaries to fall in love in the mission field. The difference in maturity between a 19-year-old boy and a 21-year-old woman is considerably more than two years! At the same time, it's not always easy for sister missionaries to follow the priesthood leadership of younger male missionaries.

Although young men serve for two years and generally stick to finding prospective converts and teaching them, young women serve for 18 months and may receive special assignments, such as staffing a Church visitors' center or helping disadvantaged people improve their health and hygiene. However, female missionaries can also be extremely effective in their evangelizing, and the demand for sister missionaries exceeds supply in many parts of the world. Male missionaries typically baptize their own converts, but female missionaries can't, because Mormon women don't hold the priesthood. Instead, the male missionaries or a local priesthood holder does it for them (for more on the priesthood, see Chapter 4).

Silver is golden

With today's prosperity and longevity, many Mormon couples find themselves with plenty of money and energy after they retire. After their children are grown, they can focus their efforts on helping the Church and its members. In particular, the Church has discovered that missionary couples provide a valuable leadership role in less-developed parts of the Church. Requests for couple missionaries have become more frequent and urgent in recent years, and it's becoming common for willing, able couples to serve multiple missions during their retirement.

Couples can choose from among several kinds of missionary assignments and locations, although most volunteer to go wherever they're needed. They may serve in a temple, gather family history data, work in a Church educational program, or fulfill many other roles. In addition, they have more flexibility in determining their length of service, and they don't have to follow the same strict schedule and rules as the single men and women (see "Living the Missionary Life," later in this chapter).

Hail to the chief

Although being a missionary is hard work, probably the most challenging assignment is to preside over one of the Church's 300-plus missions worldwide as a *mission president*. Although foot-soldier missionaries volunteer to serve when they're ready, the Church calls mission presidents at its own discretion, often surprising a man in the middle of his career.

Can you imagine being responsible for one to two hundred 19-year-old boys, plus several dozen women and couples, for a period of three years? Not only must you constantly train, motivate, organize, and discipline these people in the often-discouraging work of preaching Mormon Christianity to a largely indifferent — if not outright hostile — world, but also you must deal with the missionaries' mistakes, problems, illnesses, crises, complaints, conflicts, sins, and special requests. In addition, you must work closely with both the Church's local leaders and its General Authorities, including the highest-ranking apostles (see Chapter 8).

Sound fun? Add another factor: If you accept the calling of mission president and you're still a working man, you have to leave your job and forgo earning a salary for three years, beyond the very modest living allowance that the Church provides. If you and your wife still have children at home, you have to uproot them to live somewhere else, possibly somewhere quite foreign. We don't know how the Church identifies which men — couples, really, because the mission president's wife is usually very involved in the day-to-day running of the mission — to call, but we know that Mormons generally greatly admire these men and their wives. They probably receive a lot of spiritual help and blessings, but sheesh, what a job.

Enlisting in God's Army

A few months before the desired departure time, a young Mormon man or woman begins filling out the missionary application, which requires medical and dental exams and worthiness interviews with local Church leaders. In applying to serve a mission, young missionaries don't get to choose where they'll go and what language they'll speak. What's more, they have to pay all their own expenses, except airfare to and from the mission field, which the Church covers.

Receiving the call

After the missionary's stake president (see Chapter 6) sends the application to Church headquarters, it takes just a few weeks to process it. Because a missionary may be assigned anywhere in the world, anticipation runs high for receiving that all-important envelope from Salt Lake City. Before the missionary opens it, family and friends typically gather round, and many missionaries' hands tremble as they tear open the envelope.

Embracing the calling

Receiving a call to Wyoming when you were hoping to go to Hong Kong — or vice versa — can be a little challenging. However, Mormons believe that each mission call is divinely inspired, a hope encouraged by the fact that each letter is, by all appearances, signed by the prophet of the Church. Nevertheless, the number of calls issued each year — well over 25,000 — undoubtedly results in some bureaucratic randomness. Reports say that top-level apostles review all the calls and correct any that don't feel right.

Some Mormons believe that a person's mission call was determined in the premortal life (for more about the Mormon concept of premortality, see Chapter 2). Faith-promoting stories persist about the missionary who, while diligently knocking on doors, meets someone who seems instantly, uncannily familiar. The common explanation for such déjà vu is that in the premortal life, the missionary promised this person that during mortality, the missionary would find and teach him or her the truth. This widespread folk belief not only helps missionaries accept their callings, but also motivates them to work hard so they don't break their promise to find that special someone.

Financing the mission

Included with the mission call are specific instructions about what to purchase before reporting for duty, ranging from heavy-duty two-pant suits to durable walking shoes. Women typically wear conservative dresses or blouses with longish skirts and comfortable shoes. In Utah, several retail stores specialize in outfitting missionaries. A store is online at www.missionarymall.org, and sometimes national department stores advertise suits for missionaries at their

Utah locations. Missionaries or their parents pay for the clothing and accessories, the total cost of which can easily top 2,000 American bucks. Everything must fit into two airline-compatible suitcases, plus a carry-on bag.

Ideally, missionaries pay their own living expenses with money that they save up beforehand. Missionaries used to cover their own costs directly, an idea that was fabulous if you went to Guatemala but not so great if you went to Tokyo. Recently, the Church centralized and equalized missionary finances, with each missionary paying the same monthly amount no matter where in the world he or she serves. At the time of this writing, the monthly U.S. amount to support a missionary is $375, which totals $9,000 for a young man serving two years and $6,750 for a young woman serving 18 months.

If the missionary hasn't saved enough to pay for his or her entire mission, the parents help out. If the parents can't afford it, the local congregation pitches in. If the local congregation can't swing it, Church headquarters contributes funds under certain circumstances.

So long, farewell

When a young person is preparing to say good-bye to family and friends for such a long period of time (24 months for men and 18 months for women), people make a big deal out of the send-off. In recent years, the Church has tried to discourage several traditions connected with missionary departures, but some traditions still persist:

✔ A Sunday or two before leaving, missionaries typically give a farewell speech during *sacrament meeting,* Mormonism's main weekly congregational service. Until 2003, the missionary and his or her family typically planned the whole program, with friends and family members giving tributes and performing musical numbers. However, some congregations were being overrun with missionary farewells, so nowadays just the missionary speaks on an assigned gospel topic for only a portion of the meeting.

✔ Despite official discouragement, many missionary families continue to hold open houses directly following their son or daughter's farewell speech. The spread of food is usually quite lavish, and slipping the missionary a donation to help pay for the mission is customary. (We're not sure why the Church doesn't like farewell open houses. Perhaps they put too much pressure on some families or take time away from keeping the Sabbath, which we discuss in Chapter 17.)

✔ When the missionary reports to the missionary training center (MTC), family members are invited to come inside for a special presentation that includes inspirational videos and speeches. At the conclusion, the room erupts into frenzied hugging, and then the missionaries file through one door and sniffling family members exit out another door.

✔ In Utah, local family and friends used to see off missionaries one last time at the Salt Lake International Airport. The airport tolerated the extra people and commotion up until the 9/11 terrorist attacks in 2001, after which missionary airport send-offs were nixed.

Diving into the "Empty Sea": Missionary boot camp

A few months after receiving their calls in the mail, missionaries report on an assigned date to one of 17 *missionary training centers* around the world, which are commonly known as the *MTC* (or, as missionaries joke when writing home, the "Empty Sea"). The Church maintains an especially large MTC adjacent to Brigham Young University in Provo, Utah, where several thousand missionaries can undergo spiritual boot camp at the same time. Most American missionaries report to this flagship MTC, unless they're called to Brazil, in which case they go directly to the Church's large MTC there. After getting some training in Provo, some American missionaries continue their preparation in a smaller MTC in or near their host country, focusing on language immersion.

At the Provo MTC, English-speaking missionaries spend three weeks in intensive study and preparation, and foreign-speaking missionaries can spend up to eight weeks. Life in the MTC is extremely regimented, with a schedule similar to that followed in the mission field but much more strictly enforced. The MTC is known as a place of emotional highs and lows, where some missionaries nearly burst with enthusiasm for converting the world, while others deflate with homesickness or lack of faith. In this spiritual pressure cooker, missionaries who've attempted to hide earlier sins tend to come clean, sometimes resulting in their being sent back home temporarily — or permanently.

At the MTC, missionaries spend virtually every waking hour in the following kinds of classes and activities:

✔ Studying scriptures and a short list of LDS-published books.

✔ Memorizing and practicing the gospel principles they'll soon teach to *investigators,* or potential converts.

✔ Getting better acquainted with the local culture where they'll be serving.

✔ For those learning a foreign language, practicing and reviewing it for endless hours. (The Mormon approach to mastering languages is so effective that government agencies and companies have adopted some of the methods. However, Mormons would attribute their success at least partly to the spiritual gift of tongues, as described in the Bible's New Testament. For more on spiritual gifts, see Chapter 3.)

✔ Attending seminars on gospel topics and going through the nearby temple weekly.

✔ Exercising, laundering their clothes, scrubbing down the dorms, answering phones in the call center, eating in the cafeteria, and writing letters home.

Living the Missionary Life

A missionary's guiding purpose is to bring people to Christ through baptism. Mormons take very seriously the Great Commission at the end of the Gospel of Matthew, when Christ commands his followers to make disciples of all nations. Although Mormons respect many of the teachings and practices of other Christian faiths, they don't recognize other Christian baptisms as eternally valid (to find out why, see Chapter 4).

How many convert baptisms does the typical missionary achieve? It varies widely from place to place. It's not uncommon for a missionary to baptize dozens in South America and *none* in Europe. Approximately 243,000 converts joined the Church in 2003, making the annual worldwide average about eight or nine converts per missionary pair.

This section looks at how missionaries gain converts and what rules missionaries must follow. (By the way, for an entertaining, somewhat realistic peek into Mormon missionary life, two independent movies are available on home video: *God's Army* and *The Best Two Years*.)

Finding and teaching

Before missionaries can baptize someone, they have to find that person and teach the gospel to that person. Missionaries work in pairs for about nine hours a day in three basic activities: finding people to teach, teaching them, and working with local members.

Making initial contacts

In most missions, the task of finding people to teach takes the majority of the missionaries' time and energy. They have several ways of doing it, including the following:

✔ **Following up on referrals:** Some missionaries are given the assignment to visit people who've requested information at a Church visitors' center or who've responded to a Church advertisement, often for a free book or video. The rate of conversion from referrals is higher than that from knocking on doors, but the missionaries still sift through a lot of chaff. The most productive referrals come through local members whose friends have agreed to visit with the missionaries, often in the members' homes.

In the United States, anyone can request a visit from the local Mormon missionaries by calling 888-537-2200 or visiting www.mormon.org.

✔ **Street contacting:** Missionaries often hang out in public areas and try to strike up conversations with passersby. Parks, shopping centers, and public transportation are good places for this method. Sometimes the missionaries set up a display.

✔ **Tracting:** If this word has an air of self-torture about it, that's fitting. Knocking on doors is called *tracting* because missionaries used to hand out religious tracts, although they rarely do so anymore. Most doors go unanswered, and most answered doors result in rejection, a slam, or even verbal abuse. When missionaries are invited inside a house, it's often by a lonely elderly or unemployed person or by someone who wants to debate religion. Still, tracting yields converts slightly more often than haystacks yield needles.

Teaching people the gospel

When someone agrees to hear the Mormon message, that person becomes what the missionaries call an *investigator.* The missionaries' job is to teach the investigator a set of basic gospel principles over the course of several flexible visits. Missionaries used to recite memorized scripts, but today the Church encourages them to use their own words and rely on the guidance of the Holy Ghost.

Applying a technique called the *commitment pattern,* missionaries prepare their investigators, invite them to make commitments, and follow up to resolve any concerns.

✔ **Preparing:** The main way missionaries prepare investigators is to help them feel the influence of the Holy Ghost. During their teaching, they frequently bear solemn, earnest personal testimony that the principles are true. Other ways to help investigators feel the Holy Ghost include praying with them, singing a hymn with them, reading the scriptures aloud together, telling about personal spiritual experiences, and performing acts of service for them. Missionaries often say something like, "Do you feel a warm, good feeling right now? That's the Holy Ghost, testifying to you that what we're saying is true." (For more on the Holy Ghost, see Chapter 3.)

✔ **Inviting:** As they teach the gospel, missionaries often pause to ask investigators what they're thinking or feeling. When the time seems right, the missionaries ask the investigator to make certain commitments that move the investigator closer to baptism. The commitments include reading selected passages from the Book of Mormon, praying to know if the gospel is true, attending the local Mormon congregation, and quitting the use of tobacco or coffee. At some point, the missionaries ask the investigator to commit to a baptismal date (for more on Mormon baptism, see Chapter 6). The timeline varies from person to person — some people fulfill all the commitments within days, and others take weeks or months. Some just try to string the missionaries along because they enjoy the attention, but most missionaries will move on before too long.

✔ **Following up:** Of course, investigators face many potential roadblocks on the road to conversion, and few make it all the way to baptism. Missionaries do everything they can to assist their investigators, from researching additional scriptures to helping them find a good smoking cessation program. In the end, however, the Holy Ghost is the one who has to touch people's hearts. To encourage investigators to experience their own personal spiritual witness, missionaries share the following Book of Mormon scripture, known as *Moroni's promise:* "I would exhort you that ye would ask God, the Eternal Father, in the name of Christ, if these things are not true; and if ye shall ask with a sincere heart, with real intent, having faith in Christ, he will manifest the truth of it unto you, by the power of the Holy Ghost" (Moroni 10:4).

Working with local Church members

A big part of missionary life involves teamwork with the local Latter-day Saints, who provide the missionaries with moral support, give referrals of people to teach, and help welcome new converts into the Church. (Perhaps most important, local members often provide home-cooked meals for the missionaries. When left to their own devices, the young men in particular tend to overdose on ramen noodles or macaroni and cheese, a.k.a. the yellow death.)

When missionaries don't have teaching appointments in the evening, they usually spend that time visiting local members and giving them short gospel presentations. If the members are active churchgoers, the missionaries ask them if they have any friends or family members who may be willing to hear the gospel. If the members aren't currently active in the faith, the missionaries encourage them to start attending church again. In working with members, missionaries often use the same commitment pattern described in the preceding section (prepare, invite, and follow up). In fact, lots of returned missionaries continue using that pattern in their marriages and careers.

Church members play a vital role in conversion, because after a convert is baptized, the missionaries move on and the convert becomes the responsibility of the local congregation. All too often, that transition isn't successful. Although the new convert has usually developed a close personal relationship with the missionaries, he or she often hasn't bonded with anyone in the local congregation. For this reason, when a promising convert makes it beyond the first few missionary lessons, the missionaries often start bringing along local members to the teaching appointments, and they try to get the potential convert involved in the local Mormon social scene.

A Mormon prophet coined the phrase "Every member a missionary." The LDS Church continually urges Mormons to share the gospel with their friends and neighbors, help retain new converts, and reach out to reactivate members who've fallen away. Members are expected to hand out copies of the Book of Mormon and other Church publications, including handy little pass-along cards that offer a free LDS scripture book or video. The Church asks them to invite people into their homes to watch Church videos and, if possible, arrange for them to meet the missionaries. Although the rejection rate is still high, member referrals result in much more success than cold-calling techniques do, not only in terms of people joining the Church but also *staying* in the Church. Every Mormon congregation has members who are specifically called to help with missionary work, and they meet with the local full-time missionaries on a weekly basis to coordinate efforts.

When you hear the knock

Eventually, almost everybody in the world will encounter Mormon missionaries. Most people feel either irritated or apathetic toward them, but some feel curiosity or even compassion.

If you decide to invite the missionaries into your home, here are some suggestions to help the missionaries stay the course:

✔ If you're the opposite sex of the visiting missionaries and you're home alone or with children only, invite them to come back when an additional adult will be present.

✔ Turn off your TV and stereo, and put away magazines and newspapers.

✔ Don't smoke, drink alcohol, or use profanity in front of the missionaries. Offering them a refreshment is okay, but don't be like the guy in Melbourne, Australia, who got arrested for feeding marijuana-laced brownies to the missionaries!

✔ Be frank with them about your intentions and motivations. If you're willing to hear their message, say so. But if you just want to let them take a break or get to know them a little, be clear about that. If the weather is uncomfortably cold or hot, they'll especially appreciate it.

✔ If you must know their first names, go ahead and ask. But continue addressing them as Elder or Sister So-and-So, as indicated on their name badges. Feel free to ask about their hometowns and other small-talk stuff.

✔ If you invite the missionaries over for a meal, have it ready when they arrive, because they're not allowed to stay for more than an hour.

Following the rules

Succeeding as a missionary requires many strong qualities. A missionary must be patient, loving, persistent, and articulate. However, the Mormon missionary program seems to emphasize one virtue above all others: obedience. Over and over again, Church leaders tell missionaries that in order to effectively teach and convert people, they must follow the Holy Ghost's promptings, but they won't be able to feel the Holy Ghost unless they obey all the mission rules and regulations.

So what are the mission rules? Most of them are spelled out in a small, white booklet that missionaries are supposed to carry at all times. In addition, individual mission presidents make their own rules, which can sometimes seem arbitrary: coauthor Christopher Bigelow had one mission president who prohibited yellow neckties and asked missionaries not to use mousse in their hair. Because the mission president can't be everywhere at once, missionaries supervise each other by means of an organized system of zones and districts.

Following is an overview of the most significant rules that missionaries must follow:

- ✔ **A missionary *always* stays with his or her companion.** For many people, this rule turns out to be the most difficult aspect of serving a mission. The only time a missionary can be alone is in the bathroom — and not for too long. This policy is mainly to protect missionaries from falling into sin or danger. In most missions, missionaries can occasionally swap companions for an afternoon or evening, but they're supposed to spend most of their time working with their assigned companion, even if they can barely stand each other. On the other hand, many become lifelong friends.

- ✔ **Missionaries follow a rigid daily schedule.** They arise at 6:30, spend an hour in personal gospel study, pass another hour studying with their companion, and then work all day and evening, with one-hour breaks for lunch and dinner. If they're assigned to speak a foreign language, they take additional study time for that. Lights must be out by 10:30 p.m. Frankly, many missionaries face a big challenge in not wasting time by idling in the apartment, going shopping or sightseeing, hanging out too long at members' homes, and so on.

- ✔ **To stay spiritually pure, missionaries don't watch TV or movies, read magazines or newspapers, or listen to secular music.** Some missions allow classical music and others permit inspirational Mormon pop music, while some limit missionaries strictly to Mormon Tabernacle Choir recordings. The only reading material allowed is the scriptures, the Church magazines, and a handful of approved Church-published books.

- ✔ **One day each week, missionaries take a preparation day, or P-day.** This time isn't really a day off, because missionaries still wake up at 6:30, do their studying, and get back to work after dinner. During P-day, missionaries shop for groceries, wash their clothes, clean their apartments, fix their bicycles, write letters home, and run personal errands. If they have any time left over, they can play mission-approved sports or visit nearby tourist attractions, but they can't leave their assigned areas without permission, and they always stay with their companion.

- ✔ **With few exceptions, missionaries always wear their formal proselytizing clothes outside the apartment.** Exceptions include playing sports on P-day and performing service projects that require grubby clothes; running personal errands, however, isn't an exception. In addition, they always wear their missionary badges as a reminder of their missionary calling — some even wear them on their T-shirts while playing basketball. They must address one another by the title of Elder or Sister and not use first names or nicknames. (Yes, it's ironic that teenaged boys go by "Elder," which is a priesthood title from the Bible; see Chapter 4.)

- ✔ **Missionaries write weekly letters to their mission president and to their parents, and they're allowed to phone home only twice a year, on Mother's Day and Christmas.** Missionaries can correspond with anybody who lives outside the mission, including girlfriends or boyfriends waiting at home. One of the most common missionary clichés is receiving a Dear John letter, in which the girl back home who promised to wait for two years confesses that she's met someone else. (Dear Jane letters for the sister missionaries are less common.)

✔ **Missionaries don't date, flirt with, or even hug a member of the opposite sex.** Even in pairs, missionaries can't teach a member of the opposite sex without an additional chaperone present. If a missionary gets romantically involved with someone, the missionary is usually transferred far away, possibly even to another mission. If a missionary has sex, he or she is usually excommunicated and sent home, hopefully to repent and eventually get rebaptized. (For more on sexual standards, see Chapter 16.)

Rapid Growth: Mormonism around the World

In 1984, non-Mormon sociologist Rodney Stark made headlines when he proclaimed that The Church of Jesus Christ of Latter-day Saints was about to become the first major world religion to hit the global scene since the rise of Islam in the seventh century. Many scoffed at his prediction that by 2080, the LDS Church would claim at least 63 million adherents, and possibly as many as 265 million.

Some people believe that Stark's projections actually may have been too conservative. In 1998, Stark revisited the question and found that Mormon growth was 10 percent ahead of his timetable. Although sustaining the kind of growth the LDS Church has experienced in recent years is difficult — it grew at an average rate of 52 percent per decade for the 1980s and 1990s — the possibility certainly exists that within the lifetime of many readers of this book, Mormons will number in the tens of millions, rather than just 12 million as in 2004. However, others question the validity of Stark's projections, because Church growth seems to be slowing somewhat in the 21st century and rates of *retention* (keeping newly baptized members active in the Church) are often low.

How did this rather sudden growth in baptisms occur? After lying relatively low through the Great Depression and World War II, the Church found itself in a position to launch an unprecedented worldwide growth binge, which continues (although at a slowing pace) to this day. Under prophetic guidance, the Church poured tremendous resources into opening diplomatic relationships with individual nations, sending out more missionaries than ever, constructing meetinghouses and temples all over the globe, and providing local leadership support and resources to help the Church take root wherever it was planted. Table 14-1 illustrates how much the Church has grown since 1950, after missionary efforts were kicked into high gear.

Table 14-1	Church Growth, 1950 to 2003		
	1950	*1990*	*2003*
Total membership	About 1 million	7.3 million	12 million
Members outside the U.S. and Canada	8%	35%	54%
Number of full-time missionaries	6,000	40,000	56,000
Number of *stakes* (local clusters of 5–12 congregations)	180	1,700	2,624
Number of temples	8	44	116 (with 13 others under construction or in the planning stages)

Dealing with growing pains

The numbers in Table 14-1 certainly tell a story, but they don't tell the *whole* story. If Mormonism is going to be the next major world religion, it has to pass through adolescence before it reaches maturity — and like all adolescents, it may find that period a rather awkward time of self-definition. Religions change tremendously as they grow, and Mormonism is no exception. Consider how much it has changed since the pioneer days (see Chapter 13), when Mormons were clannish, Euro American, and polygamous. Today, they're multinational, multicultural, and most decidedly monogamous. Who knows what changes are in store for the next century, as Mormonism takes its place as a bona fide world religion?

So far in its rapid growth, several challenges have emerged, along with new Church programs and efforts to resolve those problems.

Retaining members

One of the most serious issues facing the Church at home and abroad is that of *retention,* or keeping new members active in the Church after they're baptized. In some parts of the world, baptism rates are very high, but converts may not remain active in the Church because they don't know local members, have cultural concerns about being involved in an American-based church, or simply don't yet understand the level of commitment expected of Latter-day Saints. The Church has two ways of comparing the numbers of those coming in and those actually *staying* in:

- ✔ **The percentage of baptized males who are ordained to the Melchizedek Priesthood:** In Utah, approximately 70 percent of men reach this level (usually when they're around 18 years old), but elsewhere in the world, the rate is much lower. In Mexico, for instance, it's 19 percent, and in Japan, 17 percent. These numbers mean that although men may be converting to the Church, they don't stay involved long enough to prepare for ordination. (For more on the priesthood, which all worthy Mormon males are expected to receive, see Chapter 4.)

- ✔ **Church attendance:** In the United States and Canada, the rate of weekly attendance at sacrament meeting is often thought to hover around 50 percent. So on a given Sunday, about half of all the people who are on the membership rolls of a particular congregation will actually be in church. But elsewhere in the world, attendance rates are far lower, around 20 to 30 percent. This may reflect members' difficulties in traveling to meetings that are far away when they don't have cars or reliable public transportation.

At this writing, the LDS Church has approximately 12 million people on its rolls, and it's hard to know how many of those folks actually consider themselves active Mormons. One issue to consider is that although the overall membership of the Church has grown by about 63 percent since 1990, the rate of creating wards and stakes (see Chapter 6) hasn't quite kept pace — from 1991 to 2003, the number of wards grew by about 39 percent and the number of stakes by about 43 percent. This fact is potentially significant, because new wards and stakes are created when an area has enough *active* Church members to justify a new congregation or group of congregations. Although a real growth rate of approximately 40 percent is certainly nothing to sneeze at, it's not quite the juggernaut that Stark predicted.

The Church takes retention very seriously. The Church president at the time of this writing, Gordon B. Hinckley, has made retaining converts one of the hallmark issues of his tenure as prophet, wanting to ensure that all new converts have three basic things:

- ✔ A friend in the Church to answer questions and nurture them in the faith

- ✔ A *calling* (an assignment or job to do in the local congregation; see Chapter 6)

- ✔ Training in the scriptures and the teachings of the Church through priesthood quorums, Sunday school classes, and *Relief Society,* the LDS women's organization (see Chapter 6)

During President Hinckley's time, an unprecedented change occurred: He started dispatching members of the Quorum of the Twelve Apostles for long-term assignments abroad, specifically to help members and missionaries work on retention. In 2002, he sent Apostle Dallin H. Oaks to the Philippines to help the Church strengthen new members there. Missionaries in the Philippines now work extensively on retaining new members and reactivating old ones through teaching, fellowship, and leadership opportunities. A similar strategy is being tried in Chile, where Apostle Jeffrey R. Holland was dispatched in 2002 to focus on retention.

Being sensitive to cultural differences

In the 19th century, Mormon missionaries encouraged converts abroad to gather to Ohio, Missouri, Nauvoo, or Utah — wherever Church headquarters was located at the time. Although this gave way to the bloom-where-you're-planted strategy that characterized the 20th century, it's sometimes still a struggle for Mormon converts abroad to remain true to their own culture and heritage while being involved in something that people often perceive as an American church.

As the LDS Church has expanded into many lands and cultures, it's made great strides in celebrating the local heritage of its members. Although the core teachings of the Church remain the same everywhere, its cultural expression can vary from place to place. For example, music is one area where American missionaries and Church members are learning to be more flexible with local customs in Latin America, Africa, and elsewhere. (Somehow, the staid organ music typical of American sacrament meetings just doesn't translate.)

One issue that crops up as the Church expands into many nations is the importance of training strong leaders who are native to those lands. When the Church relies too heavily on temporary missionaries to lead congregations and pass the sacrament, the congregations have no continuity of leadership, and the rising generation isn't prepared to assume those roles in the future. As you see in the next section, the Church has implemented several policies to address this issue.

Fixing retention and leadership problems

In addition to providing high-visibility leadership from headquarters, some of the Church's current strategies for improving retention and recognizing native leadership include

- ✔ **The Perpetual Education Fund:** The Church believes that its most promising asset is its young people all around the world. Through the Perpetual Education Fund, which we also discuss in Chapters 8 and 12, many young Mormons in underdeveloped countries can get an education through a revolving loan program the Church started in 2001. By 2004, the Church had granted loans to about 13,000 young men and women in Africa, Asia, Latin America, and other parts of the world. The Church believes that when young people can get an education and achieve financial stability, they're freed for greater Church activity and receive more blessings of the gospel.

✔ **Native missionaries:** In recent years, the Church has placed a greater emphasis on training missionaries who are native to the land (or at least to the language) where they're serving. For retention purposes, the immediate benefit is that native peoples don't dismiss Mormonism simply as an American church, but it also has the long-term effect of providing excellent native leadership in the years to come. Today's missionaries make tomorrow's local leaders.

✔ **Temple construction:** In the last decade, temple building has greatly accelerated around the world, and every continent except Antarctica has at least one temple. Locating temples closer to where members live increases the Church's visibility around the world and strengthens the individual members, who can make temple attendance a regular part of their spiritual life rather than a once-in-a-lifetime pilgrimage.

Getting to know the global Church

Whereas a hundred years ago Mormonism was largely an American and European faith, most of today's activity is happening in Africa, Asia, and Latin America. In fact, the Church has recently cut back its missionary force in Europe due to lack of response, and the convert growth rate in the United States is lower than it used to be. Clearly, the stage is set for the further growth of Mormonism in other key areas.

Latin America, especially Chile and Brazil

Latin America has become a hotbed of Mormon growth, and conversion rates are especially high in Chile, Argentina, Mexico, Guatemala, and Brazil. In fact, Brazil now boasts approximately 800,000 members, or about 7 percent of the Church's total membership. Most of that growth has happened in the last 25 years or so: After the Church extended the priesthood to all worthy men in 1978, including those of African heritage, racially mixed Brazil enjoyed an immediate burst of missionary activity and baptisms.

Although LDS Church members account for less than 1 percent of Brazil's total population, they're often visible. One Brazilian Mormon, pop singer Liriel Domiciano, has become something of a celebrity, known as much for wearing her distinctive LDS jewelry as for her soaring voice; for more on her, see Chapter 19.

Africa

As in Brazil, the 1978 priesthood revelation opened the floodgates for conversions in Africa. Africa is now host to over 150,000 Church members, and what's more, those numbers don't lie: Some parts of Africa have very high activity and retention rates, and the Africa West mission has almost all African missionaries.

Although meetinghouses are still few and far between because the majority of Africans live in rural areas, two temples now reside in Africa (one in South Africa and one in Ghana), with another one being constructed in Nigeria. In addition, a growing number of missionaries serve in Africa to meet the demand.

The South Pacific

Compared to its very recent growth in Latin America and Africa, Mormonism got a head start in the South Pacific. Missionaries arrived there in the late 19th century and quickly got to work converting the local populations, who already had some exposure to Christianity. (Fun fact: The 2001 film *The Other Side of Heaven,* distributed by Disney Home Video, chronicles the experiences of a Mormon missionary in Tonga in the 1950s. Check it out.)

In Tonga, about a third of the population is Mormon, and in Samoa and American Samoa, fully a quarter of the people are LDS. These three countries are, statistically, the most Mormon of any nations in the world. Incidentally, some Mormons believe that Polynesian islands were colonized long ago by Book of Mormon peoples (see Chapter 9).

Asia

Most of the Church's growth in Asia has occurred in nations that historically were colonized by Christians. In the Philippines, a Spanish colony for around 400 years, Roman Catholic Christianity was the norm when Mormon missionaries first started preaching the restored gospel there after World War II. Although Catholicism is still by far the dominant faith in the Philippines, the number of Mormon converts grows every year — despite the fact that not all those converts stick around for very long, as we mention in the preceding section.

Other Asian nations that don't have a historic base in Christianity haven't proved such fertile ground for Mormon missionaries, and the communist People's Republic of China and many Muslim nations are still closed to evangelizing missionaries. However, Japan, Hong Kong, Korea, and Taiwan all have strong LDS presences, with one or more temples located in each of those nations.

Stirring the Mormon Melting Pot

¡Bienvenidos a la Iglesia de Jesucristo de los Santos de los Últimos Días!

If you don't have a clue what we just wrote, you don't (yet) speak the second-most-popular language of The Church of Jesus Christ of Latter-day Saints. Based on current growth rates, demographers expect that Spanish will soon surpass English as the Church's most spoken language the world over. This change will result from international conversions and the conversions of Hispanics within the United States.

Although the LDS Church doesn't keep records on the ethnicity of its members, evidence suggests that even in the United States, the Church is moving away from its reputation as a white-bread institution, though it's still primarily white-led. African Americans have been quietly converting in growing numbers since the 1978 priesthood revelation (see the preceding section and Chapter 15), and several hundred African American men serve in *bishoprics* (composed of a bishop and his two counselors) and other local leadership positions. Some high-profile black converts include musician Gladys Knight, NBA star Burgess Owens, and the former Black Panther activist Eldridge Cleaver, who died in 1992.

Two recent trends may signal the future direction of the Church's increasingly diverse membership:

- ✔ **Planting churches in the inner city:** Traditionally, at least in the United States, the LDS Church has built chapels in suburban areas that are accessible only by car. Recently, the Church has been experimenting with storefront churches, renting or buying spaces in downtown areas so that members can walk or ride public transportation to meetings. One benefit of this move is that the Church gains a more discernible presence in the inner city. The strategy seems to be successful: In the Miami area, for example, the Church has tripled in membership since 1990, with most of the growth occurring among Caribbean, African American, and Hispanic converts. In New York, the Church recently adapted one of its buildings to become both a meetinghouse and a temple, with the top floors reserved for Latter-day Saints who hold a temple recommend. The place is a visible reminder of the growing Mormon presence in the midst of America's flagship city.

- ✔ **Offering services in other languages:** In larger areas, particularly urban ones, the Church offers wards and *branches* (smaller congregations; see Chapter 6) where members speak languages other than English. The most common is Spanish, but Church services are also conducted in Korean, Vietnamese, and Portuguese, among other languages. Salt Lake City even has a Tongan-speaking stake. Some Church members have discussed whether these so-called ethnic branches are helpful or whether they isolate non-English-speaking members, but the presence of these branches suggests the increasing ethnic diversity of the Church.

Chapter 15

Hot-Button Issues for Mormons

*L*ike any human organization, Mormonism has its fair share of seeming gray areas, contradictions, and conflicts that, for some members, require patience and faith to negotiate. Many of the challenges result from this young religion's dynamic, evolving nature, which leaves some people wanting to return to earlier ways, some struggling to reconcile the past with the present, and some trying to speed up the process of change.

This chapter looks at some of the key areas where Mormons and outside observers experience the most disagreement or lack of resolution. Certainly, the faith's zigzagging approach to race is troubling to many. Although Mormon views on gender roles have stayed fairly consistent — liberal for the 19th century, but conservative for the 21st — some people are dissatisfied with them. Mormon history and scripture are riddled with twists and pitfalls, and challenging voices from both inside and outside the faith continually clamor to be heard. Finally, many Mormons are still struggling to come to terms with homosexuality and polygamy (though not usually at the same time).

Race and Gender Controversies

Non-Mormons who happen to catch a session of LDS General Conference on the DISH Network may be startled by what they see: a parade of grandfatherly white men who run the show, codify the doctrine, and make all the decisions about the direction of the Church. In an age when women and African Americans have ascended to the top of many other Christian organizations, the current leadership of the LDS Church seems like a throwback to a less-enlightened age.

Of course, the situation isn't that simple, and what goes on in the upper echelons of leadership in Salt Lake City sometimes takes a while to catch up with the reality of Mormon life, which is increasingly international and multiracial. In this section, we explore the controversies that Mormonism has brought about with its leadership practices and also look at the role that women and blacks play in the Church.

Black and white and shades of gray

The Church of Jesus Christ of Latter-day Saints has experienced a lot of controversy in its history (for more on that, see just about any chapter in this book), but perhaps none so painful and long lasting as that caused by the Church's 150-year denial of the priesthood to its black members. As you see in this section, the issue wasn't *fully* resolved in 1978, when the Church finally reversed that priesthood denial.

Going back to the beginning

In the early days of the Church, when people in the southern United States still practiced slavery, outsiders generally saw the Mormons as abolitionists. In fact, when Joseph Smith ran for president of the United States in 1844, he did so on an abolitionist platform.

The prophet's commitment to rights for African Americans wasn't just civil, but also religious: Joseph Smith reportedly ordained at least one black man, Elijah Abel, to the Melchizedek Priesthood in 1836, and Abel served the Church as a seventy. (For more on the priesthood and the office of seventy, see Chapters 4 and 8.) Joseph Smith's brother William also ordained an African American barber, Walker Lewis, to be an elder. Clearly, early Mormons at least tried to apply the Book of Mormon's specific claim that the Lord "denieth none that come unto him, black and white, bond and free, male and female . . . all are alike unto God" (2 Nephi 26:33).

After Joseph Smith's death, however, Brigham Young and some other leaders increasingly preached reasons why the Church shouldn't allow African Americans to be ordained to the priesthood. No doubt the prevailing racist attitudes of 19th-century America influenced them. In 1852, Young announced that from then on, Church policy said that blacks didn't have access to priesthood ordination or to the temple and that they weren't allowed to serve as missionaries. Throughout the 19th century and continuing into the 20th, Church leaders offered two teachings as the basic justification for the ban:

✔ Leaders sometimes suggested that black skin was a consequence for individuals who were less valiant as spirits in the premortal life (for more on premortality, see Chapter 2). In this view, some individuals sided more readily with the Savior in the War in Heaven, and their reward was white skin, but others took their time to join forces with

Christ and got black skin as a result. One folk belief was that blacks stayed neutral in the War in Heaven, but several leaders taught that it was impossible to remain neutral.

✔ Even more pointedly, Brigham and others taught that those of black African descent were cursed with the *mark of Cain,* which set them apart because these spirits didn't qualify to receive the priesthood. Some felt that this consequence was because these spirits, during premortality, were somehow in cahoots with Cain, a wayward spirit who still qualified to come to earth and gain a body. But early Church leaders more commonly tied black skin to the curse of Cain in Genesis 4 of the Old Testament, saying that blackness was the direct result of Cain's sin on earth. This teaching was ironic because it seems to contradict the basic Mormon insistence that each human being is responsible only for his or her own sin, and not for someone else's transgression. (For more on that, see Chapter 2.)

The speculative belief about the mark of Cain, sadly enough, was popular in many other Christian traditions in the 19th century and into the 20th, but Mormonism had the unfortunate distinction of holding onto it longer than the Baptists, Methodists, and Presbyterians. The teaching on the premortal life was, of course, uniquely Mormon. Both ideas seem to have a basis in Mormon scripture (see Chapters 9 and 10), in which a curse of "blackness" is interpreted in a literal, physical way and not in a merely spiritual sense.

Changing Church policy

In June 1978, President Spencer W. Kimball announced that the priesthood was extended to all worthy men, regardless of race. Kimball's revelation, contained in the Doctrine and Covenants as one of two official declarations near the end of the book, obviously came as a result of deep prayer and constant questioning of the Lord.

Some outsiders dismissed the revelation as politically convenient, the Church's response to pressures from a wider culture that increasingly focused on civil rights. But if that were the case, the declaration probably would've happened a decade earlier. Instead, the catalyst seems to have been the Church's international expansion into multiracial areas such as Brazil, where it was about to dedicate a temple that many local members could never enter under the previous policy.

For many members of all races, the ban on blacks holding the priesthood caused considerable heartache. As with Kennedy's assassination, many Mormons can still tell you exactly where they were and what they were doing when they first heard the electrifying news that blacks could finally hold the priesthood. In Utah, drivers who heard the announcement on the radio turned on their car lights in the middle of the day and honked at one another, some weeping tears of gratitude and pulling over for spontaneous prayer.

Finding remnants of racism

Although the 1978 revelation was clear that all worthy males can hold the priesthood, it didn't specifically denounce the folk beliefs that people had touted for decades as justification for the old priesthood ban. Because the Church has never come out and said that blacks could've been as valiant in the premortal life as other people or refuted the notion that they all carry the mark of Cain, some Mormons continue to hold onto these politically incorrect beliefs and assume that they apply across the board as doctrine.

These old folk beliefs still linger in some LDS literature, for instance. The current edition of Apostle Bruce R. McConkie's influential work, *Mormon Doctrine,* still contains 1966 statements that the 1978 priesthood revelation surely overrode. In the book, for example, McConkie writes that those of African ancestry "have been cursed with a black skin, the mark of Cain, so they can be identified as a caste apart, a people with whom the other descendants of Adam should not intermarry." The fact that this statement, which many Mormons regard as untrue and offensive, remains in a quasi-official book written by a General Authority and published by a Church-owned press is a problem for many Latter-day Saints, black and white. Despite McConkie's statement, it's not uncommon to find interracial marriage and adoption among today's Latter-day Saints.

Mormon leaders hesitate to openly declare a past teaching to be wrong, preferring instead to quietly emphasize the Church's new direction and focus on the positive. Earlier editions of McConkie's book, for example, used to say that blacks "were less valiant in [the] pre-existence." That statement has disappeared. McConkie himself disavowed his earlier teachings shortly after the 1978 revelation, urging members to forget everything he ever said on the issue and instead to honor the "new flood of intelligence and light on this particular subject." And in 2004, a spokesman for the Public Affairs Department of the LDS Church stated, "Various opinions about the reason for this [priesthood] restriction were superseded by the 1978 revelation," which is certainly helpful, although this statement doesn't specify exactly *which* racial opinions are remnants of the past.

A prophet probably won't come right out and say, "Brigham Young was wrong about race," but he may do what LDS President Gordon B. Hinckley did in 1998 when speaking before a gathering of the National Association for the Advancement of Colored People. In his speech, President Hinckley affirmed the sacred worth and divine nature of every person, regardless of race. "Each of us is a child of God," Hinckley declared. "It matters not the race. It matters not the slant of our eyes or the color of our skin. We are sons and daughters of the Almighty."

Welcoming black Mormons today

Since the 1978 priesthood revelation, the LDS Church has experienced a mini-explosion of conversions in Africa, the Caribbean, and Brazil. (For more on this growth, see Chapter 14.) Most of these new converts are black or multiracial. Conversions among blacks in the United States have been slower, but they've still increased substantially since 1978. (The Church doesn't keep statistics on members' race and ethnicity, but anecdotal evidence and surveys suggest that black converts in the United States have a low retention rate, a possible indication that African American members' initial enthusiasm for the gospel diminishes when they find out about Mormonism's racially troubled history or don't adjust well into white-dominated Mormon culture.)

Some black members have entered the ranks of local and regional leadership in the Church, serving as bishops and in stake positions (see Chapter 6). Three men of African descent have served as General Authorities (see Chapter 8) since 1978, a number that will surely increase as more blacks rise through the ranks of Church leadership.

Meanwhile, the LDS Church has made conscious efforts to reach out to the black community in various ways, such as the following:

- A company owned by the Church publishes books on the experiences of black Mormon pioneers, raising the profile of African American Mormons.

- The Church sponsors a semiofficial organization of black Latter-day Saints called the Genesis Group (www.ldsgenesisgroup.org), which helps black members find fellowship and common ground.

- Mormons have initiated programs to help African Americans of any faith research their genealogy.

  In particular, in 2001 the Church released 11 years' worth of research on the Freedman's Bank, which in the 1870s held the financial records and family history information of thousands of former slaves. Approximately 10 million African Americans can now find out about their ancestors as far back as the 18th century. In 2004, the Church contributed time and money to creating a FamilySearch center in the new National Underground Railroad Freedom Center in Cincinnati, Ohio.

These efforts are small but promising bridges in the future relations of blacks and Mormons, who may find reconciliation by exploring the past.

Beyond Molly: Women in the LDS Church

She bakes delicious bread, wears corduroy jumpers, and shuttles her six kids around in a slightly battered minivan. She's a stay-at-home mom who decorates her suburban home with quilts she made herself and serves as president of the *Relief Society,* the Church's organization for women.

Meet Molly Mormon, who serves as most people's stereotype for a Mormon woman. (She's also the bogeywoman to Latter-day Saint women who feel they can't measure up.) Is she an accurate stereotype? Yes and no. True, every ward has at least one Molly Mormon, and the stay-at-home mom remains the gold standard for Mormon families. Mormons are totally committed to the idea that children come first and believe that no role is more fulfilling than parenthood. A popular saying in the Church is that no success outside the home can ever compensate for failure within it. Because of this claim, Mormons place a high value on keeping a parent at home full time with the children. Usually, the mom gets that job, though we do know of a few LDS families with stay-at-home dads.

But the story has another side, too. Mormon women today take up public as well as private roles on a wide and diverse spectrum. Mormon women in the United States are statistically just as likely to work outside the home as non-LDS women, though they're more likely to work part time and take off a chunk of time when their kids are young. Mormon women are in the work-place in all kinds of fields — education, medicine, law, science, business, what have you. Many resent the assumption that Mormon women are some-how oppressed.

Pointing out where Mormon theology serves women well

Mormon women often feel that their religion offers elements that are uniquely empowering to women, including

- **Belief in a Heavenly Mother:** Mormonism may be unique among Christian denominations in its conviction that God has a dynamic and holy female partner (see Chapter 3). Although Mormons don't yet know everything about Heavenly Mother because God hasn't revealed much about her, they cherish the knowledge that they have a mother in heaven as well as a mother on earth.

- **An unusually positive view of Eve and her role in creation:** As we explain in Chapter 2, Mormons don't see Eve as someone to blame for bringing sin into the world or — darn it! — forcing us all to forsake the good life in Eden. Instead, Eve was a heroine who understood that the highest and noblest task of humanity was to become more like God and that she could help open the way only by eating the forbidden fruit of mortality. You go, girl!

- **An understanding of the divine nature of each woman:** In the Mormon view, it takes two to tango up into the celestial kingdom, and women are every bit as holy and innately divine as men. (In fact, some would argue that women are naturally *more* holy, but we'll save that topic for another day.) For more info on the celestial kingdom and eternal marriage, see Chapters 2, 5, and 7.

Is abortion ever okay?

The short Mormon answer to the question of whether abortion is justified is *extremely rarely.* Mormons don't support abortion except in the following unusual circumstances:

- When a physician believes the mother's life is in serious danger
- In cases involving rape or incest
- When a physician has determined that the baby will have defects leading to death shortly after birth

Even in these circumstances, many Mormons would choose to have the baby, because LDS belief and practice are so geared toward the fundamental importance of children. For Mormons, remember, a mortal life is necessary for the progression of each spirit to the celestial kingdom. So abortion is a kind of double-whammy sin: Abortion violates the sixth commandment ("Thou shalt not kill") by taking a physical life, and it also prevents — or at least delays — a person's ability to progress spiritually.

When female converts join the LDS Church, they're typically asked during the baptismal interview if they've ever had an abortion. Mormons consider unnecessary abortion to be such a serious sin that an individual must specifically repent of it before the sacred ordinance of baptism can be administered. The Church can discipline members who receive, perform, or agree to unnecessary abortions.

Drawing a line between women and the priesthood

Although Mormon women may seem to be second-class citizens because they don't hold the priesthood, most Mormon women don't feel that way. In the first place, the priesthood, like other spiritual gifts, is a vehicle for service. The role isn't an opportunity for men to lord their position over women but to serve the Church and the world. (In fact, the first level of the Aaronic Priesthood is called *deacon,* which stems from the Greek word for servant.) Moreover, Mormon women can still receive all the blessings of the priesthood even though they aren't ordained to it. (For more on the priesthood, see Chapter 4.)

Mormon women can hold a number of nonpriesthood callings, such as teachers, auxiliary presidents, counselors (see Chapter 6 for those three positions), family-history specialists, media-relations directors, and full-time missionaries (see Chapter 14). On a practical level, women generally have as much to do with the running of local church units as men do. In fact, most Mormon women feel they have all the opportunities for service that they can handle!

A few LDS women have fought for women to be granted the priesthood, and though President Gordon B. Hinckley hasn't ruled out the idea as a future possibility, he and other Church leaders have expressed doubt about it. A number of folk rationales exist among rank-and-file Mormons for why women don't hold the priesthood, though no official doctrine on this point exists. For some possible explanations, see Chapter 20.

Hullabaloo over History and Holy Books

Some of the Church's most persistent controversies stem from ongoing debates about its history and sacred texts. In this section, we touch on some of these enduring arguments — er, *discussions* — with a special focus on the Book of Mormon and the LDS commitment to faithful history.

The Book of Mormon in the hot seat

Type **Book of Mormon problems** into any Internet search engine and you'll get tens of thousands of hits. Bitter anti-Mormons spit out criticisms of the Book of Mormon, claiming that it doesn't present real history and that the story is a big hoax. Meanwhile, zealous Latter-day Saints counter with what they say is evidence for the book's historicity and trustworthiness, answering their critics' charges and sometimes unfairly cutting down the critics themselves.

Questioning the Book of Mormon

Welcome to the Book of Mormon wars. If you thought the wars discussed *in* the Book of Mormon were fierce, wait till you get a taste of the ongoing wars *about* the book. The questions never end: Did Joseph Smith make it up? Did he plagiarize it from someone else? Can archaeological findings prove or disprove the Book of Mormon? Why haven't archaeologists discovered the great cities that the book mentions? How come today's Native Americans don't have Hebrew DNA? And on and on. Although we can't answer all these questions for you (about a gazillion more-detailed sources are available to help), see Table 15-1 for some of the more common criticisms of the Book of Mormon and the Mormon response.

Table 15-1	Questions and Answers about the Book of Mormon
Issue in Question	*The Mormon Response*
How can the Book of Mormon talk about horses, when no archaeological record of horses before the arrival of Columbus exists?	The word *horse* in the Book of Mormon may be only an approximate English translation, with a similar animal intended in the original language. (This theory is also true of the mentions of iron and steel in the Book of Mormon.) Of course, horses may have existed in ancient America, but physical evidence hasn't yet sprung up.

Issue in Question	The Mormon Response
Didn't Joseph Smith just make up a lot of biblical-sounding names to make the Book of Mormon appear to be ancient?	Mormons don't think so. At least 14 names in the Book of Mormon aren't found in the Bible but have been discovered on various Hebrew inscriptions and funeral documents from the period. Because archaeologists have discovered these names since the 1960s, Joseph Smith couldn't have known that they were authentic Hebrew names.
Doesn't the fact that Christ says almost exactly the same thing when he appears in the Book of Mormon as he does in the New Testament show that Joseph Smith merely plagiarized New Testament passages?	The texts have some minor differences, but they're indeed very similar. From the Mormon point of view, this fact doesn't present a problem. Why would Christ teach one gospel to the people in the Old World and a totally different one to the folks in the New World?
Isn't the Book of Mormon too unsophisticated in its writing style to be an authentic work of scripture?	True, the translation sometimes sounds clunky in English ("and it came to pass," repeated ad nauseam). But the Book of Mormon also features sophisticated allegories, *chiasmus* (complex, symmetrical literary patterns), and some beautiful poetry.

Putting up a defense

In 1979, some ambitious Mormons founded an organization called the *Foundation for Ancient Research and Mormon Studies,* or *FARMS* for short, to expand Book of Mormon scholarship and prove to the world that the Book of Mormon is legit. (And no, its scholars don't come to work in overalls and straw hats.)

FARMS is unapologetically *apologetic,* by which we mean that the organization exists to defend the faith. In fact, FARMS is now housed at Brigham Young University, having taken its place as a sort of officially unofficial Mormon organization. The Church doesn't directly sponsor the organization, but leaders have certainly used some FARMS findings in official writings and settings.

FARMS has raised the bar for Mormon scholarship, professionalizing it to the extent that it has answered many of the old anti-Mormon criticisms with serious research into linguistics, archaeology, biblical studies, and the like.

Ultimately, of course, the question "Is the Book of Mormon true?" is a question of faith and not of reason. But the work of FARMS makes such faith intellectually conceivable.

Conquering questions about genetics

The hot new issue these days in the Book of Mormon wars is definitely the problem of DNA studies. In a nutshell, DNA tests have shown no genetic link between modern-day Native Americans and Jews, or descendants of the original Israelites. If Native Americans are supposed to be descended from the Lamanites of the Book of Mormon (see Chapter 9), wouldn't these two groups have a direct genetic link?

Not necessarily. For starters, Mormon scholars today are very careful to note that not all Native Americans are necessarily descended from the Lamanites; in fact, given the amount of murder at the end of Book of Mormon times, it's likely that very few are. Although some 19th-century Mormons boldly claimed Lamanite ancestry for *all* American Indian peoples, Mormons today realize that the reality is probably far more complex. The Book of Mormon itself never says that all Native Americans are Lamanite descendants or that Nephites and Lamanites were the only people in the New World from 600 B.C. to A.D. 400, the 1,000-year period when Book of Mormon events took place. (In fact, the book is pretty clear that other groups were there already.) In addition, a DNA researcher at Brigham Young University has made a convincing case that although DNA studies can establish some genetic relationships, they can't prove lack of genetic relation so far back.

The DNA findings, then, don't disprove the Book of Mormon, though they may disprove former *interpretations* of the Book of Mormon.

Faithful versus accurate history

One of the other ongoing hot-button issues for Mormons is the question of how to appropriately communicate Mormon history. Some Latter-day Saints prefer to write history by highlighting how God intervened at key moments to guide his people, the Mormons, to ever-greater righteousness. Sometimes, this method risks leaving out evidence of the flaws and foibles of the human participants in history. Others write Mormon history in the same way that they'd tell the story of any group, focusing on human activity and presenting key leaders such as Joseph Smith with warts and all. Some Church leaders feel that this method inappropriately downplays the miraculous and may cause members to lose faith in the ways God acted through LDS leaders of the past.

Obviously, these two approaches can sometimes come into conflict. Such was the case in September 1993, when six members of the LDS Church were excommunicated or *disfellowshiped* (a lesser disciplinary action after which an individual remains a member of the Church but can't take the sacrament, hold a calling, or enter the temple). All six had published or spoken publicly about Mormon history, theology, or leadership; several were outspoken feminists.

At the end of the 20th century and into the 21st, the debates became quieter, with few high-profile excommunications. Perhaps because of the negative media scrutiny in 1993, or perhaps because of the gentle patience that has marked Gordon B. Hinckley's presidency (he became the prophet in 1995), the Church seems to have backed off slightly from public battles. Some signs suggest that the Church may be relaxing its opposition to secular approaches to history. Regarding the Mountain Meadows Massacre controversy, for example (see Chapter 13), the Church has agreed to open its archives to investigators and make available every document it possesses related to that tragedy.

Evolution or evil-ution?

Some Mormons view evolution as one of God's creative tools, but others deny it happens or say it's merely the byproduct of a fallen world.

Mormons don't profess to understand exactly how, when, or where God created humans or what went down prior to Adam, but most Mormon leaders teach that God's actual spiritual children have been inhabiting human bodies on this planet for only about 6,000 years. In any event, nothing in Mormon theology precludes the notion that other biological forms existed on earth millions of years ago, especially since some Mormons believe that the "days" referred to in the Genesis creation story symbolize a much longer period of time that could be consistent with the time span of organic evolution. Mormons expect God to reveal the solution to the fossil puzzle—dinosaurs, Neanderthals, and so on—in his own due time. In the meantime, Mormon biologists take comfort in the belief that scientific truth and religious truth spring from the same basic source, with a great deal still to learn in both arenas.

Various leaders of the Church have agreed or disagreed with evolutionary theory, but the Church has never taken a specific official position on the subject. Back in 1909, when evolution was a hotter topic, the LDS First Presidency affirmed that

- God created humans in his own image.

- Adam was the first human on this earth.

- Human bodies bear the characteristics of the eternal spirits dwelling within.

- Humans didn't develop from "lower orders of the animal creation" but resulted from a "fall" from a higher state of being.

According to this First Presidency statement, the only form of human evolution that really matters to Mormons is that everyone is capable of eventually evolving into a god.

Today, LDS Church–owned Brigham Young University teaches the theory of evolution, along with other scientific theories that may or may not stand the test of time.

Voices in Conflict

Inside Mormonism, freewheeling debate about all aspects of the religion bubbles up in a variety of independent venues, despite official attempts to keep matters sweet and simple. From outside the faith, people who are convinced that Mormonism isn't true, as well as ex-Mormons who are disgusted with the faith, broadcast their exposés and warnings to anyone who will listen.

Free speech on the inside

For racehorses, blinders serve a valuable purpose by keeping the horse focused on reaching the finish line. Under mandate to bring people to the Savior and prepare for his Second Coming, Mormonism uses some focusing techniques to keep people aimed at the goal. The main formal focusing technique used by the Church as an institution is the Correlation Committee, which simplifies and sanitizes all official Mormon messages to members and the world.

However, for many Mormons — especially those with an intellectual or artistic bent — there's a time and place for taking off the blinders and looking at situations from a personal, realistic slant, as opposed to just taking the Church's position at face value. The Internet, for example, is full of Mormons having frank, intimate, questioning conversations that the Correlation Committee would never approve for official Church communication channels.

When it comes to formalized publications and meetings, two independent organizations carry the torch of open Mormon expression:

- The Dialogue Foundation, which publishes *Dialogue: A Journal of Mormon Thought*
- The Sunstone Education Foundation, which publishes *Sunstone* magazine and holds symposia

Both groups provide essential outlets for freethinking Mormons, although both struggle with sometimes coming across as too critically authoritative and with not paying enough respectful attention to traditional, orthodox views.

The LDS Church has sometimes disapproved of these groups, even going so far as to excommunicate participants who won't shut up about sensitive topics. As a result, many Mormons keep these groups at arm's length, if they're aware of them at all. However, several thousand Mormons receive considerable insight and inspiration from participating, even though not personally agreeing with or accepting everything that comes up. Many people long for the day when Mormon culture grows less polarized and more capable of carrying on an open, tolerant discourse.

Sunstone

More calm and careful now than it used to be, the Sunstone Education Foundation (www.sunstoneonline.com) explores Mormon topics in two ways: by publishing a magazine and by sponsoring yearly symposia in Salt Lake City and other cities across the country. Following the motto "Faith Seeking Understanding," this group bills itself as an open, honest, and respectful forum for examining and expressing all aspects of Mormonism.

Sunstone magazine (shown in Figure 15-1), which ideally comes out six times a year, is a lively, visually appealing, 80-page smorgasbord of Mormon analysis and art, mixing heavy-duty articles with lighter reading, including cartoons and Mormon news.

Held in Salt Lake City and in smaller versions around the United States, Sunstone symposia strive for overall balance, although the more-controversial sessions tend to get blown out of proportion when the media covers them. Active, faithful Mormons publish articles in the magazine and speak in Sunstone forums, and so do inactive Mormons, excommunicants, outside observers from other faiths (or no faith), and representatives of fringe groups.

Figure 15-1: A typical edition of *Sunstone* magazine.

Cover image courtesy of Sunstone magazine.

Here's a sampling of session titles from the 2004 Sunstone symposium:

- ✔ "Internet Mormons versus Chapel Mormons"
- ✔ "Real Goddesses Have Curves (and Identities)"
- ✔ "The Best Idea in Mormonism"
- ✔ "How 'Christian' Should Mormonism Strive to Be?"

Dialogue

The main activity of the Dialogue Foundation (www.dialoguejournal.com) is publishing a quarterly journal that aims to connect Mormonism with the bigger picture of world religious thought and human experience. Published in a format somewhat like that of a loosely refereed academic periodical (with scant illustrations and occasional scholarly articles that seem to go on forever), *Dialogue* includes many provocative and groundbreaking articles, poems, short stories, and works of visual art.

Criticism from the outside

From the beginnings of Mormonism, perhaps no other U.S. religion has inspired such a large industry of critics — and yes, we mean *industry,* because some people earn their livelihoods from anti-Mormonism. This resistance isn't surprising, considering that the LDS Church claims to be the world's only true religion and aggressively evangelizes members of other faiths. From the Mormon perspective, the devil is the one who's inspiring people to attack and misrepresent God's church.

Sign-wielding anti-Mormon protestors routinely picket large Mormon events, and countless books, pamphlets, Web sites, and films attempt to expose the LDS Church as a sham. Nearly all anti-Mormons hail from evangelical Protestant Christianity, particularly the Southern Baptist denomination. In fact, many of the most dedicated anti-Mormons are former Mormons who "found Christ." Their purpose is twofold: helping people leave Mormonism and keeping members of their own flocks from converting to Mormonism.

What's the beef?

Common anti-Mormon complaints include the following:

- ✔ **The Bible:** Much of the Protestant objection to Mormonism arises from different interpretations of Bible teachings, particularly the Godhead's nature and identity, how and why people are saved, and what happened to the Savior's church after he left the earth. In addition, conservative

Protestants object to Mormonism's acceptance of scripture beyond the Bible. (For more on Mormon views regarding the Bible, see Chapter 9.)

✔ **The Book of Mormon:** As we discuss earlier in this chapter, critics find many problems with Mormonism's key scripture, mostly along the lines of alleged chronological errors and lack of scientific proof. (For more on the Book of Mormon, see Chapter 9.)

✔ **Brigham Young:** Joseph Smith's prophetic successor made several statements that haven't aged well, including racist teachings and the concept that Adam was in fact God, which today's Church doesn't accept as doctrine. (For more on Brigham Young, see Chapters 12 and 13.)

✔ **Cult:** In sociological lingo, a *cult* is a small and intense religious group that unites around a single charismatic individual. Some Mormons acknowledge that their faith began as a cult of Christianity, in much the same way that Christianity began as a cult of Judaism. However, the term has taken on extremely negative connotations, and many anti-Mormons claim that Mormonism is *still* a cult, even 175 years and 12 million members later. (For more on Mormonism's founding, see Chapter 4.)

✔ **Joseph Smith:** The Angel Moroni told Mormonism's founding prophet that his name would "be both good and evil spoken of among all people" (Joseph Smith — History 1:33 in the Pearl of Great Price; see Chapter 10). Some of the most vicious anti-Mormon attacks focus on Joseph's own alleged character flaws, such as his youthful treasure digging and adult practice of polygamy. (For more on Joseph, see Chapters 4, 9, 10, and 11.)

✔ **Masonry:** Much has been made about the similarities between Mormon temple rites and Masonic rituals. (For more on Mormon temples, see Chapter 7.)

The Mormon response

As with most controversies in the religious arena, countering or proving anti-Mormon claims with hard evidence that either side would accept is difficult. Some Mormons enjoy debating, but most simply express their hope that truth seekers will learn about the religion from fair, trustworthy sources; take their questions and concerns directly to God in prayer; and then follow their own hearts.

Mormons sometimes warn each other to shun faith-destroying anti-Mormon literature, because it's not unheard of for members to abandon the faith due to doubts raised by anti-Mormons. The LDS Church itself doesn't typically respond directly to anti-Mormon claims, but some groups make an effort to defend the faith, most notably the Brigham Young University–based FARMS (farms.byu.edu), which we discuss earlier in this chapter, and the independent Foundation for Apologetic Information & Research (www.fairlds.com).

Getting along with other religions

Brigham Young famously urged tolerance and the right of all people to worship as they see fit. He told the Mormons to leave their neighbors alone and "let them worship the sun, moon, a white dog, or anything else they please, being mindful that every knee has got to bow and every tongue confess." So although Mormons believe that in the afterlife all people will acknowledge Jesus Christ as Lord, in this world we all have to get along despite our religious differences.

How does that idea play out in daily life? Mormons believe very strongly in not allowing any one religion to be fused with civic government and in permitting all people to worship or not worship as they please. (See D&C 134 and the 11th Article of Faith.) Mormons do, of course, try to persuade governments to pass legislation that they view as moral and just — however, they feel the government doesn't have the right to sponsor or suppress anyone's religion.

Although they believe that their church is the only institution that Christ established on the earth, Mormons applaud the many righteous works of members of other denominations who are inspired by the Savior's love and example. President Gordon B. Hinckley, the LDS prophet at this writing, speaks often and very positively about the strong friendships he enjoys with individuals of other faiths and the good that he believes they're achieving in the world. Most Mormons — especially those who live outside of the U.S. Intermountain West and are therefore part of a minority religion — value the moral contributions of their non-Mormon neighbors, though they may agree to disagree about points of theology. In addition, the LDS Church sometimes donates money to other religions, such as in 2000 when it gave a Hindu society in Utah $25,000 to help build a Hindu temple there.

Beyond Heterosexual Monogamy

In Mormonism, the two most troublesome forms of sexuality usually overlap with opposite ends of the ideological spectrum. Polygamists tend to be conservative fundamentalists who claim that they're upholding true Mormon tradition and that the mainstream LDS Church has drifted astray. Practicing Mormon homosexuals, on the other hand, tend to be progressive liberals who celebrate change and hope the LDS Church will one day grow to accept them.

Ultimately, however, the LDS Church excommunicates people who persist in either taboo sexual behavior. Meanwhile, many members struggle to resist homosexual desires or come to terms with their polygamous heritage.

Born that way?

For Mormons, heterosexual procreation is a basic principle of the universe and an essential element of God's nature. In addition, the LDS Church's recent

Proclamation on the Family (see Chapter 10) declares that gender is an eternal attribute of each person's soul. When it comes to homosexual tendencies and gender ambiguities, Mormons see those challenges as symptoms of an imperfect, fallen world that the Savior will eventually heal.

In the meantime, the LDS Church says that homosexual *behavior* is a sinful moral choice rather than an acceptable lifestyle option or unavoidable part of someone's personality. However, most Mormons recognize that some people — for complex reasons probably related to both temperament and environment — truly struggle with unwanted homosexual impulses. In the Mormon view, involuntarily feeling homosexual attraction isn't sinful; acting on the temptation — or failing to resist it — is where the sin comes in. In addition, Mormon authorities frequently affirm that people must treat homosexuals with kindness and charity — in other words, "Hate the sin, but love the sinner," as it's commonly said.

Mormons don't like to use the word *gay* because it implies acceptance of the gay cultural identity. Instead, Latter-day Saint authorities use terms such as *same-gender attraction,* which describes the temptation rather than the person. Although Mormons believe that God doesn't allow people to be tempted beyond what they can bear, they understand that some battles may last an entire lifetime, with victory only gradually emerging after years of effort and resistance.

Overcoming the sin

In bygone times, Mormons were among those who tried to cure homosexuality via extreme measures, such as aversion therapy, shock treatments, and — perhaps most ill-advisedly of all — heterosexual marriage. Nowadays, however, Mormons struggling with same-gender attraction can usually get enlightened assistance from LDS-affiliated therapists. In general, these therapists help their clients reclaim what the Church teaches is their God-given heterosexuality. They try to help patients figure out where their gender development went off-kilter so that those people can rebuild a proper sexual identity. Some Mormons eventually overcome same-gender attraction enough to become successful heterosexuals, and some never do.

Several support groups are available for Mormons dealing with same-gender attraction, whether their own or that of a loved one. An independent group called Evergreen International (www.evergreeninternational.org) finds the most favor among mainstream Mormons, with LDS General Authorities often speaking at its conferences. Evergreen's mission is to help individuals "overcome homosexual behavior and diminish same-sex attraction."

However, some people remain in the Church while defining themselves as gay. In general, the LDS Church doesn't discipline its members for having a homosexual *orientation,* only for acting upon it by engaging in any form of nonmarital sex. A few organizations and support groups cater to homosexual

Latter-day Saints, including Affirmation (www.affirmation.org), which seeks to help gay, lesbian, bisexual, and transgender Mormons come to terms with their identities.

Fighting gay marriage

Although Mormon authorities warn against any abuse or mistreatment of people with a homosexual orientation, the LDS Church formally opposes gay marriage. In fact, it has donated funds to support anti-gay-marriage campaigns and urges members to exercise their political muscle against it. Not since the LDS Church helped defeat the Equal Rights Amendment in the 1970s has the official organization spoken out so prominently on a national social issue — and the fight's only just beginning.

I do, I do, and I do again . . .

Ah, the P-word that just won't go away: *polygamy*. If there's one thing that most Mormons — especially missionaries and public relations workers — wish they could change about the religion's image, it may be the 19th-century practice of polygamy. Although the mainstream LDS Church completely abandoned the earthly practice of polygamy by the early 20th century, Mormon-style polygamy is still going strong among rebel sects in Utah and elsewhere, to the mainstream Church's chagrin. (For more on Mormon polygamy's historical roots and rationales, see Chapter 13.)

Nowadays, the way most Mormons feel about contemporary polygamists is similar to how many Protestant Christians feel about Mormons. Not only does the LDS Church excommunicate polygamists, but also Church officials insist that polygamists shouldn't be called Mormons or linked in any way with the LDS Church. On the other hand, polygamists claim they're the only true Mormons, because they've stayed true to founding prophet Joseph Smith's teachings instead of allowing themselves to become corrupted by the pressures of the world.

For those who don't care much about religious issues, Mormon polygamists still hold considerable fascination, as if the Amish had adopted free love. Increasingly, Mormon-related polygamists pop up in the national news, often for crimes such as child or spousal abuse, incest, statutory rape, child abandonment, welfare fraud, kidnapping, and murder. (Mainstream Mormons point to these crimes as evidence that polygamy without God's sanction is corrupt.) In addition, polygamists are starting to crop up more often in popular culture. In 2004, for example, cable giant HBO announced that it's developing — with the help of producer Tom Hanks — a new drama called *Big Love* about a polygamous family living in Utah.

The LDS Church and politics

The LDS Church has gotten involved in some key political efforts to defeat same-sex marriage legislation in states such as Alaska, Hawaii, and California, pouring money into the fight to prevent gay marriage from being recognized by the government. However, that departure is unusual for the Church, which typically shies away from direct involvement in politics. The Church makes exceptions to its general rule of nonintervention when issues arise that the First Presidency sees as a moral threat to the nuclear family, such as same-sex marriage or, in the 1970s, the Equal Rights Amendment.

That's not to say that individual Mormons aren't involved in politics. Latter-day Saints consider voting a religious imperative, and they're active in all aspects of the political process. Utah remained pretty Democratic through the Great Depression, even going against the suggestion of the Church president (published on the front page of the Church-owned *Deseret News*) to vote against Franklin D. Roosevelt in 1932. But after World War II a seismic political shift occurred, in which most of the Latter-day Saints followed their leaders, almost all of whom were at least leaning toward the Republican Party.

This shift was due, at least in some measure, to the connection of LDS leader Ezra Taft Benson serving during President Eisenhower's oh-so-Republican cabinet as secretary of agriculture in the 1950s. At that time, Mormons gravitated to the Republican Party because it strongly opposed communism, which many Mormons considered to be a serious threat.

Although the communist menace is a thing of the past, many U.S. Mormons still self-identify with the Republican Party today, especially because it seems to most closely embrace their conservative social stance. However, a vocal minority of Mormon Democrats is ever present, including the highly visible Nevada politician Harry Reid, who became the U.S. Senate Minority Leader in November 2004.

On a regular basis, the First Presidency issues an official statement that local leaders read from the pulpit of every LDS congregation around the world, reiterating the Church's policy of neutrality when it comes to political parties, platforms, and candidates and encouraging individual members to study the issues and exercise their right to vote.

Although many grassroots Mormons appreciate the Church's refusal to talk about its polygamous past, others wish the Church could find a way to more openly and positively come to terms with its history. After all, many born-and-bred Mormons have polygamous ancestors, and LDS scriptures still proclaim doctrines of plural marriage (most notably section 132 of the Doctrine and Covenants). Even today, many mainstream Mormons believe — or perhaps *fear* is a better word — that some people will practice polygamy in heaven. In fact, in today's LDS temples men can still get eternally sealed to more than one woman, usually in the case of remarriage after the first wife dies (see Chapter 7).

Chapter 16

Sacrificing on Earth to Receive Blessings in Heaven

. . . .

In This Chapter

▶ Obeying a strict code of sexual purity

▶ Following Mormon dietary regulations

▶ Donating a tenth of your income

▶ Going without food and drink once a month

. . . .

*I*n a distinctively Mormon hymn written during the pioneer era and still widely sung, Mormons croon, "Sacrifice brings forth the blessings of heaven." For Mormons, sacrifice is the essence of life's mortal test, because sacrificing earthly things is how people become pure and obedient enough to one day reenter Heavenly Father's presence and become like him.

Fortunately, Mormonism no longer typically requires the extreme, all-encompassing sacrifices common in 19th-century pioneer days, when persecution drove Mormons to give up their possessions and comforts, their places in society, their homes, and sometimes even their lives for faith's sake (see Chapters 11 through 13 for more on Mormon history). These days, Mormonism's most challenging sacrifices come mostly in the form of disciplined lifestyle choices that are increasingly at odds with what mainstream culture accepts and values.

The most difficult area is probably sexuality, which Mormons believe must be strictly channeled into marriage between one man and one woman. Famously, Mormons abstain from coffee, tea, tobacco, alcohol, and harmful, addictive substances (which doesn't include sugar, thank heavens). In addition, committed Mormons donate 10 percent of their income to the Church, and once a month they skip two meals as an exercise in spiritual discipline and charitable giving. In this chapter, we discuss these major sacrifices and why Mormons believe that making them is the road to holiness and, ultimately, heaven.

Chase and Be Chaste: The Law of Chastity

At an independent Mormon dating Web site called HotSaints.com (check it out yourself if you don't believe this site actually exists), the motto is "Chase and Be Chaste," which is a pretty accurate summary of the Mormon attitude toward sexuality. Far from being a debased-but-necessary earthly function or even simply a gift of God to humankind, sexuality is nothing less than a divine attribute of the Heavenly Parents themselves (see Chapter 3 for a more-detailed discussion of Mormon views on Heavenly Father and Heavenly Mother). Although it's not a topic that comes up in Mormon Sunday school today, earlier leaders taught that the eternal parents procreated human spirits through a glorified version of the same procreative act that humans use on earth.

Stated in the simplest terms, the Mormon Law of Chastity prohibits any sexual relations outside of lawful, heterosexual marriage. Chastity is one of the covenants that adult Mormons make in the temple (see Chapter 7 for more on the temple covenants). For Mormons, practicing chastity includes not only abstaining from sexual activity outside of marriage, but also actively seeking a suitable marriage partner, because self-imposed celibacy thwarts God's designs for humankind. In fact, some Mormons believe that the Savior himself may have been married during his earthly ministry.

Understanding the purposes of sexuality

Mormons believe that Heavenly Father entrusted humans with sexuality not only to populate this planet but also as one of the key elements of their mortal test (for more info on the mortal test, see Chapter 2). In fact, how people conduct themselves sexually and parent any resulting offspring may be one of the most important factors in determining their eternal status. Those who live worthily and become eternally sealed to their mate in a Mormon temple can become heavenly fathers and mothers themselves, giving birth to spirit children and creating earthly planets to house those children during their own mortal tests. Considered from an eternal perspective, the reasons why Mormons consider sex a sacred privilege that the Law of Chastity must govern are clear.

When other Christians express concern that the Mormon concepts of God's sexuality and humankind's eternal potential are blasphemous, Mormons point to certain biblical passages for support. During his New Testament ministry, for example, Jesus Christ commanded his followers to "be ye therefore perfect, even as your Father which is in heaven is perfect" (Matthew 5:48). To Mormons, the meaning of *perfect* includes not only freedom from mistakes and blemishes but also completeness and wholeness. In fact, one dictionary definition of the word *perfect* is full sexual maturity, which is what Mormons are striving for on the eternal level, as commanded by the Savior.

Staying chaste

The Law of Chastity not only forbids any form of fornication or adultery, but also encompasses "anything like unto it," including pornography, immodesty, and masturbation. For married Mormons, Church leaders caution them never to be alone with a member of the opposite sex except family members. For dating couples, the Church warns against intimacy beyond holding hands, hugging, and mild kissing.

Steering clear of pornography and masturbation

In the Mormon view, pornography damages spirituality, degrades the actors and viewers, and plants the seeds of sexual sin. Mormon authorities constantly warn members of all ages to be vigilant against pornography, particularly on the Internet. Mormon sensitivity to anything resembling pornography is so high that some LDS authorities advise members to avoid all R-rated movies, although that area remains controversial. Church leaders counsel youth, in particular, to avoid such movies. (For more about R-rated movies, see Chapter 18.)

As far as masturbation is concerned, Mormons consider it an impure practice that thwarts self-discipline, dulls spirituality, and can become a gateway to other sins, including pornography and homosexual activity. It's nowhere near as serious as other sex-related sins, of course, but Mormons say it requires repentance — in fact, young people aren't cleared to go on missions until they're free of the practice. When it comes to public sex education, Mormon parents are responsible for correcting any teachings that go against Mormon standards, particularly the notion that masturbation is acceptable.

Maintaining modesty

In the area of modesty, the main sacrifice adult Mormons make is avoiding any clothing style that isn't compatible with the temple-issued underwear commonly known as *garments,* which cover the entire torso to the knee and shoulder, with the front neckline dipping down almost to the bottom of the breastbone (for more information about temple garments, see Chapter 7). For sports and swimming, adult Mormons can remove their temple garments and don appropriate gear. Mormon females generally don't wear two-piece bathing suits, and a new industry has emerged to provide Mormon girls with modest prom dresses.

Another aspect of Mormon modesty is that members don't defile the sanctity of the bodily temple with tattoos or piercings, except for *one* piercing per ear for women. However, as we point out in Chapter 8, this one-piercing standard is more cultural than doctrinal, and standards vary somewhat throughout the

Church (especially outside the United States). If someone got a tattoo before joining or becoming active in the LDS Church, he or she isn't necessarily expected to have it removed, but members in good standing don't get new ones.

Keeping hands and tongues under control

Whether teens or adults, dating Mormons ideally don't do more than hold hands, hug, and exchange closed-mouth kisses. Some Mormons even believe that a couple's first kiss shouldn't happen until across the altar, right after their temple marriage.

According to the Church-produced pamphlet *For the Strength of Youth,* Mormon teens shouldn't date before age 16, and they're instructed not to

- ✔ Kiss anyone passionately (commonly interpreted as French kissing)
- ✔ Lie on top of anybody
- ✔ Touch anyone's private areas or allow anyone to touch theirs, clothed or unclothed

Leaders urge unmarried adults to follow these guidelines as well. Of course, many couples venture into riskier territory. Those who end up having sex must confess to their local congregational leader as part of the repentance process (see the later section "Dealing with sexual sin"). For those who manage to stop short of fornication, many Mormons would say they need to see the bishop too, if they've gone far enough to feel guilty about it. However, some couples who've reached second or third base try to repent without the bishop's involvement.

Enjoying marital intimacy

Although Mormons view procreation as one of the primary purposes of sex, they also place a high value on its role in expressing marital love and binding couples together emotionally and spiritually. Mormon publishers put out detailed books about how to enhance sexual pleasure and compatibility, and couples enjoy wide latitude for sexual expression within marriage, as long as they avoid "unholy and impure practices" and put their temple garments back on afterward.

You can find statements against oral sex from Mormon leaders, but the practice isn't unheard of in Mormon marriages, and the official policy seems to be "don't ask, don't tell." When a married person does inquire about the acceptability of oral sex, local authorities typically answer along the following lines: "If you're uncomfortable enough that you needed to ask, the act probably isn't a good idea." As far as anything more adventurous than oral sex, the command to avoid all "unholy and impure practices" pretty much prohibits a practicing Mormon from even thinking about it.

What about birth control?

Statements against birth control used to be much stronger in Mormonism, with warnings that limiting the number of children could force spirits intended for one's own family to be born into other families, perhaps even a non-Mormon family. Authorities urged Mormon parents to sacrifice their own plans, preferences, and conveniences in order to fully accommodate Heavenly Father's ordained course of nature, with the warning not to put the mother's health at undue risk. As a result, unusually large families, with children sometimes numbering in the double digits, used to be more common in Mormonism.

Today, nearly all forms of contraception are in fairly wide use among Mormons. Under "Birth Control," the current Church handbook of instructions for local leaders simply states, "The decision as to how many children to have and when to have them is extremely intimate and private and should be left between the couple and the Lord. Church members should not judge one another in this matter." The only form of elective birth control that LDS leaders forbid is abortion, although the Church makes the rare exception in cases of rape, incest, and medical necessity (see Chapter 15). The Church discourages surgical sterilization except when medically necessary, but it's not unheard of for a Mormon couple to get snipped or tied when they feel they're finished having children.

Receiving the blessings of chastity

All in all, Mormons see the Law of Chastity as the only safe, sane way to deal with sexuality, which leaders sometimes compare to electricity. Although electricity can be a powerful, life-changing force for good when properly channeled, it can be devastating when unleashed through misuse or negligence. Mormons take pride in statistics demonstrating that they enjoy some of the world's lowest rates of venereal disease, teenage pregnancy, divorce, and other problems. That's not to say, however, that Mormon statistics don't sometimes match or even exceed the mainstream average in certain areas, depending on the study. As Joseph Smith himself warned it would be, sexual immorality in all its varieties is the main besetting sin of Church members.

Being chaste requires constant vigilance against tempting thoughts, flirtations, and entertainments. Mormons strive to continually subdue their unchaste desires and impulses. The blessings from doing so include not only peace of mind, stronger marriages and families, and freedom from the consequences of sin, but also the hope of a full and complete resurrection, including eternal procreative powers (see Chapter 2).

Dealing with sexual sin

According to the Mormon outlook, mortals who crash during their earthly test-drive of procreative powers — and fail to fully repent — will be resurrected to a lesser degree of glory that doesn't include the opportunity for eternal parenthood (see Chapter 2 for more on the afterlife). Although Mormon authorities understand that a predatory pedophile is in a completely different class from an engaged couple who has sex before their wedding ceremony — and treat such offenders very differently — leaders collectively refer to sexual sins as second only to murder in degree of seriousness. Mormons believe that God will fully forgive most sexual sins, but that forgiveness doesn't come easily.

Finding forgiveness for sexual mistakes

If a Mormon succumbs to sexual temptation, the process of repentance includes the following steps:

1. **The sinner confesses his or her sexual misbehavior to the local bishop during a private interview in the bishop's office, located inside the meetinghouse.**

   Members are encouraged to consult with the bishop at the earliest signs of sexual weakness instead of waiting until they've fallen completely into sin, because sexual sin is like spiritual cancer — better to catch it early.

2. **The bishop offers support and guidance for repentance, emphasizing how the Savior's Atonement applies to the sinner and can help him or her repent.**

3. **The bishop gives practical advice for overcoming the sin, including referring the sinner to a professional if he or she needs extra help to overcome addictions or compulsions.**

   Repenters are expected to make lifestyle changes similar to those advisable for a recovering alcoholic, in terms of avoiding places, people, situations, thoughts, and emotions that lead to sin.

4. **The bishop decides what disciplinary action is necessary to protect the Church's integrity and help motivate the sinner in the repentance process (see the next section).**

5. **To gain institutional forgiveness, the sinner usually needs to demonstrate several months of renewed religious devotion under the bishop's supervision, including increased prayer, fasting, scripture study, charitable service, and — of course — complete chastity.**

   If a couple experiences an unwed pregnancy and decides not to marry, the Church urges them to place the baby for adoption through LDS Family Services (www.itsaboutlove.org).

Facing the music

Although Mormon disciplinary actions aren't common occurrences, the vast majority of the punishments that do occur are triggered by unchaste behavior. Discipline varies from situation to situation, depending on the frequency of the sin, the sinner's level of responsibility, his or her degree of remorse, and other factors. In making disciplinary decisions, Mormon leaders seek inspiration, because only Heavenly Father fully knows the sinner's heart and what consequences will best foster full repentance.

In general, the following disciplinary pattern seems to apply for cases of unlawful intercourse:

- Youth usually face probation, which temporarily prohibits them from certain aspects of worship and participation.

- Single adults who've received their temple endowments (see Chapter 7) usually face *disfellowshipment,* a lengthier, more-formal probation imposed and overseen by a committee of local church leaders.

- Full-time missionaries and married adults often face *excommunication,* which means the complete loss of their Church membership. An excommunicated person may, however, eventually qualify for rebaptism after a period of repentance.

Sexual sins that stop short of intercourse usually prompt a lesser sanction, but sex crimes such as rape, incest, and pedophilia virtually always result in excommunication. Local leaders are expected to do everything possible to protect innocents and involve law enforcement authorities without violating confidentiality. In fact, the Church maintains a special hotline to help local leaders correctly handle situations involving sexual abuse.

As we discuss in Chapter 15, homosexuality is a troublesome issue for the LDS Church. Mormons don't blame anybody for feeling involuntary same-sex attraction, but homosexual *behavior* is always sinful and can result in Church discipline. LDS bishops and therapists strive to help individuals reduce their same-sex attraction and prevent or stop any homosexual behavior.

Whaddya Mean, No Coffee? Living the Word of Wisdom

Many non-Mormons know very little about what their Mormon friends believe about Christ, the afterlife, or the plan of salvation. But they almost always know about the Mormon health code! Maybe they had neighbors who didn't drink beer at the block's annual Super Bowl party or worked with a woman who refused the coffee served at Friday morning department meetings. The Mormon commitment to good health usually makes an impression.

Where did this commitment come from? Well, like many aspects of the LDS religion, the duty to maintain good health has its roots in revelation, in this case a section of the Doctrine and Covenants (see Chapter 10) that Mormons call the *Word of Wisdom.* The legend surrounding its origin is that Joseph Smith and other early LDS leaders used to chew tobacco during Church meetings, spitting juices on the floor. Joseph's wife, Emma Hale Smith, was disgusted by this act, and her complaints led the Prophet to ask God whether tobacco use was really appropriate for Latter-day Saints.

The Lord's response, contained in D&C section 89, covered far more than just tobacco; it also restricted the consumption of wine, liquor, meat, and hot drinks (today interpreted to mean tea and coffee of any temperature). Although many Mormons understand this scripture as suggesting that all caffeine is bad and should be avoided, this idea isn't official Church doctrine; the Church allows members to decide that issue for themselves, and some members choose to drink cola.

Some people wonder whether Mormons get kicked out of the Church for kicking back a few. The answer is no: Basic Church membership isn't contingent upon keeping the Word of Wisdom. However, members with Word of Wisdom problems can't hold priesthood callings or get a temple recommend. So although nobody gets excommunicated for smoking a cigarette or being spotted in Starbuck's, the full blessings of Church membership, including temple attendance, are reserved for those who walk the straight and narrow path.

Interpreting the Word of Wisdom

For most of the 19th century, Latter-day Saints interpreted the Word of Wisdom a little more loosely than they did in the 1830s or do today. Moderation, rather than entire abstinence, was the key:

- ✔ Coffee, tea, and alcohol were among the list of provisions that the Church recommended for the westward trek in 1846 (see Chapter 12).

- ✔ Church leaders used wine for the sacrament at Sunday meetings and at the dedication celebrations for the temples in Kirtland, Ohio, and Nauvoo, Illinois.

- ✔ Brigham Young chewed tobacco for most of his adult life. (He acquired this nasty habit before he converted to Mormonism, and he struggled valiantly to give it up, managing to quit for a nine-year period between 1848 and 1857.)

- ✔ Young encouraged some early Latter-day Saints to begin vineyards in Utah, sending one group of Swiss immigrants to southern Utah to start the *Dixie Wine Mission.* Their vineyards were very successful, and they sold wine all over the Western United States in the late 19th century. Young had no tolerance for drunkenness, vulgar behavior, or the domestic violence that sometimes resulted from alcohol abuse, but he and other Latter-day Saints in the late 19th century did permit a small intake of wine or Danish beer.

So why are Mormons today teetotalers, when their pioneer ancestors weren't? The fact that early Latter-day Saints regarded the Word of Wisdom differently than Mormons do today isn't evidence of hypocrisy but of historical change. Here are some reasons:

- ✔ **It allied Mormons with the temperance movement.** In the early 20th century, American culture began examining food and health issues more strictly, with alcohol being a particular concern. The LDS Church was in favor of the temperance measures of the day and began substituting water for wine in sacrament meetings in July 1906. Fifteen years later, the Church made strict adherence to the Word of Wisdom a requirement for temple admittance, with no exceptions.

- ✔ **It helps build a Mormon identity today.** After the Latter-day Saints gave up the practice of plural marriage, strict compliance in living the Word of Wisdom became another way of signifying Mormon identity. Today, keeping the Word of Wisdom helps bond the Mormon community as well as strengthen individual Latter-day Saints.

- ✔ **It saves Mormons from modern addictions that are potentially very serious.** This reason could be the most compelling one of all for today's zero-tolerance policy. Nowadays, addictive substances are more widely available than ever before, and a Mormon has to learn to say no to the small things so that she's in the habit of saying no when someone offers her a drug that could ruin (or take) her life.

By the way, the Word of Wisdom contains an explicit mention that Mormons should eat meat sparingly and in times of cold or famine, if at all. Also, Joseph Smith taught that animals have spirits. But most U.S. Mormons are unabashed carnivores, and the Church has never taken an official position on vegetarianism. Lorenzo Snow, the Church's president in the early 20th century, emphasized his wish that all Latter-day Saints would stop eating meat, but Joseph F. Smith, the prophet who followed him, didn't stress this counsel.

Live long and prosper: A principle with promise

Although non-Mormons tend to focus on all the things that Mormons give up in order to practice the Word of Wisdom, most Latter-day Saints view the principle differently. They feel that keeping these precepts enhances their health and that they enjoy a greater well-being.

Soda and other gray areas

Although individual General Authorities have expressed opinions against the consumption of caffeine in soft drinks, the Church has never taken an official position on the subject. We know from a *60 Minutes* interview that President Gordon B. Hinckley doesn't drink caffeinated sodas, but plenty of rank-and-file Mormons do.

By the same token, the Word of Wisdom doesn't expressly forbid decaffeinated coffee, though many Church members would say this substance falls under the biblical urging to "avoid the very appearance of evil." In other words, although decaf isn't an official or absolute no-no, most Mormons would frown upon it because it looks, smells, and tastes like regular coffee.

In such matters, the Church urges its members to resolve the issue themselves through prayer and study. When thinking about whether the Word of Wisdom forbids a certain substance, Mormons should ask themselves these questions:

✔ Is it habit forming, illegal, or potentially addictive?

✔ Is it known to be harmful to health or spiritual well-being?

Some longevity studies support this notion. In the United States, Mormon men who are active in the Church live about seven and a half years longer than non-Mormon men, and religiously active Mormon women live about five and a half years longer than their non-Mormon peers. Active Latter-day Saints also enjoy lower rates of cancers of the colon, stomach, pancreas, uterus, ovary, and prostate than do non-Mormons. The Word of Wisdom certainly seems to live up to its billing as a principle with promise, helping Latter-day Saints enjoy robust health and longer lives.

In addition to its physical benefits, Mormons believe they can enjoy spiritual rewards from keeping the Word of Wisdom, including greater awareness of and thankfulness for God's gifts of food and drink. Mormons also know that they're protecting their bodies — which they believe to be temples for their spirits — from potentially harmful substances.

The last word on the Word of Wisdom

Here's a quick rundown of what's kosher for Mormons and what's not, food-wise:

✔ **Definitely okay:**

• Hot apple cider and hot cocoa.

• Caffeine-free soft drinks.

- Chocolate (which entertainer Marie Osmond has labeled "Mormon medication").

- Moderate quantities of meat.

- Postum (which is fine from the perspective of Mormon orthodoxy, though maybe not from the standpoint of good taste).

- A diet rich in grains and vegetables.

✔ **Probably okay:**

- Herbal tea (according to the Word of Wisdom, herbs are "to be used with prudence and thanksgiving").

- Cooking with wine, because the alcoholic content burns off during cooking. Some very conservative Mormons, however, won't use so much as a teaspoon of vanilla extract in a batch of chocolate-chip cookies.

✔ **Possibly okay:** Nonalcoholic beer and sparkling cider rather than champagne. However, some Mormons think they should avoid even *looking* like they're drinking forbidden substances, because drinking them may confuse people.

✔ **Probably not okay, but no one knows for sure:** Decaffeinated coffee. A June 1988 article in the official Church magazine never said that decaf is forbidden, but it did take pains to point out that decaf drinkers suffer elevated risk for ulcers and other gastrointestinal difficulties. However, bishops and stake presidents aren't supposed to deny a member a temple recommend for drinking decaf, and Apostle John Widtsoe advised members that consumption of decaffeinated drinks isn't against the Word of Wisdom.

✔ **Definitely not okay:**

- Alcohol, including wine and beer.

- Black tea, green tea, and other caffeinated teas.

- Coffee and recipes that use it (which may even include desserts like tiramisu, though the authors hope not).

- Iced coffee and iced caffeinated tea.

- Illegal drugs, recreational drugs, and illicit prescription medications.

- Tobacco.

✔ **The subject of endless debate:** Caffeinated soft drinks (see the sidebar, "Soda and other gray areas").

Clear as mud? Great.

Tithing: Paying the Lord's Tax

Many Churches apply the word *tithe* to any donation, but Mormons take the word's meaning of "tenth" literally. The LDS Church expects its members to give the Church a full 10 percent of their *increase,* which most people understand to mean all the money they earn, after business expenses but before personal living expenses.

Sound hard? It is. For many families who faithfully pay tithing, the cost is one of the biggest household budget items, in some cases second only to the mortgage check. For this reason, tithing is often the most difficult day-to-day commandment to obey, requiring some real spiritual and financial discipline to develop the habit and stay consistent. To get a head start, Mormon children typically start handing coin-filled tithing envelopes to the bishop before they're even baptized at age 8, and the financial clerk faithfully deposits these donations with the rest of the tithing.

Paying tithing gladly

Prophets have taught that paying tithing is a commandment essential to both full *salvation* (returning to live with God) and *exaltation* (becoming like God). Obeying this law is a requirement for entering the holy temple (see Chapter 7), although not for participation in local meetinghouse activities.

By paying tithing, Latter-day Saints demonstrate their love for the Savior and devotion to his earthly kingdom. Tithing funds provide the main means for the Church to carry out its missions, but members don't get to vote on how the Church spends or invests their tithing dollars. The Church expects them to pay their tithing without grudge or reservation, and failure to do so is considered the same as robbing God. It counts as tithing only if it's paid to the Church; members can't allocate their tithing dollars to other charities and causes.

Even in Old Testament times, people tithed. This principle was part of the *Law of Moses* (the law that governed the Israelites until Christ came), and the prophet Malachi recorded the following words, which Mormons often quote from the Bible: "Bring ye all the tithes into the storehouse, that there may be meat in mine house, and prove me now herewith, saith the Lord of hosts, if I will not open you the windows of heaven, and pour you out a blessing, that there shall not be room enough to receive it. And I will rebuke the devourer for your sakes, and he shall not destroy the fruits of your ground; neither shall your vine cast her fruit before the time" (Malachi 3:10). In other words, when God's people demonstrate their faithfulness by tithing, God responds by pouring out his spiritual blessings.

Tithing is only a warm-up exercise

As much of a sacrifice as paying tithing is, Mormons see it as a lesser law that God gave because people couldn't live the higher law. Basically, tithing is God's Plan B, a first step in learning to live Plan A, which Mormons call the Law of Consecration.

Revealed by God to the Prophet Joseph Smith early in the Church's history, the *Law of Consecration* basically meant that the Latter-day Saints should give everything they owned to God's kingdom. In practical terms, the Mormons pooled together all their worldly possessions under a central Church authority and received only enough back to meet their personal needs. The goal was to live together in complete harmony and abolish economic

inequalities. According to scripture, some ancient groups succeeded at living this law — but for the most part, the 19th-century Latter-day Saints couldn't make it work for long.

Many prophets have taught that the principles that living the Law of Consecration requires, such as selflessness and cooperation, are necessary to become like God. At some point, when God feels they're ready to handle it, the Latter-day Saints expect to start fully living the Law of Consecration, which includes devoting all their time and talents to God's kingdom. In the meantime, individuals pay tithing and strive to maintain an attitude of consecration in their own minds and hearts.

Figuring the tithing bill

The Church doesn't specify exactly how members should calculate their tithing, instead urging them to seek the guidance of the Holy Spirit. Some Latter-day Saints pay 10 percent of their *gross income,* meaning the total amount before Uncle Sam claims his share, and some pay 10 percent of their *net income,* after taxes. In addition to wages and salaries, tithing is generally understood to apply to cash gifts, inheritances, unemployment benefits, and interest and dividends. Some Mormons, if they received a car as a gift, would even look up the Kelley Blue Book value and pay 10 percent of that amount.

Rather than pass around a collection plate during meetings, Mormons pay tithing privately. In a small holder hanging on the wall outside the bishop's office, the Church provides donation forms and gray envelopes imprinted with the bishop's home mailing address. After filling out the form and enclosing a check or cash, the member hands the sealed envelope directly to the bishop or one of his two counselors, or they can mail it to the bishop if it doesn't contain cash. The financial clerk, a ward's volunteer bean counter, keeps track of donations and issues each member a statement at the end of the year to use for tax purposes. Members can pay tithing at whatever frequency they choose, up to yearly.

Settling up at year-end

At the end of the year, the bishop invites each family to meet with him to review whether their tithing donations have been accurately accounted for and to declare whether the total represents a full tithe or not. Typically, parents and their children all attend the annual tithing settlement together.

The LDS Church encourages members to attend tithing settlement even if they haven't paid a full tithe. This meeting provides a good opportunity to sit down with the bishop, and often, he can point the way to budgeting or employment help, which can enable members to start paying a full tithe in the future.

Knowing where your tithe is going

The Church doesn't disclose financial information, but outsider estimates of annual tithing income usually fall in the $4 billion to $6 billion range. In addition, the Church maintains several for-profit businesses and investments, which outsiders estimate net several hundred million more dollars annually. In response to such estimates, the Church usually claims they're exaggerated, and spokesmen point out that overall, the Church's assets consume far more income than they produce.

The Church uses tithing to pay for the following:

- ✔ Family-history facilities and equipment
- ✔ Local congregational activities and expenses
- ✔ Meetinghouse and temple construction, including land acquisition
- ✔ Modest living allowances for full-time Church leaders (local leaders aren't paid for their volunteer efforts)
- ✔ Salaries and facilities for a few thousand Church administrative employees

In addition, tithing can make up shortfalls not covered by members' payment of donations, tuition, and fees for the following:

- ✔ Charitable welfare efforts
- ✔ Church publications and materials, including over 100 million copies of the Book of Mormon to date
- ✔ Church universities, schools, and educational programs, including the nation's largest private university, Brigham Young University in Provo, Utah
- ✔ The worldwide missionary program

To some members' dismay, the Church has occasionally used tithing dollars to fight for conservative social values in the political arena, whether through anti–Equal Rights Amendment activities in the late 1970s or opposition to same-sex unions in Alaska and Hawaii in the late 1990s. However, such use isn't common; for more on politics, see Chapter 15.

From the practical standpoint, tithing money lends an equality to Mormonism that is missing in many other denominations. All tithing funds flow through Church headquarters. Wards with affluent members send more tithing money to Church headquarters than the ward receives in return, while wards with lower-income members send less tithing money to headquarters than the ward receives. The result is a high level of ward equality across the Church, rather than a few upscale wards with elaborate programs and many wards that have to manage their programs on meager resources.

Receiving tithing dividends

Although tithing is a test and a sacrifice, Mormons consider it the source of many blessings, both material and spiritual. Tithing may appear to lop off 10 percent of the family budget, but Mormons believe the Lord compensates them with other blessings, sometimes including economic benefits.

In Mormon speeches and magazines, inspiring stories dramatize the benefits of faithfully paying tithing even when the immediate financial outlook is bleak. A typical tithing story may involve a family deciding to use its last hundred dollars to pay tithing rather than buy food. The next morning, they wake up to find bags of groceries anonymously left on the porch.

However, paying tithing is no guarantee of prosperity. Tithing doesn't cancel out foolish financial choices, and money problems can still happen to those who faithfully obey this commandment, although they exercise faith that the Lord will hasten their economic recovery.

Making the sacrifice of paying tithing has a profound effect on members' lives, binding them more closely to the religion. Sitting in a meetinghouse or temple, a tithe-paying member can take pride in having made a substantial personal investment in the beautiful facilities. In addition, obeying this commandment helps with discipline, humility, and other traits that bring a person closer to the Savior.

Reinstating the importance of tithing

At the end of the 1800s, the Church faced serious financial trouble, due mainly to legal problems related to polygamy. Fewer than a quarter of the Latter-day Saints were paying tithing, and only about a third of those paid in cash. Most people paid their tithing *in kind,* donating every tenth chicken, bushel of wheat, or whatever form their material increase took.

Sustained as the Church's fifth prophet in 1898 at the age of 84, President Lorenzo Snow launched a campaign to reemphasize tithing, and the Latter-day Saints heeded their prophet's call. By the time President Snow died in 1901, the Church had regained financial stability. Before long, the Church started discouraging payment of tithing in kind, and tithing became a requirement for entering the temple.

Fast Sunday: The Slowest Sabbath of the Month

The first Sunday of the month is likely to find some Mormons a little grumpy. Their patience with their children is at a low ebb, and they grab at the sacrament bread with a little more enthusiasm than usual. The sound of their church meetings is occasionally punctuated by prominent abdominal growling. Yet throughout the day, they often feel the Spirit more strongly than usual. Welcome to Fast Sunday.

Mormons have fasted since the 1830s, though members during the 19th century usually observed the fast on the first Thursday of the month. Not until 1896 did the all-church fast begin occurring on Sunday.

Then as now, Mormons often paired their once-a-month fast with a special testimony meeting. For sacrament meetings held on other Sundays of the month, members of the three-man bishopric choose speakers beforehand from ward members and visiting area leaders. But the monthly fast-and-testimony meeting has an open-mike tradition allowing any Mormons, including small children, to speak about their beliefs and experiences and testify about the Savior. (For more on testimony meetings, see Chapter 6.)

Fast Sunday can be difficult for some people (and the Church doesn't recommend it for everyone — see the section "How and when to fast (And who shouldn't)" for more information about who the Church *doesn't* ask to fast). A full two-meal fast (about 24 hours) is tough to do; the only food or liquid that passes the lips of observant Mormons during this period is the sacrament bread and water. But fasting is one of the regular spiritual disciplines that can bring people closer to God and each other and offer new insights into spiritual questions.

Why Mormons fast

Mormons point to three basic reasons why they fast once a month, which we explain in this section.

Mastering the body

Much of life's energy is consumed with meeting physical needs and wants. You spend time earning a living to buy food; you spend time shopping for and preparing that food; you linger over that food and then wonder if maybe you also deserve some dessert. In fact, many people expend a whole lot of energy each day just thinking about food.

To Mormons, fasting offers an opportunity to step off the food treadmill for a while and think more about God, who gave us food and every other good thing. It gives Mormons the chance to test their bodies and cleanse them. Church leader Melvin Ballard once said that self-control over the physical body is one of the greatest achievements humans can attain, because "the greatest battle any of us shall ever fight is with [the] self."

Helping the poor

When Mormons fast, even those who are affluent and well fed gain a short-term understanding of what going hungry feels like. From this experience, they grow in compassion and desire to serve others.

True to the Mormon character, members act out this compassion in a very concrete, practical way. When Church members fast, they contribute money to the Church welfare fund by checking the fast offering option on the tithing form. The Church encourages members to donate, at a minimum, the money that their family would've spent on the two meals they skipped. The bishop of each ward decides how to apply fast offering money, which he and the Relief Society president (the woman who oversees the ward's women's organization) can discreetly use to help members in need pay for food, clothing, and shelter.

If members can afford to give more, the Church encourages them to do so. When Mormons pay a generous fast offering, they can feel good that they're helping others, both locally and internationally. As we explain in Chapter 8, any money in the welfare fund that isn't needed to help Church members spills over into the Humanitarian Relief Fund, which provides aid to people of other religions all over the world.

Growing spiritually

The most important and lasting benefits of fasting are spiritual. Doctrine and Covenants section 59, for example, equates fasting with joy and rejoicing. (See Chapter 10 for more on the D&C, one of the four standard works of scripture in the LDS canon.) At times, this idea seems like a daunting task for Mormons — fasting is hard enough, and doing so with joy can seem impossible when your blood sugar is plummeting. But Mormons aspire to fast as the Bible says Jesus instructed, not with a sad countenance but with quiet joy (Matthew 6:16).

The key element is prayer. For Mormons, the fast begins and ends with a prayer and is often characterized by spontaneous prayers for strength in between ("Heavenly Father, please help me not to steal my toddler's Cheerios!"). On a serious note, Mormons believe that fasting makes prayer more meaningful — and prayer, in turn, gives meaning to the fast.

Here are two key spiritual benefits of fasting:

- ✔ **Fasting helps Mormons grow closer to each other.** Because all Mormons around the world fast on the same Sunday, everyone's in the same pickle. (Oops, a food reference — amazing how many of these words pop up when people are trying not to think about food.) Fasting also has a communal element to it that happens on the local level. Sometimes, a whole ward fasts and prays on behalf of a church member who's sick or injured. Other times, the ward fasts and prays together for a particular spiritual purpose — for example, for the missionaries to be able to find people who want to study the gospel.

- ✔ **Fasting makes Mormons feel closer to God.** In addition to the monthly fast, many Mormons fast before they attend the temple (though in recent years, the Church has encouraged members to be cautious about fasting before a temple session, because too many people were passing out during temple rituals). Mormons also do extra fasts on an individual level when they're seeking inspiration about a particular issue in their lives, such as how to reconcile with a family member, prepare for a new *calling* (see Chapter 6), face a health challenge, or know the truth regarding a specific gospel principle. However, Church leaders don't recommend fasting for more than 24 hours at a time or more than about once a week.

A fast becomes an acceptable sacrifice to God when humility and honest searching accompany it. Giving up food isn't enough; Mormons believe they have to do so in a spirit of prayer and delight. When a fast just involves not eating, it has little spiritual benefit and actually focuses *more* attention on food. The goal is to think less about food and other worldly concerns by praying more purposefully than usual. (By the way, many people find that eating a big meal before starting a fast makes them feel hungrier during the fast than eating a smaller meal.)

How and when to fast (And who shouldn't)

The basic guideline is that Mormons abstain from food and drink for two meals, or about 24 hours, though some individuals vary in how they fast. The regular monthly fast usually begins after dinner on Saturday evening and continues until dinner on Sunday evening — well, maybe midafternoon. In addition to praying during the fast, Mormons usually begin and end the fast with a personal or family prayer that says, in essence, "Heavenly Father, I'm now beginning a fast for such-and-such a purpose" or "Heavenly Father, I'm now ending my fast and going into the kitchen to stuff my face with crackers, even though dinner is only ten minutes away."

Because the first Sundays in April and October are always General Conference Sundays, those monthly fasts take place on the last Sundays of March and September. A ward can also move Fast Sunday if a ward or stake conference conflicts with it. (For more information on these Church conferences, see Chapters 6 and 8.) One of the most simultaneously sinking and exhilarating feelings in Mormonism comes when a member, while munching breakfast on a Sunday morning, suddenly remembers it's Fast Sunday: "Darn, I forgot! I guess I may as well eat another piece of bacon."

In general, the following groups are exempt from the fast:

- ✔ Pregnant and nursing women.

- ✔ Those who are "delicate in health" or otherwise "subject to weakness," including the elderly and the sick.

- ✔ Young children (often, Mormon kids start fasting for one meal around the time they're baptized at age 8 and graduate to two meals when they advance from Primary to Young Men or Young Women at age 12. But the Church has no ironclad rules on this matter.)

The Church encourages those who can't fast to get involved as much as they can by making the day a time of prayer and meditation and by taking part in testimony meeting if they feel so inspired.

President Heber J. Grant counseled Mormons to not get too hung up on the technical details of fasting. The main thing, he cautioned, is to promote the *spirit* of fasting, drawing closer to Heavenly Father and Jesus Christ.

Chapter 17

Connecting with God and Each Other

Mormonism isn't just a Sunday religion. It's a 24/7 commitment to God and his people. Although much of Mormonism is outwardly focused — knocking on doors to do missionary work, feeding the poor, and so on — the religion also fosters a rich inner life. In this chapter, we focus on how today's Mormons participate in certain daily, weekly, and monthly spiritual practices so they can grow closer together, retain the constant companionship of the Holy Ghost (see Chapter 3), and become more like their Heavenly Father.

Note: We should point out that the daily, weekly, and monthly frequencies represent the ideal. Most Mormons don't keep every single Sabbath, pray on their knees every morning and evening, or complete their home and visiting teaching assignments without fail. But most Mormons try to do most of these things most of the time, and they believe that these practices contribute to their spiritual growth.

What Mormons Do Daily . . . Ideally

In the Mormon view, each day is a gift from God and represents an opportunity to grow closer to him and his Son, Jesus Christ. That belief translates into some daily practices that are designed to help Mormons nurture their relationships with God and the Savior and make them more aware of the spiritual things in everyday life.

It's been said that when Mormons want to talk to God, they pray, and when they want God to talk to them, they read the scriptures.

Talking with the Big Guy

Mormons believe strongly in making time every day for Heavenly Father. Of course, Mormons call on God for help when they're sick, in trouble, or worried. But God isn't just a foul-weather friend; Mormons believe that if they want to have a strong relationship with him, they need to talk to him even when everything's swell. Heavenly Father loves all his children and wants to communicate with them daily.

Although the prime times for routine, formal prayer are in the morning, evening, and before meals, Mormons also zoom up prayers to God at appropriate times throughout the day: when asking for patience with a cranky toddler, strength to overcome temptation, or wisdom on some complex spiritual issue. There's no *wrong* time to pray.

When Mormon families gather together, they say their prayers out loud, but when individuals pray, they can do so either aloud or silently. Mormons believe that God hears both kinds.

Spending a little time alone with God

Mormons pray directly to God the Father. They don't believe that having an *intermediary* (one who stands in between the person praying and God) is necessary in order to access the Father. Therefore, they don't pray to Jesus Christ, Mary, or any saints (anyway, in Mormonism, the term *saint* applies to all members). Although Mormons sometimes don't feel like praying, they know that these times are when they especially need to pray, in order to maintain that close connection with their Heavenly Father and remain sensitive to his will for their lives.

As Mormon missionaries teach anyone who will listen, LDS-style prayer has four basic steps:

1. **Call on Heavenly Father.**

   The most common opening phrase is simply "Dear Heavenly Father," but variations are okay.

2. **Thank him for blessings.**

   Before getting into needs and desires, Mormons meditate on blessings and express gratitude for specific ones. Such blessings may include family members, good health, or the knowledge of the gospel. Many Latter-day Saints regularly thank God for the Atonement of Christ.

3. **Ask for blessings.**

   This part of the prayer is nearly always the longest. Mormons try to understand God's will and pray for it to come about, instead of treating him like Santa Claus. Here, Mormons may ask for strength to withstand temptation or meet new challenges; confess their sins to Heavenly Father and ask for forgiveness; remember loved ones who are ill or troubled; or pray about conflicts in the nation or the world.

4. **Close in the Savior's name.**

   Every Mormon prayer closes with this basic phrase: "In the name of Jesus Christ, amen." This practice stems from a verse in the Book of Mormon, where Jesus tells the Nephites to "always pray unto the Father in my name" (3 Nephi 18:19).

Navigating "thee" and "thou"

New converts and non-Mormons are sometimes surprised by the formal language that English-speaking Latter-day Saints typically use for prayer. The prayers that Mormons say in public (in sacrament meeting, Relief Society, and so on) sound like King James English, and many Latter-day Saints pray this way at home, too.

The key point to remember is that Mormons use the formal language to refer to God, not other people. So it's correct to say, "Heavenly Father, we thank thee for thy blessings and ask for thy protection for our son Jared, who's leaving this week for BYU." But Mormons don't use the lofty language throughout, so "Heavenly Father, our son Jared, who tarries here before departing for college, requireth thy protection" would be over the top.

Why do Mormons pray in this Shakespearean way? Church leaders teach that having a special language reserved just for God is appropriate because it shows him our respect and love. (Ironically enough, from a historical perspective this language is *not* particularly formal; folks in King James's day considered "thee" and "thou" to be vernacular and familiar and used those pronouns with family members and social inferiors, while they reserved "you" for high-ranking nobility. Now that "you" is common, the positions have reversed, and so the formerly informal pronouns are the ones Mormons use for God.)

This language is sometimes tricky for new converts to get used to, and using it certainly isn't a requirement, though it's customary in the English-speaking Church. Other languages often adopt other terminology for prayer — sometimes formal, sometimes not.

Minding body language

One of the unique aspects of the Mormon approach to prayer is the emphasis on a particular body posture (see Figure 17-1). Although Mormons believe that sincere prayer can occur in any position, many choose to pray on their

knees with their arms folded, heads bowed, and eyes closed. (However, closing the eyes wouldn't work for one of this book's coauthors, who says nearly
all his personal prayers aloud while driving the car. Or maybe he's just not
exercising enough faith yet.)

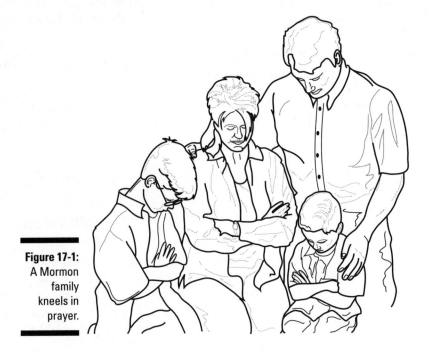

Figure 17-1:
A Mormon
family
kneels in
prayer.

Christianity has a long-held tradition of kneeling for prayer, so its prevalence
among Mormons isn't surprising. The posture shows humility and respect to
Heavenly Father. Considering how often Mormons get on their knees for personal prayer, though, newcomers are often surprised that Mormons don't do
it in their church services. In sacrament meeting and other church meetings,
the person who gives the opening or closing prayer does so standing up, and
members of the congregation stay in their seats.

Mormon arm-folding, on the other hand, occurs in church services and also
at home in private or family prayer. Generally, Mormons cross their arms
over their chests while they bow their heads in prayer. This practice is actually pretty recent in Church history and seems to have become popular in the
middle of the 20th century. The most common theory about this stance is
that Primary teachers dreamed it up to stop little kids from smacking each
other or fidgeting during prayer time. Although many Mormons pray this
way, they certainly aren't obligated to do so.

Getting answers to prayer

In the Book of Mormon, the Savior tells the Nephites that whatever they ask God for in Christ's name will be given to them, provided that they do so in faith and ask for something "which is right" (3 Nephi 18:20). Yeah, that last part is a bit of a catch, isn't it? In other words, if they pray for something and expect Heavenly Father to come through, they'd better be praying for something righteous and in harmony with his will.

Mormons believe that when they pray, one of several outcomes typically happens:

- ✔ They immediately receive whatever they asked for in prayer, whether it be a tangible item, a person who helps them, or guidance on a decision or problem.

- ✔ They eventually receive what they asked for.

- ✔ They don't seem to receive any answer at all and may later realize that what they were asking for wasn't part of God's holy plan.

Although it'd be nice if the first outcome happened more often, the last one is often more conducive to long-term spiritual growth, because it teaches patience and humility.

One final note on answered prayers: Although Mormons believe that any time or place is appropriate for sincere prayer, many report receiving special inspiration when they're in a temple. Mormons can sit in the celestial room of the temple for as long as they want after an endowment session has ended. In this quiet room, Mormons feel a unique connection with Heavenly Father. Maybe they sense this connection because when they're away from the hustle-and-bustle of daily life, they have time to truly listen for the Spirit's voice. (For more on temples, see Chapter 7.)

Praying together helps with staying together

The LDS Church encourages Mormon families to pray together each day, both morning and night if possible. Ideally, they do so in addition to each family member's individual prayers. Families pray for their spiritual and material needs and give thanks for their blessings. In addition, many spend a few minutes reading the scriptures aloud together. (More on that practice in the next section.)

Most families try to pray together first thing in the morning, before everyone heads off for work or school. Yes, getting teens to sacrifice precious minutes of sleep for this ritual is a tough task. (It's especially difficult when the teens are getting up super-early anyway to attend morning seminary — see Chapter 8.) As an alternative, some Mormon families schedule their devotional time around a family meal or after school, depending on what works best for the family's schedule. Although getting everyone assembled and holding the kids' interest is a challenge, Mormon parents believe that family prayer and scripture study are their best lines of defense in raising spiritual children in a secular world.

Studying scriptures

In addition to daily prayer, most Mormons strive to study the scriptures every day. (Those who don't at least have the decency to feel guilty about it.) For some Mormons, scripture study happens apart from personal or family prayer, although others incorporate a one-stop-shopping approach and have a single devotional time that incorporates both elements.

You can flip back to Chapters 9 and 10 for more on the LDS scriptures, but for now all you need to know is that Mormons have four books (known as *standard works*) that they regard as canonized scripture: the Bible (including the Old and New Testaments), the Book of Mormon, the Doctrine and Covenants (D&C), and the Pearl of Great Price. Many Mormons possess something called a *quadruple combination*. That term may sound like a complicated figure-skating move, but it's actually just a heavy volume with all four of these standard works conveniently bound together. Mormons call it the *quad* for short. The Church also publishes scripture sets with the Bible separate and the other three books bound together as a *triple combination*.

Mormons use all kinds of methods for studying the scriptures, including the following:

- ✔ Some mark up their texts with colored pencils, make notes in the margins, and check the cross-references in the Bible Dictionary and the Topical Guide, two alphabetical resources included in LDS editions of the scriptures.

- ✔ Some read doctrinal books or go on the Internet to compare their daily scripture reading with what various LDS authorities say about the passage, helping them understand it in the wider context of what the Church teaches.

- ✔ Some methodically work their way through one of the standard works each year, and others study whatever sections the Holy Spirit seems to suggest to them on a given day. Often, members will focus their daily reading on the reading assignments given in Sunday school class.

One thing you don't normally see in Mormon circles is the group Bible study beyond Sunday school class, as you do in most Protestant and some Catholic churches. Some informal groups of Mormon friends get together to talk about gospel issues, but the Church doesn't officially sponsor such scripture study groups. For Mormons, the emphasis is more on individual and family scripture study, in addition to Sunday school and other formal classes. However, Mormons do often hold evening lectures commonly known as *firesides*, presumably because they used to be held in members' living rooms; nowadays, these occasional events usually take place in a meetinghouse.

What Mormons Do Weekly . . . Ideally

Fifty-two weeks a year, Mormons are expected to keep the Sabbath day holy and devote some focused, gospel-oriented time to their families on Sunday. Although honoring the Sabbath is a commandment for Mormons, the Church leaves some room for individual interpretation and emphasis regarding the details of observance. In addition, the Church strongly suggests that members hold a weekly family home evening.

Observing the Sabbath

If you've ever known a Mormon, you've probably seen firsthand that they don't do some things on Sundays. They aren't as rigid about Sabbath observance as Orthodox Jews are — Mormons drive cars and turn on electric lights, for example — but they're stricter about Sabbath-keeping than most Christians nowadays. In this section, we examine why and how Mormons keep the Sabbath.

Why Mormons keep the Sabbath

In the Old Testament, God commanded the Israelites to rest from all their labors on the seventh day, as he did when he created the world. In Hebrew, the verb *shabbat* means "to cease or desist" — an important indicator of what a Sabbath ought to be like. For Mormons, as well as for Jews and other Christians, keeping the Sabbath means setting apart one day a week for spiritual renewal. Mormons "cease and desist" from the cares of the world in order to pursue holiness.

For Mormons, the rhythm of the whole week revolves around the Sabbath. They try to get their work, household chores, and shopping done by Saturday evening so that Sunday can be entirely free of worldly concerns. Most Mormons look forward to the Sabbath, seeing it as a time set aside to celebrate God and rejoice in his rich blessings.

God commanded people to observe the Sabbath for the following two reasons:

✔ **Worship:** The Old Testament is clear that the Sabbath is meant to be "a day to the Lord" (Leviticus 23:3) — in other words, it's God's day. The whole point is to honor God. Mormons keep that commandment by spending part of Sunday in church, where they learn more about God and Jesus Christ (for more on LDS church services, see Chapter 6). Mormons also worship privately as individuals and families on Sunday, through prayer and scripture study.

✔ **Rest:** Worshiping God while also taking care of all the daily worries and stresses that mar our ordinary lives is tough. So in order to worship sincerely, Mormons step back from those day-to-day activities and aim for Sabbath rest. God set the pattern for this situation: After he created the world, he took a much-needed daylong vacation. He blessed the Sabbath day and made it holy (Genesis 2:3) by resting — a model that Mormons take as their example.

Don't get us wrong. Mormons believe very strongly in the value of hard work, and the Mormon work ethic is a wonder to behold. But Mormons believe that Sunday is a day for rest and that they should forgo any activity that's intended to make money or to increase their worldly productivity. One problem in Mormonism is that sometimes people do so much Church volunteer work on Sunday that they don't spend enough time with their families — but hey, at least Church work is a change of pace from earning a living.

How Mormons keep the Sabbath

Like most Christians, Mormons observe the Sabbath on Sunday, not Saturday. They regard it as a morning-to-bedtime affair rather than a day that begins at sundown on Saturday night and ends at sundown on Sunday. Some newbies are surprised to discover that Mormon temples are actually closed on Sundays, to encourage members to focus on worshipping in their local meetinghouses and homes (for more on temples, see Chapter 7).

Mormons are very diverse in terms of what they do or don't do on the Sabbath. Newly married LDS couples often have to reconcile their differences on this score: One may have grown up in a conservative family in which everyone stayed dressed in their Sunday best all day, while the other was raised in a more free-wheeling environment in which they listened to secular music on Sunday and played touch football on the lawn. Our goal in this section isn't to present a one-size-fits-all approach to the Sabbath or to suggest what LDS Church members should or shouldn't do on Sundays, but merely to show a range of approaches.

In general, keeping the Sabbath means doing the following:

✔ **Attending church services and leadership meetings:** As we say in the preceding section, worship is one of the two most important aspects of the Sabbath, and the communal part of that worship happens in church. During church services, Mormons gather together to hear spiritual talks, take the sacrament, sing hymns, and learn about the gospel (see Chapter 6). In addition, some members have callings that require them to stay after the three-hour block of meetings ends (or, egads, in the early-morning hours before church begins) for attending leadership meetings, singing at choir practice, or helping manage the affairs of the congregation.

✔ **Paying extra attention to the spiritual side:** If attending church is the public, visible component of Sunday worship, then the private component involves concentrated individual attention to spiritual matters. Many Mormons see Sunday as a chance to spend a little extra time in prayer and scripture study, beyond what they do on regular days. They may take up additional reading, sing hymns at home, or prepare a gospel lesson for next Sunday at church. Whatever they do, their aim is to love and understand God a little better.

✔ **Refraining from work:** Some Mormons, of course, have no choice but to work on Sunday, especially if they're in the healthcare profession or some other occupation that doesn't easily accommodate normal business hours. (Remember, the Savior himself healed the sick on the Sabbath.) But Church leaders routinely emphasize that members shouldn't work on Sundays if they have any choice in the matter. This ideal may mean turning off the computer and leaving that briefcase full of papers resolutely closed. Some Mormons do no housework at all on Sundays; others do the barebones stuff like dishes and snow shoveling but leave the more demanding chores for another day. Many students refrain from homework on Sundays, but some don't.

✔ **Resting:** Not working is a start to obtaining Sunday rest, but it's just the beginning. Mormons like their Sundays to be rejuvenating and relaxing, so they take it easy. At least one Mormon prophet has said that naps are an acceptable Sabbath activity, prophetic counsel that both of your coauthors keep faithfully; Sunday is the only day of the week when naps are usually possible and guilt free. However, some Mormons would feel lazy if they were caught napping on the Lord's day.

✔ **Not spending money:** In general, most Mormons try to avoid spending money on the Sabbath. The idea is that Sunday should be a noncommercial day that you spend thinking about spiritual things, not material concerns, and Mormons don't want to encourage businesses to hire people to work on the Sabbath. Obviously, avoiding commercial interaction is impossible on some Sundays, such as when traveling, which is the only time most Mormons will eat in a restaurant on the Sabbath (although some avoid eating out on Sundays even while on vacation). They feel more flexible about bending the no-spending rule when they urgently need to buy something, like gas for the car or medicine for the flu, than when facing a nonessential purchase that they can easily delay. (New Nikes are *not* considered urgent.)

✔ **Making time for family:** Mormons feel that one important aspect of the Sabbath is the opportunity it gives them to spend time with family members when the daily pressures of work, school, shopping, and chores are taken out of the equation. Mormons run the gamut on how they strengthen their families through Sabbath observance. Some, for example, make an enormous meal and invite extended family over for a warm, lively evening of dinner and board games. Others interpret the Sabbath to mean that meals should be simple or prepared in advance so that they don't spend the day slaving over a hot stove. Mormon families

> decide for themselves what kind of recreation they feel is appropriate for the Sabbath. Some allow their children to play with neighborhood kids, and others don't. Some allow TV, and others don't, not even on Super Bowl Sunday. Most Mormons don't play sports on Sunday, and swimming is widely understood to be a Sabbath no-no.
>
> ✔ **Serving others:** Some Mormons do their home and visiting teaching on Sunday (see the section "Ding, dong, Mormons calling") or take the opportunity to visit sick or aged members of the congregation. Many Mormons use the Sabbath to write letters to loved ones or call them on the phone.

However Mormon families choose to navigate the small stuff about Sabbath observance, the key point to remember is that Sabbath activities must center on two ideas: worshiping God and resting. Mormons try to avoid *legalism,* or adhering solely to the letter of the law, by focusing instead on the spirit of the law and the purpose of the Sabbath.

Family Home Evening (Sorry, no Monday Night Football)

Sunday may be the LDS Sabbath, but Monday evenings hold nearly as much spiritual significance for Mormons. This evening is so sacred that all Mormon buildings are deserted and locked by 6 p.m., and even telephoning another family on that night is considered poor form. In communities where lots of Mormons live, they often lobby schools, sports teams, and other organizations to schedule activities on other evenings.

What's all the fuss about? Well, the LDS Church expects its members to spend Monday evenings together as families. As we discuss in Chapter 5, the family has eternal potential for Mormons, and they put lots of effort into building family unity. Far more than an occasion to simply gather around the television or go on a picnic, the Church's *family home evening* program includes praying, singing, and studying the gospel together.

A typical Monday night

On many Mormon refrigerator doors, next to A+ spelling tests and soccer schedules, you find a little homemade poster listing several family home evening tasks, such as *prayer, song, lesson, game,* and *refreshments.* Each family member's name is written on a movable marker, and the markers are rotated from task to task each week.

In most Mormon homes, family night — as it's often called — begins right after dinner on Monday. Ideally, each family member has prepared his or her assignment by then, particularly those in charge of the lesson and refreshments. In the case of young children, a parent or older sibling helps them get ready. Here's how the typical family home evening usually progresses:

- ✔ **Prayer:** Most families begin and end the evening with prayer. Some families kneel, and others remain in their seats.

- ✔ **Song:** It's typical to sing a song before the opening and closing prayers. These songs often come from the Church's official songbook for children, but nonreligious songs are okay too, especially at holiday times.

- ✔ **Lesson:** The heart of family home evening is a gospel lesson geared toward the kids. Quite often, the lesson includes visual aids, such as cutout figures on a flannel board. No standardized curriculum exists — instead, every family comes up with lessons to meet their individual needs and circumstances. However, the LDS Church publishes a family home evening resource manual, and some Mormons exchange lesson materials.

- ✔ **Planning and discussion:** Many Mormon families take time during family night to discuss family plans and problems. They may decide whether to visit Yellowstone or Disneyland for summer vacation or agree on new family rules about borrowing each other's toys or clothes.

- ✔ **Activities and refreshments:** Many families build a component of fun into the evening, such as going bowling or playing a board game. Some families do service projects for the needy as part of family night.

- ✔ **Other traditions:** Customizing the basic family home evening program is easy. For example, coauthor Christopher Bigelow's parents invited each family member to report the best and worst thing that happened to him or her during the previous week. In addition, one of the rotating weekly assignments was *conduct,* which meant acting as emcee for the evening.

Although the preceding list reflects some common approaches to family home evening, each family finds what works best at different stages of life. To avoid family home *screaming,* it's important to keep the evening fun and flexible. You want the kids to look forward to it, not dread it!

Other kinds of family home evening

Of course, not everyone is available on Monday evenings, so they can set aside a different time for family home evening, as long as they're consistent. New and older married couples without children at home are still encouraged to hold family home evening, and Mormons without spouses often group together on Monday nights. Brigham Young University organizes single students living in the dorms into family home evening groups, which act as a kind of substitute family for each other. In addition, many members of other faiths adapt Mormonism's family home evening model to meet their own needs.

What Mormons Do Monthly . . . Ideally

At least 12 times a year, Mormons pay assigned visits to fellow members in their local congregation, skip two meals, and attend the temple, if one is located reasonably close. Of course, a Mormon can do these things *more* than once a month, if desired, but monthly is the minimum standard.

Ding, dong, Mormons calling

No, we're not talking about Mormon missionaries ringing your doorbell — we cover that in Chapter 14. This section describes two unique LDS practices of members making assigned visits to each other within a local *ward,* or congregation. Each month, the men pair off to *home teach* each household in the ward, and the women pair off to *visit teach* each other.

Home teaching

In a Mormon ward, leaders assign each adult priesthood holder to a home teaching partner, and each partnership visits specific households each month, usually two to four households, but sometimes more. Often, a man is paired with a teenage priesthood holder so the boy can start learning the ropes.

The main purpose of home teaching is to help the *bishop* — or congregational leader — and other local leaders look after all the sheep in their flock. This is a major part of how Mormons fulfill what they see as a religious responsibility to look after each other, in the absence of full-time paid clergy. Home teaching is a two-way street: The home teachers bring gospel messages, invitations, and support to each household, and they take back information about any concerns or needs of the household.

A home teaching visit can occur at any mutually agreed upon time, and it typically takes about a half-hour. Many home teachers wear the usual Mormon priesthood uniform of a white shirt and tie during their visits, but some dress casually. Here's the rundown on what home teachers do:

- ✔ **Deliver a gospel message:** Each month in the Church's official *Ensign* magazine, the prophet or one of his counselors provides a gospel message, and the magazine includes a sidebar of tips on how home teachers can use the message to teach their assigned families. Sometimes, the home teachers may prepare a special message — for example, talking about baptism if a child's 8th birthday is coming up soon. In addition, home teachers often make sure the families know about any special upcoming Church parties or events, particularly if the family doesn't regularly attend church.

✔ **Pray with the family:** Typically, the home teaching partner who doesn't give the message offers a prayer for the family. However, home teachers let the head of the household decide who prays at the beginning and/or end of a home teaching visit.

✔ **Assess the family's welfare:** Home teachers make sure their assigned families have food, warmth, and other basic needs. In addition, they find out if any family member is facing a particular challenge or needs help with anything, including spiritual and religious matters. If necessary, the home teachers inform leaders about the situation so the Church can provide assistance.

✔ **Provide help:** When a father needs to give his sick child a blessing of healing, an ordinance that normally requires two priesthood holders (see Chapter 4), he often calls the family's home teachers to assist. Help can also be practical as well as spiritual: Home teachers could help a single mother paint her house, a family load its moving truck, or a widow fix her plumbing.

✔ **Report to the supervisor:** Even if the families don't need anything, home teachers report to their supervisor about whether or not they completed their assignments. The Church records home teaching statistics, and leaders take pains to make sure percentages stay up. In priesthood lessons, leaders frequently emphasize home teaching — ad nauseam, it sometimes seems — as one of the most crucial priesthood duties.

In addition to the monthly visits, the home teaching system also functions as an information network and calling tree for all the families in a ward. If the bishop wants to get out a particular assignment or message to everyone, the home teachers often spread the word. In times of emergency, priesthood holders are generally expected to check on the status of their assigned home teaching families and be prepared to report the information, including any needs, to local leaders.

Home teaching may sound well and good on paper, but we're going to be honest here. The majority of the time, home teaching seems pretty mundane, and a lot of the time people don't do it consistently. Lining up appointments at a mutually satisfactory time is often inconvenient, especially where members live far apart from each other, and the small talk and gospel messages can seem superficial. One of Mormonism's most common clichés is putting off home teaching until the end of the month, which makes it seem even more like merely jumping through a hoop. (How many home teachers does it take to change a light bulb? Just two — but you have to wait until the last day of the month.)

However, from time to time something magical happens with home teaching. Once in a while, home teachers make a real impact on people's lives, such as helping a less-active family come back into church activity or providing a positive role model for the son of a single mother. After months of seemingly routine visits, a home teacher may suddenly realize that he's come to know and love a particular family. Despite its seeming tediousness, the practice of home teaching brings Mormon congregations closer together.

Visiting teaching

Mormon men aren't the only ones who head out to teach Church members once a month. Women also teach other women, an initiative organized through the Relief Society (see Chapter 6). This practice is called *visiting teaching,* and it happens separately and in addition to the home teaching that the men organize.

Because visiting teaching is more intimate than home teaching — one or at most two teachers visit one woman at a time — the opportunity exists for marvelous friendships to build. Ideally, each visit includes a prayer and a short lesson. Mormons find suggestions for these monthly lessons in the "Visiting Teacher Message" column of the *Ensign* magazine, which provides scripture references and quotes by male and female LDS leaders. If a teacher has the time and inclination, she may create her own lesson, so long as it helps meet the spiritual needs of the sisters she teaches. Sometimes, visiting teaching can be a bit chaotic if there are small children around, so one companion might entertain the kids while the other teaches the lesson.

But visiting teaching has more to it than sharing a monthly lesson. Visiting teachers are the first people on the job when a woman needs help with something. If a sister in the ward can't stop throwing up from morning sickness, her visiting teacher is the one who offers to take care of her other children for a few hours and to cook dinner so the pregnant lady doesn't have to smell ground beef. When another sister is so elderly that she can't come to church on Sunday, her visiting teacher is the one who brings her flowers and catches her up on all the news. Visiting teachers keep the Relief Society president updated on any needs in a family.

The best visiting teachers are ones who step in to help without having to be asked, because Mormons aren't always good about asking for help even when they desperately need it. Though it's not necessary, many visiting teachers bring goodies, treats, or little pick-me-ups to the women on their route. A bag of homemade cookies, for example, may come with a note bearing a favorite scripture, such as "let your soul delight in fatness" (2 Nephi 9:51).

Break out the breath mints: Fasting

On the first Sunday of the month, Mormons skip two meals, going without food and water for about 24 hours. No, they're not trying to lose weight — they're trying to master their physical appetites, tune up their spiritual sensitivity, and draw closer to Heavenly Father. In addition, they donate the money they would've spent on food — and more, if they're able — to the Church's fund for supporting those in need. During church on *Fast Sunday*, people share their testimonies about the Savior (see Chapter 6).

Mormons consider fasting to be a commandment, and it's not effective unless coupled with focused prayer. While fasting, some Mormons keep breath mints handy, because going without food and water takes a toll on oral freshness (on the other hand, some Mormons would see sucking breath mints as breaking their fast). Mormons can fast more often than monthly, if they choose, but the Church discourages going longer than 24 hours at a time. (We discuss fasting in more detail in Chapter 16. Also, for more information about what happens to the money collected during the monthly fast, see Chapter 8 on the Church's welfare program.)

A trip to the temple (a.k.a. Mormon date night)

Although home teaching, visiting teaching, and fasting are all nonnegotiable monthly expectations, attending the temple monthly is more of a commonly accepted guideline than a firm requirement. Perhaps one reason is that many Mormons don't live close enough to a temple to attend often — after all, the Church has built only about 130 temples worldwide, as opposed to more than 10,000 meetinghouses for regular Sunday worship.

Friday and Saturday nights are some of the busiest times at temples, because many couples make temple attendance a monthly date. Inside the temple, Mormons perform a number of different *ordinances,* or physical rituals necessary for returning to live with God and become like him. In Chapter 7, we discuss these ordinances in more detail, along with other aspects of the temple.

Here are two reasons why Mormons strive to attend the temple monthly, if not more often:

- ✔ **Keeping spiritually in tune:** Although temple ordinances are always the same, with little or no freestyle preachin' and prayin', Mormons draw continual spiritual sustenance and eternal perspective from them. The levels of reverence and sacredness are much higher in a temple than in a meetinghouse, and there's no other place on earth where Mormons feel closer to God, the Savior, and the Holy Ghost than in a temple.

- ✔ **Helping to redeem the dead:** Each time a Mormon completes another temple ordinance, he or she does so on behalf of a particular person who died without performing his or her own ordinances. Mormons are trying to perform temple ordinances for everyone who's ever lived, and billions of ordinances still need to be completed — so every little bit helps, even just once a month. Deceased persons must choose whether to accept or reject the ordinances performed on their behalf.

Chapter 18

In the World but Not *of* the World

Mormonism has always been a hands-on religion, and especially so when Mormons are trying to live spiritual lives in a secular world. They want to be *in* the world but not *of* it, a careful negotiation that involves a little bit of improv and a whole lot of prayer. In the New Testament, one of the letters attributed to Peter speaks of the need to become "a chosen generation, a royal priesthood, an holy nation, a peculiar people" (1 Peter 2:9). That goal is hard to reach in this day and age, but Mormons aim for it, knowing that their quest for holiness is — at the very least — going to make them a little bit different from their peers.

In addition to the spiritual practices we explore in Chapter 17, Mormons engage in a variety of other, more-practical activities that are religious as well as worldly. In the Mormon view, faithfulness in taking care of this life's temporal responsibilities is an important part of preparing for the responsibilities of eternity and developing the attributes of divinity. For theological and practical reasons, Mormons make the habit of hoarding food and being prepared for emergencies. Similarly, both spiritual and financial reasons spur Mormons to stay out of debt. And partly in response to a prophet's inspired advice, they seek to make a record of their lives through journals and scrapbooks. In entertainment and the arts, Mormons are creating their own increasingly distinct subculture. In this chapter, we take you through all these aspects of Mormon life.

Becoming Self-Reliant

Even people who aren't big fans of Mormons or their religion often acknowledge with grudging admiration that Mormons know how to take care of themselves and each other. To Mormons, part of being a "peculiar people" is making every effort to become independent and self-sufficient so they don't have to depend on non-Mormons or the government for help. (For more on the LDS Church's extensive private welfare system, see Chapter 8.)

In the Mormon view, becoming self-reliant has several basic components, such as

- ✔ Being financially prepared
- ✔ Storing enough food and supplies to weather any emergency
- ✔ Having a disaster plan in place at all times

Mormons say that the Lord told them that if they're prepared, they don't need to be afraid of anything (see Doctrine and Covenants 38:30; for more on the D&C, see Chapter 10).

Staying out of debt

Since the 19th century, LDS prophets have consistently emphasized two duties with regard to money: Pay an honest tithe and stay out of debt. (For the scoop on tithing, see Chapter 16.) Getting out of debt — and staying there — can be tricky. People are constantly surrounded by advertisements that promise them a better life if only they'll buy this widget or that gadget. And with the easy availability of credit, it's no wonder that Mormons seem as prone as anyone else to sink into a financial quagmire. Because Mormons often have large families and try to keep one parent at home full time with the children, they absolutely must learn to manage their resources wisely.

Being in debt doesn't just charge a financial price. Debt also places a spiritual burden on a family, because it often leads to depression, overwork, and marital tension. From Brigham Young on down, LDS leaders have taught that thrift, not material possessions, is the key to security. True happiness doesn't come from having a new car or the latest high-definition TV; in the Mormon view, it comes from having a strong relationship with God, serving others, and staying free from all forms of bondage, including severe financial anxiety.

In fact, even Mormon scriptures put in two cents on the debt issue: In D&C 104:78, the Lord declares his will that his children remain debt free, and in D&C 19:35 he equates debt with bondage. Mormons believe that God wants people to be entirely free — and that human *agency* (see Chapter 2), or free will, is an essential principle of the gospel. With this idea in mind, the belief that God hates debt, which takes away people's freedom, makes perfect sense.

The Church recommends four basic steps for staying out of debt:

- ✔ **Live within your income.** This step is obviously the most important one. If you regularly exceed your income, spending more money than you make, debt is inevitable. You have to step off the debt treadmill and make a habit of living within your means.

✔ **Save for the future.** The Church encourages its members to put aside a portion of their income — ideally, at least 10 percent — into retirement funds, college savings, and other investments for the future. Mormons also try to maintain an emergency fund to cover several months of living expenses in case of illness or unemployment.

✔ **Have adequate insurance.** Many people who get by from paycheck to paycheck are completely flattened when they have major medical bills or an unexpected death in the family. Adequate insurance — including health, life, and disability insurance — is vital to every family's financial stability. In other words, Mormons believe that God wants people to make wise provisions for possible misfortunes instead of just trusting God to make sure nothing bad happens to them.

✔ **Be wise about credit.** Mormon leaders would love to see Latter-day Saints borrow money only to pay for their homes and educations — assets that either appreciate in value or help people increase their incomes. However, many Mormons borrow money to pay for their cars and some other purchases. Sadly, Mormon-dominated Utah has one of the highest rates of personal bankruptcy of any U.S. state, so many Mormons are clearly borrowing more than they can afford.

President Heber J. Grant — a Mormon prophet who was in debt himself at one point — said, "If there is any one thing that will bring peace and contentment into the human heart, and into the family, it is to live within our means, and if there is any one thing that is grinding, and discouraging and disheartening, it is to have debts and obligations that one cannot meet." Although being frugal is tough when so many voices say, "Buy now and pay later," most Mormons strive to meet their financial obligations and put aside a nest egg for the future.

Getting squirrelly: Food storage

A little-known fact about Mormons is that they're pack rats and food hoarders. What's more, The Church of Jesus Christ of Latter-day Saints encourages this behavior, advising members to store food for emergencies. In the old days, the Church counseled people to store enough food to last their families for two years. Now they store enough only for one year, but that's still a heck of a tall order. Why do Mormons store food? Here are some reasons:

✔ **As a result of the Mormons' turbulent and crisis-laden history (see Chapters 11–13):** Having been persecuted and driven from their homes, and having survived the grueling westward trek and the travails of settling the desert, Mormons learned to be careful with every resource. This idea is ingrained in the Mormon mindset, like your grandmother who lived through the Depression and World War II and now has a fit every time you leave a trace of food on your plate. People who've lived through lean times don't soon forget.

✔ **Just in case the Second Coming happens sooner rather than later:**
Most Mormons don't believe Jesus will come back anytime soon,
because scriptures speak of several conditions that haven't yet happened (see Chapter 3). Still, being prepared can't hurt, in case society
breaks down to such an extent before the Second Coming that a reliable
infrastructure for food and other needs doesn't exist.

✔ **To handle small or large emergencies:** It's nice to have extra supplies
on hand when a blizzard causes a three-day power outage. When
Mormons use food storage long term, they usually do so because a
breadwinner is disabled, sick, or unemployed.

✔ **So they can help other people during *their* emergencies:** Mormons are
some of the best donators of canned goods to community food bank
donation drives. In tougher times closer to home, a Mormon family's
stored food can help their neighbors weather a weeklong storm or a difficult financial period.

✔ **Because it's financially prudent:** Maintaining a large food supply allows
Mormons to save money by buying items in bulk when they go on sale.
In addition, by making fewer trips to the grocery store, they spend less
time and energy and reduce their temptations to buy things on impulse.
Next time you pass a woman at the supermarket whose cart is full of
canned tuna, she may well be a Mormon.

Finding a place to put it all

Storing an entire year's worth of food isn't easy. Some folks just don't have
the space — imagine living in a tiny Manhattan or Tokyo apartment. It's not
unusual to see Mormons who live in urban apartments or other small spaces
creatively storing canned food under furniture or behind the coats in a
closet. More than one Mormon family has even used a large food bin — clev-
erly disguised under an embroidered cloth — as a coffee table. (Well, not literally for *coffee*.)

Ideally, Mormons devote a large pantry closet or even a small room to food
storage (see Figure 18-1). This spot should be cool, because warmth acceler-
ates the decay process for many foods. Basements are good places, as long
as the food is off the floor and flooding isn't an issue.

An even more serious problem than storing food is storing water, which
doesn't exactly lend itself to space-saving techniques. Most Mormons store
enough water for a short period, such as a week, and also buy water purification tablets in case they experience a disaster that keeps them from a safe
water supply for a longer period. Other items that the Church urges Mormons
to store include a year's supply of clothing, medical supplies, and, where possible, fuel for warmth and cooking.

Photo by Rick Egan/The Salt Lake Tribune

Figure 18-1:
A Brazilian
Mormon
family's food
storage.

Establishing a system

Many Mormons initially feel overwhelmed when they think about storing a year's supply of food. The fact is that probably only a minority of Mormons has an entire year's supply (not to mention a reliable way to cook their food if electricity is unavailable), but most Mormons have *something* set aside. They may have enough for only a few weeks or months, but they feel that's far better than having nothing at all.

Here are the three basic rules of food storage:

✔ **Store what you eat.** Many people, including some Mormons, figure that if disaster ever strikes, they'll eat anything they can get their hands on, so it's okay to just store a bunch of raw wheat and dehydrated food. However, research says otherwise. During World War II, for example, the British government conducted a study on emotions and food during times of extreme stress (such as, say, a war). What they found was surprising. Although lots of people *say* they'd eat anything if their lives depended on it, most actually don't — when it comes right down to it, they'd rather starve than eat strange or disgusting foods. In other words, not just any port will do in a storm; comfort food never matters more than during a catastrophe.

With this fact in mind, obeying the first rule of food storage and storing mostly foods you know your family will eat is important. A financial setback or natural disaster isn't the best situation to try that recipe for pinto bean fudge for the very first time. If the kids devour boxed macaroni and cheese, buy a couple caseloads plus canned milk and supplement with multivitamins if a crisis strikes. If you can't imagine getting through a snowstorm without your particular brand of chicken noodle soup, have some to spare.

✔ **Eat what you store.** Unless you're regularly eating the foods you put in food storage, they may be too old or rotten to consume when an emergency hits. Lots of Mormons think their food storage worries are over after they buy a few hundred-pound bins of wheat and dried beans. But if they never open those bins and use the food inside, it eventually becomes the favorite breakfast of untold varieties of critters. To prevent this dilemma, some Mormon families routinely grind their stored wheat to make bread and cereal and include some dehydrated foods in day-to-day meals. This way, everyone gets used to the new tastes.

✔ **Eat the foods on a rotating basis, so you consume the oldest stuff first.** After Mormons go grocery shopping, they often date the food they've just purchased. If a can doesn't have an expiration date on it already, they use a permanent marker to write the date they bought it. Then — and this part is important — they move the new purchases to the back and push the older items to the front so the older foods are the first items available the next time Mom sends a kid to get a bottle of ketchup or a cake mix.

Getting started with food storage

Storing food doesn't have to cost a fortune or drain a family's time. One tip provided by experts Clark and Kathryn Kidd in their book *Food Storage for the Clueless,* published by Deseret Book (hey, they can't all be Dummies books), is to adopt what they call the 5-5 plan: Spend an extra five minutes and five dollars a week to build up food storage. At the beginning, you just buy, say, a couple of jars of peanut butter and an extra box of crackers each week. Then begin adding some canned soups. After a few months, you'll have enough basics to last your family through a short-term crisis, and you can then start thinking about storing for the long term.

When you get to this second stage, take advantage of the numerous companies that sell dried and packaged food-storage products that can last 15 or even 20 years (though we'll pass on the textured vegetable protein taco meat, thanks).

The Church also emphasizes home production: canning food, grinding wheat to make bread, raising vegetable gardens, and so on. Many Mormons still do their own canning, making jams, pickles, preserves, and all manner of foods that have a long shelf life. In the spirit of home production, some Mormons also sew some of their own clothes, though not as often as in the past.

Don't forget the other basics, too: pet and baby needs, an alternate source of heat for warmth and cooking, a battery-operated radio, candles, and so on. You can find more information and helpful lists in the emergency preparedness section at www.providentliving.org.

Preparing for emergencies

Visitors to Mormon meetings are sometimes surprised at how much practical attention the Church gives to preparing for emergencies. At Relief Society and priesthood meetings and even in sacrament talks (see Chapter 6), speakers and teachers routinely emphasize the need to be prepared, Boy Scout style. The Church's official family home evening resource book is filled with lessons on how to give mouth-to-mouth resuscitation, how to behave in an earthquake or tornado, and how to arrange where kids should meet up with parents in case family members are separated.

In addition to staying out of debt and storing as much food as possible, most Mormons have what they call a *72-hour kit* for each member of the family. Basically, a 72-hour kit should contain everything a human being needs in order to survive for three days anywhere. (The family had better pray that an emergency doesn't stretch to 73 hours, or they're in real trouble.)

Unlike food storage, a 72-hour kit needs to be portable. Say you experience a flood and your entire town is evacuated. Or imagine that emergency officials have declared your high-rise apartment building in Los Angeles a disaster area because of a nearby earthquake. You grab your 72-hour kit and hit the road.

Many people keep their 72-hour kits in a backpack or other convenient bag. Some Mormons place their entire family's individual kits in one large rolling bin and wheel it wherever they need to go (this option is especially practical if the family will be driving and not walking).

Typical items in a 72-hour kit include

- Cold, hard cash (possibly a couple hundred dollars, though there's no standard amount)
- An extra set of warm, dry clothes, plus an emergency blanket or sleeping bag
- A first-aid kit
- Meals for three days (such as military-style MREs — yummy)
- A radio with extra batteries, a flashlight, and cell phones
- Toiletries and toilet paper
- Water for three days (the heaviest item)

Sometimes, Mormon families take a dry run at an emergency situation and practice leaving the house with their 72-hour kits. Through this experience, they figure out what works and what doesn't about their disaster plan and fine-tune accordingly. When they stop to have a meal somewhere, for example, they may discover that their planned supper of Progresso soup doesn't work because they didn't think to bring a can opener. Practice makes perfect, and they hope that by preparing, they'll be ready should the unthinkable ever happen.

Crafting, Chronicling, and Stuffing Face: Mormon Traditions

Another practical way that Mormons put their religious values into daily life is by keeping records of what goes on at home and in the family. Putting it all down on paper isn't just a nice thing to do; the Book of Mormon says that recordkeeping can enlarge the memory and enhance the lives of an entire people (Alma 37:8).

Just as the present-day Mormons still feel a pull toward their pioneer ancestors (see Chapter 12), future Mormons may look to the journals and scrapbooks that Latter-day Saints are making now for inspiration and information.

Keeping a record

In 1980, LDS president Spencer W. Kimball spoke out about the need for Mormons to keep a journal for themselves and for their descendants. (President Kimball, at the time he was called to be the prophet, had already filled 33 black binders with his own accounts of his life, so he clearly practiced what he preached.)

Not all Mormons keep a journal, and certainly not everyone does so consistently from elementary school to the grave. Obviously, some members are naturally more gifted at writing than others and gravitate toward this kind of counsel anyway, but for others, the task is a struggle. Journaling requires a significant chunk of time for it to be an effective spiritual and mental discipline. However, most Mormons at least make the attempt at some point.

Why journal? By keeping a journal, Mormons record their hopes and dreams, their challenges and responses to obstacles. Venting and analyzing one's problems in a journal can yield peace and solutions. Some young people keep journals for their future spouses so their marriage partners can one day get to know the people they were as children and teenagers. Missionaries keep journals of their missionary experiences — for many Mormons, that's the only time they really succeed at journaling. Most Mormons expect that their children or grandchildren will someday read their journals, so they try to record the experiences that they think may be helpful or interesting to later generations. They may edit out whatever makes them look bad, but they may include spiritual experiences that are too personal or sacred to share with most people.

The scrapbooking craze

"Crop till you drop," reads a sign posted in the window of a Utah scrapbooking store. And Mormon women do. (_Crop,_ in scrapbooking lingo, means to cut or shape a photograph.) They also embellish, emboss, stamp, create borders, write detailed captions, and spend hours searching for the perfect stickers for each page.

To some degree, Mormons have always practiced the hobby of making scrapbooks — they've been creating photo albums since the invention of the daguerreotype. A scrapbook, however, is a whole different animal, because it involves not just photos but also journaling and decorating. The pastime is huge in Mormon culture. Some of scrapbooking's most visible product lines, stores, magazines, and national companies were founded by Mormon women who turned their leisure pursuit into full-fledged businesses.

Since the 1990s, scrapbooking has transformed from a cottage industry into a $2.5 billion — yes, that's with a _b_ — annual business. What started out as a small-scale hobby at Relief Society meetings and elsewhere has spread to millions of people who aren't Mormon. In the United States alone, approximately 25 million scrapbookers (including one of your coauthors and the wife of the other) mob the scrapbooking stores (over 2,000 of them).

Most Mormons who scrapbook do so to make a beautiful record of family life. The sky's the limit, with the only restrictions being the scrapbooker's time, creativity, and budget. (Scrapbooking can be a costly activity, with two-thirds of American scrapbookers spending at least $25 a month on supplies.) And perhaps someday, future generations will look at the items preserved on acid-free paper — always use acid-free paper! — and get to know a bit about our era and its people. For the lowdown on this hobby and tips on how to get started, pick up _Scrapbooking For Dummies_ by Jeanne Wines-Reed and Joan Wines (Wiley) from a bookstore near you.

Mormon handicrafts

Mormons are known for their handicrafts — witness the quilt hanging in the ward's Relief Society room or the zippered floral scripture tote that a Mormon sister threw together with leftover fabric. A few weeks after coauthor Jana Riess was baptized, she attended her first all-day-Saturday crafting event at her ward. One of the sisters congratulated her on having her "real" baptism into LDS womanhood — she had done a craft! Apparently, this event made the new Mormon identity official.

Mormons routinely gather for crafting events — sewing circles, quilting bees, and scrapbooking crop nights (see the previous section), for example. Crafts have become so associated with Mormon culture that Mormon Handicraft, a Utah company that specializes in handmade quilts and other artifacts of Mormon culture, now sells its wares at every Deseret Book store, a for-profit chain owned by the LDS Church. (Mormon Handicraft used to be a charitable arm of the Relief Society, which used the proceeds from the sale of its craft items to help the poor and needy. For more on the Relief Society, see Chapter 6.)

In addition to quilts and the like, Mormon Handicraft also sells handmade afghans, embroidered cloths, aprons, and "quiet books" to help occupy babies and toddlers during church meetings. For examples of what they have for sale, check out www.mormonhandicraft.com. (No, we don't get a kickback.)

Mormon comfort food

Rumor has it that whatever Mormons *can't* have (in the way of alcohol, coffee, and tobacco), they often make up for with voracious overeating, especially in the sugar category. Although it hurts us to admit it, that theory has truth to it, and we'll ease any sadness about the cold, hard truth by drowning our sorrows in some turkey tetrazzini and yeast rolls, followed by a big bowl of mint chocolate chip ice cream.

Go to any Mormon potluck and you'll see an abundance of a particular kind of white-bread, country cooking that has become known as "Mormon comfort food." In addition to stick-to-your-ribs favorites such as pot roast, mashed potatoes, chocolate cake, and homemade breads, Mormons enjoy a dish that many of them call *funeral potatoes,* because it shows up at the luncheon following many U.S. and Canadian Mormon funerals. As with other favorite LDS recipes, this one buries the potatoes in mounds of cream-of-chicken soup and sour cream.

And if you're brave enough to try it, green gelatin salad can't be beat. The green variety of Jell-O sells about four times as many boxes in Utah as it does in other states, and this recipe is largely to blame. Another food item beloved by Mormons is *fry sauce,* a pink-colored combination of ketchup, mayo, and spices that's available in many Utah fast-food restaurants.

We can't vouch for the exclusivity of all this food, because favorite Mormon items such as green bean casserole with French-fried onions on top seem to be religiously universal. (For example, Lutherans in the upper Midwest also eat funeral potatoes, though they call it a "potato hot dish.") But some recipes appear to be distinctively Mormon, such as many of those included in *The Essential Mormon Cookbook: Green Jell-O, Funeral Potatoes, and Other Secret Combinations,* by Julie Badger Jensen (Deseret Book).

Taking in a Bit of Culture

In Mormonism's 13th Article of Faith, founding prophet Joseph Smith echoes the words of the Apostle Paul: "If there is anything virtuous, lovely, or of good report or praiseworthy, we seek after these things" (for more on the Articles of Faith, see Chapter 10). Mormons pride themselves on seeking — and, to a less-successful degree, helping create — the world's most inspiring artistic entertainment and enlightenment.

Although Mormon prophets have called upon members to achieve the highest artistic goals, Mormonism has yet to cough up any Shakespeares or Michaelangelos, let alone Lennons or Spielbergs. On the other hand, they've given the world the Osmond family (see Chapter 19) and best-selling sci-fi author Orson Scott Card. Perhaps Mormonism's artistic culture hasn't yet fully blossomed because too many Mormons prize creative expression more for what it *isn't* than for what it *is.* When asked their opinion about a movie or novel, many Mormons will recommend it — or not — based on how few swear words or sex scenes it has, rather than its artistic merits.

When creating their own art, many Mormons flee from anything too dark, graphic, skeptical, or frank. Nearly all Mormon art strives to be uplifting, which often translates into self-conscious propaganda for the faith instead of striking originality, groundbreaking exploration, or cathartic honesty. At the same time, although Mormonism hasn't yet given rise to a Philip Roth or a Woody Allen, a surprising number of maverick-minded artists are creating Mormon-themed works that may one day break out of the LDS artistic ghetto and gain significant audiences and critical notice. In this section, we look at some of the most interesting Mormon music, literature, drama, and film.

Lifting a chorus to the Lord: America's choir

The Mormon Tabernacle Choir is the 800-pound gorilla of Mormon artistic culture. Tracing its roots at least as far back as the small choir that debuted shortly after the first pioneers arrived in the Salt Lake Valley, the choir has achieved considerable worldwide fame. Since hitting its stride early in the 20th century, the Mormon Tabernacle Choir has accomplished the following:

- Performed in many of the world's finest concert halls
- Made more than 150 recordings and launched its own record label
- Earned five gold and two platinum records, in addition to winning a Grammy Award
- Anchored the nation's longest-running weekly radio program, *Music and the Spoken Word,* which reached the 75-year mark in 2004
- Sung at five U.S. presidential inaugurations

Staffed by about 360 rigorously screened volunteer singers who rehearse for hours every week (see Figure 18-2), the choir functions both as an enhancer of Mormon worship and as an ambassador for the faith. Many a door-knocking Mormon missionary has gained entry into a household because the person's heart was previously touched by a choir performance, recording, or broadcast.

Although the choir emphasizes worshipful music, it also performs pieces in a wide variety of traditional and classical forms. Their music isn't necessarily a big hit with younger audiences, but the choir has done much to improve the Church's public image and secure its place in mainstream American culture. Current information on the choir is available at www.mormontabernacle choir.org.

Figure 18-2:
The
Mormon
Tabernacle
Choir in the
Conference
Center.

Photo by Trent Nelson/The Salt Lake Tribune

Onward Christian crooners: Mormon pop music

Mirroring the recent rise of contemporary Christian music, the Mormon culture is spawning its own commercial pop music, with notable success by artists such as Michael McLean and Kenneth Cope. Most recently, Mormon pop music has sprouted LDS boy bands and rock-and-roll adaptations of classic Mormon hymns. Mormon bookstores sell these CDs for home use, but churches don't play them during Mormon worship services, where generally only sedate hymns are welcome.

As far as Mormons breaking into mainstream pop music, the Osmonds are still the highest achievers, although another fairly big name is Randy Bachman of the Guess Who and Bachman-Turner Overdrive. Gladys Knight didn't join Mormonism until 1997, so her career doesn't count as Mormon, though at this writing she was heading up a 100-voice Mormon gospel choir in Las Vegas. (Yes, really.) Mormon converts occasionally pop up in unexpected places, such as New York Dolls bassist Arthur "Killer" Kane, who died in 2004. More recently, one group with Mormon ties, The Used, made the national charts with its pioneering music in the "screamo" genre.

Concerning Mormon attitudes toward secular music, Church authorities and motivational speakers regularly warn young Mormons against listening to inappropriate music. Nevertheless, Mormon youth typically listen to the same music as their non-Mormon peers, except for the most graphic and profane stuff. At youth dances held in the recreational halls of Mormon meetinghouses, the DJs play mostly mainstream radio hits.

Reading between the lines: Mormon books

With its emphasis on education and literacy, Mormonism has given rise to a thriving, multimillion-dollar industry of publishers and bookstores. However, you generally won't see Mormon books on national bestseller lists, because the Mormon book industry isn't yet fully plugged into the national publishing grid. To spot a Mormon bookstore, look for a distinctively Mormon word in the store's name, such as *deseret, seagull,* or *beehive.*

In addition to popular novels, Mormon publishers crank out plenty of inspirational and doctrinal nonfiction, including many written by top Church authorities (see this book's appendix). And Stephen R. Covey has successfully adapted some Mormon principles for a national audience with his blockbuster *The 7 Habits of Highly Effective People* (Free Press). To get an idea of all that Mormons are currently reading — or at least *buying* — browse the Web sites of the most influential Mormon presses, as shown in Table 18-1. In this section, we focus on Mormon fiction.

Table 18-1	Mormon Presses	
Publisher	**Description**	**Web Site**
Cedar Fort	Small, conservative, popular	www.cedarfort.com
Covenant Communications	Larger, conservative, popular	www.covenant-lds.com
Deseret Book	The largest, and the only one owned by the LDS Church	www.deseretbook.com
Signature Books	Small, liberal, intellectual	www.signaturebooks.com

Commercial novels

Thirty years ago, only a handful of Mormon novels existed. However, in more-recent years, popular Mormon fiction has boomed, and Mormon authors have started to see success in specific categories, both within the Mormon market and nationally.

- ✔ **Historical:** By far, the biggest-selling novels within Mormonism have been the nine-volume *Work and the Glory* series by Gerald Lund (Deseret Book), which has sold more than 2 million copies and given rise to a film adaptation. This series traces the steps of Mormonism's founding pioneers through the eyes of a fictional family. Other popular Mormon historical fiction series have dramatized the Book of Mormon, the Bible, the African American Mormon experience, and Mormon perspectives on the World War II and Vietnam eras. Issued by a national publisher, Orson Scott Card's *Saints* (Forge) tells the story of an English convert who becomes one of Joseph Smith's polygamous wives.

- ✔ **Mystery:** Although mystery isn't as successful as romance within the Mormon market, LDS publishers regularly put out mysteries and thrillers, with LDS characters confronting murder, kidnappings, and other perils. The biggest Mormon author who's broken into the mainstream mystery genre is Anne Perry, a convert to Mormonism who lives in Scotland. (By the way, *Lord of the Rings* director Peter Jackson's early film *Heavenly Creatures* is based on a girlhood experience of Perry's.)

- ✔ **Romance:** This genre has sold hundreds of thousands of copies inside the Mormon culture, with authors Rachel Nunes, Anita Stansfield, and Jack Weyland leading the way. In these stories, converting or recommitting to Mormonism typically plays as big a role as falling in love. Some of these novels have dealt with more-troubling themes, such as rape or adultery, but Mormon publishers and retail chains are cautious about books that contain challenging material.

✔ **Science fiction and fantasy:** This kind of writing doesn't get published much inside Mormon circles, but newspapers have reported that a whole mess of Mormons read and write sci-fi and fantasy at the national level. The most prominent Mormon writer in this area is Orson Scott Card (see Chapter 19), who's famous for *Ender's Game* (Tor Books) and is also known for his novels based on thinly veiled allegories of the Book of Mormon and Joseph Smith's life and times. Another big-selling Mormon sci-fi novelist is Dave Wolverton, who also writes as David Farland. Yet another well-known Mormon author is Tracy Hickman, coauthor of the *Dragonlance* series based on the Dungeons and Dragons universe. Surprisingly, Mormonism hasn't yet produced any hot-selling apocalyptic fiction, like evangelical Christianity's *Left Behind* series.

✔ **Young adult:** Perhaps because Mormonism's tender cultural sensibilities are well suited to writing for teens, several Mormon authors have won national contests and published young adult books with national publishers. However, these Mormon writers still manage to tackle some challenging issues for their audience. Notable names include Ann Cannon, Chris Crowe, Lael Littke, Louise Plummer, Carol Lynch Williams, and several others.

Literary fiction and poetry

Most mainstream Mormons don't know it, but the culture includes a small, passionate intellectual literary scene, in which books are wildly successful if they sell 1,000 copies. In addition, some writers with Mormon affiliations have made ripples on the national literary scene.

For literary novels and collections of stories and poems, culturally liberal Mormons turn to Signature Books (www.signaturebooks.com). For the newest short stories and poems, sources include the nonprofit journals *Dialogue, Irreantum,* and *Sunstone* (for more info, use an Internet search engine to find their Web sites). In addition, a small arts organization called the Association for Mormon Letters serves as a Mormon literary hub by sponsoring conferences, an e-mail discussion list, and various publications. For more info, including over 700 online reviews of Mormon literary works, visit www.aml-online.org.

In the mid-20th century, national publishers released Mormon-themed works by two authors — Virginia Sorensen and Maurine Whipple — whose books are still worth seeking out today. Within Mormon culture, one of the most highly regarded literary authors is Levi Peterson, particularly for his novel *The Backslider* (Signature). In today's national literary scene, the handful of Mormon-connected contemporary authors who are making those aforementioned ripples include Brian Evenson, Judith Freeman, Walter Kirn, Brady Udall, and Terry Tempest Williams. However, several of these authors have publicly acknowledged that they're no longer active in the faith.

Hams and cheese: Mormon drama

Mormons are fairly big on plays, musicals, pageants, and other forms of live drama. One of the first things the prophet Brigham Young did after the pioneers arrived in the Salt Lake Valley was establish a theater, and he even played some roles himself.

Today, Mormonism's biggest manifestation of live drama is outdoor pageants. Dramatizing Mormon scripture and history, these annual shows typically run for a week or two during the summer at historical Mormon locations around the country. The largest, most lavishly produced event is the Hill Cumorah Pageant, staged near Palmyra, New York, on the hill where Joseph Smith found the golden plates that he later translated as the Book of Mormon (for more on that topic, see Chapter 9). To find out about Mormon pageants, including performance schedules, type **LDS pageants** into an Internet search engine.

Homegrown pop musicals used to be a major part of Mormon culture, but not much anymore. *Saturday's Warrior* and *My Turn on Earth* made a big splash among Mormon audiences during the 1970s, and you can still enjoy their camp appeal on home video. Each year, Mormon youth used to cook up cheesy "road show" minimusicals and perform them throughout the *stake* (a grouping of local congregations), but that practice has almost died out.

As far as literarily significant Mormon plays, a surprising number of somewhat edgy, envelope-pushing pieces are produced at or near Brigham Young University in Provo, Utah, including several by LDS playwright Eric Samuelsen. On the national and international scene, Mormon convert Neil LaBute creates stirs with his challenging plays about people doing each other wrong, including some Mormon characters. Gay Jewish playwright Tony Kushner included many Mormon characters and themes in his award-winning *Angels in America,* which debuted on Broadway and also got adapted by HBO, but Mormons generally don't consider it accurate.

Going Dutcher: The rise of Mormon cinema

Mormon movies existed before the turn of the 21st century, but not like they do today. Over the years, the LDS Church has put out various kinds of films, including high-quality, crowd-pleasing movies for its state-of-the-art theater in downtown Salt Lake City. In addition, Church-owned Brigham Young University has produced short moralizing films for many years, several of which have achieved camp status within the Mormon culture (especially *Johnny Lingo* and *Cipher in the Snow,* which are available on video). But the real fun didn't start until 2001.

Carving out a niche

Down in Hollywood, a Mormon filmmaker named Richard Dutcher noticed that small films serving niches such as the gay community succeeded, so he decided to try his hand doing the same for Mormons. Released in 2001, his first feature film, *God's Army,* tells the story of full-time missionaries in the Los Angeles area, with more humor and realism than institutional films ever dared. Dutcher managed to get the film into some theaters in heavily Mormon areas. A few million dollars later, the independent Mormon film movement was born.

Since Dutcher's debut, more than a dozen independent Mormon films have followed, with several new ones appearing each year, most of them primarily comedic in tone. Unfortunately, poor scriptwriting, hammy acting, and amateur production values have marred most of them. Mormon filmmakers drool for a crossover hit like *My Big Fat Greek Wedding,* but the closest attempt so far has been a safe, earnest, beautifully produced South Pacific Mormon missionary story called *The Other Side of Heaven.* Disney Home Video picked it up for distribution, but it didn't exactly create a stir. However, Dutcher and some other talented LDS filmmakers still have a few tricks up their sleeves, including Dutcher's much-anticipated biopic on founding Mormon prophet Joseph Smith.

You can find out anything you ever wanted to know about the connection between Mormonism and film at the exhaustively fascinating `www.ldsfilm.com`, an independent site maintained by Mormon film buffs.

Showing up in Hollywood

Believe it or not, Hollywood has a few Mormon producers, directors, and other movie folk.

- In terms of audience size and critical response, one of the highest-achieving Mormon artists in any field is writer/director Neil LaBute, who has turned several of his plays into films.

- In 2004, BYU-trained filmmaker Jared Hess created a nationwide indie sensation with his screwball comedy *Napoleon Dynamite,* which doesn't include any explicitly Mormon elements but avoids sex and profanity.

- Mormon filmmakers Don Bluth and Richard Rich have made many well-known animated movies for the likes of Disney.

- Mormon filmmaker Kieth Merrill won an Oscar for his feature documentary *The Great American Cowboy.*

- Mormon producer Gerald R. Molen has worked on several of Steven Spielberg's films.

Here are some of the best-known Mormon-affiliated actors, including a few TV ones: *Erin Brockovich*'s Aaron Eckhart (the biker boyfriend), *WKRP in Cincinnati*'s Gordon Jump, *Bring It On*'s Eliza Dushku, *The Brady Bunch*'s Mike Lookinland (Bobby), *Family Affair*'s Johnny Whitaker (Jody), little person Billy Barty, and oatmeal huckster Wilford Brimley. In addition, actors Matthew Modine and Ryan Gosling were raised Mormon.

An R-rated controversy

One of Mormonism's biggest cultural controversies is whether or not members should watch R-rated movies. Several years ago, an apostle warned Mormon teens not to see R-rated movies, and since then other Church authorities have echoed the counsel as a semi-commandment for all Mormons, regardless of age.

However, many faithful Mormons choose to watch carefully chosen R-rated movies, and the LDS Church shows signs of acknowledging that the U.S. movie rating system isn't a reliable viewing guide, especially for members in other nations. Many Mormons have discovered that some R-rated movies are more morally edifying than some PG-13 ones, even if the *F*-word count is a little higher. Still, you'll find some Mormons who are quite strict about avoiding all R-rated movies as a spiritual discipline, just as some are stricter than others about drinking cola.

Some enterprising Mormons, including the folks at CleanFlix and ClearPlay, offer the public different methods of viewing movies without the offensive parts, including editing videocassettes and providing filters for DVD players. However, Hollywood doesn't like people tinkering with its films — well, except for the airlines — and has filed several lawsuits.

Part V
The Part of Tens

The 5th Wave   By Rich Tennant

"You know how you're always saying we can learn a spiritual lesson when bad things happen to us? Well, you're about to get a spiritual lesson from Herb's Towing and Collision and the Able Auto Insurance Company."

In this part . . .

You meet ten (or so) famous Latter-day Saints, get answers to ten frequently asked questions about Mormonism, and find out about ten places to visit where you can discover more about Mormon history and belief.

Chapter 19

Ten Famous Mormons

*M*ost of the Mormons who've achieved national fame and fortune in non-religious arenas are still alive, which perhaps isn't surprising when you consider that Mormonism isn't even 200 years old as a faith. Keep in mind, however, that a handful of prominent Mormons have already kicked the bucket. In this chapter, we focus on well-known Mormons who are still with us at the time of this writing.

Jane Clayson

Moving up the broadcast television career ladder in Salt Lake City and Los Angeles, Brigham Young University (BYU) graduate Jane Clayson reached a national pinnacle in 1999, when she was named as coanchor of CBS's *The Early Show,* along with Bryant Gumbel. In 2002, she became a CBS news correspondent, with stints substituting for anchor Dan Rather, doing "Eye on America" news segments, contributing stories to *48 Hours,* and fulfilling other high-profile assignments.

Already a hero to Mormons for maintaining LDS values and standards during her top-shelf career, Clayson upped the ante in 2004 by turning her back on the TV industry to become a full-time wife and mother. "I didn't ever want to look back in 15 years and point to a bookshelf of videotapes and say, that's been my life," she told a 2004 university graduating class in Utah. Today, she's known as Jane Clayson Johnson.

Stephen R. Covey

When Mormons read *The 7 Habits of Highly Effective People* (Free Press), Covey's self-help book that's sold more than 15 million copies in 32 languages and 75 countries, many of them recognize glimmers of LDS gospel principles. But hey, that's okay — presumably, Covey gives the LDS Church 10 percent of his millions of dollars in royalties (for more on Mormon tithing, see Chapter 16). Covey's impact on the business world prompted *Time* magazine to recognize him as one of America's 25 most influential people — and led Scott Adams to title one of his Dilbert cartoon collections *Seven Years of Highly Defective People*.

A former BYU professor in organizational behavior and business management, Covey cofounded and co-chairs the Franklin Covey Company, which bills itself as the world's largest management and leadership development organization. (The company produces those elaborate daily planners that Mormons helped originate and still use widely.) Additional books authored or coauthored by Covey include *Principle-Centered Leadership* (Free Press), the time-management guide *First Things First* (Free Press), the parenting manual *The 7 Habits of Highly Effective Families* (Golden Books Adult Publishing), and the 2004 business bestseller *The 8th Habit: From Effectiveness to Greatness* (Free Press).

Liriel Domiciano

You may not have heard this Mormon singer's name before — but if you're from Brazil, you likely know her by just her first name. Liriel performed for eight months on Brazil's version of the amateur-talent TV show *American Idol,* and since then her CDs have sold millions of copies, including Brazil's sixth-best-selling CD ever.

Born in 1981 and reared in a poor Sao Paulo suburb, Liriel converted to Mormonism as a teen in 1996, along with other family members. After LDS Church President Gordon B. Hinckley heard her sing during the rededication of a temple in Brazil — which, with 800,000 Mormons, has the world's third-highest Mormon population, after the United States and Mexico — he requested her to perform as a soloist with the Mormon Tabernacle Choir during the LDS Church's semiannual General Conference in 2004, the first soloist to do so since the 1930s (see Figure 19-1; for more on General Conference, see Chapter 8). "This means everything to me," she told a Salt Lake newspaper. "It's better than Disneyland."

Figure 19-1:
In 2004,
Liriel
performed
with the
Mormon
Tabernacle
Choir.

Photo by Rick Egan/The Salt Lake Tribune

Richard Paul Evans

When Richard Paul Evans wrote *The Christmas Box,* his sentimental story of a young family befriending a widow, he initially intended it for his two daughters. As a Christmas gift in 1993, he made 20 copies of the short book for friends and family members, and soon bookstores started calling for copies. An advertising executive by profession, Evans successfully published the book himself. After a national publisher (Simon & Schuster) picked up the book, it topped bestseller lists in hardcover and paperback editions simultaneously, with more than 8 million copies eventually printed in 18 languages. In 1995, producers made the story into a top-rated TV movie that won an Emmy Award.

Since then, Evans has gone on to write several more novels, and although he's not exactly a critic's darling, he still charts on the bestseller lists. He's donated some of his proceeds to a charitable foundation that provides services for abused and neglected children, and he's active on the motivational speaking circuit.

Orrin Hatch

A metalworker and lawyer by training, Utah's best-known politician — for better or worse — initially won his U.S. Senate seat in 1976 and, at press time for this book, has served continuously since then. As a powerful Republican with some heavy-duty committee responsibilities, Hatch has worked to slow the growth of the federal bureaucracy and hold the line against expensive, prohibitive government regulations. People have called him "Mr. Free Enterprise" and "Guardian of Small Business."

Some of Hatch's most public efforts have included defending Supreme Court Justice Clarence Thomas during his confirmation brouhaha, supporting a constitutional amendment that prohibits desecration of the U.S. flag, safeguarding the nutritional supplement industry — much of which is based in Utah — against government regulation, speaking out in favor of stem cell research, and running for U.S. president in 2000. As a somewhat surrealistic sideline, Hatch writes and performs patriotic and religious songs.

Gladys Knight

Back during her days in Motown with the Pips, singer Gladys Knight surely never imagined she'd one day hear about Mormonism through the grapevine and take the midnight train to Utah (see Figure 19-2). Sure enough, however, in 1997 one of her children introduced her to the faith, and she got baptized. (As far as we know, no Pips have taken the plunge yet.)

Since then, Knight has performed and recorded what some call Mormon gospel music, including gospel versions of Mormon hymns. Invited to perform at several high-profile events at Church headquarters, Knight once commented that she loved Mormon music but then added, "I just think some of it could use a little zip!" Today she lives in Las Vegas, where she leads a Mormon gospel choir.

Figure 19-2: Gladys Knight sings at the 2004 funeral of the LDS prophet's wife, Marjorie Hinckley.

Photo by Rick Egan/The Salt Lake Tribune

The Osmond Family

This toothsome family has given rise to what are probably still the most famous Mormon entertainers ever. Like white doppelgangers of the Jackson Five, the five Osmond brothers arose in the national consciousness in the late 1960s through appearances on *The Andy Williams Show,* and the brothers made several hits together, including "One Bad Apple" and "Yo Yo." Before breaking up in 1980, they expressed their Mormon beliefs in a concept album called _The Plan_. Today, some of the brothers still perform together, and several of their sons have formed a singing group.

Like Michael Jackson, Donny emerged as the family's breakout star, becoming one of the biggest teen idols of the 1970s. However, his younger sister Marie gave him a run for his money as a multifaceted entertainer, and both continue occasionally popping up in TV shows, Broadway musicals, charities, recordings, and other venues. Most famously, the two combined forces for TV's _The Donny & Marie Show_ in the late 1970s and again for a daytime TV talk show in the late 1990s. Donny told about his panic attacks in his 1999 memoir _Life Is Just What You Make It: My Story So Far_ (Hyperion), and in 2002 Marie published a memoir titled _Behind the Smile: My Journey Out of Postpartum Depression_ (Warner Books). Donny devotes a section of his personal Web site at www.donny.com to Mormonism.

Mitt Romney

When moderate Republican Mitt Romney was elected in 2002 as governor of Massachusetts, where Mormons are only somewhat less exotic than the Amish, many Latter-day Saints celebrated the victory as evidence of the faith's increasing acceptance. The real test, however, may come in 2008, when many expect Romney — like his father, George Romney, did before him — to run for president. Hillary versus Mitt, anyone?

With degrees from BYU and Harvard, Mitt built a successful career in management consulting and venture capitalizing, gaining a reputation for turning around troubled companies. He rose to international prominence as the savior of the scandal-mired and deficit-hobbled Salt Lake Olympics, successfully pulling off the world's first major post-9/11 event. If that credit isn't enough, in 2002 _People_ magazine named him one of the year's most beautiful people. In 2004, Mitt published a memoir entitled _Turnaround: Crisis, Leadership, and the Olympic Games_ (Regnery).

Sharlene Wells

Back in 1985, Sharlene Wells became the first foreign-born Miss America, and her daddy was a high-ranking General Authority in the LDS Church at the time of her victory. Was it coincidence that such a clean, wholesome person won the year after 1984's Miss America resigned over some nude _Penthouse_ photos? You be the judge.

Born in Asunción, Paraguay, where her Nevada-born father was working as a banking executive, Wells played the Paraguayan harp and sang in Spanish for her Miss America talent, performing for a record-breaking television audience of more than 100 million people. After her reign, she graduated from BYU and became one of the first female reporters at ESPN, where she covered sporting events ranging from college football to the Kentucky Derby. Married with four children and today known as Sharlene Wells Hawkes, she works in communications, makes public appearances, and gives speeches. In 2002, she published the self-help book *Kissing a Frog: Four Steps to Finding Comfort Outside Your Comfort Zone* (Shadow Mountain/Deseret).

Steve Young

Masterful at both running and throwing the football, Steve Young is perhaps the most successful product of BYU's once-mighty quarterback factory, which also turned out Robbie Bosco, Ty Detmer, Jim McMahon, Gifford Nielsen, and Marc Wilson. A great-great-great-grandson of Mormon prophet Brigham Young, Steve played in the National Football League from 1985 to 1999, most of those years with the San Francisco 49ers, where he learned quarterbacking from Joe Montana.

Although many Mormon athletes have sacrificed their professional careers by refusing to play on the Sabbath, Steve Young set a Super Bowl record with six touchdown passes in 1994's Sunday match. However, Mormons still generally respect and admire him, especially now that he's finally married. He's often been a spokesperson for the LDS Church, including on *60 Minutes*. Other famous Mormon athletes include golfer Johnny Miller and baseball star Dale Murphy.

Chapter 20

Quick Answers to Ten Common Questions About Mormonism

*M*ormonism may not be the world's most unusual religion, but it's far enough off the beaten path to generate lots of questions from outside observers and people who are new to the faith. In this chapter, we address some of the most common questions that Mormons typically encounter at one time or another. We cover nearly all these topics more deeply elsewhere in this book, so the answers in this chapter are the boiled-down versions.

Are Mormons Christian?

Perhaps no other question is raised as frequently as this $64,000 one: Are Mormons Christian? Mormons, of course, absolutely believe that they're Christians, because they love and worship the Savior, Jesus Christ, and endeavor to follow his example in all things. To paraphrase the Book of Mormon, they talk about Christ, rejoice in Christ, preach about Christ, prophesy about Christ, and look to him alone for the forgiveness of their sins (see 2 Nephi 25:26). In what way could they not be Christian?

Well, it seems that the deciding factor depends on how you define the word *Christian.* If the word means its primary dictionary definition — "one who professes belief in the teachings of Jesus Christ" — then the answer is an absolute yes. But the people who ask this question sometimes don't think that this belief is enough. For example, they may call Mormons non-Christians because Mormons reject the concept of the Trinity as other Christian churches have traditionally defined it: that God is one ultimate being with three persons. (For more on Mormon views of God, see Chapter 3.) So if that's the litmus test, Mormons don't make the grade.

Other issues are at stake as well. For example, some people believe that Mormons can't be Christians because they've added other books to the canon of what God has revealed as scripture (the Bible). What's more, Mormons believe that revelation is still open ended and claim that God reveals new doctrine today through his prophet. So if the definition of *Christian* rules out any additional scriptures or revelation, once again, Mormons don't qualify.

Another point of contention centers on priesthood authority. Many different Christian churches, even when they disagree with each other over matters of doctrine, still accept each other's ordinances, such as baptism, as being essentially valid. However, Mormons believe that the priesthood was lost from the earth until God restored it through Joseph Smith. As a result, Mormons believe that other churches, no matter how much good they do, don't possess full authority from God, and converts to Mormonism have to be baptized again even if they were already baptized into another Christian church. (For more on Mormon views about the priesthood and its restoration, see Chapter 4.) As you can imagine, members of some Christian churches find this view insulting.

In recent years, the LDS Church has been using the tagline "Christian but different." In other words, Mormons consider themselves Christians, but their beliefs and practices are sometimes quite different from traditional creedal Christianity. It's helpful to think about adding "Mormon Christian" to the other kinds of Christians already out there: evangelical Protestant Christians, Eastern Orthodox Christians, Roman Catholic Christians, and on and on. Mormon Christians believe that although their doctrines may sound unusual to other Christians, their good works and spiritual sincerity reflect well on the Savior that all Christians seek to emulate. And as Christ himself said, his followers will be known by their fruits.

How Can Mormons Give Up 10 Percent of Their Income?

True — faithful Mormons give the Church a full 10 percent of their income (some pay 10 percent of their gross income, and others pay on their take-home amount). For many Mormon households, tithing is one of the largest monthly budget items. When Mormons face the choice between paying tithing and buying groceries, the Church expects them to exercise faith, put the Lord first, and trust in his providence, which the Church itself sometimes provides through its welfare program. (To find out more about the Mormon practice of tithing, see Chapter 16.)

Certainly, tithing sometimes causes Mormon families to miss out on luxuries that they may have otherwise enjoyed, and in some situations the sacrifice may be even greater. On the other hand, Latter-day Saints aren't generally known for being materially needy or economically underprivileged (in the United States, at least). Mormons believe that tithing helps them grow spiritually, but the real key to gladly obeying this commandment is the Mormon belief that the Lord increases one's blessings in return for supporting his kingdom. Paying tithing doesn't guarantee riches or protection from temporary setbacks, but most Mormon tithe-payers believe that, at the end of the day, they come out ahead materially as well as spiritually.

For new LDS converts, disciplining their budgetary habits to accommodate the tithe can be one of the hardest parts of coming up to speed as a Mormon. However, Church classes and magazines frequently give advice about managing finances wisely, and developing a consistent tithing habit is quite possible. For faithful Mormons, the question isn't how they can afford to pay tithing, but how they could afford *not* to pay it.

What Happens inside an LDS Temple?

After the prophet or an apostle dedicates a Mormon temple for sacred use, only Church members who've proven their moral and spiritual worthiness can enter. Inside, they reverently participate in a number of different *ordinances,* or physical rituals necessary for returning to live with God and becoming like him. Mormons perform these ordinances not only for their own spiritual benefit, but also on behalf of those who died without receiving them. (For detailed info on temples, including how they differ from regular LDS meetinghouses, see Chapter 7.)

Although Mormons don't receive their own baptism, confirmation, and — for all worthy males — priesthood ordination inside a temple, they can perform these ordinances on behalf of the deceased only inside a temple. Living and dead people alike may receive Mormonism's three higher ordinances only inside a temple: being symbolically washed and anointed with water and olive oil, participating in a two-hour *endowment* session that rehearses God's entire plan of salvation, and getting sealed as a family for eternity.

Mormons perform their own temple ordinances only once; after that, they visit the temple to perform ordinances for the dead. In the spirit world, each deceased person's spirit must choose whether to accept or reject the ordinances that people on earth perform for him or her.

Why Don't Mormons Drink Alcohol or Coffee?

Like Jews, Muslims, and Hindus, Mormons have a list of substances that they're forbidden to consume if they want to remain orthodox. Sort of like Mormon kosher, the list is a cradle-to-grave program for maintaining spiritual and physical health. In a nutshell, Mormons stay away from alcohol (wine, beer, and liquor), coffee, tea, tobacco, and any drug that they can't buy over the counter or that wasn't prescribed to them by a doctor.

This guideline, called the *Word of Wisdom,* comes from revelation that God gave to the prophet Joseph Smith in the 1830s. Interpreted slightly differently over time, this advice has held the status of commandment since the early 20th century. The Word of Wisdom is important enough now that the LDS Church requires members to obey it in order to be admitted into the temple. (For more on the temple, see Chapter 7.)

Mormons believe that bodily purity and spiritual holiness are connected, and they consider the requirements of the Word of Wisdom to be easy to keep when compared with their spiritual benefit. Mormons aren't free to drink a Sea Breeze, for example, but they're free *from* addiction or the potential for it. In addition, they're protected from the impaired judgment and bodily harm that often result from intoxicants. These freedoms are a tremendous blessing in an age of excess and dependence.

The basic guidelines of the Word of Wisdom are crystal clear, but some of the small stuff falls into gray areas. Is caffeinated soda okay? What about decaf coffee or herbal tea? You'll find Mormons on both sides of such issues. For more-specific information on the Word of Wisdom, see Chapter 16.

Why Do Mormons Have Such Large, Strong Families?

To Mormons, the nuclear family is an eternal principle, with husband and wives *sealed* together eternally and their children sealed to them. Therefore, when Mormon families put effort into strengthening their harmony and togetherness, they're mindful that the investment extends beyond this life. In other words, if they're going to be stuck together forever, they may as well learn to enjoy it. (For more on Mormon families, see Chapter 5.)

Although the Mormon birthrate has declined in recent years, Mormons still have larger families on average than the typical citizen. One of the main reasons is rooted in the Mormon belief that before birth all human spirits exist in a state that Mormons call *premortality* (refer to Chapter 2). Those spirits who are currently embodied on earth are responsible for bringing still-waiting spirits into righteous Mormon homes and shouldn't put off having children for selfish or worldly reasons. In addition, some Mormons believe they formed spiritual family relationships in the premortal state, and they don't want to leave behind any spirits who belong in their earthly family.

On the practical level, Mormons use several techniques for strengthening their families. Throughout Mormondom, families reserve Monday evenings for *family home evening,* which they devote to learning the gospel, discussing plans and problems, and enjoying activities together (refer to Chapter 17 for more). In addition, Mormon families ideally read scriptures and kneel in prayer together daily, and the Church constantly teaches good parenting skills and other family-enhancing principles. Mormons can divorce and even apply to cancel an eternal sealing, but the rate of divorce among temple-sealed couples is less than half the national average.

Do Mormons Believe in the Bible or Just the Book of Mormon?

In the Mormon view, the Bible and the Book of Mormon go together like rama-lama . . . um, we mean that Mormons love both of them and regard them both as scripture. The Book of Mormon isn't a replacement for the Bible, but a companion to it. As its subtitle says, this book is "Another Testament of Jesus Christ," pointing readers to the Savior and further describing his role and ministry.

Mormonism's eighth Article of Faith states, "We believe the Bible to be the word of God as far as it is translated correctly; we also believe the Book of Mormon to be the word of God." Mormons look to the Bible for guidance, knowledge, teachings, and spiritual consolation. They don't, however, think that God stopped there. Although the Bible is primarily an account of God's dealings with the house of Israel in the ancient Near East, God also gave the world the Book of Mormon, a record of Israelites who fled to the Western Hemisphere. In the Mormon mind, both books flow together to tell the story of how God redeems humanity through the atoning sacrifice of Jesus Christ, and both reveal his ultimate plan for creation.

As we explore in Chapter 9, the main event of the Book of Mormon is the appearance of Christ in the New World. The Book of Mormon clarifies some points of doctrine that the Bible doesn't resolve, such as the proper method and reasons for baptism (2 Nephi 31; 3 Nephi 11:23–26) and the nuts and bolts of the eventual resurrection of our bodies (Alma 40). The Book of Mormon complements the Bible but doesn't compete with it. In addition, Mormons believe in other works of scripture from both ancient and modern prophets, including the Doctrine and Covenants and Pearl of Great Price (see Chapter 10).

Do Mormons Really Believe that Humans Can Become Gods?

Nowadays, Mormons prefer to say that humans can eventually become *like* God, which sounds less presumptuous. But Mormons don't expect it to happen any time soon. It's not like LDS Sunday schools teach members how to create planets and parent billions of offspring. And it's not like Mormons will ever stop honoring and obeying their Heavenly Father, even if they become eternal parents like him.

To Mormons, the idea that God's children can grow up to become like him makes perfect sense, even if humans are still only in the embryonic phase. Other kinds of Christians see this belief as blasphemous, but Mormons find justification right in the New Testament, where the Lord commands, "Be ye therefore perfect, even as your Father in Heaven is perfect" (Matthew 5:48). The word *perfect* means not only pure and unblemished, but also complete and whole. (For more on the nature of God, see Chapter 3.)

The best summary of this Mormon belief is a phrase that LDS Prophet Lorenzo Snow coined: "As man now is, God once was; as God is now, man may become." For Mormons, this belief is basic to understanding the purpose of life and the answers to the great questions: Where did we come from? Why are we here? Where are we going? In a nutshell, this life is a test to see who's worthy of godhood, which is attainable only by living the full gospel of Jesus Christ as offered by the LDS Church. (For more about the plan of salvation, see Chapter 2.)

Why Can't Women Hold the Priesthood?

Women have never held the priesthood in The Church of Jesus Christ of Latter-day Saints, although until the 1940s they did perform healing ordinances for sick women and children. (For a quick explanation of the meaning of priesthood to Latter-day Saints, see Chapter 4.)

The LDS Church has never published an official statement about why LDS women don't hold the priesthood, although various General Authorities and individual members have floated some ideas. One widely held theory is that women are so innately spiritual and righteous that they don't need the priesthood in order to grow and become more like God. This kind of reverse sexism says that women are naturally superior to men, so many Mormons who feel the explanation is inadequate have rejected it. Another theory is that God simply ordained it that way, and it's not our place to ask why what's good for the gander isn't also good for the goose.

Most Mormons, however, aren't very ruffled over the issue. As we discuss in Chapter 15, Mormonism offers some ideas that are uniquely empowering to women, such as the belief in a Heavenly Mother (see Chapter 3) and a positive view of Eve and her role in elevating humankind (see Chapter 2). To outsiders, the fact that women don't hold the priesthood may appear limiting, but Mormons don't usually feel that way. Women can receive all the blessings of the priesthood even if they don't hold the priesthood themselves. As President Gordon B. Hinckley, the Mormon prophet at this writing, put it, "In this Church the man neither walks ahead of his wife nor behind his wife but at her side. They are coequals in this life in a great enterprise."

Do Mormons Still Practice Polygamy?

No. No, no, no, no, and no. Any questions?

Seriously, Mormons are often surprised and frustrated at just how often this question comes up. The LDS Church hasn't approved of earthly polygamy since 1890, and the Church even excommunicates people who practice it nowadays. So the fact that the question never dies is kind of irritating.

In part, this persistence is due to the fact that dozens of fringe groups with ties to old-timey Mormonism still practice polygamy and have taken their case to the court of public opinion in the form of TV talk shows and books. Some claim that they're the real Mormons and that the LDS Church has betrayed God by forbidding polygamy (see Chapter 15). The official LDS Church has distanced itself from these small but high-profile groups, urging members of the media to appreciate the distinction between polygamists and mainstream Mormons. Church PR spokespeople clarify until they're blue that the term *Mormon polygamist* is an oxymoron, because no polygamist can remain a member of The Church of Jesus Christ of Latter-day Saints.

Some Mormons complain that in its zeal to be distinguished from contemporary polygamists, the LDS Church has gone too far in the other direction, downplaying the vital role that polygamy played in its own history prior to 1890 (see Chapter 13). Church leaders have de-emphasized or ignored polygamy in recent Church curricula and instruction manuals. But who can wonder why the Church wants to avoid any confusion, when people continue to mistakenly believe that Mormons still practice polygamy?

How Can Mormons Revere Joseph Smith?

An angel told Mormonism's founding prophet that his name would "be both good and evil spoken of among all people," and that claim has certainly come to pass. Although Mormons revere Joseph Smith as a prophet, they realize that he was an imperfect mortal who made some mistakes and needed to repent of some sins. In fact, Joseph himself admitted that he was subject to the faults of human nature, although not a committer of any glaring sins.

If the young Joseph was involved in some of the loopy trends of his time, such as digging for treasure and dabbling in folk magic, perhaps that idea simply demonstrates his keen imagination and openness to new things, useful attributes for an emerging prophet of God. In fact, Mormons love Joseph all the more for his vibrant, down-to-earth personality. The product of a hardscrabble rural upbringing, he was known for roughhousing with children, playing sports, and enjoying a good laugh. Regarding his practice of polygamy, Mormons don't see it as a character flaw but as his reluctant obedience to one of God's most difficult commandments.

Many anti-Mormons unjustly criticize Joseph Smith, and some observers make the mistake of thinking that Mormons worship Joseph or put him on an equal footing with the Savior. Although Mormons believe that Joseph Smith is the world's greatest prophet who ever lived, in terms of his revelatory output and contribution to humankind's potential salvation, he nevertheless remains in the same class as Moses, Abraham, Peter, and other biblical prophets. (For more on Joseph Smith, see Chapters 4, 9, 10, 11, and 12.)

Chapter 21

Ten Mormon Places to Visit

In This Chapter

▶ Visiting Mormon history sites from coast to coast

▶ Knowing the most interesting sites and activities

*L*DS Church members aren't the only ones who are interested in visiting Mormon sites. Many people's first experience of Mormonism comes by either intentionally visiting or haphazardly stumbling upon a historic site that has special significance for Mormons. Going to some of the places listed in this chapter is a terrific way to find out about Mormon history and Mormonism today firsthand.

In this chapter we offer a brief overview of some of the most important sites connected with Mormon history and culture, organized in rough chronological order. Except where noted, all these places are open to the public six days a week and are free. Some Church-owned sites are also open for limited hours on Sundays. You can find up-to-date schedules and driving directions at www.lds.org.

Sharon, Vermont

Sharon, Vermont (also called South Royalton), the birthplace of Mormon founder Joseph Smith, is a little off the radar but well worth a visit. Here you'll see Joseph Smith's birth site, with a small stone marking the place where the Smith family home stood in 1805. A visitors' center offers a permanent exhibit telling the story of the Smith family's years in Vermont, and you can see a 38.5-foot granite monument — one foot for each year of the prophet's life — that the Church dedicated in 1905.

The year 2005 will be full of special bicentennial celebrations at the birthplace, with pageants and meetings to commemorate the life of Joseph Smith during the bicentennial of his birth. Plan to spend half a day in Sharon to see the Smith family sites. If you're tooling around Vermont, you can also check out Brigham Young's birthplace in Whittington in the southern part of the state. Though Brigham's house no longer stands, you can see a 12-foot granite monument to him, as well as a plaque marking the road where his birthplace once stood.

Palmyra, New York

As the site of many of Mormonism's most sacred events, Palmyra has become a Mormon tourist hot spot in recent years, especially since the Church dedicated a temple there in 2000. Among the many places to visit in and around Palmyra, some highlights include

- **The Sacred Grove:** This place is a forest clearing where the teenage Joseph Smith prayed and received the First Vision in the early 1820s. (For a recap, see Chapter 4.) Modern-day Mormons and people of other faiths take advantage of this quiet spot for prayer and reflection.

- **The Grandin Building:** Located in downtown Palmyra, this building is where the Book of Mormon was first printed in 1830. Unlike many other historic buildings from the Church's founding days, the Grandin is still standin', making it a particularly interesting place to see.

- **The Smith family farm:** Here you can walk through a replica of the Smiths' log home on the exact site of the one where they lived with eight of their kids. (See, contemporary Mormons aren't the only people who raise large families in cramped quarters.)

Plan to spend two days in the area, if possible. One especially neat time to go is during the *Hill Cumorah Pageant,* when thousands of people gather for a few days in July to witness a blockbuster theatrical production about the Book of Mormon. Hotel and campsite reservations fill up early, and the whole Palmyra region is more crowded during the pageant than any other time of year, but the show is a real spectacle. For more info, try www.hillcumorah.org.

Kirtland, Ohio

The Mormons' first full-fledged community, located in Kirtland, near Cleveland, Ohio, has gotten a superb facelift. In 2002 and 2003, the Church restored numerous buildings in the town to what they looked like in the 1830s, when more than 2,000 Mormons lived there. More buildings will be renovated in future years. Some places to visit in Kirtland include

✔ **The Kirtland Temple:** Shown in Chapter 11, this historic temple is now owned by the Community of Christ and is open to the public. For more on the Community of Christ, see Chapter 12.

✔ **The Newel K. Whitney home and store:** Located on Kirtland's main drag, this building is the original place where Mormons shopped for provisions and where, in an upper room, Joseph Smith received many of the revelations that Mormons regard as scripture. Even those people who don't share the LDS belief in continuing revelation can appreciate this meticulously kept store as a window into the American past, from the bolts of calico on the wall to the hard candy at the counter.

✔ **The Kirtland Visitors' Center:** This center, which opened in 2003, offers tourists historical exhibits and a short film about Kirtland in the 1830s.

You can see most of Kirtland in one very full day, and this place is excellent to visit year-round. Other things to see include an old Mormon schoolhouse and the homes of Sidney Rigdon and Hyrum Smith, brother of Joseph. (For more on Mormonism's Kirtland era, see Chapter 11.)

Nauvoo and Carthage, Illinois

Nauvoo is the pinnacle of the Church's restoration efforts, welcoming approximately 350,000 visitors annually. As such, this city has become quite a tourist mecca, especially since the 2002 dedication of the reconstructed Nauvoo Temple, shown in Figure 21-1. (Be sure to make your reservations early if you want to stay at the Hotel Nauvoo, for example, or eat at the stomach-stretching smorgasbord there.)

Figure 21-1: The reconstructed Nauvoo Temple, dedicated in 2002.

Photo courtesy of Phil Smith

Nauvoo and Carthage have so much to see that we can only mention a few of the most significant places:

- **The Nauvoo Visitors' Center:** This center is a good place to start because you get an overview of Nauvoo history from the Mormon point of view and can arm yourself with maps and brochures of nearby attractions.

- **Joseph Smith's home and redbrick store:** This home, called the Mansion House, also functioned as an inn where the Prophet and his wife Emma housed visitors to the city. The upper floor of the store was the site of many significant events in Mormon history, including the organization of the women's Relief Society (see Chapter 6) and the introduction of the temple endowment (see Chapter 7). The Community of Christ owns both the home and the store.

- **The Scovil bakery:** No, this place doesn't have great historical significance, but while you're learning about 1840s baking techniques you can munch on their free gingerbread cookies.

- **Cultural Hall:** This three-story building is where Mormons held lectures, concerts, dances, and plays. Besides the temple, this building is the most impressive one in Nauvoo.

- **Carthage Jail:** Here is where Joseph and Hyrum Smith were assassinated on June 27, 1844. Visitors can put their fingers in a bullet hole in the door to the second-floor room where the brothers were held.

Nauvoo takes a good two days just for the highlights, and longer if you want to explore the dozens of restored buildings. You can tour the homes of Brigham Young, Wilford Woodruff, Lucy Mack Smith, and Heber C. Kimball (ancestor of coauthor Christopher Kimball Bigelow), or see on-site demonstrations of blacksmithing, woodworking, and other trades and crafts from the period. Anyone can walk around the grounds of the 2002 temple, although you need a temple recommend to get inside (see Chapter 7).

Missouri

Missouri was the site of great heartache and persecution for the Mormons — for a rehearsal of that litany of woe, read Chapter 11 — so visitors to Mormon sites in Missouri today are treated to a mostly sad story of persecution, mob violence, and exile. Many of the sites related to Mormon history are in and around Independence, the Saints' first major settlement in the state. The city is important not just to Latter-day Saints but also to several other Mormon-related denominations that still have a presence in the area. Things to see include

✔ **The Community of Christ's auditorium and temple:** The auditorium is the Community of Christ's gathering place for their world conferences; their lovely temple, dedicated in 1994, is open to the public for tours, prayer, and worship. (For more on this Mormon-related denomination, see Chapter 12.)

✔ **The LDS Visitors' Center:** This visitors' center, which is across the street from the auditorium, occupies a small portion of the land that Joseph Smith declared would be home to Christ's great temple in the Millennium (see Chapter 3). The Community of Christ and other groups own the rest of this choice parcel.

But the Independence area isn't the only place to visit in Missouri. Be sure to stop at the Liberty Jail in Liberty. (Liberty's actually the place where Joseph was behind bars, so the name must've seemed a bit absurd to him.) While he was in jail, though, he received some of the most beautiful revelations of the Doctrine and Covenants (D&C 121–23), which discuss how to deal with adversity and hardship. The Church has rebuilt the jail in cutaway fashion — almost like a movie set — so that visitors can get a whole panoramic view of the place where Joseph spent the cold winter of 1838–39.

Winter Quarters, Nebraska, and Council Bluffs, Iowa

Although the sites in this section are in two different states, they're both right on the border between Iowa and Nebraska. In case you haven't heard enough about the Mormons' sufferings and persecutions, just wait — there's more! The winter of 1846–47, which the Saints spent at the place they called *Winter Quarters* (the Mormons sometimes aren't very poetic about place names), was one of the most difficult periods of Mormon history. About 600 people died here from cold, hunger, and disease. Today, the site is called the *Mormon Trail Center* and is an interesting place to visit if you're in the Omaha area. Here are some things to see and do:

✔ **Check out the pioneer memorial and museum.** The trail center itself features a pioneer memorial, a small museum, and interactive activities for kids, such as pulling a handcart. The center also features a short film about the hardships the Mormons faced in Winter Quarters.

✔ **Peek around the cemetery.** The adjacent Mormon Pioneer Cemetery was the final resting place for about 325 Latter-day Saints, but the names of all 600 who died here are listed on a memorial plaque. The most memorable object is probably the arresting life-size sculpture of a Mormon couple burying their child in an open grave. Many Mormons consider this statue to be a beautiful tribute to the sacrifices and courage of the pioneers.

✔ **Stand in the place where Brigham Young became the LDS president.** Just on the other side of the Missouri River was the Mormon settlement in Kanesville (now Council Bluffs), Iowa, where the Church owns a log tabernacle near the site where a church building stood in 1847. This tabernacle represents the place where Brigham Young was sustained the second president of the Church three and a half years following Joseph Smith's death. (Mormon prophetic succession is much faster nowadays; for more on Brigham Young and the challenges of this first transition of power, see Chapter 12.)

Martin's Cove, Wyoming

Did we mention that the pioneer Mormons' sufferings aren't yet over? No east-to-west, roughly chronological road trip would be complete without a stop at Martin's Cove, the death site for some unfortunate Mormons who were part of the Martin Handcart Company of 1856. Because of their late start in heading west, this pioneer company was trapped by fall blizzards in Wyoming, and 145 of them died before help arrived. (See Chapter 12 for the story.)

In the late 1990s, the Church bought the land and opened it as a living-history museum, where individuals can try wheeling 150-pound handcarts on fairly challenging expeditions. (Less-hardy pioneers may want to opt out of this exercise.)

Salt Lake City, Utah

Obviously, Salt Lake City, which has been Mormonism Central ever since the Latter-day Saints arrived in July 1847, has dozens of Mormon history sites to visit. Try to spend several days in Salt Lake City, and stay right downtown if you're not renting a car. Here are the highlights:

✔ **Temple Square:** This is the place to start if you're staying a few days, and the one place you can't miss if you have only a few hours. (In fact, people with layovers at the Salt Lake International Airport can grab a special shuttle to Temple Square for a quick visit.) Guided tours of the square are available in 40 languages, and reservations aren't necessary. Tours include the following buildings:

• **The Salt Lake Temple:** The temple itself isn't open to the public (sorry, Charlie), but you walk around much of it on the tour, taking in the exterior architecture and the beautiful grounds. This six-spire temple is the pinnacle of LDS architecture and took 40 years to build.

- **The tabernacle:** Home of the Mormon Tabernacle Choir (see Chapter 18), this dome-shaped building resembles half an egg. The coolest part of the tabernacle is its amazing acoustical resonance; you can literally hear a whisper from one end of the building to the other. For a real treat, drop by the building at 8 p.m. on most Thursday evenings. The choir rehearses at this time, and the rehearsals are free to the public.

- **Assembly Hall:** This former worship building that Mormons now use for concerts and the like is another must for music lovers. You can catch a free concert almost any weekend evening.

- **Visitors' centers:** Temple Square now has two visitors' centers. In the north one you can see a famous 11-foot sculpture of Christ, an image that many Mormons adore.

✔ **Joseph Smith Memorial Building:** Across from Temple Square is the Joseph Smith Memorial Building, formerly a glamorous hotel that the Church now owns and uses for wedding receptions, office space, movie screenings, restaurants, and local congregational meetings. For fun, take the elevator up to the top floor and gaze out at Temple Square below. Even on weekdays, you'll be amazed by the number of brides having their pictures taken on the grounds below.

✔ **Family History Library and Museum of Church History and Art:** Located west of Temple Square, the library houses the world's largest collection of genealogical records (see Chapter 5), and the museum exhibits art and artifacts related to the Mormon experience.

✔ **The LDS Conference Center:** This center takes up an entire block just north of Temple Square and is open daily for free tours. The 21,000-seat building was completed in 2000; for details, see Chapter 8.

✔ **Beehive House:** Get a glimpse into 19th-century polygamous life by touring Brigham Young's home, the Beehive House. This national historic landmark is open for free half-hour tours and is a great window into President Young's private and public life, even though many of the guides never mention plural marriage.

After the tour, go around the corner of the building to have lunch in the Lion House Pantry, a cafeteria that offers the best of Mormon country cooking. Be sure to check your low-carb diet at the door and feast on the homemade rolls, cakes, and pies.

✔ **LDS Humanitarian Center:** Catch a shuttle from Temple Square to the LDS Humanitarian Center for a free two-hour tour. The center offers a great way to see the Church's welfare and humanitarian relief programs in action (see Chapter 8). You can taste whatever food they're making that day, watch as volunteers can beets or sort through clothing donations, and tour an exhibit detailing the ways the Church helps the needy.

Provo, Utah

Unlike Salt Lake City, Provo's highlights are easy to see in a day, and the town is remarkable mostly for the fact that there are just *so . . . many . . . Mormons.* They're everywhere, gosh darn it. Although Salt Lake City is less than half Mormon now, Provo is one of the most Mormon towns in Utah, with a population of around 95 percent Mormon in some pockets. So remember that the idiot who cuts you off in traffic in Provo is probably a Mormon.

The most important site in Provo is Brigham Young University (BYU), which regards itself as the Lord's university and proclaims the motto of "Enter to learn; go forth to serve." Even Mormons find it strange to enter buildings that are named after people and places in the Book of Mormon (Deseret Towers and Helaman Halls, for example) or individuals from LDS history. While visiting BYU, hit the bookstore and check out the great range of Mormon books, modest knee-length shorts, and Mormon gifts for sale. Also be sure to gape at all the chocolate for sale at the candy counter; you won't find coffee or caffeinated soda for sale in the BYU student center, but by heavens, you can get all the sugar your heart desires.

Polynesian Cultural Center, Hawaii

Unlike all the other sites in this list, the Polynesian Cultural Center charges admission, and it's not a Mormon history site per se. Begun by the LDS Church in 1963 to call attention to the various cultures of Polynesia, this place is the most-visited paid attraction in Hawaii, with more than 1 million visitors annually. Think of it as a very wholesome theme park, with shows, music, craft demonstrations, Polynesian foods, and entertainment (sorry, no roller coasters).

The park is staffed by students from nearby BYU-Hawaii, many of whom are natives of Fiji, Tonga, Samoa, Tahiti, New Zealand, and Hawaii. Although the center isn't directly related to Mormon history, it offers a great window into the Mormon present, because it showcases some of the cultures where Mormonism has taken a strong hold. For more on the international growth of the Church, particularly in the South Pacific, see Chapter 14; for information on the Polynesian Cultural Center, check out www.polynesia.com.

While you're in Hawaii, stop by the Hawaii Temple visitors' center (not all Mormon temples have visitors' centers, but some do). One of the oldest LDS temples and the first outside the continental United States, the Hawaii Temple was dedicated in 1919. Like the Polynesian Cultural Center, the temple is located in Laie, a high-density Mormon town on the North Shore of Oahu. Regular shuttles connect the cultural center with Waikiki and other places.

Index

• M •

quilt, 144, 315–316
Quorum of the Twelve Apostles (Church leaders), 134, 178

• R •

racial issues
  attitudes toward Native Americans, 216
  Brigham Young, 184, 252–253
  changes in Church policy, 253
  continuing problems, 254
  history, 252–253
  overview, 251–252
  premortality effects, 26
  priesthood, 181, 253
  progress, 254–255
radio program, 318
rapist, 35
referral, 238
reincarnation, 17
Relief Society (women's organization), 107, 109, 133, 139
Reorganized Church of Jesus Christ of Latter Day Saints (RLDS). *See* Community of Christ
repentance, 167–168, 274, 276
Republican Party, 269
rest, 298, 299
restoration
  Aaronic Priesthood, 67–68
  beginnings, 60–64
  establishment of LDS Church, 64–66
  gospel gap, 60
  Joseph Smith's role, 14, 60–65
  Melchizedek Priesthood, 69–70
  overview, 60
  priesthood function, 66–67
resurrection, 47
retention, 243, 244–247
revelation
  Church leadership, 137
  Doctrine and Covenants, 177–178
  Ohio history, 186
  recent, 182–184
Rich, Richard (filmmaker), 323
Rigdon, Sidney (early Church leader), 186, 200
ritual, 12, 17, 126

RLDS. *See* Community of Christ
road show, 112
romance, 76
romance novel, 320
Romney, Mitt (politician), 331
routine. *See* daily life

• S •

Sabbath (Sunday)
  first Sunday fast, 286–289
  ideal practice, 297–300
  overview, 17
  rationale, 297–298
  schedule, 92
  Sunday School, 106–108
  temple closure, 123
sacrament, 93, 98–99
sacrament meeting
  attendance, 245
  deacon's duty, 67
  definition, 67, 92
  first Sunday fast, 286
  kneeling in prayer, 294
  missionary send-off, 236
  protocol, 96–101
Sacred Grove (location of First Vision), 63
sacrifice, 271
saint, 65
Saints (Card, Orson Scott), 320
Salt Lake City. *See* Utah
Salt Lake Tabernacle Choir, 226
Salt Lake Temple, 214
salvation. *See also* plan of salvation
  versus exaltation, 115–116
  importance of baptism, 101
  tithing, 282
  uniqueness of Mormonism, 18–19
San Bernadino, California, 217
sanctifying members, 57–58
Satan. *See* devil
Saturday's Warrior (musical), 25
savings, 309
Savior. *See* Jesus Christ
science fiction, 321
scrapbooking, 315
Scrapbooking For Dummies (Wines-Reed, Jeanne and Wines, Joan), 315

Notes